Latino Catholicism

WITHDRAWN

PRINCETON UNIVERSITY PRESS
PRINCETON AND OXFORD

# LATINO

# Catholicism

Transformation in
America's Largest Church

Timothy Matovina

Copyright © 2012 by Princeton University Press
Published by Princeton University Press,
41 William Street, Princeton, New Jersey 08540
In the United Kingdom: Princeton University Press,
6 Oxford Street, Woodstock, Oxfordshire OX20 1TW

press.princeton.edu

*Jacket photo*: Cross © JLP/Deimos/Corbis
All Rights Reserved

Library of Congress Cataloging-in-Publication Data

Matovina, Timothy M., 1955–
Latino Catholicism : transformation in America's largest church / Timothy Matovina.
    p. cm.
Includes bibliographical references (p.      ) and index.
ISBN 978-0-691-13979-1 (alk. paper)
1. Hispanic American Catholics—Religious life.    2. Catholic Church—United States.
I. Title.
BX1407.H55M38 2012
282.089′68073–dc23        2011029592

British Library Cataloging-in-Publication Data is available

This book has been composed in Kepler and Neuzeit S
Printed on acid-free paper. ∞
Printed in the United States of America
3  5  7  9  10  8  6  4  2

# CONTENTS

# PREFACE

Catholics comprise the largest religious group in the United States, encompassing nearly a fourth of all U.S. residents. Hispanics constitute more than a third of U.S. Catholics. They are the reason why Catholicism is holding its own relative to other religions in the United States. According to researchers of the American Religious Identification Survey, without the ever-growing number of Latinos in this country, the U.S. Catholic population would be declining at a rate similar to mainline Protestant groups. And given the relative youthfulness of the Latino community, Hispanic Catholics will continue to represent an increasing percentage of U.S. Catholics over time. They already comprise more than half of U.S. Catholics under the age of twenty-five and more than three-fourths of Catholics under eighteen in Texas, New Mexico, Arizona, and California. Robert Putnam and David Campbell succinctly sum up these demographics in their much-discussed 2010 study about the state of American religion, avowing that the Catholic Church in the United States "is on its way to becoming a majority-Latino institution."[1]

The expanding number of Latinos alters the overall demographics of U.S. Catholicism in several ways. Although the traditional Catholic institutional base is in the Northeast, the Latino presence has helped shift the demographic weight of U.S. Catholics to the Southwest. Revealingly, from 1990 to 2008 the proportion of Catholics in the populations of Texas and California increased by 9 and 8 percent respectively, while that of Massachusetts and New York respectively decreased by 15 and 7 percent. The demographic changes are especially dramatic in states with a historically weak Catholic presence, like Georgia, where Hispanic Catholics now outnumber Catholics of European descent. Catholic dioceses with the largest Hispanic population growth since 1990 include locales that previously had few Latinos, such as Charlotte, North Carolina; Savannah, Georgia; and Boise, Idaho.[2]

But numbers alone do not define the significance of the Latino presence in the U.S. Catholic Church. The mutual influence of Catholicism and Hispanic peoples in the United States is shaping not just the future of American Catholic life but also the life of the nation. Latinos are altering U.S. church and society through their responses to demands that they become "Americanized" and adopt the English language; their advocacy for Hispanic ministry and for immigration rights; their participation in parishes, apostolic movements, and denominational switching; their responses to the crisis of clergy sex abuse and bishops' knowing transfer of offenders; and their voting patterns, involvement in faith-based community organizing, and proclivity for public ritual and devotional traditions. At the same time, the lives and faith of Latino Catholics are being refashioned in dramatic ways: through the multiple pressures of assimilation, English-only movements, civil rights struggles, conservative political forces, the fact of religious pluralism and growing secularization, the rise of small faith communities and of Pentecostal and evangelical religion, and the ongoing controversies over immigration and clergy sexual abuse of children.

This book examines these mutual influences in detail. As such, it adopts an approach unlike previous book-length examinations of Latino Catholicism or Latino religion, which have tended to focus on one particular theme—the interplay between Latino religion and ethnic identity, for example—or a particular region or Latino group. The three largest populations—ethnic Mexicans, Puerto Ricans, and Cubans—have been the subject of various monographs.[3] While I treat a number of themes and distinctions between particular Latino groups when they are pertinent to the point under discussion, the primary interpretive lens of this book is how the U.S. context, the U.S. Catholic Church, and Latinos mutually transform one another.

After an opening chapter on Hispanics in U.S. Catholic history, subsequent chapters examine Latinos' integration in church and society, initiatives to develop structures and a core vision for Hispanic ministry, participation in parishes and apostolic movements, pastoral leadership, worship and devotion, faith-based activism and voting patterns, and efforts to pass on the faith to their young. An epilogue offers a final assessment and view toward the future of Latino Catholics and the mutual transformations examined in the book. The challenges posed by Pentecostal and evangelical churches and by rising numbers of Latinos who claim to have no religious affiliation are treated in various sections throughout the volume, particularly in chapter 4. Latino involvement in and response to the crisis of Catholic clergy sex abuse and bishops' knowing transfer of offenders are also examined in several sections, especially in chapter 3. Likewise, past and present influences of Latin America on Hispanic Catholics in the United States are addressed, most extensively in chapters 1 and 3. Finally, insights of Latina and Latino theologians, both individually and collectively through the Academy of Catholic Hispanic Theologians of the United States, are interspersed throughout the various chapters that comprise this work.

It is difficult to make simple generalizations about Latinos. Although "Latino Catholics" may be a convenient term to distinguish those with ancestral or personal origins in the Spanish-speaking world from U.S. Catholics with ties to the majority culture or other ethnic and racial groups, the idea of a generic Latino Catholic is no more useful than that of a generic African, Asian, European, or Native American Catholic. Spanish is a primary language in twenty-two countries, all of which have native daughters and sons now residing in the United States, the fifth largest and most diverse Spanish-speaking nation in the world. Historically, of course, Spanish-speaking people share a common Iberian heritage in which Roman Catholicism plays a significant role. At the same time, indigenous and African roots have come to influence Spanish-speaking peoples to varying degrees. In the Caribbean, where Spanish colonizers decimated native populations and forcibly resettled numerous African slaves, the African influence remains particularly strong. In countries such as Peru, Guatemala, and Mexico, where many significant elements of the Inca, Maya, and Aztec civilizations survived the Spanish conquest, these and other indigenous cultures continue to shape contemporary life. The mixing, or *mestizaje*, of Iberian, African, and indigenous cultures has proven to be a complex process with numerous local, regional, and national variations. Moreover, differences of socioeconomic status as well as regional and generational differences further contribute to the tremendous diversity among U.S. Hispanics.

Even the terms Latinos use to identify themselves vary. While some prefer to describe themselves with reference to their nation of origin, and others insist on "American" to highlight their U.S. association or identity, many Latinos employ terms such as "Mexican American" or "Cuban American" to accent their dual heritage. Persons of Mexican descent and some others embrace the term "Chicano" or its feminine form, "Chicana," usually as a means of expressing a strong ethnic consciousness and orientation toward social struggle and justice. As Puerto Ricans, Cubans, Mexicans, and other groups come into greater contact and collaborate on mutual concerns, they more frequently employ umbrella designations such as "Hispanic," "Latino," and "Latina" to accentuate commonalties of language and ethnic heritage, as well as perceived differences with other U.S. residents. "Hispanic" is more commonly used in official Catholic documents and among Catholic leaders, while "Latino" and the gender-inclusive "Latino/a" are gaining ascendancy among scholars and activists. Regional differences can influence which label one chooses; for example, "Latino" is strongly preferred in California and elsewhere on the West Coast.[4] Since no one label enjoys universal acceptance, the most common ones are employed interchangeably in this book. Moreover, every attempt is made to respect the terminology that particular individuals and groups use in referring to themselves.

Where appropriate this book draws on recent sociological surveys of Latinos, such as those of the Pew Hispanic Center and Pew Forum on Religion and Public Life; the Program for the Analysis of Religion among Latinos; the Hispanic Churches in American Public Life project; the Center for Applied Research in the Apostolate ; the National Research and Resource Center for Hispanic Youth and Young Adult Ministry; the National Study of Youth and Religion; the American Religious Identification Survey; the Latino National Survey; and studies conducted by leading scholars such as Andrew Greeley, Dean Hoge, Edwin Hernández, Robert Putnam, and David Campbell, among others. The book also benefitted from interviews with key Latino Catholic leaders and grassroots Hispanic Catholic faithful and has drawn on published presentations and sermons, newspaper reports, editorials, magazine articles, websites of Catholic organizations, official church documents, and pertinent secondary literature on Latino religion from a variety of disciplines.

Although I hope to provide a balanced view, it would be misleading to describe this book as a work of strictly dispassionate analysis. My scholarly work, teaching, and public speaking have enabled me to get to know many of the people who appear in these pages. In writing this book I hope to engage scholars, interested general readers, and the many Hispanic ministry leaders whose dedication I admire. I will consider my mission accomplished if some of these ministry leaders find this book a source of useful reflection.

I am indebted to colleagues and Hispanic ministry leaders who commented on chapter drafts as I developed the manuscript, especially Alejandro Aguilera-Titus; Petra Alexander; Andrés Arango; Jay Caponigro; Arturo Chávez; Kathleen Sprows Cummings; Kenneth Davis, O.F.M. Conv.; Jay P. Dolan; Erika Doss; Cynthia Duarte; Virgilio Elizondo; James Empereur, S.J.; Allan Figueroa Deck, S.J.; Thomas Florek, S.J.; Lucille Flores, S.S.M.; María Eva Flores, C.D.P.; Raúl Gómez, S.D.S.; Gilberto Hinojosa; Brett Hoover, C.S.P.; Ken Johnson-Mondragón; Thomas Kselman; John McGreevy; José Antonio Medina; Kristy Nabhan-Warren; Mark Noll; David O'Brien; Hosffman Ospino; Arturo Pérez-Rodríguez; Nancy Pineda-Madrid; Gerald Poyo; Alberto Pulido; Bill Purcell; Gary Riebe-Estrella, S.V.D.; Alberto Rojas; Juan Romero; Moises

Sandoval; Katarina Schuth, O.S.F.; Luis Tampe, S.J.; Feliciano Tapia; Richard Wood; and Robert Wright, O.M.I.

An earlier version of chapter 1 in this volume was published in the fall 2010 issue of the *U.S. Catholic Historian* and is reprinted here with permission. I gratefully acknowledge Christopher Kauffman, the editor of that journal and a longtime friend and mentor, for granting the reprint permission and providing insightful commentaries on an earlier draft of the chapter.

Bill and Anna Jean Cushwa have been generous supporters in every conceivable way of Notre Dame's Cushwa Center for the Study of American Catholicism. I appreciate deeply their friendship and support and the intellectual life of the Cushwa Center, which has enhanced my research for decades. Paula Brach of the Cushwa Center provided her typically effective and invaluable work on numerous research tasks. A grant from the Louisville Institute supported the sabbatical leave that afforded me the writing time to complete this project. I am grateful to those who provided me with that opportunity: Dr. James W. Lewis and his colleagues at the Louisville Institute, as well as my own colleagues and administrators at the University of Notre Dame. Thanks also to Fred Appel for his outstanding guidance on this project and to his colleagues at Princeton University Press for their editorial expertise, and to Michael Anthony Abril for his careful work in preparing an index for the volume. Finally, my debt of gratitude is deepest to the numerous Hispanic ministry leaders and Latino Catholics whose commitments and insights have enriched me. Above all else, I hope this book illuminates and animates their struggles, their hopes, and their faith.

# ABBREVIATIONS

| | |
|---|---|
| ACE | Alliance for Catholic Education |
| ACHTUS | Academy of Catholic Hispanic Theologians of the United States |
| ACORN | Association of Community Organizations for Reform Now |
| ACU | Agrupación Católica Universitaria |
| ARIS | American Religious Identification Survey |
| BCHA | Bishops' Committee on Hispanic Affairs |
| CARA | Center for Applied Research in the Apostolate |
| CCHD | Catholic Campaign for Human Development |
| CCR | Catholic Charismatic Renewal |
| CNSH | Comité Nacional de Servicio Hispano |
| COPS | Communities Organized for Public Service |
| HCAPL | Hispanic Churches in American Public Life |
| IAF | Industrial Areas Foundation |
| La Red | National Catholic Network de Pastoral Juvenil Hispana–La Red |
| MACC | Mexican American Cultural Center/Mexican American Catholic College |
| MCDPs | Missionary Catechists of Divine Providence |
| NCCB | National Conference of Catholic Bishops |
| NCCB/SHA | NCCB Secretariat for Hispanic Affairs |
| NCCHM | National Catholic Council for Hispanic Ministry |
| NORC | National Opinion Research Center |
| NSYR | National Study of Youth and Religion |
| PADRES | Padres Asociados por los Derechos Religiosos, Educativos, y Sociales (Priests Associated for Religious, Educational, and Social Rights) |

| | |
|---|---|
| PARAL | Program for the Analysis of Religion among Latinos |
| PFRPL | Pew Forum on Religion and Public Life |
| PHC/PFRPL | Pew Hispanic Center and Pew Forum on Religion and Public Life |
| PICO | Pacific Institute for Community Organizations |
| SEPI | Southeast Pastoral Institute |
| UFW | United Farm Workers |
| USCCB | United States Conference of Catholic Bishops |

Latino Catholicism

# 1
## CHAPTER

# Remapping American Catholicism

Father José Antonio Díaz de León, the last Franciscan priest serving in Texas when it was still part of Mexico, died mysteriously in 1834 near the east Texas town of Nacogdoches. A judge exonerated an Anglo-American accused of murdering Díaz de León amid rumors that the priest's death of a gunshot wound was a suicide. Mexican Catholics decried this decision as a sham. How could their pastor, who had served faithfully on the Texas frontier for nearly all his years as a priest, have committed such a desperate act?[1]

Seven years later Vincentian priests John Timon and Jean Marie Odin made a pastoral visit to Nacogdoches. They deplored the conditions of Mexican Catholics, whom, they said, Anglo-Americans had indiscriminately killed, driven away, and robbed of their lands. Father Odin also reported that Anglo-Americans had burned the local Catholic church building to the ground. Yet these and other visitors observed that Mexican Catholic laity continued to gather in private homes for feast days and weekly worship services and celebrated various rituals, such as funerals. Catholicism in Nacogdoches remained almost entirely a lay-led effort until 1847 when (by then) Bishop Odin was finally able to appoint two priests to replace Father Díaz de León. Parishioners' eager reception of the sacraments from their new pastors testified to their enduring faith amid a tumultuous period of social upheaval.

These largely forgotten events occurred simultaneously with more widely known episodes in U.S. Catholic history. General histories and survey courses of U.S. Catholicism inevitably examine the atrocities of the anti-Catholic mob that burned the Ursuline convent to the ground at Charlestown, Massachusetts (across the river from Boston), in 1834, the same year of Father Díaz de León's assassination and concurrent with the burning of the Nacogdoches parish church. Historical overviews also explore the saga of European Catholic

1

immigrants, such as the Irish and the Germans, whose migration flows increased significantly during the very same decades that Mexican Catholics at Nacogdoches struggled in faith for their very survival as a community. Irish-born John Hughes became bishop (later archbishop) of New York in 1842, the same year that Odin, the first bishop of Texas (and later archbishop of New Orleans), was ordained to the episcopacy. But Odin's two decades of endeavor to advance the Catholic Church and faith in Texas are far less recognized than Hughes's simultaneous labors in New York.

U.S. Catholic historians' strong focus on the eastern seaboard and European settlers and immigrants mirror long-standing emphases in the broader scholarship of North American religious history. Studies in recent decades have addressed lacunae in this historiography such as the role of regionalism, the frontier, women, African Americans, and Asian Americans, to name but a few.[2] Collectively these studies reveal that while documenting "forgotten" peoples, histories, and regions is an essential intellectual endeavor, it is only a first step toward the longer-range goal of investigating how to remap general narratives of the past in a manner that more adequately encompasses the various peoples, places, and events that formed it. Building on the groundbreaking work of colleagues like Moises Sandoval, the leading figure in the 1975 founding and subsequent development of the U.S. chapter of the Comisión para el Estudio de la Historia de la Iglesia en Latinoamerica (CEHILA, the Commission for the Study of the History of the Church in Latin America), this chapter is part of the larger effort to rethink the narratives of U.S. religious history, and U.S. Catholicism in particular—in this case, through the lens of Latino Catholic experience.[3]

Interpreting the past is never a neutral endeavor, of course. A basic truism of historical studies is that those who control the present construct the past in order to shape the future. With this challenge in mind, how can we understand the past in a way that sheds light on the tragedies of Father Díaz de León and the Ursulines at Charleston; Catholicism in Nacogdoches and in New York; the contributions of bishops Odin and Hughes; and the experiences of Mexican, Irish, German, and other Catholics? More broadly, what are the basic themes of U.S. Catholic history? What gradual trends or dramatic turning points mark it into distinct time periods? How do Latinos fit into and shape the overall narrative? Obviously the answers to these questions are matters of interpretation, and no single response is unilaterally comprehensive. But how one responds is decisive for a number of the issues and topics that are fundamental to understanding the Hispanic presence and the future of Catholics in the United States. So we begin with an assessment of the historiography of U.S. Catholicism.

It is no surprise that for Latinos the most contentious renderings of the U.S. Catholic past are those that obscure their contributions, sometimes to the point of near invisibility. While the strongest expressions of this critique are usually directed at more dated scholarly works, as recently as 2008 James O'Toole's *The Faithful: A History of Catholics in America* encompasses only two brief references to Hispanics from the origins of U.S. Catholicism to the dawn of the twenty-first century. The final chapter of O'Toole's examination of U.S. Catholic history from the perspective of the lay faithful depicts Latinos as an important component of Catholicism's ongoing evolution in the United States in the new century, but unfortunately this leaves the impression that only now are Hispanics becoming a noteworthy element of the U.S. Catholic story.[4]

To varying degrees other recent general histories of U.S. Catholicism address the Hispanic presence and contribution more adequately. A number of historians begin their rendering of the U.S. Catholic story with the Spanish colonial era rather than the establishment of the later and overwhelmingly Protestant British colonies. Woven into the narrative of general works such as those of James Hennesey, Jay Dolan, Charles Morris, and James Fisher are discussions of immigration patterns, demographic shifts, and Latino Catholic leaders, organizations, movements, religious traditions, political involvement, and social activism. But these historical treatments often subsume Hispanics into an Americanization paradigm that is presumed to hold true for all Catholics in the United States. Morris concluded his acclaimed 1997 work with the assertion that there is a "standoff between the tradition of Rome and the tradition of America [the United States]." His claim is based on an understanding of U.S. Catholicism as, in the words of Dolan, a fledgling "republican" church after U.S. independence that expanded into an "immigrant church" in the nineteenth and early twentieth centuries and after World War II had "come of age" as "American," a process often depicted as culminating in John F. Kennedy's election as president, which signaled for numerous Catholics the authentication of their full acceptance in U.S. society. Explicitly or implicitly, scholars contend that these developments expanded Catholics' benefits and contributions as U.S. citizens.[5]

Even those who protest Americanization as a detriment to Catholicism divide the U.S. Catholic past into a similar series of historical eras. Distancing himself from previous authors he deemed "one-sided in a progressivist direction," Joseph Varacalli presented his 2006 work *The Catholic Experience in America* as "one of many more balanced and orthodox pieces of scholarship that . . . should be viewed, partly at least, as a result of the intellectual legacy of Pope John Paul II." Yet Varacalli follows the same basic pattern of historical periods as the predecessors he critiques, albeit with his own interpretive slant. He depicts Catholicism in the United States as evolving from modest beginnings as a "minority church" in the first decades of the new republic to a period of nearly a century and a half in which mass immigration and effective episcopal leadership enabled Catholics to forge a subculture that "successfully propagated" the faith. In his view the zenith of Catholic subculture and its defense against "a then Protestant and a mostly unsympathetic civilization" was the period following World War II. But upward mobility, progressive interpretations of the Second Vatican Council (1962–1965), and secularization in society at large significantly diminished the countercultural edge of the subculture and the vitality of Catholic faith. While Varacalli diverges from previous authors in his addition of a fourth historical era he calls the Catholic "restorationist" movement under the pontificates of popes John Paul II and Benedict XVI, he does not depart from the dominant schema. Instead he critiques the process of Americanization that others depict in a more positive light.[6]

Some scholars question whether the immigrant-to-Americanization paradigm is the best lens through which to examine the U.S. Catholic experience, even for the experience of European Catholic immigrants and their descendants. Others critique the language of "coming of age," noting that whatever their level of formal education and status, European immigrants did not sojourn in a perpetual state of childhood immaturity, nor did adopting the English language and U.S. social norms indicate that their descendants had advanced to the age of adulthood.[7] Nonetheless, the contention that U.S. Catholics have become "Americanized" to a significant degree remains an important interpretive lens through which most scholars, pastoral leaders, and other observers examine Catholicism in the United States.

The core question about the Americanization paradigm is this: in the long view, will the undeniably profound assimilation that transpired in the period from roughly 1920 to 1980 end up appearing more as an anomaly in U.S. Catholic history, or as the norm? Are there interpretive lenses that illuminate important alternative understandings of the historical trajectories of U.S. Catholicism? From the perspective of many ecclesial leaders, for example, a more pressing concern is the loosening of attachment to the institutional church in recent decades as reflected in data such as the relatively fewer vocations to the priesthood and religious life and the lower rates of Catholic school enrollment and Sunday Mass attendance, trends that are evident to varying but significant degrees among both immigrant and U.S.-born "Americanized" Catholics. How will future historians assess trends such as these, their interrelation with the Americanization paradigm, and the relative explanatory significance of each for understanding Catholicism in the United States? Are there other interpretive lenses no one has yet articulated that will rise to the fore in analyses of the U.S. Catholic past? At this juncture the most tenable conclusion about the Americanization paradigm is that it offers considerable insight into the experience of European immigrants' descendants from the interwar period until the two decades following the Second Vatican Council, as well as into the subsequent contentious debates about the stance Catholics should take vis-à-vis the wider U.S. society. To presume that the Americanization paradigm is the best or even the sole organizational schema for U.S. Catholic history, and in particular for examining the place of groups such as African Americans and Latinos within that history, remains unsubstantiated.

Thus a decisive challenge is to construct a history of U.S. Catholicism that incorporates Latinos, and other non-European groups, but is not modeled exclusively on European Catholic immigrants and their descendants' societal ascent and assimilation during the middle six decades of the twentieth century. Indeed, in broad strokes the history of Latino Catholics inverts the standard depiction of their counterparts from nations such as Ireland, Germany, Poland, and Italy. While Catholics were a small minority in the British colonies, in lands from Florida to California they comprised a more substantial population under Catholic Spain. The first mass group of Catholics to settle in the United States was nineteenth-century European immigrants, but the first large group of Hispanic Catholics became part of the nation during that same era without ever leaving home, as they were incorporated into its boundaries during U.S. territorial expansion into Florida and then westward. Just as European immigration diminished to relatively minuscule numbers as a result of 1920s restrictive immigration legislation, Hispanic immigration began in earnest with the Mexican Revolution. The counter trajectory of Latino Catholic history in the United States in relation to that of their European-descent coreligionists necessitates a reanalysis of each epoch delineated in the standard historiography, particularly the period since World War II, as waves of Hispanic immigrants have comprised an increasingly significant portion of what was purportedly an established, Americanized, post-immigrant church.

A Latino perspective on U.S. Catholic history also necessitates sharper attention to its international dimensions, especially the intersections of U.S. and Latin American history. Following the Spanish colonial presence in lands that are now part of the United States, U.S. political and economic expansionism led to the conquest of nearly half of Mexico's national territory at the midpoint of the nineteenth century, consolidated U.S. occupation of Puerto

Rico five decades later, fueled economic shifts that led to the origins of late nineteenth- and early twentieth-century immigration from Mexico, resulted in a U.S. presence throughout the Caribbean and Central America that helped induce migrations from those regions, and has driven the globalization process that in recent decades fed an immigration explosion from throughout Latin America. This latter process blurred the border between Latin and North America, accelerating the development of previous links between Catholicism in the United States and Catholicism in the rest of the Americas. It also produced an unprecedented degree of diversification of national origin groups among Latinos in U.S. Catholicism. Examining the U.S. Catholic past through the lens of this diverse Hispanic experience—as well as through the experience of Europeans and other groups—expands on a unilateral Americanization paradigm with a hemispheric perspective that is essential for understanding the current demographic Hispanicization of Catholicism in the United States.

## Colonial Origins

Jay Dolan's introduction to the U.S. history survey course exemplifies a fundamental revision that a number of contemporary scholars have adopted for U.S. Catholic historiography. Dolan's custom on the first day of class was to ask his students the significance of three years in North American history: 1607, 1608, and 1610. At least one student was always able to recognize 1607 as the date for the founding of the first British colony, Jamestown. But rarely could anyone identify 1608 as the founding date for Québec, and 1610 for Santa Fe. Dolan attests that "the reasoning behind my pedagogical cunning is to impress upon the students the French and Spanish dimension of American history as well as the more familiar English aspect." Colonial U.S. historians like Alan Taylor have expanded on Dolan's treatment, noting even less-acknowledged developments within territories that later became part of the United States, such as the Dutch colonies, Russian settlement in Alaska, and British incursions into Hawaii.[8] Implicitly, this approach answers an essential question for any overview of U.S. history: does the subject matter encompass solely the British colonists and other peoples and territories *only when* they become part of the U.S. nation, or does it encompass the inhabitants of regions that are now part of the United States both *before and after* their incorporation? Rather than a story of thirteen original colonies and their westward expansion, the latter perspective accentuates the encounter and conflict of peoples, primarily the southward-moving French, the northward-moving Spanish, the westward-moving British, the natives who already lived on the land, and the slaves and immigrants who settled among them. Given that both the French and Spanish colonists were from Catholic countries, any comprehensive analysis of U.S. Catholic history must examine their foundational presence and the extent of their influence on subsequent developments.

Spanish-speaking Catholics have lived in what is now the United States for twice as long as the nation has existed. The first diocese in the New World was established in 1511 at San Juan, Puerto Rico, now a commonwealth associated with the United States. Subjects of the Spanish Crown founded the first permanent European settlement within the current borders of the fifty states at St. Augustine, Florida, in 1565, four decades before the establishment of Jamestown, and around 1620 established at that settlement the first Marian shrine in what is now the continental United States, Nuestra Señora de la Leche y Buen Parto (Our Nursing Mother of Happy Delivery). Before the end of the sixteenth century, Spanish Jesuits and Franciscans initiated missionary activities in present-day Georgia and even as far north as Virginia. In 1598 Spanish subjects traversed present-day El Paso, Texas, and proceeded north to establish the permanent foundation of Catholicism in what is now the Southwest.

Catholics in the thirteen British colonies were a repressed minority in a Protestant land, eventually even losing the elective franchise in Maryland, the only British colony that Catholics founded. They comprised scarcely 1 percent of the population at the signing of the Declaration of Independence. Meanwhile, in Hispanic settlements from Florida to California, Catholicism was the established religion under Spain and, in the Southwest, under Mexico after it won independence in 1821. This prescription led newcomers to the region—such as escaped slaves from Georgia who were granted freedom in Spanish Florida, famed Alamo defender James Bowie in Texas, and renowned scout Kit Carson in New Mexico—to accept Catholic baptism and at least nominal practice of the faith. From the standpoints of original settlement, societal influence, and institutional presence, the origins of Catholicism in what is now the United States were decidedly Hispanic.

Contemporary Latinos acclaim the foundational role of their ancestors in various ways. El Paso residents maintain that members of the Juan de Oñate expedition celebrated the "first Thanksgiving" in the United States on April 30, 1598, in gratitude for surviving their trek across the Chihuahuan Desert. The Oñate expedition festivities included a Catholic Mass and a meal for which the Spaniards provided game and natives from the region supplied fish. Since 1989 the El Paso Mission Trail Association has commemorated the event annually with a community picnic and festivities and Mass in historic sites like the San Elizario Presidio Chapel. Costumed participants and members of the local Tigua Indians reenact the Oñate expedition's day of thanks. In 1991 a delegation from El Paso visited Plymouth Rock dressed as Spanish conquistadores and, according to an El Paso Mission Trail Association press release, was amicably "arrested and charged with blasphemy and spreading malicious rumors for stating that the real First Thanksgiving took place in Texas." Though this staged confrontation was aimed at drawing publicity to both parties involved, the same press release also proudly noted, "The Plymouth trial judge ordered a delegation of Pilgrims to travel to El Paso the following year to observe the Texas Thanksgiving."[9]

Yet, on the whole, popular perceptions have frequently relegated the historical significance of Hispanic Catholicism in the colonial period to a romanticized and bygone day of the Spanish missions. Such depictions appeared in print immediately after the U.S. takeover of northern Mexico in the U.S.-Mexican War (1846–1848), such as Francis Baylies's eyewitness account of the U.S. Army's overland advance from San Antonio down to the heart of Mexico, which encompassed his laudatory observations about the missionary efforts of Spanish friars among the native peoples of Texas. Baylies marveled at the "magnificent traces" of the missioners' labors during the Spanish colonial era that were noteworthy in the ruins of the mission compounds near San Antonio. He also bemoaned the general decline in local conditions since Mexican independence, including the deterioration of the "magnificent churches [and] monasteries," which "once the outposts of christianity [*sic*], were now moss-covered ruins." According to Baylies, after Mexico won independence, "everything went to decay. Agriculture, learning, the mechanic arts, shared the common fate; and when the banners of the United States were unfurled in these distant and desolate places, the descendants of the noble and chivalric Castilians had sunk to the level, perhaps beneath it, of the aboriginal savages."[10]

Baylies's justification of the U.S. conquest as a redemption of Mexican backwardness and corruption induced his sharp, Eurocentric contrast between the decline of the missions under Mexico and the previous "golden age" of the missions, in which Spanish friars selflessly taught Christianity, Spanish culture, and European civilization to native peoples. Writer Helen Hunt Jackson extended this view to a national audience through a series of 1883 *Century Magazine* articles on Fray Junípero Serra, the founder of the California missions. Though Jackson was the daughter of a strict Massachusetts Congregationalist family, she found spiritual inspiration in her hagiographic perception of Serra and his fellow Franciscans, even considering their labors superior to those of the Puritans, whom, she claimed, "drove the Indians farther and farther into the wilderness every year, fighting and killing them," while the Spanish friars "were gathering the Indians by thousands into communities and feeding and teaching them." Jackson's best-selling novel *Ramona*, first published in 1884, solidified this idealized view of the missions in the popular mind-set. A love story set against her presentation of the social upheaval after the passing of the missions, Jackson's literary success cast a long shadow of "Ramonamania": rail tours of the California missions, a 1919 D. W. Griffith film starring Mary Pickford as Ramona, an annual Ramona theatrical pageant that continues to this day, initiatives to restore Spanish missions, and, most conspicuously, the development of Mission and Spanish Revival architectural styles that mark the landscape of towns and cities across the Southwest and beyond.[11]

A number of scholars and other commentators have noted that many restored missions and writings about them fail to account for indigenous perspectives on the mission system, including the cultural shock, harsh treatment, and death from European diseases that many Native Americans endured in mission communities. Yet even professional historians often fall into the false presumptions that the missions were the only Catholic religious institutions in the Spanish colonies and Mexican territories and that *all* the missions underwent a period of abandonment and decline. In fact, parishes, military chapels, private shrines, and some missions have been the homes of active Catholic faith communities from colonial times until the present day.[12]

The "arrival" of Christianity in lands that are now part of the continental United States began with Spanish expeditions into the area, such as Juan Ponce de León's famous excursions into Florida and the fated Pánfilo de Narváez expedition, from which only Alvar Núñez Cabeza de Vaca and a handful of companions survived after an eight-year ordeal of hunger, captivity, and an overland trek from Florida to New Spain (present-day Mexico).[13] Later, Spanish subjects established settlements to stake territorial claims for the Spanish Crown, pursue economic gain, and propagate Catholicism among native populations. *Villas* (towns) with formal civil and church institutions, military garrisons, and missions provided historically tested structures around which Hispanic frontier communities emerged.[14]

Catholic missionaries, usually Franciscan friars, with the major exception being Eusebio Kino and his fellow Jesuits in Arizona, accompanied exploratory expeditions and then were an integral part of Spanish efforts to establish settlements. Sometimes the friars founded missions within or near settled indigenous communities. In other cases they induced nomadic peoples to settle down at newly established missions, usually in the vicinity of Spanish

9

towns and military garrisons. Since they typically had but a single or small group of friars and perhaps a few Spanish military personnel, the mission settlements were in effect missionary-led Indian towns. Initially the prospect of entering the missions to stave off enemies, starvation, and harsh winters seemed attractive to some Native Americans, but a number of them eventually found mission life too alien and coercive. They were not accustomed to the Spanish work routines and religious lifestyles, and they also found unacceptable the friars' demands that they shed their traditional ways. Many became resentful and left the missions. In some cases outright rebellion ensued, most famously in 1680 when New Mexico's Pueblo Indians exploded into open violence under the leadership of a shaman or spiritual leader named Popé, driving the Spaniards and their loyal indigenous subjects from the region and seeking to purge their communities of Catholic symbols and everything Spanish.[15] Though the Spanish reconquered them beginning in 1692 and Franciscan missionary efforts resumed, the revolt highlighted the potential clash of civilizations in mission life.

On the other hand, a number of Native Americans remained within the world of the missions, accepted Christianity, and took on Hispanic and Catholic identities. In various locales the native peoples revered missionaries for their faith, dedication, and willingness to advocate for them within the Spanish colonial system. Julio César, who identified himself as a "pure-blooded Indian" of California, recalled with fondness that as a resident of Mission San Luís Rey (near San Diego) during his youth, a Padre Francisco was the priest in charge of the mission, and "the Indians called him 'Tequedeuma,' an Indian word which signified that the padre was very sympathetic and considerate toward the Indians; in fact, he was very loving and good."[16] For the missionaries, Hispanicizing the natives entailed creating living spaces for their charges around impressive churches that became centers of everyday life. The missionaries worked diligently to inculcate Catholicism, define work regimes, establish predictable daily life routines, teach the Spanish language, oversee social interactions, enforce Christian-appropriate gender relations, and strive to modify cultural practices among the natives that they believed were contrary to Christianity.

At the same time, even as natives were incorporated into Catholicism and Hispanic society, to varying degrees they exerted their own cultural influence on the Hispanic newcomers. For example, archeological research reveals the presence of Coahuiltecan artifacts such as pottery, tools, and blankets in San Antonio's Hispanic households during the colonial period. Coahuiltecans and other native peoples also brought to Catholic worship some of the spirit and elements of their communal rituals called *mitotes*, which included singing, dancing, and feasting to mark occasions like the summer harvest, hunting or fishing expeditions, or the return of the full moon.[17]

The Spanish Crown viewed the missions as temporary institutions whose role was to prepare Native Americans to become good Spanish subjects. Officially, from their inception the missions were destined for secularization—that is, transference from missionary to civil authorities and diocesan clergy once the friars completed the work of Hispanicizing the natives. But in fact secularization varied from region to region, depending on socioeconomic realities, central government policies, the level of cooperation among Native Americans, and the often competing interests of missionaries and local officials.

In theory, the indigenous converts at the missions were to receive individual land allotments and other assets in the secularization process to aid them in their transition to a new status as Hispanicized Catholics. But in numerous cases this did not occur: the Native Americans simply lost everything to unscrupulous officials or other Hispanic residents, often moving into Hispanic towns where they occupied the bottom of the social structure. However the mission residents fared, the secularization process transformed their communities from corporate entities under the authority and protection of specific missionary orders to independent communities that became another element of Hispanic civil society. In the process many missions no longer had resident clergy. A large number fell into disrepair, many of them later rebuilt. Nonetheless, the church structures at locales like Santa Barbara, California; Ysleta, Texas (near El Paso); and San Xavier del Bac, south of Tucson, Arizona, among others, continued to function as Catholic houses of worship and do so even today.

Male friars produced the vast majority of extant mission records, which consequently tend to accentuate their perspectives, accomplishments, and struggles. Nonetheless, the missions reveal a long-standing, significant element of Latino Catholicism: the faith and leadership of women like Eulalia Pérez, who became a prominent figure at Mission San Gabriel (near Los Angeles). A native of Loreto, Baja California, Pérez moved to the mission in the early nineteenth century with her husband, who was assigned there as a guard. After her husband's death, Pérez and her son and five daughters lived at the mission, where she became the head housekeeper, a leadership position in the mission community that grew increasingly significant as the number of friars decreased. Her duties included managing supplies and their distribution, as well as supervising Native American workers. The elderly Eulalia noted modestly in a memoir she dictated to an interviewer that as the mission's "mistress of the keys" (*llavera*), she "was responsible for a variety of duties." In fact she was the lay overseer of the mission community's daily life.[18]

Though missions were numerically the predominant Catholic institution in the northern stretches of New Spain, parishes, military chaplaincies, and private chapels also played a crucial role in establishing and maintaining Catholicism. Unlike the missions in which the population consisted exclusively of Native Americans, save for a few friars and Hispanic military personnel, these other religious foundations provided for the spiritual welfare of Hispanic civilian and military settlers and their descendants, as well as some natives who eventually joined their communities. Parishes first appeared with the establishment of formal towns and grew in number as some missions were secularized and became ordinary parishes. Local residents built the churches and sought to obtain the services of clergy, either religious-order priests like the Franciscans, or diocesan priests, who were primarily trained to serve existing Spanish-speaking Catholic communities rather than to work for the conversion of Native Americans. In Spanish colonial times, Hispanic Catholics established parishes in places like St. Augustine, San Antonio, Laredo, Santa Fe, Albuquerque, and Los Angeles, along with military chapels in other locales, such as Santa Barbara and Monterey, California, where the current Catholic cathedral has its origins in a colonial military chapel.

The construction of the first church edifice in San José, California, demonstrates local initiative in establishing parishes. In 1802 settlers at San José, which had been founded in 1777, petitioned for permission to build a chapel. From its foundation the community had relied on Mission Santa Clara, about four miles away, for their spiritual needs. When they received the required permission, the 217 settlers immediately began building their church. In 1804 an earthquake destroyed their newly completed chapel, but the community persisted and rebuilt it, at one juncture receiving help from the military commander at nearby Monterey, who sent individuals under judicial sanction to work on the church building. Once built, the settlers took it upon themselves to negotiate with the Franciscans at Mission Santa Clara for their spiritual services.[19]

Private chapels and pilgrimage sites also reveal local initiative and the origins of contemporary Hispanic Catholicism in the colonial past, most famously the sanctuary of Chimayó in New Mexico. Tewa Indians acclaimed the healing properties of Chimayó's sacred earth long before Catholic settlers arrived at this locale on the western side of the Sangre de Cristo Mountains. Spanish subjects completed the first chapel at the site in 1816 and dedicated the Santuario de Chimayó to Nuestro Señor de Esquipulas (Our Lord of Esquipulas), a Guatemalan representation of the crucifixion associated with a Mayan sacred place of healing earth. During the 1850s, however, devotees of the Santuario de Chimayó added a statue of the Santo Niño de Atocha (Holy

Child of Atocha) in response to a new local shrine dedicated to the Santo Niño. Subsequently the Santo Niño and the miraculous dirt became the focal points for most Santuario devotees. They remain so today for thousands of pilgrims who visit Chimayó annually.[20]

Though Louisiana was under Spanish control from 1766 to 1803 and Spain controlled Florida for well over two centuries until 1821 (with one hiatus of British rule from 1763 to 1783), most Hispanic Catholics in what is now the United States resided in the Southwest. During the Spanish colonial era and the subsequent period after Mexican independence in 1821, New Mexico was in their most populous territory and thus the one with the largest number of Catholics. By the beginning of the nineteenth century, the diocesan clergy in New Mexico had begun the process of slowly displacing the Franciscan missionaries who had served in the region since the late sixteenth century. This was, of course, a natural and predictable course of events, since the missions had always been viewed as temporary institutions dedicated to preparing the indigenous communities for parish life as Hispanic citizens. In 1798 the diocese of Durango, which encompassed New Mexico, introduced the first diocesan pastors to the region, one for the parish at Santa Fe and the other at Santa Cruz. As the Franciscan numbers declined, particularly after Mexican independence, when many Spanish friars were forcibly exiled or left the new republic out of loyalty to their native Spain, the diocesan priests increased thanks to recruitment of local youth who went to seminary in Durango. Between 1823 and 1826 four New Mexicans completed their training and returned home to begin their ministries. By the end of the 1840s the Franciscans had all left or died, and some seventeen or eighteen diocesan priests, most of them recruited locally, served the spiritual needs of New Mexico's parish communities. In the end, the church's viability in New Mexico depended on the communities themselves, including their ability to recruit their youth into the priesthood.[21]

One such local vocation, Father Ramón Ortiz (1814–1896), was born in Santa Fe, attended seminary at Durango, and was ordained there in 1837. Within a matter of months he began a parochial assignment in the El Paso district that lasted nearly sixty years. An activist priest, Ortiz was a staunch defender of Mexican sovereignty. As U.S. troops prepared to occupy his local area during the U.S.-Mexican War, Ortiz wrote his bishop, vowing that the local populace would defend their nation at all costs. The curate later served as an elected delegate to the national congress in Mexico City, where he opposed the 1848 Treaty of Guadalupe Hidalgo, which ended the war and ceded nearly half of Mexico's territory to the United States. When New Mexican territorial governor William Carr Lane sought to occupy Mexican territory in

1853 (land later ceded to the United States through the 1854 Gadsden Purchase), Ortiz rode out to confront the governor. The curate then returned to El Paso and alerted local authorities, who mounted a force of eight hundred men to defend their borders. Unitl his death in 1896, Ortiz offered dedicated pastoral service on both sides of the river that formed the new international boundary between Mexico and the United States.[22]

Priests and their lay parishioners enacted cultural ways and traditions that included Catholic religious expressions. Communities drew on rituals, devotions, and celebrations of their ancestors such as the celebration of saint days and other feasts, processions, Mass, initiation rites, *compadrazgo* (godparentage), and dramatic proclamations of Christ's death and removal from the cross, among others. One ritual practiced during the Spanish colonial era at the parish church of San Francisco de Asís in Santa Fe was a Good Friday service in which devotees symbolically removed Jesus's body from the cross, placed it in the arms of his grieving mother, and then accompanied the corpse through the streets in a solemn procession. The church sanctuary served as the hill of Calvary for this occasion, with the statue of Our Lady of Solitude placed prominently to depict Mary at the foot of the cross. A priest's *Sermón de la Soledad* (Sermon of Solitude) accompanied the ritual, inviting congregants to "travel by meditation and contemplation to Golgatha, also called Mount Calvary," and then dramatizing in great detail what "our eyes see in this sad, ill-fated, and mournful place."[23]

The intensity of Catholic devotion and commitment is difficult to assess precisely, but it undoubtedly varied from place to place, from household to household, and from person to person. Michael Carroll has noted the unfortunate tendency of commentators' "taking the sort of Hispano Catholicism that existed in New Mexico during the late nineteenth and early twentieth centuries and projecting it onto the colonial past." At the same time, Carroll's contention that colonial New Mexicans were only nominally Catholic is unconvincing. He alleges that widely documented religious practices in colonial New Mexico, such as feast days, initiation rites, and the like primarily reflected social norms and not religious sensibilities. Carroll bases his conclusion on the argument that primary sources do not reveal New Mexicans engaged extensively in practices evident in other locales of Latin America and Spain: apparitions, cults for sacred images, painted ex-votos, and the ecclesial reforms that church leaders promoted after the Council of Trent, such as increased Mass attendance and knowledge of doctrine. Yet Carroll did not consider that difficult economic conditions, lower population density, and isolation mitigated against a broad manifestation of these particular religious expressions in New Mexico, as well as against the influence of ecclesial authority more prevalent elsewhere among Spanish-speaking populations. Nor does Carroll offer comparisons to settlements in Texas, California, and other areas of New Spain's northern frontier, which in fact evidenced patterns of religious practice similar to those in New Mexico. In the end he does not offer compelling evidence to sustain his argument that widespread Catholic practices constituted an overwhelmingly social phenomenon largely devoid of religious significance. Nonetheless, Carroll's cautionary note about not presuming a uniformly fervent Hispanic Catholicism is well taken. The Hispanic colonial enterprise differs from subsequent eras in that Catholicism was the prescribed religion, but romanticized views of a pristine and unvarying Catholic faith among all residents are unfounded.[24]

Latino Catholicism in places from St. Augustine, Florida, to Sonoma, California, originated with communities planted during the sixteenth through the nineteenth centuries. As the United States expanded from the original thirteen colonies to span the North American continent during the first half of the nineteenth century, Hispanic Catholic places of worship and some eighty thousand Spanish-speaking Catholics were incorporated into the growing nation. Extant faith communities, religious traditions, and clergy in various locales belie presuppositions of a radical break with the Spanish colonial past that dismiss Hispanic foundations of Catholicism in what became the United States.

## Enduring Communities of Faith

Famine in Ireland and revolution in the German states accelerated Catholic immigration during the mid-nineteenth century, making Catholicism the largest denomination in the United States by the 1850 census. Commenting on these and subsequent waves of immigrants, Pulitzer Prize winner Oscar Handlin would later famously remark, "Once I thought to write a history of the immigrants in America. Then I discovered that the immigrants *were* American history."[25] His sweeping thesis does not account for the experience of mid-nineteenth-century Mexican Catholics in the Southwest who, as a common quip puts it, did not cross the border but had the border cross them during U.S. territorial expansion. Unlike the saga of their contemporary European coreligionists, who as émigrés sought haven in a new land, the story of the first large group of Hispanic Catholics in the United States is primarily a tale of faith, struggle, and endurance in places where their Spanish and Mexican forebears had already created a homeland. In one often-repeated phrase, they were "foreigners in our native land" who survived the U.S. takeover of northern Mexico.[26] German immigrants and their descendants recalled 1848 as a year of revolution; the Irish remembered it as a moment at the height of the potato famine. But the same date is etched in the consciousness of Mexicans and Mexican Americans as the pivotal juncture when military defeat led Mexico's president to cede nearly half his nation's territory to the United States. While historians, immigrant descendants, and national symbols like the Statue of Liberty enshrine immigrant ascendancy as a quintessential American story, Hispanics who were incorporated into the United States underwent the disestablishment of their religion along with widespread loss of their lands, economic well-being, political clout, and cultural hegemony. Their *aguante* (unyielding endurance) and faith during this time of social upheaval is one of the most frequently overlooked chapters in U.S. Catholic history.

The conquest of northern Mexico began with the war between Texas and Mexico (1835–1836), which resulted in the establishment of an independent Texas Republic. Nine years later the United States annexed Texas and another war erupted in disputed territory along the Rio Grande near present-day Brownsville, Texas. The 1848 Treaty of Guadalupe Hidalgo brought an official end to this war; established new borders between Mexico and the United States; and purportedly guaranteed the citizenship, property, and religious rights of Mexican citizens who chose to remain in the conquered territories. Mexico lost the present-day states of Texas, Nevada, California, Utah, and parts of New Mexico, Arizona, Colorado, and Wyoming. Six years later the Gadsden Purchase—or, as Mexicans call it, the *Tratado de Mesilla* (Treaty of Mesilla)—completed the U.S. takeover of former Mexican territories. With the threat of another U.S. invasion as the backdrop for negotiations, James Gadsden "purchased" the southern sections of present-day Arizona and New Mexico for $10 million. This land acquisition enabled U.S. entrepreneurs to expropriate the profits from this territory's rich mine deposits and its suitability as a route for expanding rail transportation networks.

The futility of direct resistance to U.S. occupation was painfully evident in events like the 1847 Taos Rebellion, an uprising in which Hispanic and Native American allies attempted to overthrow U.S. rule that had been established in New Mexico the previous year. Insurrectionists assassinated territorial governor Charles Bent and at least fifteen other Anglo-Americans, but U.S. forces quickly suppressed the rebellion and publicly hanged its leaders. Military defeat merely initiated the process of U.S. conquest and expansion, as law enforcement personnel, judicial and political officials, occupying troops, and a growing Anglo-American populace imposed U.S. rule. Violence against Mexicans at times reached extreme proportions, but the judicial system afforded little if any protection for them despite their U.S. citizenship. The frequent lynching of Mexican residents even included the hanging of a woman. In California a vigilante mob of Anglo-Americans condemned a woman named Josefa to avenge the death of their fellow miner Fred Cannon, whom Josefa had killed with a knife after he broke down her door in a drunken rage. Anglo-American newcomers further consolidated the conquest by asserting their dominion over political and economic life. When Texas became a state in 1845, for example, Mexican San Antonians lost control of the city council their ancestors had established and led for more than a century. They also lost most of their land holdings, often in biased legal proceedings and in some cases through outright criminal removal from their homes and property. Increasingly Mexicans became a working underclass.[27] Demographic shifts facilitated the diminishment of their political and economic influence. Nowhere was this shift more dramatic than in Northern California, where the Gold Rush altered the demographic profile almost overnight.

Hispanic hegemony in religious life and public celebrations also dissipated in the half century after the U.S. takeover of the Southwest. By 1890 in the formerly "Catholic" town of Los Angeles there were seventy-eight religious organizations, including groups such as Congregationalists, Jews, Buddhists, Baptists, Unitarians, and an African Methodist Episcopal congregation. In various locales Anglo-Americans promoted the participation of Mexican-descent residents in the parades and ceremonies of newly organized U.S. holidays like the Fourth of July. As one report of an 1851 celebration in San Antonio stated: "We have many foreigners among us who know nothing of our government, who have no national feeling in common with us.... Let us induce them to partake with us in our festivities, they will soon partake our feelings, and when so, they will be citizens indeed."[28]

Parishes and other elements of Catholic life were not immune to change during the turbulent period of transition. Dioceses were established at places like Galveston (1847), Santa Fe (1853), San Francisco (1853), Denver (1887), and Tucson (1897). European clergy served in many areas of the Southwest, with the French predominating in Texas, New Mexico, and Arizona; the Irish in Northern California; and the Spanish in Southern California. During the second half of the nineteenth century, the appointment of Catholic bishops in the region reflected this same pattern, with the exception of a Spaniard in Northern California. Scores of religious sisters and some religious brothers also crossed the Atlantic or came from the eastern United States and began schools, hospitals, orphanages, and other apostolic work in the Southwest.

Differences in culture and religious practice led some newly arrived Catholic leaders to misunderstand and criticize their Mexican coreligionists in some respects. The first resident bishop of Los Angeles, Thaddeus Amat, C.M., oversaw an 1862 synod meeting that forbade Mexican Catholic faith expressions like *los pastores*, a festive proclamation of the shepherds who worshiped the newborn infant Jesus. Reflecting the nineteenth-century ultramontane posture that many European clergy brought with them to the United States, one that stressed loyalty to the pope and the standardization of Catholic ritual and devotion, Amat and the synod fathers repeatedly cited the decrees of the sixteenth-century Council of Trent as the authoritative source for their ecclesial legislation. They ordered priests to "carefully avoid introducing any practices or rites foreign to Roman [practices]" and bemoaned "the scandal which often arises" from Mexican traditions they found too boisterous and indecorous. Thus they demanded that public processions, funeral traditions, and religious feasts strictly adhere to the rubrics of the Roman Ritual and banned long-standing local practices such as festive displays of devotion during processions, cannon salutes as a form of religious devotion, and the fiestas and entertainment that accompanied religious celebrations.[29]

A number of Protestants were utterly condemnatory in their assessment of Mexican Catholicism. After observing public devotion during the feast of the Mexican national patroness, Our Lady of Guadalupe, at Monterey, California, Congregationalist minister Walter Colton mockingly quipped that Guadalupe probably knew or cared little about such religious exhibitions. Baptist minister Lewis Smith wrote from Santa Fe that along with various other rituals, Mexicans reenacted the "farce" of Jesus's crucifixion. Undoubtedly the most renowned of the attacks on Hispanic traditions was directed at Los Hermanos de Nuestro Padre Jesús Nazareno (Brothers of Our Father Jesus the Nazarene), or Penitentes, in northern New Mexico and southern Colorado. Local residents frequently deemed outside observers of their rites "Penitente hunters" because of their intrusive presence and the sensationalistic reports they wrote about the brotherhoods' religious practices.[30]

Protestant leaders attributed U.S. expansion to divine providence and adopted a view of religious "manifest destiny." They saw Hispanic Catholicism as inherently inferior and Protestantism as a force that would inevitably conquer all of the Americas. One minister wrote that the Anglo-American takeover of Texas was "an indication of Providence in relation to the propagation of divine truth in other parts of the Mexican dominions[,]. . . Guatemala and all South America" as well as "the beginning of the downfall of [the] Antichrist, and the spread of the Savior's power of the gospel." Three years before the outbreak of war with Mexico, William Hickling Prescott published his best-selling *History of the Conquest of Mexico*, a romanticized portrayal of Hernán Cortés and the sixteenth-century Spanish invasion of the Aztec empire. In the judgment of historian Jenny Franchot, this influential treatise "subtly modulates into a critique of the vitiated Hispanic civilization that results from the conquest, thus providing an ancestor narrative justifying Mexican subordination to an expansionist Protestant United States."[31]

Explicitly or not, the presumed superiority of civilization and Christianity in the United States has been the most consistent justification for the nation's history of expansionism. Willa Cather's best-selling 1927 novel, *Death Comes for the Archbishop*, played a large part in popularizing this justification. Set in nineteenth-century New Mexico, the novel sharply contrasts the life of Jean Baptiste Lamy (1814–1888), a French priest who became the first bishop (and later archbishop) of Santa Fe, with that of native New Mexican priest Antonio José Martínez (1793–1867). Fictionalized as Bishop Latour, Lamy is idealized as a saintly and civilizing force whose heroic efforts rescued deluded New Mexican Catholics from his antagonist, the allegedly decadent and despotic Martínez. Even Cather's physical description of Martínez—"his mouth was the very assertion of violent, uncurbed passions and tyrannical self-will; the full lips thrust out and taut, like the flesh of animals distended by fear or desire"—evoke disdain and repulsion. Her plotline leaves no doubt that the imposition of U.S. rule and new religious leadership in New Mexico and the greater Southwest was both a sacred duty and a moral imperative.[32]

Cather's depiction of Father Martínez parallels the vitriol of earlier anti-Catholic literature such as Maria Monk's *Awful Disclosures of the Hotel Dieu Nunnery in Montreal* (1836), a slanderous and unfounded account of convent life that became the best-selling literary work of its day. Yet numerous European-descent Catholics were effusive in their praise of *Death Comes for the Archbishop*. Their acclamation of Cather, who was raised Baptist and became an Episcopalian, coincided with a period of rising influence of the Ku Klux Klan and anti-Catholic nativism. Focusing on the laudatory depiction of Lamy as a holy priest and an Americanizing influence, rather than the derogatory figure of Martínez, a number of priests and nuns wrote Cather congratulatory letters. The editor of *Catholic Library World* regarded Cather as "the outstanding American woman novelist of the day" and *Death Comes for the Archbishop* as "her greatest book." A columnist in the national lay Catholic opinion journal *Commonweal* extolled the book's depiction of Lamy and his French clerical companions, who gave "all their powers, their endurance, their courage, their strength, their culture, their riches of European experience" to the task of "saving souls" among Native Americans and "the scanty and static Mexican population." This writer went so far as to say it was "the duty of Catholics to buy and read and spread Willa Cather's masterpiece."[33] Cather's clear-cut delineation between a normative Euro-American Catholicism and its purportedly deficient Hispanic counterpart clearly struck a chord with

European-descent Catholics who were struggling to cast aside their stigmatization as foreigners and achieve social acceptability in the United States.

As renowned historian of the Southwest David Weber noted, "Even scholarly writers must reckon with Cather's imagination." Robert Wright and Gilberto Hinojosa concur that historians of the Southwest—both historians of religion and those who study other topics—have generally "adhered to the basic outline of the received historiographical tradition" reflected in Cather's novel. In his 1981 work *American Catholics*, the distinguished U.S. Catholic historian James Hennesey states that in nineteenth-century New Mexico, the church under Mexican leadership was "decadent" and "sacramental life was virtually non-existent." He argues that "Padre José Antonio [*sic*] Martínez of Taos, depicted under his own name in Willa Cather's *Death Comes for the Archbishop*, was a classic case" of corrupt native priests who "extorted exorbitant fees" and neglected their pastoral duties, leaving local religious culture plagued by "ignorance, neglect, and permissiveness." Regarding Lamy, Hennesey concludes that "the diocese and then the archdiocese of Santa Fe stand as a monument to [his] energy and organizing genius." Though later he offers a more sympathetic overview of Mexican Catholic leaders in California, in his initial treatment of their legacy Hennesey contends that after the secularization of the California missions in 1834, "religion declined" and the Californios were "innocent of cultural influence" and spent their days in "a free and lazy life, riding madly about the countryside, enjoying brutal blood sports."[34]

Mexican Catholics have contested such scandalously deprecating portrayals from the first years of their incorporation into the United States. In December 1848 Bishop John Hughes of New York wrote José de la Guerra y Noriega of Santa Barbara seeking information about conditions in California for the Provincial Council of Baltimore held the following May. Hughes's inquiry included the assertion that all Mexican clergy had abandoned California, leaving Catholics there "destitute of all spiritual aid." In his response, De la Guerra politely but firmly insisted "with due respect to the Mexican priests, that the information which has been given to Your Illustrious Lordship regarding their conduct [abandoning their parishioners] during these latter times does not correspond with the facts." He reported that there were still sixteen priests in California.[35]

Mexican residents employed various strategies to accommodate the new regime. In many locales where ethnic Mexicans remained the majority, Anglo-Americans consolidated control by means of a "peace structure," a "post-war arrangement that allows the victors to maintain law and order without the constant use of force." The peace structure entailed an arrangement between Anglo-American newcomers and the elites of Mexican communities that did not alter traditional authority structures but placed Anglo-Americans atop the existing hierarchy. Often marriages between Anglo-American men and daughters from the elite families of a locale played a key role in this arrangement. These marriages offered Anglo-Americans the advantages of land, inherited wealth, and social status. At the same time, they offered Mexican residents allies to help protect familial interests and land holdings within the new political and economic structures. After the U.S. takeover, such allies were particularly useful, as many Mexicans did not speak English, were unfamiliar with the legal system, and were vulnerable to accusations of disloyalty toward the United States. It is not surprising, then, that during the time of transition, in places like San Antonio "at least one daughter from almost every *rico* [rich] family . . . married an Anglo."[36]

Some residents of the former Mexican territories survived the effects of the U.S. takeover through isolation. In places like northern New Mexico, some degree of autonomy was possible because of the physical distance from U.S. institutions and influence. While this isolation was often the result of circumstance as much as design, Hispanic communities embraced the opportunities for cultural continuity. Nonetheless, in the end, even the most isolated settlements did not fully escape U.S. influence. In the towns and the urban areas that expanded with the arrival of the railroads in the 1870s and 1880s, Mexican *barrios* (neighborhoods) resulted from forced segregation as well as the desire for separation from Anglo-American society. As an ethnic enclave, the barrio mediated a sense of split existence between the familiarity of Mexican home and neighborhood and the alienation of the Anglo-American world where barrio residents often worked and sometimes went to school. At the same time, however, the barrio provided a strong base for group survival, cultural retention, and ethnic pride. In this way it was a structure that enabled Mexicans to sustain themselves despite the social changes they endured.[37]

Hispanic residents like New Mexican Rafael Romero drew on their heritage as natives of the region to defend themselves more directly against what they perceived as the impositions of newcomers. When the territorial governor blocked Jesuit attempts to establish the tax-exempt and degree-granting status of their new school in Las Vegas, New Mexico, in 1878, Romero made a spirited defense of Catholics' rights. His public address during festivities for the close of the school's first academic year acclaimed his audience as native New Mexicans whose "ancestors penetrated into these deserted and dangerous regions many years before the Mayflower floated over the dancing waves that washed Plymouth Rock." He went on to remind his listeners that Jesus was also "tormented by a provincial governor," claiming that the oppressive actions of their current territorial governor were worse than the misdeeds of Pontius Pilate, whose sin, according to Romero, was one of omission rather than direct persecution of the innocent. Defending himself against possible retorts that he spoke too harshly, he went on to ask rhetorically: "Am I not a Catholic citizen of a Catholic land, New Mexico? And have I not, as a New Mexican Catholic, been grossly insulted by a pathetic public official? What does it mean when a man sent to be the governor of a Catholic land, in an official message directed to Catholic legislators and to our Catholic people, piles insult upon insult against a religious order of the Catholic Church?"[38]

Mexican resistance to the consolidation of U.S. rule was not limited to rhetoric. During the war between Mexico and the United States, some offered military resistance to the foreign invaders, such as Californians who defeated U.S. forces at battles in the Los Angeles area and at the hamlet of San Pasqual before peaceably coming to terms with their more numerous and heavily armed foes. Violent resistance erupted in various locales even after the U.S. conquest. In the decades following the U.S. Civil War, guerrilla leaders such as Tiburcio Vásquez in California and Juan Cortina in Texas led retaliatory movements protesting the endemic violence and injustice their people suffered at the hands of Anglo-Americans. Mexican residents also defended their rights in the political arena, as at the 1845 Texas Constitutional Convention when delegate José Antonio Navarro was able to prevent passage of a law that restricted voting rights to Anglo-American residents.[39]

Conflicts between Mexicans and Catholic leaders at times resulted in public controversy and even open resistance, as in the infamous and frequently cited conflict between Padre Martínez and (Arch)bishop Lamy. In 1875 Bishop Dominic Manucy of Brownsville rejected a request that twenty-two exiled Mexican sisters reside in the area and serve Mexican-descent Catholics. Local Spanish-speaking Catholics were incensed at Manucy's decision, particularly since they offered to pay the living costs for the sisters. On the day the women religious were to board the train and depart from Brownsville, an angry crowd removed their train from its tracks and refused to let authorities replace it.[40]

But a number of foreign Catholic clergy and religious became beloved among the Mexican Catholics they served and energetically supported and enhanced their people's faith life and religious practices. Bishop Jean Marie Odin offered ministrations in Spanish and insisted that other priests coming to Texas do the same. He participated in Mexican religious feasts and spoke enthusiastically of the religious zeal demonstrated in these celebrations. San Francisco's first archbishop, Joseph Alemany, O.P., enjoyed a similar rapport with Spanish-speaking Catholics under his care. Women religious led Catholic initiatives in numerous locales, such as Los Angeles, where the Daughters of Charity of St. Vincent de Paul arrived in 1856 to establish a school and orphanage, but soon expanded their ministries to meet other needs such as health care, disaster relief, catechetical instruction, and job placement for women. Most of the sisters who served during the nineteenth century were of Irish descent, but their numbers included women from Mexico and Spain as well as several local Hispanic women who joined the order after receiving their education from the sisters. In Colorado, New Mexico, and the El Paso district, exiled Italian Jesuits served in parishes and as circuit riders to scores of mission stations. They also founded a college at Las Vegas, New Mexico, which they later moved to its current location in Denver and eventually renamed Regis University, and established *La Revista Cátolica*, the first Spanish-language Catholic newspaper in the United States.[41]

A number of local communities asserted their Mexican Catholic heritage in the public spaces of civic life through their long-standing rituals and devotions—sometimes on their own, as in the case of Nacogdoches after Father Díaz de León's murder or of Los Angeles after Bishop Amat's restrictive decrees, at other times with the support of sympathetic priests and religious. From Texas to California, various communities continued to enthusiastically celebrate established local traditions such as pilgrimages, *los pastores*, Holy Week, Corpus Christi, and established patronal feast days like that of Our Lady of Guadalupe. The persistence of religious traditions is particularly striking in light of some Catholic and Protestant leaders' attempts to ban, replace, and condemn them. In the face of such initiatives, as well as military conquest and occupation, violence and lawlessness, political and economic displacement, rapid demographic change, and the erosion of cultural hegemony, Hispanic Catholic feasts and devotions had a heightened significance. These religious traditions provided an ongoing means of public communal expression, affirmation, faith, and resistance to newcomers who criticized or attempted to suppress the heritage of Mexican-descent residents. Undoubtedly fear and anger at their subjugation intensified religious fervor among many devotees.

The most renowned lay group that served as the protectors of treasured local traditions was the aforementioned Penitentes of northern New Mexico and southern Colorado. Penitente brotherhoods evolved in towns and villages well before the U.S. takeover of the area. Their most noticeable function was to commemorate Christ's passion and death, although they also provided community leadership and fostered social integration. Organized as separate local entities, Penitente brotherhoods had a leader named the

*Hermano Mayor* (literally "older brother") and a *morada* (literally "habitation"), or chapter house, where they held meetings and religious devotions. Despite the sharp criticism they often received from outsiders, the Penitentes continued providing leadership for prayer and social life in numerous local communities.[42]

In more urban areas, which tended to have a greater presence of priests and religious, activist Mexican lay women and men continued traditional feast days and faith expressions in Catholic parishes. The annual series of celebrations for Tucson's original patron saint, St. Augustine, lasted for an entire month at San Agustín parish. Similarly, San Fernando parishioners in San Antonio organized public rituals and festivities for Our Lady of Guadalupe, Christmas, San Fernando, San Antonio, San Juan, San Pedro, and other feasts. Most conspicuous among these rites was the annual Guadalupe feast, celebrated with a colorful outdoor procession, elaborate decorations adorning the Guadalupe image and their parish church, gun and cannon salutes, extended ringing of the church bells, and large crowds for services conducted in Spanish.[43]

Women frequently played key leadership roles in public worship and devotion. Doña María Cornelia Salazar and Señora Juana Epifanía de Jesús Valdéz were *madrinas* (godmothers) for the solemn blessing of a new statue for the 1874 Guadalupe feast day at Our Lady of Guadalupe parish in Conejos, Colorado. Throughout the region young women served in processions as the immediate attendants for the Guadalupe image in her annual feast-day celebration.[44] They occupied similar places of prominence in processions for other Marian feast days, such as the Assumption.[45] Even when male Penitentes provided significant leadership for communal worship, women played vital roles in local traditions like the annual procession for the feast of St. John the Baptist.[46] Often these leadership roles did not significantly alter restrictions on women in other public functions, reinforced the notion that women were naturally more pious than men, and symbolically linked the purity of young girls dressed in white with icons like the Virgin Mary, a communal accentuation of feminine chastity that lacked a corresponding association between young boys and Jesus. Yet Mexican-descent women extended their familial efforts to transmit cultural and devotional traditions into a public role of community leadership that shaped Mexican Catholics' ritual expressions. Their leadership demonstrates what Ana María Díaz-Stevens calls the "matriarchal core" of Latino Catholicism—that is, women's exercise of autonomous authority in communal devotions despite the ongoing patriarchal limitations of institutional Catholicism and Latin American societies.[47]

A number of communities in the Southwest struggled for their very survival. In the process their observance of long-standing traditions often abated or even ceased. Nonetheless, as Bishop Henry Granjon of Tucson noted in 1902 during his first pastoral visit to Las Cruces, New Mexico, many Mexican-descent Catholics in the Southwest continued to practice their own customs and traditions decades after the U.S. takeover of their lands. According to Bishop Granjon, in the Southwest these traditions served to "maintain the unity of the Mexican population and permit them to resist, to a certain extent, the invasions of the Anglo-Saxon race."[48] The waves of newly arrived women religious and clergy like Granjon vastly increased the Catholic institutional presence and support structures in the region, enhancing leadership initiatives among Mexican Catholics that enabled a number of local populations to adapt and continue their traditional expressions of faith, defend their sense of dignity, collectively respond to the effects of conquest, and express their own ethnic legitimation.

## New Immigrants

Israel Zangwill's play *The Melting-Pot* opened on Broadway in 1908 and extended into popular parlance the term "melting pot," a concept first articulated in a famous passage of French American writer Hector St. John de Crèvecoeur's 1782 book, *Letters from an American Farmer.* The success of *The Melting-Pot* was rooted in an assimilationist perspective that many Americans endorsed, including President Theodore Roosevelt, who at the conclusion of the opening performance in the nation's capital leaned over the edge of his box and shouted, "That's a great play, Mr. Zangwill, that's a great play." In one of the play's most memorable lines, its hero, a Russian Jewish immigrant named David Quixano, refers to the United States as "the great Melting-Pot" in which the "blood hatreds and rivalries" of Europe dissolve in the "fires of God," the crucible through which "God is making the American." As scholars like Philip Gleason have shown, even more than the dissipation of one's native language and customs, at its core the ideology of the melting pot required the acceptance that the U.S. experiment in democracy represents a decisive break with the past and a new order and model for the future.[49] Zangwill's success was somewhat ironic, given its bold proclamation of the power of a U.S. melting pot to assimilate newcomers and the national sentiment to restrict European immigration that arose concurrently with his play. By the 1920s new legislation severely curtailed the flow of European émigrés that had continued almost unabated over the previous century.

The consequent waning numbers of first-generation Catholics from Europe hastened their transition to monolingual English and the acceptance of U.S. cultural norms. John Tracy Ellis, widely regarded as the premier historian of U.S. Catholicism, observed in his influential general history of American Catholics that the 1920s immigration laws "made a direct contribution to the maturity of the Church in the sense that during the [following] generation its faithful for the first time had an opportunity to become more or less stabilized." Assessing Ellis's scholarly achievement, Daniel J. Boorstin, the editor of the Chicago History of American Civilization book series, in which the Ellis volume appeared, wrote in his 1969 editor's preface to the second edition of the book that recent American Catholic history "is a peculiarly significant and inspiring chapter in the growth and fulfillment of American institutions." More recently, Charles Morris has concluded that "except for the newest waves of Hispanic immigrants, American Catholics have long since made it in America. As much as any other religious body, they are middle-class, suburban, educated, affluent. They exercise control over their own lives in ways that their grandparents never did."[50]

U.S. Catholics had long argued that Boorstin's and Morris's affirmation was true: Catholics were no less American than their counterparts of other faiths. In a 1948 *New York Times* interview, Archbishop John T. McNicholas of Cincinnati, chairman of the administrative board of the U.S. bishops' National Catholic Welfare Conference, contested accusations of Catholic disloyalty from the newly formed organization Protestants and Other Americans United for Separation of Church and State. McNicholas avowed that he and his fellow bishops "deny absolutely and without any qualification that the Catholic bishops of the United States are seeking a union of church and state by any endeavors whatsoever" and that Catholics would not do so even if one day they constituted a majority in the country. Catholic political candidates also vigorously protested accusations that they were unable to uphold the Constitution because their first loyalty was to the Vatican, such as the 1960 indictment of Dr. Ramsey Pollard, president of the Southern Baptist Convention: "No matter what [John F.] Kennedy might say, he cannot separate himself from his church if he is a true Catholic. . . . All we ask is that Roman Catholicism lift its bloody hand from the throats of those that want to worship in the church of their choice." Kennedy and the only previous Catholic national party nominee for president, Alfred E. Smith, famously stated their support for the separation of church and state and the U.S. Constitution, Smith in a 1927 article in the *Atlantic Monthly* and Kennedy in a speech to the Greater Houston Ministerial Association. Kennedy's election was a watershed moment for Catholics, an electoral victory that, in the words of journalist William Shannon, "wiped away the bitterness and disappointment of Al Smith's defeat in 1928; it removed any lingering sense of social inferiority and insecurity."[51]

Hispanics were a small part of the nineteenth-century immigration that gave rise to the Americanizing process of the twentieth century. Though an open border between the United States and Mexico allowed Mexican citizens to migrate even after the Treaty of Guadalupe Hidalgo, their numbers were relatively low until the last three decades of the nineteenth century, when gradually a larger group of immigrants and refugees began to arrive. After the U.S. Civil War ended in 1865, mining, agriculture, and railroad construction in the regions from Texas to California, and then in Mexico itself, linked the regions economically, creating migration flows of Mexican labor north. The Porfirio Díaz regime (1876–1911) in Mexico promoted economic growth linked to foreign interests, leading to prosperity for some but displacement and migration for others, who went to the United States looking for work. U.S. interests in Caribbean products, particularly sugar and tobacco, also encouraged the movement of Puerto Ricans and Cubans to the United States. Intermittent struggles for independence in both Puerto Rico and Cuba led some political activists into U.S. exile. While many political exiles were skeptical if not antagonistic toward the Catholic Church and its leaders, who in their native lands consisted largely of Spaniards and others who supported Spanish colonial rule, Caribbean newcomers augmented the diversity of Hispanic Catholics in the United States.[52]

Like European Catholic émigrés, many Hispanics advocated for national or ethnic parishes as a means to retain their language, cultural practices, sense of group identity, and Catholic faith. As early as 1871, Catholics at San Francisco proposed a national parish to serve the Spanish-speaking population in their growing city. Although most Spanish-speaking residents were of Mexican descent, representatives from the consulates of Chile, Peru, Nicaragua, Colombia, Bolivia, Costa Rica, and Spain were among the leaders in this effort, making it one of if not the first pan-Hispanic Catholic initiatives in the United States. Four years later, San Francisco archbishop Joseph Alemany established the national parish of Our Lady of Guadalupe. In 1879 Cuban lay Catholics in Key West, Florida, worked with church officials to establish a chapel named after Nuestra Señora de la Caridad del Cobre (Our Lady of Charity of El Cobre), the most prominent Marian icon and devotional tradition in Cuban Catholicism. Worshipers at the chapel organized the Caridad del Cobre feast, other Marian devotions, Christmas pageants, and even a celebrated pastoral visit from the archbishop of Santiago, Cuba.[53]

One of the earliest Cuban exiles was the influential Father Félix Varela (1788–1853), who fled to New York in 1823 after the Spanish regime he opposed as a Cuban delegate to the Spanish Cortes (parliament) condemned him to death. In exile Varela worked as a parish priest and eventually rose to the position of vicar general for the diocese of New York. But even in the midst of a busy pastoral life among Irish and other New York Catholics, he continued to advocate for Cuban independence from Spain and the abolition of the slave trade, along with writing and thinking about politics, philosophy, and religion. He published an important exile newspaper, *El Habanero*, in which he promoted Cuban independence, and maintained active correspondence and intellectual exchange with his compatriots on the island. Although the Spanish government pardoned him in 1833, Varela refused to acknowledge that his support for constitutional rule represented criminal activity. He remained in exile and never returned to Cuba. Now a candidate for official canonization as a Catholic saint, Varela is also recognized as a precursor of Cuban pro-independence thought. Cubans often describe him as "the one who first taught us to think."[54]

As European immigration declined and the process of their incorporation into American life quickened over the course of the twentieth century, nascent Hispanic immigration accelerated. The expansion of cities and agribusiness in the Southwest, the enticement of railroad and industrial jobs in the Midwest, and exemption from the exclusionary 1920s legislation that curtailed European immigration were key factors attracting Mexican émigrés. Massive Mexican immigration began after the outbreak of the Mexican Revolution in 1910, expanding the population of existing ethnic Mexican communities in the Southwest and establishing scores of new populations in that region and beyond. Intermittent periods of relative calm followed the enactment of the 1917 Mexican constitution, but violence erupted once again in central and western Mexico when President Plutarco Elías Calles (1924–1928) vigorously enforced anticlerical articles of that constitution. The resulting guerrilla war, known as the Cristero Rebellion (1926–1929), drove even more émigrés north to the United States, many fleeing religious persecution. During the Depression era of the 1930s Mexican migration all but came to a halt, and a wave of nativist fever led to the repatriation of numerous Mexicans and the illegal deportation of many native-born Mexican American citizens. But the northward flow resumed with growing work opportunities during World War II. The infamous *Bracero*, or guest worker, program (1942–1964) brought some five million contracted workers north from Mexico, a number of whom stayed or eventually returned to establish homes in the United States. A number of undocumented migrants also crossed into the United States. Many of them stayed permanently. After the Bracero program ended, the number of undocumented workers increased dramatically, a trend that continues into the twenty-first century. Today ethnic Mexicans in the United States comprise about two-thirds of the nearly 50 million Latinos in the country. Though the Latino population is widely dispersed across the nation, half of them live in California or Texas due primarily to the heavy concentration of ethnic Mexicans in those two states.[55]

The Puerto Rican case illustrates economic dynamics that led migrants from the Caribbean and Latin America northward. Following the U.S. occupation of the island in 1898 after the Spanish-American War, Puerto Rico's subsistence farming and primarily agricultural economy increasingly became a single, cash crop enterprise. During the last decade of Spanish rule, the island produced 57,000 tons of sugar a year. Five years after the U.S. takeover that rate had increased to 200,000 tons per year. By 1930 it was 900,000 tons a year. This transition to a single export commodity subject to price fluctuations on international markets placed a great deal of pressure on the traditional subsistence economy. As owners concentrated their landholdings to facilitate productivity and growth, Puerto Rican farmers were displaced. Also problematic was that sugar production provided work only during the harvests, leaving workers unemployed or underemployed the rest of the year. Puerto Ricans left home in increasing numbers, searching for a more stable livelihood. The number of Puerto Ricans living on the mainland increased from 1,513 in 1910 to nearly 53,000 in 1930. Migratory pressures became even more dramatic after World War II when policymakers introduced incentives to create a manufacturing base, a program known as Operation Bootstrap. Industrialization initiated a new era in the island's economic history, producing a nascent middle class. At the same time, the urbanization of a primarily rural people and the uneven participation in the economic benefits of industrialization led many more to leave home in an unprecedented migration to the mainland. The first great waves of Puerto Rican migrants after World War II went to New York City, where more than 80 percent of the Puerto Rican population on the mainland lived in 1950. But over time Puerto Ricans increasingly moved beyond New York to other locales, including a growing number who gained higher education during the transformations of Puerto Rico's economy. Today approximately 10 percent of the Latino population on the U.S. mainland is Puerto Rican.[56]

Thousands of Cubans also left their homeland, in their case largely as a result of Fidel Castro's 1959 rise to power in the Cuban Revolution, a struggle that a number of Catholics initially supported. Castro's radicalizing of the revolution led to confrontations between his government and Catholic Church leaders. In November 1959 they convened a National Catholic Congress that drew some one million supporters to Havana's Plaza Cívica—or Plaza de la Revolución, as it later became known—to reaffirm their Catholic allegiance and, implicitly, protest the country's political direction. The following year Cuban Catholic bishops and lay leaders publicly acknowledged the need for reforms to advance the well-being of the poor, but also called for human rights for all citizens and expressed alarm at the government's growing relations with Communist bloc nations. Thousands of Catholics subsequently fled the island, some joining exile counter-revolutionary groups like those that conducted the failed 1961 Bay of Pigs invasion. Castro cited such actions as a rationale to repress church leaders. By 1963 some 200,000 Cubans had arrived in the United States, including the core of Cuba's Catholic militant laity and leadership. The majority of Cubans initially established themselves in the Miami area, but the federally run Cuban Refugee Program settled others in locales across the country. Though many of these first exiles were educated, professional, and Catholic, over the following decades as Castro's stance shifted back and forth between restrictive and more open immigration policies, those who abandoned the island encompassed a wider spectrum of Cuban society. The largest group after the initial exodus came in 1980 when the Cuban government opened the port of Mariel for exiles wishing to pick up family members. As the boats arrived from Florida, authorities filled them with people who wanted to leave but also with others who had been forcibly deported, about 125,000 Cubans in all. All told, more than a million Cubans arrived in the United States in the half century since the Cuban Revolution.[57]

Countries from throughout the Western hemisphere were represented in the U.S. immigration flows by the 1990s, making the U.S. Latino population more complex and diverse than ever. Civil wars during the 1970s and 1980s in Central America, especially in El Salvador, Guatemala, and Nicaragua, were the catalyst for growing numbers of refugees from that region. In El Salvador, for example, a civil war ravaged between 1979 and 1992, claiming the lives of more than seventy-five thousand victims, until a 1992 peace accord brought some alleviation to hostilities. Refugees numbering in the hundreds of thousands fled the country. Economic dynamics, urbanization, increases in birth rates and life expectancies, growing aspirations for better lives, improved transportation, ties with family members already in the United States, and the communications revolution led people from across Latin America and the Caribbean to immigrate. The Dominican presence in the United States was fairly limited until the last years of dictator General Rafael Leónidas Trujillo, who ruled the Dominican Republic from 1930 to 1961 and severely restricted international migration. After Trujillo's 1961 assassination the migrant flow accelerated, with the majority of émigrés settling in New York and the environs. By 1990, Dominicans in New York numbered some seven hundred thousand and rivaled the local Puerto Rican population in size. Though South Americans comprise a relatively small minority of U.S. Hispanics, in recent decades their numbers have also increased, with Colombians, Peruvians, and Ecuadorians predominating, but with additional émigrés from nations such as Argentina, Chile, and Brazil. Given the distance involved in their migration, those who are able to make it to the United States tend to have a higher income and level of education. Consequently they are disproportionately represented among the clergy and lay leaders in dioceses and parishes, exercising an influence beyond their numbers.[58]

The profound but vastly diverse formative experiences of émigrés from the Caribbean, Mexico, and Central and South America defy easy generalization. Church-state relations have a long history, as evidenced in the acrimonious episodes of conflict in Mexico and, in more recent decades, in the elections of a Catholic priest and bishop as presidents of Haiti and Paraguay, respectively, in both cases leading these clergy to desist from exercising their priestly functions at the behest of Vatican officials. Historically, the number of available clergy is another key factor shaping Catholic impact, in some cases a sufficient number of priests to wield significant influence but usually not enough to address large and dispersed Catholic populations. Devotional expressions of faith are widely practiced in a Catholicism that values direct—what theologians call sacramental—encounters with God, Mary, and the saints in everyday life. Every country in Latin America has at least one shrine dedicated to a Marian image that is a center of national veneration and identity. Yet the faith stance among local populations ranges from those who engage Catholicism as primarily a heritage of devotional traditions, as a means to struggle for justice, or as an institution with a defined body of doctrines and teachings. Not surprisingly, many Latin Americans believe Catholicism entails some combination of these or other elements, though a substantial number are involved with Catholicism only nominally or not at all. Protestantism, especially in its Pentecostal and evangelical forms, has expanded rapidly though unevenly throughout the continent. Mexico remains one of the most staunchly Catholic nations in terms of the preferred denominational allegiance of its population, while Puerto Rico, where the U.S. government and churches conducted an energetic program of Americanization and Protestant proselytizing after annexing the island in 1898, is among the most Protestant. Such historical and religious legacies mark in myriad ways the perceptions of any Latino émigré who spent his or her formative years at home before arriving in the United States.[59]

Latin America's most direct influence on Catholicism in the United States is the formative experiences that immigrants carry with them. Nicaraguan refugee Sara García fled the civil war in her country with her husband and three children in 1984. Resettled as an undocumented resident in Newark, García noted in an interview that her fear of deportation to a native country where she would be punished or even killed led to a deepening of her trust in God: "All we can do is commend ourselves to God whenever we leave the house and, when we return, thank the Lord we made it safe and sound." Yet she also said that her Catholic faith was rooted in her childhood experiences in rural Nicaragua. García received only a first-grade education but remembered the nuns who came to offer the catechesis that prepared her for her first communion. Though her family's poverty was so acute that her mother worked day and night and had little time to take her children to church, the influence of her mother's example and the Catholic culture of her childhood were lasting. Regarding her faith, García echoed the sentiments of many Hispanic Catholics: "I was born a Catholic and, God willing, I will die a Catholic."[60]

Catholic ministries to Hispanic newcomers expanded with the rising tide of immigration. Émigré clergy, women religious, and lay leaders ministered among their compatriots, as during the Mexican Revolution, the Cristero Rebellion, and their aftermath, when Mexican Catholics collaborated with U.S. church officials to establish new parishes in such diverse places as Los Angeles, Houston, Dallas, Kansas City, Milwaukee, St. Paul, and Toledo. Twelve Mexican parishes opened in Los Angeles alone between 1923 and 1928, with the total number of predominantly Mexican parishes in the archdiocese increasing to sixty-four by 1947. In other instances U.S. Catholics engaged in outreach to the newcomers, such as the visionary lay apostolic endeavors of Mary Julia Workman in settlement house ministry in Los Angeles and Veronica Miriam Spellmire in establishing and fostering the phenomenal growth of the Confraternity of Christian Doctrine in San Antonio, as well as the response of the New York archdiocese to Puerto Rican migration under the leadership of Cardinal Francis Spellman and priests such as Joseph Fitzpatrick, S.J.; Robert Fox, Ivan Illich, and Robert Stern. U.S.-born Hispanics also engaged in dedicated ecclesial service to their own communities, such as the Missionary Catechists of Divine Providence, the first and only religious order of Mexican American women founded in the United States, who have provided leadership in evangelization and catechesis in the Southwest and beyond for more than eighty years.[61]

Like European Catholic immigrants before them, each group of Latino newcomers fostered ministries and church structures that served the needs of their compatriots. None illustrate such initiatives more clearly than Cuban exiles. Historically, Catholicism had a relatively minor role in Cuban society.

The church hierarchy never wielded the political influence it did in Latin American locales like Mexico. Practice of the faith was far stronger among the elite and more nominal among the masses of the working class, especially in the island's predominantly rural areas. Yet a Catholic renaissance gradually emerged during the first half of the twentieth century, which, while still largely focused on the middle and upper classes, led to an array of schools, lay movements, and social action initiatives that helped form strong cohorts of Catholic leaders. The strength and public activism of this leadership was sufficient enough that under Castro all foreign priests and a significant portion of Cuban priests were deported or left the island under duress. Proportionally these clergy provided exile communities with substantially more priests of their own than any other Latino group. Because the first exiles were drawn heavily from Cuba's middle and upper classes, lay Catholic leaders who had received substantial faith formation in Cuba were also well prepared to play a key role in organizing educational and pastoral initiatives once they arrived in the United States.[62]

Cuban Catholics in Miami wasted little time creating a formal presence. Catholic schools opened to accommodate the demand among Cubans, including the continuation in exile of several academies that the Castro government had closed in Cuba, such as the highly regarded Belén and La Salle. These schools offered an English-language Catholic education within a Cuban cultural environment that promoted the Spanish language, Cuban identity, and an exile consciousness. By 1962 sixteen parishes in the Miami area had Spanish-speaking priests on staff. A year later a predominantly Cuban congregation, San Juan Bosco, was established in Miami's Little Havana district. Substantial numbers of Cuban Catholics helped found or participated in other parishes. Shortly after the 1965 closing of the Second Vatican Council and the enactment of its decrees that led to the celebration of the Eucharist in vernacular languages rather than Latin, Miami-area parishes had a combined total of thirty weekly Masses in Spanish. Nearly one hundred Cuban priests were serving in the Miami archdiocese by 1975.[63]

Though Cubans found U.S. Catholicism more parish-based than had been the case in their homeland, where lay apostolic movements played a central role in their practice of the faith, Cuban lay initiatives helped nurture their Catholicism in exile. The "transplanting" of the Agrupación Católica Universitaria (ACU) exemplifies the dynamism of lay organizations. Spanish Jesuit Felipe Rey de Castro founded the ACU in 1931 to form select university students and professional men as Catholic leaders through the spiritual exercises of St. Ignatius of Loyola. On the eve of the Cuban Revolution, the sodality had nearly six hundred members, or *agrupados*, as they refer to themselves. They had fostered from among their numbers the vocations of more than two dozen Jesuits and four diocesan priests, including Bishop Eduardo Boza Masvidal, who became the most influential Cuban bishop in exile. The ACU also engaged extensively in charitable works and in social reform efforts like its influential 1958 report on rural workers, *¿Por qué reforma agraria?* (Why Agrarian Reform?). Father Rey de Castro's successor as ACU spiritual director, his fellow Jesuit Amando Llorente, gathered ACU members for a retreat within a month of his exile to Miami. Shortly thereafter exiled ACU members began to publish the organization's newspaper, *Esto Vir*, and by 1963 they had convened an international ACU convention in Atlanta. These efforts enabled Cubans who had not settled in Miami to remain involved, as did Father Llorente's pastoral visits to dispersed ACU members and the distribution of his taped weekly homilies. Adapting to their new circumstances, by 1966 the ACU had accepted non-Cubans as members, a decision that enabled the group to grow in numbers and remain viable into the twenty-first century.[64]

Cuba's Nuestra Señora de la Caridad del Cobre is the most important symbol of Cuban exile Catholicism. Though the original image of the patroness resides in a shrine at El Cobre in eastern Cuba, a replica from a parish church in Guanabo Beach near Havana arrived in Miami for the Virgin's feast-day celebration on September 8, 1961, and Cuban exiles continued to fervently commemorate the annual feast of their patroness. Their 1966 celebration inspired Miami bishop (later archbishop) Coleman Carroll to call for the construction of a sanctuary dedicated to her. At Bishop Carroll's invitation, the leader for this initiative was Msgr. Agustín Román, a highly regarded priest who later became the first Cuban to be named a bishop in the United States. Over the next seven years, exiles helped fund the construction of the sanctuary that Carroll consecrated upon its completion in 1973. The shrine quickly became a place of pilgrimage for Cubans who linked La Caridad to their sense of Cuban nationality.[65]

Cuban Catholics expressed deep gratitude for Carroll's endorsement of La Caridad shrine and for the Miami (arch)diocese's outreach efforts to exiles through its Centro Hispano Católico. Msgr. Bryan Walsh was a tireless advocate for Cubans during their resettlement and led the famous Operation Peter Pan, which found accommodations for young Cubans whose parents sent them ahead out of fear they would be conscripted into Communist-led schools or military service. But there were also tensions between Cubans and U.S. church leaders. ACU members accused Archbishop Carroll and his assistants of being heavy-handed in their imposition of an assimilationist agenda on Cubans, arguing that the U.S. clergy "feared the cultural expression of Catholicism that Cubans brought with them would disrupt the ecclesial unity of the diocese of Miami." *Agrupados* bemoaned what they perceived as "a thorough attempt to force Cubans to adhere to American patterns and to swiftly transform themselves into American Catholics." Whether intended or not, many Cubans perceived that Miami church officials sought to purge their intense exile consciousness and anti-Communism, as when Archbishop Carroll prohibited popular Cuban priest Father Ramón O'Farrill from delivering an invocation at the 1972 Republican National Convention. A report in the Spanish-language Miami newspaper *Alerta* outlined the situation of Cuban priests like O'Farrill, concluding that "the Cuban Catholic priests of Miami are the object of a severe and unprecedented discrimination on the part of this city's archbishop." Not surprisingly, Archbishop Carroll disagreed with such charges, citing his considerable effort to welcome Cuban exiles in the archdiocese and make them part of its structures and life of faith. He avowed that Cuban initiatives conducted without diocesan approval and oversight weakened episcopal authority and ecclesial unity.[66]

The Cuban case illustrates two parallel forces in motion within U.S. Catholicism since World War II. Latino Catholics, previously a largely Mexican and Puerto Rican population concentrated in New York, the Southwest, and various Midwestern cities and towns, now encompass expanded contingents from every nation of Latin America and the Caribbean and extend from Seattle to Boston, from Miami to Alaska. The growth of their population occurred contiguously with European-descent Catholics' rise to respectability as full-fledged Americans. Many Euro-American Catholics have only vague memories of their immigrant heritage. Today there are more Catholic millionaires and more Catholics in Congress than any other denomination. Six of nine justices on the Supreme Court are Catholic. As Allan Figueroa Deck, S.J., has noted, the Hispanic "second wave" of Catholic immigration to the United States has occurred just as "U.S. Catholics have become comfortable with their hard-earned [U.S. American] identity" and "achieved acceptance in a predominantly Protestant and rather anti-Catholic country."[67] The relations between early Cuban exiles and officials of the Miami (arch)diocese—a mix of compassionate outreach, misunderstanding, frustration, and collaboration—illustrate the varied exchanges occurring between Latinos and their coreligionists in parishes and dioceses throughout the country.

## Catholicism in America

The Cuban exile experience is but one example of the myriad ways that, for good and for ill, Catholics throughout the American hemisphere mutually influence their fellow Catholics in other locales. Recognizing this reality,

contemporary church officials have promoted vital links they believe are conducive to stronger Catholic faith and evangelization in the hemisphere. The
Latin American episcopal conferences at Medellín, Puebla, Santo Domingo,
and Aparecida, as well as the 1999 Synod on America, have increasingly taken
a more hemispheric focus. In a homily at Yankee Stadium on his first visit to
the United States, Pope John Paul II boldly likened the split between the richer
and more powerful nations and the more economically impoverished nations
of the world to the rich man and Lazarus of Luke 16. He avowed that one of
the great challenges in the American hemisphere and in our world today is
to see that the destinies of the richer northern and poorer southern halves
of the planet are intimately conjoined. Significantly, in subsequent teachings
John Paul did not speak of "America" in the plural, but in the singular. In his
apostolic exhortation *Ecclesia in America*, the title of which itself denotes the
interconnectedness of the hemisphere, he noted explicitly that his "decision
to speak of *America* in the singular was an attempt to express not only the
unity which in some way already exists, but also to point to that closer bond
that the peoples of the continent seek and that the church wishes to foster as
part of her own mission."[68]

Interpreters of the past do well to adopt such a vision of the hemisphere,
reimagining national histories within the context of an international American Catholicism and social reality. In this approach the term "American" itself, usually employed in the United States to designate the national ethos,
connotes historical links and the need for solidarity across international borders. Without discounting the interpretive contribution of the Americanization paradigm, particularly for understanding the experience of European-
descent Catholics, a hemispheric American perspective enhances the effort
to construct a narrative of the U.S. Catholic past that encompasses the struggles and contributions of Father Díaz de León, his Nacogdoches parishioners,
and Bishop Odin, as well as their East Coast contemporaries and numerous
other Catholics.

One implication of this broader perspective is the need to articulate the
multiple origins of Catholicism in what is now the United States. The first
French Catholic settlement within the current U.S. borders was on Ste. Croix
(De Monts) Island in present-day Maine and, like early Hispanic settlements,
also preceded the first British colony. Escaped slaves from the Carolinas and
Georgia, whom Spanish officials in Florida welcomed as free persons on the
condition that they converted to Catholicism, were the first people of African
descent to establish a settlement in territories that are now part of the United
States. They founded Gracia Real de Santa Teresa de Mose near St. Augustine
in 1738. Afro-Latino Catholic influence was also evident in places like Los

Angeles, where more than half of the *primer pobladores* (first settlers) in 1781 were at least partially African. Native peoples became Catholic in response to colonial missionary efforts, most notably Blessed Kateri Tekakwitha (1656–1680), a child of Algonquin and Mohawk parents born in what is now Auriesville, New York. Tekakwitha was baptized when she was twenty and, though weakened with various physical complications from a bout with smallpox, inspired many through her life of prayer, fasting, and service.[69] Historical studies of the United States usually focus on the British and then U.S. ascent over French, native, and Spanish rivals in the formation of a new nation. But the story of U.S. Catholicism must treat the various peoples who first lived the Catholic faith and established Catholic institutional presence in places that are now part of the United States, and then examine the contact and conflict between these groups as the European powers, the natives, and the nascent U.S. nation vied for territorial control.

The subsequent growth and development of Catholicism in the United States during the great century of European immigration (1820–1920) cannot be fully explicated without due attention to nonimmigrant Catholics. Like Mexicans in the Southwest, Native Americans struggled to endure—some in communities that Spanish and French missioners had previously sought to evangelize, others within the new system of U.S. laws, Indian reservations, and government-sanctioned Christianization efforts. The travails of African Americans were no less traumatic. Catholic laity, priests, and religious orders had slaves, a number of whom were baptized Catholic and instructed in the faith. When President Abraham Lincoln signed into law a military draft to support the northern Civil War cause in 1863, New Yorkers, many of them immigrant Irish Catholics who vied with African Americans for unskilled labor jobs, assaulted black residents in one of the bloodiest riots in the history of the city. Yet both African and Native Americans exhibited uncommon steadfastness in their faith against all odds. Venerable Pierre Toussaint (1766–1853), born a slave in the French colony of Santo Domingo (Haiti), resettled with his master in New York. There he became a successful hairdresser among the city's aristocratic women, obtained his freedom, and was renowned for his devotion to daily Mass and his remarkable life of charity. Henriette Delille (c. 1813–1862) accomplished the amazing feat of founding an African American order of women religious in antebellum New Orleans. She is acclaimed as a "servant of slaves" and "witness to the poor." As with Delille, the cause for sainthood of Augustus Tolton (1854–1897) has been introduced in the Vatican. A former slave who became the first African American priest, Tolton had to study in Rome because segregated U.S. seminaries would not admit him. He endured racism and ridicule as the first African American to breach the "color line" of the priesthood in the United States. Nicholas Black Elk (c. 1863–1950) was celebrated both as a medicine man among the Lakota Sioux of the Northern Plains and as a lay Catholic catechist.[70] Historically, Catholics such as these cannot be subsumed into a saga of immigrants. The conquered, the enslaved, and freed former slaves—along with the more numerous and influential immigrants—necessitate examining more deeply how the distinct experiences of entry into the United States shaped participation in church and society and thus to varying degrees the formation of U.S. Catholicism.

The Americanization of émigrés' descendants in the course of the twentieth century occurred simultaneously with another crucial historical trend: the significant new immigration of Catholics to the United States. Demographic growth in U.S. Catholicism over the past half century is heavily rooted in immigration from Asia, the Pacific Islands, Africa, and particularly Latin America. Officials of the United States Conference of Catholic Bishops estimate that more than half the Catholics in the United States today are not of Euro-American ancestry. In the archdiocese of Los Angeles alone, the Eucharist is regularly celebrated in forty-two languages. The Roman Catholic Church in the United States is the most ethnically and racially diverse national ecclesial body in the world. Historical analyses must explore the implications of this striking phenomenon.

Today the international and especially the hemispheric connections of Catholicism in the United States are more extensive than ever. Interaction between émigrés and their fellow U.S. residents is the most common means through which church and society in the United States and various other nations shape one another. Immigrants also exert influence on their ancestral homelands, particularly Hispanics who live in greater proximity to their native countries. Certainly their major economic influence is the remittances immigrant workers send home, which in some years has averaged as much as $2 billion per month to Mexico alone. Remittances do not solely support family members; they also fund community projects such as the sponsorship of feast-day celebrations and the construction and upkeep of churches, religious shrines, and schools. The conspicuous flow of fiscal resources reflects less often noted cultural and religious exchanges, such as the experiences immigrants have in parishes, prayer groups, and church renewal movements in the United States that they carry with them when they return home to visit or resettle. Mexican parishioners from Nuestra Señora del Rosario parish in Coeneo, Michoacán, illustrate the capacity of immigrants to transform religious practice in their native land. The numerous baptisms and marriages which émigrés return home to celebrate, especially during the weeks surrounding the Christmas holiday, has notably shifted the ritual calendar of parish life from a cycle of traditional devotions and feast days to a cycle of sacraments and family gatherings that revolve around the schedules of returning immigrants. Hispanic Catholics in the United States have also initiated outreach efforts to Latin America, such as the Amor en Acción lay missionary community in the archdiocese of Miami, which was formally established in 1976 under the inspiration of Alicia Marill and Adriano Garcia to foster ministerial collaboration in the Dominican Republic and Haiti.[71]

A hemispheric perspective on Catholicism requires attention to migratory flows in all directions, which in the last half century have encompassed a relatively small but influential group of U.S. Catholics who have visited Latin America or served in church ministries there. Often their experiences transform their understanding of Catholicism, as well as their attitudes toward the foreign policy of the United States. Catholics from the United States have received ministerial training at centers such as the Institute of Intercultural Communication, which Father Ivan Illich founded in Puerto Rico in 1957. During its fifteen years in operation the institute staff trained numerous priests, seminarians, and other pastoral workers for the archdiocese of New York. Women religious, priests, and lay missioners have also established significant and vital links between the United States and the rest of the Americas through missionary institutes, most notably Maryknoll. Other Latin American links include U.S. Catholics' awareness and involvement with liberation theology; the civil wars in Central America during the 1970s and 1980s; well-known incidents like the 1980 murders of Archbishop Oscar Romero and four U.S. church women serving in El Salvador; and the numerous delegations of students, scholars, and church leaders who have visited and established contacts in Central and South America and the Caribbean.

The ambitious project of a hemispheric approach holds great promise for studies of U.S. Catholicism, first and foremost through placing those investigations within the broad context of one of the most momentous events of Christianity's second millennium: the encounter and clash of the Old and the New Worlds. Conquest, settlement, enslavement, immigration, and exile were the human—and too often inhuman—experiences that constituted this massive intermingling of diverse peoples. Wars to establish nation-states independent of European rule and struggles to this day for life, dignity, and self-determination are part of the painful legacy of violence and conquest that gave birth to the hemisphere Europeans named America. Despite rampant injustices, Native Americans, Africans, Europeans, their mixed-race offspring, and to a lesser extent Asians have all contributed to the formation of new societies, cultures, and traditions. Interpreters of U.S. Catholic history need to address all of these peoples and experiences within the current borders of the United States but against the backdrop and comparative framework of the American continent. This entails the recognition that the U.S. Catholic Church was never exclusively an immigrant church, nor is it solely an "Americanized" church today. Rather, it is a church built on the founding faith of migratory, conquered, and enslaved peoples that currently is largely run by middle-class, European-descent Catholics with growing numbers of Latino, Asian, and African immigrants, along with sizable contingents of U.S.-born Latinos, African Americans, Asian Americans, and some Native Americans.

Consciously or not, on the practical level the long-standing links between Latin and North America already lead many Latinos to adopt a more hemispheric perspective to Catholicism in the United States. Though the number of Hispanic Catholics in the regions from Florida to California at the time of their U.S. incorporation was comparatively small, the memory that Hispanics established faith communities in Spanish and Mexican territories before the United States expanded into them shaped the historical development of those communities as they, their descendants, and even later immigrants became part of the United States. Marking the landscape with hundreds of Spanish place-names and churches like San Antonio's San Fernando Cathedral—which has remained a predominantly Hispanic congregation under the flags of Spain, Mexico, the Republic of Texas, the United States, the Confederate States of America, and then the United States again—enduring communities of faith provided a foundation on which Mexicans and other Latinos later built. More importantly, they fostered a sense among these subsequent émigrés that places to which they came were not entirely foreign, but an extension of home. As a Mexican immigrant to San Antonio commented after experiencing the ambiance and public worship of the cathedral congregation, San Fernando "is the one place in San Antonio that's still part of Mexico."[72]

Such perceptions conflict with the presumption that European immigrants and their descendants set a unilateral paradigm for assimilating newcomers into church and society. Since the early 1990s the geographic dispersion of Latinos across the United States and the growing diversity of their national backgrounds, a number of them immigrants whose Catholicism is rooted in formative years spent in their native lands, have brought the historical perspectives of Catholics from Latin America and the United States into unprecedented levels of daily contact. In numerous dioceses and parishes where a significant Hispanic presence has arisen for the first time—and in many others where the Hispanic presence is long-standing—Latinos and their fellow Catholics encounter in the quotidian relations of ecclesial life not just unfamiliar customs and languages, but also the intersection of different histories. The profound historical convergences underlying these encounters intensify the potency of everyday experiences to cause trust or apprehension, collaboration or isolation. These convergences also shape the dynamics of Hispanic integration into church and society that are crucial for the next chapter in U.S. Catholic history.

CHAPTER 2

# Integration

I mmigrant clergy can border on the hagiographic when they exalt the influence of Catholicism in their native land. One priest lauded his compatriots' "simple yet strong piety and trust in God," the influence of a Catholic ethos in everyday life, and the "deep religious feeling [and] love for the Madonna," which "alone would be proof of the strength of their religion." His depiction elicited a two-month dispute in the pages of the national Catholic weekly *America*. The first respondent retorted that "piety does not consist in processions or carrying lighted candles, in prostrations before a statue of the Madonna, in processions in honor of the patron saints of villages." Others characterized immigrants as ignorant of their Catholic faith, infrequent in church attendance, and unwilling to offer financial or other support to parishes. For these reasons critics regarded the émigrés as "easy victim[s] to the Protestant proselytizer." Immigrant defenders questioned the legitimacy of such claims. They opined that immigrants' practice of their faith was remarkable when one considered that most of them were poor workers struggling for their very survival. Most had endured the ordeal of migrating from their homelands to blighted neighborhoods in U.S. cities, where they found relatively few priests prepared to serve them in their native tongue. Several respondents in the debate pointed out the enthusiastic immigrant response to pastoral outreach efforts. Some considered the real issue to be the hostility the immigrants so frequently meet in the United States, even from members of their own church.[1]

The short statement with which the editors of *America* closed this controversy sided with the critics: "When all has been said and due discount has been made for the insufficiency of the data offered as the basis of a judgment, the conviction, we think, will cling to most readers' minds that there is an Italian problem, and that it clamors for solution." The year was 1914, three decades after debate about the "Italian problem" surfaced among U.S. Catholic bishops at their 1884 Plenary Council of Baltimore. Pope Leo XIII even weighed in on the situation in an 1888 letter urging the U.S. bishops to provide his immigrant compatriots "the saving care of ministers of God familiar with the Italian language."[2]

Accusations and rebuttals regarding the Italian immigrants of yesteryear are strikingly parallel to perceptions of today's Latino Catholics. Indeed, the protracted debate about Italians reveals a central and long-standing feature of U.S. Catholicism: the varied attempts to incorporate diverse groups into a unified body of faith. Gerald Shaughnessy's 1925 book, *Has the Immigrant Kept the Faith?* reflected the core concerns and fears of numerous priests and prelates in this regard.[3] Was the Catholic Church losing millions of adherents during the process of integration into the United States? Should pastoral leaders actively foster integration, as many Irish bishops advised, or promote linguistic and cultural retention in order to fortify the émigrés' Catholic loyalties, as German immigrant leaders frequently exhorted?

Unlike European émigrés from the great century of migration between 1820 and 1920, today's Hispanic newcomers tend to have not only ethnic differences but also class and educational differences from descendants of previous immigrant groups. The challenge of forging unity among such an increasingly diverse ecclesial body is more acute than ever. Central to this challenge is the hotly debated question of whether Latinos will—or should— adopt the language and cultural ethos of the United States.

Many Catholic scholars and pastoral leaders presume the experience of European immigrants and their descendants established an Americanization paradigm that other newcomers will inevitably follow. The late Samuel Huntington's book *Who Are We? The Challenges to America's National Identity* forecasted that the United States is well on its way to precisely the opposite scenario: the emergence of a precipitously bifurcated English-Spanish society due to support for multiculturalism, extensive Latino and especially Mexican immigration, and the singular tendency of Spanish-speaking émigrés to retain their language and culture. Huntington forewarned that these trends threaten to refashion a "[United States of] America with two languages and two cultures [that] will be fundamentally different from the America with one language and one core Anglo-Protestant culture that has existed for over three centuries." Commenting on marketing executive Lionel Sosa's book *The Americano Dream: How Latinos Can Achieve Success in Business and in Life*, Huntington unambiguously revealed his convictions on the matter of assimilation: "There is no Americano dream. There is only the American dream created by an Anglo-Protestant society. Mexican-Americans will share in that dream and in that society only if they dream in English." In a similar vein, Victor Davis Hanson's book, provocatively titled *Mexifornia: A State of Becoming*, addressed citizens of the state that most consider the epicenter of Hispanicization with the dire warning, "If we do not change by either adopting an assimilationist program or insisting on metered and legal immigration, or both, we shall soon see a culture in southern and central California that really is a hybrid civilization." Such fears and proposed remedies to address them have undergirded various state ballot initiatives for English-only laws and limiting government services to immigrants.[4]

The controversial theses of Hanson and Huntington have unexpected resonance with the views of prominent Latinos. As New America Foundation senior fellow Gregory Rodriguez relates, many Chicano activists and scholars—who perceive both Huntington and Hanson as ideologues, and vice versa—see the Mexican American experience as one of enduring racial separateness and subjugation, more akin to African Americans' experience than to the immigration and Americanization of European émigrés. This view led numerous Chicanos to the conviction that "assimilation and integration were acts of betrayal." In Rodriguez's assessment, this "Chicano portrayal of Mexican Americans as a unified, downtrodden people preternaturally loyal to their ancestral culture was astonishingly similar to the way Anglo racists had been characterizing Mexican Americans for more than a hundred years. Racists had long enjoyed portraying Mexicans as a race apart [and] unassimilable." Chicano adulation of their people's resistance to what they perceive as the imperialistic impositions of the United States is diametrically opposed to Huntington's and Hanson's demands that Latinos acquiesce to those same assimilationist expectations. But in an ironic twist both sides agree on the same fundamental point: Latinos have not substantially integrated into the predominant U.S. cultural ethos. According to Rodriguez, Hispanic advertisers have proffered a similar stance as they sought to segment a lucrative consumer market by "ignoring the existence of U.S.-born English-dominant Latinos" in their market research so that they could "convince mainstream corporations that Latinos would continue to speak Spanish no matter how many generations their families live in the United States." Thus financial rewards stimulate marketers to depict Latinos as a group for whom assimilation is at best a distant possibility.[5]

Conversely, anthropologist Arlene Dávila examines media and survey reports that embellish indicators of Hispanic integration and collectively comprise another reaction to Samuel Huntington's "well-publicized tirade" and to the "xenophobic attitudes enveloping the immigration debate." Dávila unveils "a growing consensus among pundits, advocates, and scholars who insist and provide proof that Latinos are not a social liability; that they are moving up and contributing; and that, in fact, their values make them more American than 'the Americans.'" She explores highly publicized claims such as the rise of Latinos to the middle class and their alleged political realignment with the Republican Party. In each case she demonstrates that such claims are partially true but inflated. Though she recognizes they are a welcome relief from stereotypical images like those that emphasize undocumented status and criminality, Dávila perceives these more positive depictions of Latinos' work ethic, values, and contributions to U.S. life as distortions of the current situation among Latinos, the majority of whom are not middle class or Republican. She asserts that, while never explicitly stated, these portrayals presume the United States is a color-blind society and implicitly contrast Latinos' "coming of age" with African Americans' purported stagnation. The false impression that Latinos are rapidly advancing and assimilating exacerbates tensions between African Americans and Latinos and ignores the struggles of numerous Latinos or, worse, blames them for not becoming more prosperous or integrated into U.S. society.[6]

Like Dávila, other analysts accentuate the need to transcend facile depictions of either wholesale assimilation or wholesale resistance to it. Douglas Massey maintained that Huntington's interpretation of existing data "exaggerates several challenges to assimilation in the twenty-first century while minimizing the many positive indications of ongoing incorporation of new immigrants into American society." Leo Chavez asserted that writers like Huntington have concocted "the Latino Threat Narrative," a discourse that accuses Latinos of being an invading force with destructive effects on U.S. society. Davíd Carrasco publicly debated Huntington after the release of *Who Are We?* and charged that the book "ignores the significant dynamics of the many cultural crossroads and religious borderlands that have always done more to generate American identity as lived experiences than his [Huntington's] provincial 'cultural cores.'" Focusing on "hybridity" rather than a zero-sum approach to assimilation versus cultural resistance, Carrasco urged his audience "to move our discourse on race to a discourse on race mixture" and thus focus on the mutual transformations that he argued have long marked the encounters of peoples in the Americas.[7]

The U.S. Catholic bishops characterized "assimilation" in their 1987 National Pastoral Plan for Hispanic Ministry as a process through which newcomers "are forced to give up their language, culture, values, and traditions and adopt a form of life and worship foreign to them in order to be accepted." Conversely, "integration" is an attempt to foster "mutual enrichment through interaction among all our cultures" in an ambiance of reciprocal respect for one another's language, heritage, faith expressions, and participation in church life and decisions that shape it. In their most recent official statement on Hispanic ministry, the 2002 document *Encuentro and Mission: A Renewed Pastoral Framework for Hispanic Ministry*, the bishops urge that Hispanics "must be seen as an integral part of the life and mission of the Church in this country. We must be relentless in seeking ways to promote and facilitate the full incorporation of Hispanic Catholics into the life of the Church and its mission."[8]

Yet initiatives to promote Hispanic ministry have evidenced tensions between the goals of promoting unity with Catholics of other backgrounds, on the one hand, and advocating for separate structures that tend to foster vibrant Hispanic faith communities, on the other. Interviews of diocesan and parish leaders conducted for a 1999 report of the U.S. Catholic Bishops' Committee on Hispanic Affairs reveal disagreements within U.S. Catholicism akin to those in the wider society regarding the issue of "incorporation versus assimilation." The study report noted, "There is an ongoing tension between those who propose that the best way to bring Hispanics into the Church is by assimilating them into mainstream Catholicism and culture in the United States as fast as possible, and those who advocate that true incorporation requires that Hispanics be welcomed first on their own terms." One group contended that "forcing Hispanics to assimilate immediately only reproduces their subaltern status within the Church" and advocated for offering sacraments and other activities in Spanish, calling forth and nurturing Hispanic leaders, and, "once the Hispanic Catholic community has gained sufficient strength, then and only then" incorporating them more broadly into parish life. Another group held that such a "gradualist view" runs the "danger of making the same mistakes of the past, of producing exclusionary 'mini national parishes' that divide the Church."[9]

Consciously or not, like interlocutors in the wider societal debates about Latino integration, many Catholics fail to see that collectively Latinos neither rapidly assimilate nor indefinitely retain the Spanish language and their allegiance to Hispanic cultural ways. Indeed, what most observers fail to note is that the ongoing accommodation to U.S. church and society among Latinos has transpired concurrently with the arrival of other Hispanic newcomers since at least the first decades of the twentieth century. Recognizing the trajectories of Latinos' cultural retention, their adaptation to the U.S. milieu, and the role of Catholicism in these dynamics is essential for understanding the ongoing efforts of Hispanic ministry leaders to articulate and enact a vision of integration rooted in Catholic faith and teaching.

The Italian experience is a good starting point for assessing Catholic impact on ecclesial and societal integration. A 1975 landmark study by Silvano

Tomasi identified three stages in the development of New York's Italian parishes from 1880 to 1950, the peak years of Italian immigration and adjustment to life in New York. The initial stage consisted of attempts to incorporate immigrants into existing structures, usually into predominantly Irish parishes. These "duplex parishes" were attempts to economize by avoiding the construction of multiple parishes in the same neighborhood. But this plan failed because of language problems, the perceived economic strain that poor immigrants put on existing congregations, the precedent of national or "ethnic" parishes among German Catholics, Italian resentment of Irish control of the U.S. hierarchy, the complaints of Italian clergy against the plan, and the prejudice that Italians felt from other Catholics, often symbolized by their relegation to worshiping in the basement of existing parishes. Many church leaders also feared the loss of Italians to Protestant denominations. Thus they supported the formation of Italian parishes where the immigrants could find a home within their own church.[10]

The failure of the "duplex parish" led to the second stage of Italian parish development: the creation of Italian national parishes. These parishes—and in many instances the parochial schools that played a prominent role in parish life—were often the first institutions that Italian immigrants could call their own. National parishes were part of a larger social process: many stood at the symbolic if not the geographic center of ethnic enclaves that both sustained them and were sustained by them. Tomasi argues that the Italian national parish had the character of a "quasi-sect," since "it became the place where immigrant Italians who were on the religious and social periphery of society, could fulfill their religious needs, find opportunity for self-expression, [and] preserve their self-perception of being human in the face of an unknown social environment."[11] As quasi-sects, the intended purpose of Italian parishes was to preserve immigrant faith and their "sacred cosmos," a combination of saints, devotions, sacred things, and view of the world that informs the rest of life. The parishes strengthened the internal structure of Italian communities in that they preserved symbols and other carriers of immigrant culture, provided an arena for the emergence of Italian leadership, and facilitated adjustment to U.S. society.

In time Italian national parishes gave way to interethnic, territorial parishes in which the children and grandchildren of immigrants integrated into the "middle American" milieu with Catholics of other backgrounds. Among the conditions facilitating this change was the loss of the Italian language among the descendants of émigrés, declining immigration resulting from fluctuations in the job market and restrictive immigration legislation, and the mobility of immigrants' descendants as they made advances in education and employment. But Tomasi asserts that the role of the national parish was also significant in the integration of Italians into more heterogeneous parishes and into the wider society, since national parishes allowed immigrants a period of adjustment with the support of an institution that was familiar. In Tomasi's words, while facilitating the ongoing Catholic allegiance of immigrants and their descendants, the national parish simultaneously mediated the process of "integration through separation."[12] Tomasi's widely accepted thesis unveils no small irony: while Italians and other immigrant groups labored to found national parishes as enclaves to preserve their language, culture, and ethnic expressions of faith in a new land, over time these segregated congregations enabled their descendants to integrate into U.S. society and ecclesial life from a position of strength. National parishes built unity by allowing newcomers to integrate in their own time and, to an extent, on their own terms rather than those of their established predecessors.

Shortly after becoming archbishop of New York in 1939, Cardinal Francis Spellman reversed a policy of establishing national parishes that had shaped New York Catholicism for nearly a century. The official report of the first "Conference on the Spiritual Care of Puerto Rican Migrants" explains his approach to the national parish issue. Held in April 1955 at San Juan, Puerto Rico, this conference brought together some of the leading thinkers and pastoral agents involved with Puerto Ricans, both from the island and from the mainland. Spellman wrote an introductory dedication for the conference report, extolling "integration" as the goal of Catholic ministry among Puerto Ricans on the mainland. The final summary of the conference proceedings stated that although "the national parish has always been the usual arrangement that provided for the spiritual care of previous immigrant groups," it was no longer a viable pastoral strategy, because the third generation of an immigrant group frequently moves out of these parishes, leaving the congregation depleted and the church building in disrepair. Furthermore, the children of immigrants too often abandon their ancestral religion because they identify the Catholic faith with the archaic practices of their national parish community. The summary also cautioned that some one-third of baptized Catholics in New York would belong to national parishes, a number presumably prohibitive given available resources and personnel. Finally, conference participants concluded that "since the people [Puerto Ricans] will eventually become integrated with the established population, it would be wiser to begin the process of integration from the very beginning."[13]

Not all conference participants agreed with this analysis. Although he assented to the archdiocesan policy, Jesuit priest Joseph Fitzpatrick also stated that the national parish had enabled previous immigrants to assimilate gradually while at the same time preserving their faith and giving them a sense of security during the difficult transition to life in a new land. Other conferees requested "a number of times that some effort be made to learn the sentiments of the Puerto Rican people themselves" on the national parish question, since conference sessions (as well as the archdiocesan policy) were predicated on the untested presumption that "the Puerto Rican people are quite willing to be integrated with the territorial parishes."[14]

Although conference delegates took no action to ascertain Puerto Ricans' views, Father Phillip Bardeck, the Redemptorist pastor of New York's St. Cecilia parish, presented a paper that inadvertently illuminated the perspective of one group of Puerto Rican parishioners. Bardeck defended the practice of fostering integrated parishes like St. Cecilia, where English- and Spanish-speaking congregants worshiped under the same roof. To the pastor's surprise, however, Puerto Rican parishioners objected when he sought to move their weekly Mass with Spanish homily (the Mass itself was still prayed in Latin) from its original site in the basement to the church itself. He then put the matter to a secret ballot, and an "overwhelming" number of Puerto Ricans voted to retain the Mass in the basement. According to Bardeck, this vote reflected the Puerto Rican perception that in the tight schedule of the upper church, "they would have to give up some of the customs that they had brought up with them from Puerto Rico." This implicit plea for a parish structure that supported their culture and faith expressions illustrates the desire of many Puerto Ricans and other Latinos who arrived on the U.S. scene after Catholic leaders abandoned the national parish as a relic of their church's immigrant past. As Jaime Vidal notes in his history of Puerto Rican Catholics, many newcomers disagreed with what they perceived as the U.S. clergy's intention to "promote the Americanization of the Puerto Ricans . . . at the speediest possible pace."[15]

The significance of Catholic parishes for newcomers was not lost on Puerto Rican migrants, whose numbers increased dramatically in New York after World War II, just as Italian and other immigrant parishes were in the midst of losing members to more heterogeneous, suburban parishes. Encarnación Padilla de Armas arrived in the city in 1945 as a young widow with a small boy at her side and $150 in her pocket. Subsequently she met Father Fitzpatrick, with whom she shared her concern that the archdiocese of New York was neglecting the Puerto Rican community. Fitzpatrick asked her to write a report on the situation and promised that he would deliver it personally to Cardinal Spellman. Padilla de Armas gathered and led a small group of Puerto Rican women to prepare this 1951 report, which claimed, "The most striking aspect of the Puerto Rican situation is the constant and energetic activity of

Protestants." The report emphasized that some eight hundred Puerto Rican ministers served in New York, where there was "not a single Catholic priest of Puerto Rican origin." It also asserted unequivocally that "Puerto Ricans must be received as regular parishioners" in existing Catholic parishes and that established congregants must be taught "their obligation of receiving these new people as brothers in Christ."[16]

The developments in Hispanic ministry that Padilla de Armas and her companions helped initiate in New York elucidate what could be called the "national parish dynamic," which is arguably the most significant trend underlying the many Hispanic ministry efforts since World War II. Consciously or not, like European immigrants who built national parishes, Latinos attempt to establish and nurture structures of Catholic life that enable them to move from, at best, feeling hospitality in someone else's church to a sense of homecoming in a church that is their own. Archdiocesan officials established the Spanish Catholic Action Office two years after the Puerto Rican women produced their report. The women's efforts revealed that the Puerto Rican response to the official decline of the national parish was to replace it with structures that met their desire to feel the sense of belonging and ownership national parishes provided.

Puerto Rican Catholics created other means to congregate themselves despite the lack of national parishes. During the 1950s tens of thousands celebrated the June 24 feast of Puerto Rico's patron San Juan Bautista (St John the Baptist) with an annual archdiocesan Mass, procession, and daylong festivities that included a civic and cultural program of events. Archdiocesan leader of Hispanic ministry Father Robert Stern has observed that this celebration "offered an opportunity for a public demonstration of the religious and cultural values of the Puerto Rican community. . . . It was the first citywide event that gave presence to the Puerto Ricans." The renewal movement Cursillo de Cristiandad (Short Course in Christianity) weekends began on a regular basis in the New York archdiocese in 1960. They were immensely popular and influential among Puerto Ricans and other Latinos, according to Stern, in large part because they "provided a framework and community to the individual Hispanic immigrant otherwise submerged in New York's dominant non-Hispanic culture and in danger of losing his identity as Hispanic and Catholic." Similarly, though U.S. clergy promoted the Caballeros de San Juan Bautista (Knights of St. John the Baptist) as a temporary Puerto Rican pious association that would foster "integration" and "assimilation," many Puerto Ricans saw the Caballeros as on organization that would help them maintain their religious practices, ethnic identity, and group cohesion on the mainland.[17]

Nonetheless, Hispanic leaders have claimed that the absence of the national parish cost the church "the good will and loyalty [of many Puerto Ricans and other Hispanics] which the national parishes created in earlier ethnic groups" and that "the lack of juridically sanctioned Hispanic parishes with strong pastors identified with their people is perhaps the single greatest reason for the ineffectiveness of our outreach to Hispanics." The consequences of this lack were poignantly illuminated in March 1990 when a terrible fire gutted a social club in the South Bronx and left eighty-seven people dead, most of them Hondurans. Joseph Fitzpatrick noted that one of New York Hondurans' "greatest pains was that they had no place to grieve; no place to gather where they could feel *en su casa* (at home), a familiar spot where relatives and friends would meet, a tiny bit of turf in a large and complicated city that would be a little bit of home, of Tegucigalpa, or San Pedro Sula or La Ceiba; a place where they would know, without distraction, that they were still Hondurans, *El Pueblo de Honduras*." Analyzing this tragedy, Fitzpatrick concluded poignantly, "Therefore, the central problem still remains: How can the church minister to Hispanic people . . . and fulfill the same function that the national parish fulfilled a century ago?"[18]

Recognizing this challenge, many bishops, clergy, and lay leaders nurture the national parish dynamic as a means of strengthening their coreligionists' Catholic allegiance and faith. Not surprisingly, Hispanic ministry initiatives in the U.S. Catholic Church tend to be strongest among immigrants who respond enthusiastically to the national parish dynamic: their traditional rituals and devotions, recognizable spiritual and material needs, preference for Spanish, and deep resonance with pastors who express solidarity with them make them relatively easier to form into vibrant faith communities. The preponderance of foreign-born Latino clergy—five of every six among some three thousand Latino priests in the United States are foreign born—undergirds the prevalence of an immigrant-focused, Spanish-language approach in Hispanic ministry.[19]

Today various Catholic parishes are in effect national parishes, because they serve overwhelmingly Hispanic congregations. The impulse to found and support such faith communities is evident among all Latino groups, as is evident in the predominantly Puerto Rican parish of Santa Agonía (Holy Agony) in New York, the Cuban parishioners of San Juan Bosco in Miami, the largely Mexican immigrant congregation of St. Pius V in Chicago's Pilsen neighborhood, and the multiethnic Latino immigrant communities of the Misión Católica de Nuestra Señora de las Americas on the outskirts of Atlanta and of Our Lady of the Angels in Los Angeles, or La Placita, as it is commonly known. Congregations like these engage parishioners at multiple levels, providing social services and sacraments, English classes and traditional devotions, religious education and legal aid, parenting classes and prayer groups. Chicago priest Ezéquiel Sánchez, former archdiocesan director of Hispanic ministry, noted about one Chicago congregation, "A lot of people are not very welcoming toward Hispanics, and, consequently, Mission Juan Diego ends up being an island of refuge for them. It's their own place."[20] Similar dynamics often ensue when Latinos are congregated in multicultural rather than ethnic parishes: they establish and support Hispanic feast-day celebrations, devotional practices, renewal movements, and parish organizations. These widespread initiatives reflect Latinos' desire to stake out their own turf within U.S. Catholicism, just as Germans, Poles, Italians, Slovaks, Czechs, Ukrainians, and others did previously in their national parishes.

The 2007 Pew Latino religion survey confirms the ongoing influence of the national parish dynamic. Seventy percent of Latino Catholics reported that their congregation has services in Spanish, at least one Hispanic serving as clergy, and that the Mass in which they typically participate has a predominantly Latino worship assembly. Foreign birth and residence in an area densely populated with Latinos increase these percentages but do not account exclusively for the phenomenon of Latino ethnic solidarity in parishes. For example, 57 percent of respondents who live in an area where the population is less than 15 percent Latino report they regularly worship in a predominantly Latino assembly.[21]

Various factors bode for a more prolonged vitality of the national parish dynamic among Latinos than among Italian and other previous European émigrés. The restrictive immigration legislation of the 1920s severed European ties by discontinuing the large influx of first-generation immigrants who could have reinforced language, culture, and the vitality of national parishes. Despite efforts to restrict Hispanic immigration and the growth of Protestantism in Latin America, however, family unification and the flow of people in a global economy continue to attract numerous Latino Catholics to the United States. Ongoing immigration reinforces retention of the Spanish language, elements of Latinos' respective cultures, and the desire for faith communities that foster group solidarity.

European immigrants who crossed the Atlantic Ocean tended to make a more decisive break with their past. The possibilities of return during the nineteenth and early twentieth centuries were in many cases rather limited because of economic factors, the political situation in their native land, or both. Leaving their ancestral homelands behind disposed them and especially their U.S.-born descendants to accept the ways and identity of their adopted homeland. Today, however, though Cubans and some other exiled or refugee groups may be unable to return home, contact with their countries of origin and other countries where Spanish is spoken is more frequent for Hispanics. This is particularly the case in the Southwest, where proximity with Mexico can literally be as close as several hundred yards. Puerto Ricans have the unique distinction of being "citizen immigrants," U.S. citizens by birth who travel freely between the island of Puerto Rico and the U.S. mainland. Spanish television programs, the Internet, and improved transportation add to the trend of greater contact with one's homeland and the larger Hispanic world. With good reason, scholars of Latinos in the Americas today often speak of transnational migration—underscoring the frequent contact and back-and-forth travel among families and kinship networks that span national boundaries—rather than the more unidirectional concept of immigration. Ongoing contact augments the desire at the core of the national parish dynamic: a faith community that is resonant with one's sense of identity and belonging.

Hispanic émigrés number roughly half the newcomers to the United States, and, given that Spanish is the primary language in multiple countries, collectively they comprise the largest proportion of immigrants speaking a single non-English language in the nation's history. The sheer size of this linguistic cohort expands use of Spanish and associated cultural mores. It further neutralizes assimilation through fostering ethnic enclaves, a feature of many European-immigrant settlement patterns that dissipated with the suburbanization of the émigrés' descendants and the discontinuance of extensive immigration from their respective homelands.

Today's Latinos also encounter greater support for diversity. Hispanic activists, pastoral leaders, and theologians have joined a chorus of voices that call for respect for pluralism in U.S. society and churches. Some propose an image like the stew pot to replace that of the melting pot, arguing that as in a stew pot the various ingredients remain distinct but mix to bring out the flavor in one another, so too different cultures and ethnic groups should be mutually enriching. Within the Catholic Church, while teachings on the church's missionary effort in foreign lands are long-standing, Pope Benedict XV's 1919 statement *Maximum Illud* was the first papal apostolic letter dedicated exclusively to the subject. Since then nearly every pope has issued at least one encyclical letter on this topic, increasingly critiquing evangelization efforts that promote Western culture as if it were intrinsic to the Gospel and Catholic faith. The Vatican II document *Ad Gentes* (Decree on the Mission Activity of the Church) added further to this teaching, as did the U.S. Catholic bishops' 1983 pastoral letter on Hispanic ministry and 1987 National Pastoral Plan for Hispanic Ministry, both of which promoted "pluralism, not assimilation and uniformity," as "the guiding principle in the life of communities in both the ecclesial and secular societies."[22] Unlike nineteenth-century Catholics like the Germans who petitioned Pope Leo XIII to grant them an independent church structure in the United States to protect them from the assimilationist demands of Irish clergy, contemporary Latinos draw on official church teaching and more widespread advocacy for diversity in U.S. society to buttress their efforts to retain their culture and faith traditions.

Another factor augmenting the drive for ethnic solidarity is numerous Latinos' experiences of being disdained or discriminated against. This struggle has not afflicted them alone, of course. Almost every immigrant group had to endure prejudice upon arriving in the United States. With Latinos and other groups (most notably African Americans) from outside of Europe, however, there is frequently a critical difference: skin color. The descendants of European immigrants could blend into U.S. society once they knew the language and culture, a process that typically entailed what various contemporary studies have deemed "whitening," or their reclassification from unwelcome foreigners to acceptable white Americans. But the ethnic origin of many Hispanics remains readily apparent. Too frequently, subtle—and not so subtle—racist treatment is the result. The 2006 Latino National Survey revealed that nearly half of U.S.-born Latinos report they have been treated unfairly at work, in contacts with police officers, in their search for housing, or in stores or restaurants. As scholars like Cynthia Duarte have shown, even third- and subsequent-generation Latinos who are well adapted to life in the United States have to deal in daily life with the social, political, and economic ramifications of their ethnicity.[23] Continuing experiences of prejudice lead Latinos to band together for mutual support and to oppose wholesale incorporation into a society perceived as unappreciative of the Hispanic presence.

Finally, as Joseph Fitzpatrick has argued, unlike Europeans who arrived to the "immigrant church" of the nineteenth and early twentieth centuries, more recent Hispanic newcomers encounter a U.S. Catholic Church that is "now a middle-class institution." A 2008 survey showed that 60 percent of "white Catholics" earn incomes of at least $50,000 annually, with nearly half that number earning more than $100,000, while a 55 percent majority of Hispanic Catholics earn less than $30,000. Differences of social class between numerous Latinos and the descendants of European immigrants who occupy the majority of leadership position in parishes and dioceses further inhibit working-class Latinos from developing a "consciousness that this is their church" apart from the national parish dynamic.[24]

The history of U.S. Catholicism reveals that many newcomers do not accept forced integration readily, but, consciously or not, when given the freedom to do so, many have integrated from a position of strength. From the perspective of immigrants ranging from Italians, Germans, and other nineteenth-century Europeans to today's Hispanics, the fundamental issue in such disputes is moving beyond mandated assimilation to voluntary integration, beyond an established "host" group controlling parish life to a sense of mutual belonging, beyond receiving hospitality in someone else's parish to a homecoming in one's own church. As the U.S. bishops' National Pastoral Plan for Hispanic Ministry eloquently put it, effective Hispanic evangelization requires their movement *de ser lugar a ser hogar* (from a place to a home) within U.S. Catholicism, since "the great majority of our Hispanic people feel distant or marginated [*sic*] from the Catholic Church."[25] Theologically, Latinos' considerable ecclesial activism over the past half century reflects the bishops' statement as well as the core conviction of millions of other newcomers throughout the long saga of U.S. Catholicism: God's house is not holy just because all are welcome. God's house is holy because all belong as valued members of the household. The national parish dynamic among Latinos, which from all indications will persist into the foreseeable future, is yet another step in the long process to forge Catholic faith communities in a pluralistic church and society.

But this is not the full story. Historian Rudolph Vecoli echoed the sentiments of millions of immigrant Catholics when he concluded that "the 'Italian Problem' was many things to many people, but to the Italian immigrants themselves it may have been that the Church in the United States was more American and Irish than Catholic." Italians' sense of ethnic distinctiveness, and their resentment of perceived impositions from their more established Irish coreligionists, fueled their desire to establish and maintain national parishes. Yet, with the help of a gradual transition period in these parishes they built and led, Italian immigrants did in time identify as Italian Americans and many of them simply as Americans. Indeed, as historian Timothy Smith has argued, while ethnic identity and its mobilization are often thought to be fixated on the past, frequently they are far more "aimed at the future." Smith contends that the "religious piety that flourished in immigrant churches from the beginnings of American settlement w[as] not merely traditional, but progressive. Belief and devotion were powerful impulses to accommodation and innovation; and both helped legitimate the behavior, the perceptions, and the structures of association that sustained the process of change."[26] Thus Italians and other immigrants sought to preserve their language and traditions, but they also brought their heritage and ethnic pride to bear on personal and familial aspirations such as education, employment opportunities, economic well-being, and in general a better life as citizens of the United States. Their social advancement enabled them and especially their descendants to not only participate in but also to shape the society and the church of which they formed a part.

Similarly, while ethnic consciousness remains strong among many Hispanics, their hopes and dreams for a brighter future entice them to engage the opportunities they encounter in the United States, especially those for educational and economic advancement. The research of Brian Duncan and Stephen J. Trejo shows that the reliance on self-reporting of ethnic background in most surveys of the largest Hispanic group, Mexican Americans, in fact tends to omit significant numbers of those who are most successful because they do not identify themselves as being of Mexican heritage. Duncan and Trejo found that nearly 30 percent of third- and subsequent-generation descendants of Mexican immigrants did not identify that ancestry when responding to the Current Population Survey. The third- and subsequent-generation descendants who intermarry with non-Latinos are particularly likely to have higher levels of income and education and lower levels of self-identifying as being Mexican American. Consequently, "some of the most successful descendants of Mexican immigrants assimilate to such an extent that they fade from empirical observation."[27]

Sociologists Richard Alba and Victor Nee note distinctions between immigrants today and those of yesteryear but contend that the impact of their different historical circumstances on the language and cultural retention of émigrés is often overstated. They argue that predictions of ongoing Latino immigration are at least somewhat tentative, that transnational dynamics are more a difference in degree than in kind between present and past migrants, and that we have forgotten how European immigrant groups such as Jews, Italians, and the Irish suffered from racist theories and did not pass into the status of "whites" as easily as we now anachronistically imagine. The influence of transnationalism is often ambiguous, as contact with one's ancestral home can both nourish ties of affection and also remind U.S. residents of the differences between their native and adopted lands that affected the original decision to migrate. Furthermore, "even if the United States were to embrace officially an affirmative policy of multiculturalism, of lending support to group efforts to maintain cultural differences, it is far from clear that this would have much impact on the informal, ground-level pressures to assimilate." Alba and Nee caution strongly against the presumption that the historical circumstances of today's émigrés portend a permanent retention of their language and culture of origin, noting "evidence of contemporary assimilation" among immigrants and their descendants in the areas of language and cultural acquisition, socioeconomic attainment, emerging patterns of geographic dispersion, and social relations. Their analyses discount neither the ethnic cohesion evidenced in phenomena like the national parish dynamic nor, conversely, the potent assimilatory forces in U.S. society. They conclude that "assimilation is unlikely to achieve the same preeminence among the descendants of contemporary immigrants [as it did among earlier immigrants], but that it will be a force of major consequence we have no doubt."[28]

In the process of adapting to life in the U.S. milieu, many Hispanics lose substantially their connections to their ancestors' homeland and their Spanish language ability. Despite misconceptions about the Hispanic population exacerbated in recent public debates about immigration, the majority of Latinos in the United States—nearly 70 percent, according to preliminary data for the 2010 census—are not immigrants. A 2003 study revealed that while 60 percent of Hispanics above age thirty-five are immigrants, only 13 percent of those below age twenty are. The study also showed the linguistic impact of U.S. birth and residence: among Latino Catholics of high school age, 15 percent primarily speak Spanish, 60 percent are bilingual, and 25 percent speak English with little or no Spanish. Though more than half of Latino adults speak exclusively or primarily Spanish in their home, two-thirds of Latino teens speak exclusively or primarily English among their friends. The 2006 Latino National Survey showed that while half of Latino immigrants report making contact with family and friends in their country of origin at least once a week, by the third generation a similar number of their descendants say they make such contacts "never."[29] These statistics and the pleas from Latino leaders for greater initiatives in ministry among U.S.-born Latino youth, a need articulated in the 2006 gathering of 1,680 Latino youth delegates from across the United States for the First National Encuentro for Hispanic Youth and Young Adult Ministry, are just some of the indicators that an analysis of Latino Catholicism that solely emphasizes immigrants and ethnic solidarity is woefully inadequate.

Indeed, historically, even as the national parish dynamic emerged, many Hispanics adapted to their new environs in the United States. Various Hispanic leaders have bemoaned this development as detrimental to their practice of Catholicism, such as Puerto Rican migrant Sylvia María Quiñones Martínez in her 1955 address to the National Conference of Catholic Charities. Earlier that year Quiñones Martínez had served as secretary for the first "Conference on the Spiritual Care of Puerto Rican Migrants" held in Puerto Rico. She was also a parish leader at New York's Incarnation parish, where she worked among Puerto Rican families as a member of the Legion of Mary. Quiñones Martínez's 1955 oration idealized Puerto Rican culture on the island but went on to observe that after migration, "in their attempts to be accepted and considered as equals, Puerto Ricans tend to imitate mainlanders and discard their customary manner of living." She noted that the young were especially susceptible to this loss, and she was saddened that among many migrants "it is considered old-fashioned to cover walls with religious pictures and the practice of religion becomes cold and formal." Quiñones Martínez concluded that "by discarding long-established customs and traditions and adopting an entirely new way of living, Puerto Ricans are depriving others of something that is simple and beautiful which could contribute tremendously to Catholic life here [on the mainland]."[30]

Even first-generation immigrants have made considerable accommodation to their adopted homeland. One 1920 Mexican immigrant to Chicago, identified in an interview as Mrs. Mesa, attested that she attended the mixed-nationality school at Guardian Angel parish, where her best friend was Italian and another friend was "American." She received her first communion in Mexico and usually worshiped at the predominantly Mexican St. Francis of Assisi parish. Yet she had her first child baptized within the multiethnic Guardian Angel congregation, continued to visit her non-Hispanic friends there regularly, and said, "I nearly always make my confessions [in English] at Guardian Angel because I like it better." Another Latina, named Gloria, who emigrated to New York from the Dominican Republic around 1965 at the age of ten, described herself in an early 1980s interview as "assimilated" and "the most integrated into U.S. society" among her eight siblings and other family members. While insisting that she will always be *Dominicana*, Gloria noted that she adopted U.S. ways more rapidly than other family members because she so consistently interacted with non-Hispanics during her university studies, in her profession, and in her social circle. She said that the people who most influenced her adaptation to U.S. society were her former boyfriends, whom she identified as "Jews, Italians, and Puerto Ricans." As she forged a new life in the United States, Gloria also became "disillusioned with the church" and Catholic teachings because of the "cultural conflict" she encountered living between *las dos culturas* of her native and adopted homelands.[31]

Today a growing number of Latinos participate in English-dominant parishes, where they are often exposed to the U.S. ethos and become more a part of it. Frequently a decline in their practice of Hispanic traditions accompanies their participation in these parishes. In his recent study of Latinos and the new immigrant church, David Badillo observed graduates from the University of Puerto Rico who were recruited to work in suburban Chicago, noting how young Hispanic professionals such as these can "blend smoothly into local, English-speaking parishes for regular worship." His claim is consistent with a study of William D'Antonio and his colleagues on Catholic generations in the United States. Though the survey focused solely on English-speaking, "assimilated Hispanic Catholics"—the education and income levels of the Hispanic sample for the study were on par with those of the non-Hispanic sample—it showed that this group of Hispanics is "relatively well integrated into parish life" and does "not differ significantly from non-Hispanic Catholics" on most indicators of religious behavior, core beliefs, church commitment, Catholic identity, and attitudes about their parish. Some Hispanics intentionally seek out parishes that facilitate their integration. After the family of Puerto Rican Marta Vargas moved to the mainland, her father insisted that she and her siblings live in an English-dominant neighborhood and worship in English at the neighborhood parish, because "you are in this country now and you need to learn its language and culture." Unlike Gloria, Marta's experiences in an English-dominant ambiance did not diminish her participation in the Catholic Church. Her formation in parish life built upon the Catholic faith she received from her family and led her to serve as a campus minister within the archdiocese of Miami.[32]

The experiences of Marta, Gloria, and Mrs. Mesa shed light on several influential factors that dispose immigrants and their descendants toward adopting U.S. ways. Not surprisingly, those who have a higher degree of contact with non-Hispanics frequently accommodate themselves more readily to the U.S. milieu. Dating and marriage of non-Hispanics usually intensifies the influence of this contact, as it did in Gloria's case. Statistically most children with only one Hispanic parent still tend to self-identify as Latinos. But given that scholars have long contended that intermarriage trends are a key indicator of assimilation, it is noteworthy that the Latino National Survey found marriage to non-Latinos increased fourfold from 13 percent in the first generation to nearly 50 percent in the fourth generation. Marta's experience reveals the motivating factor of parental or personal desire to adapt quickly to the U.S. milieu. Her story and those of Gloria and Mrs. Mesa show that immigration at a young age—or U.S. birth—further increases the possibility of a more rapid adoption of the English language and U.S. cultural ways. Higher levels of formal education also tend to enhance assimilatory inclinations. Distance from home is yet another factor, as evidenced in the experience of Mrs. Mesa, whose resettlement in Chicago removed her much farther from her Mexican homeland than the more numerous émigrés of her generation who relocated to the Southwest. The influence of regionalism on the acculturation of Latinos has become more pronounced in recent decades, as the dispersion of Latinos across the United States means that more of them live in areas where they comprise a smaller numerical minority, in many cases facilitating more frequent interaction with non-Hispanics. Data from the U.S. Census confirms the influence of regionalism: while 85 percent of U.S.-born Mexican American adults who lived near the U.S.-Mexican border in 1990 spoke Spanish at home at least occasionally, fewer than half of those who lived outside the border region did so. Yet on aggregate more than 95 percent of both groups could speak English well.[33]

Most distinctive about Latinos as a group within U.S. Catholicism as well as the wider society is that, although they evidence both the national parish dynamic and the same tendency to integrate as did their European coreligionists, in their case *both* dynamics are taking place concurrently over a more extended period of time. Even the notion of generations commonly invoked as a collective process in discussions of assimilation is misleading when applied to Latinos. As sociologists Edward Telles and Vilma Ortiz have shown, this is especially true for Mexican Americans, among whom frequently "four (or more) different generations-since-immigration intermarry, live together, interact, and often share a common ethnic identity." Moreover, like other groups, because of social and individual circumstances, Latinos do not integrate in a singular manner or on a singular timeline. No previous group has encompassed such an expansive population of immigrants and their descendants, English speakers and those who speak another tongue, newcomers and established residents as do today's Latinos. National surveys confirm that Latinos value both their ethnic heritage and their life in the United States: a 2000 poll showed that although 89 percent of self-identified Latinos agreed it is important "for Latinos to maintain their distinct cultures," 84 percent of the same group also said it is important "for Latinos to change so that they blend into the larger society as in the idea of the melting pot." An overwhelming majority of young self-identified Hispanics also express a dual identification: more than 90 percent of second- and subsequent-generation young Latinos surveyed for a 2009 Pew Hispanic Center study stated that they describe themselves both by their family's country of origin and "as American."[34]

A recent longitudinal study of Mexican Americans reveals some of the simultaneous indicators of both accommodation and cultural retention. Telles and Ortiz updated the 1960s research of Leo Grebler, Joan Moore, and Ralph Guzmán, published in the landmark 1970 book *The Mexican American People: The Nation's Second Largest Minority*. The Telles and Ortiz research team interviewed nearly 60 percent of respondents who were under age fifty at the time of the original survey. On the one hand, they found that most Mexican Americans inhabit "a world largely shaped by their race and ethnicity" and that even to the third and fourth generation "ethnicity continues to influence their language, who they choose as friends and marriage partners, where they live, how they see themselves, and how they vote." The single most influential factor that retards assimilation is low educational opportunity and attainment, which has a domino effect on socioeconomic, marital, residential, cultural, social, and political integration. Yet signs of gradual integration are present in these and other dimensions of life, most notably in language, with the second generation largely proficient in English and, by the fifth generation, the curtailment of households in which parents speak Spanish to their children to well under 10 percent. Though limited to Mexican Americans in the heavily Latino population centers of San Antonio and Los Angeles, the Telles and Ortiz study argues persuasively that both the three-generation assimilation and the permanent racial underclass explanations comprise inadequate lenses through which to scrutinize Latino integration in U.S. society.[35]

The complexity and the prolongation of the integration process in Latino lives is further evident among those Latinos whom scholars like David Hayes-Bautista call "retro-assimilators." Upbringing and education in the United States immerses young Hispanics into the U.S. ethos and teaches nearly all of them to be English-proficient, if not English-dominant. But factors such as increased Spanish-language media and Spanish-speaking celebrities, opportunities to study Spanish and Latino cultures in schools, Spanish-speaking peers and even dating and marriage partners, grandparents and other relatives, discrimination and the search for identity, and the professional and economic benefits of being bilingual entice many young Latinos to deepen their connections to their ancestral heritage. Ongoing immigration and the size of the Hispanic population extend the conditions for retro-assimilation to many locales across the United States and even down to third- and subsequent-generation Latinos whose families have long since become enmeshed in U.S. society.[36]

Eddie Gutierrez is one of a number of students I have met who could easily focus their energies solely on personal success and comfort, yet elect to reconnect with their Hispanic roots and serve those who have not had the opportunities they enjoy. Echoing Hayes-Bautista's depiction of retro-assimilators, Gutierrez describes himself as "an English-household, Mexican American boy raised under the American spotlight of education and opportunity." But Sunday visits back to his father's childhood parish, Our Lady of Guadalupe on the south side of Milwaukee; the spiritual influence of his grandfather who served as a deacon there; and education in a Jesuit middle school for predominantly Latino young men induced him to become more connected to his Hispanic origins and learn to speak Spanish. At the University of Notre Dame he majored in premed and Spanish, studied abroad in Ecuador and Mexico, was a leader in Latino student organizations, and did extensive volunteer service, including internships for community organizing among Hispanics in Chicago and among the homeless in Milwaukee. Motivated by his Catholic faith and his desire to help address the need for mentors and leaders among his fellow Hispanics, his goal is to complete medical school and serve in a community that needs bilingual medical professionals.[37]

The *simultaneity* of ethnic solidarity, ongoing immigration, and even retro-assimilation *along with* transition into U.S. church and society—which has been evident among Latino Catholics since at least the 1920s—remains frequently unacknowledged among Hispanic and other Catholics. On the one hand, one often hears statements like: "They'll assimilate in another generation or so anyway. By offering services in Spanish, you're just holding them back. Other immigrant groups also felt 'put upon' when they first got here. This is just one more group going through the adjustment to American life. This too will pass." Such statements presume that European immigrants and their descendants set a pattern that all other Catholics in the United States will inevitably follow, ignoring realities such as the continuing arrival of new Hispanic immigrants, the influence that proximity to the border has on language and cultural retention, and the resilience of many U.S.-born Latinos in preserving their customs and their Spanish-speaking ability. On the other hand, advocates for Hispanic ministry focus on these same realities and proceed to underestimate or discount the considerable number of Latinos who are monolingual English speakers, have weakened ties to their Hispanic heritage, worship in largely non-Latino parishes, or even have switched from Catholicism to another denomination or to no religion at all. The vibrant faith among Hispanic immigrants in many Catholic parishes feeds the misconception that the vast majority of Hispanics will retain indefinitely their cultural ties and Spanish-language ability. To understand the Hispanic presence in U.S. Catholicism, one must comprehend that the future possibilities are not the dichotomous options between assimilation and cultural retention but a comingling of both realities that will persist much longer than it did for European immigrant groups, even as U.S. and Latino cultures are continuously refashioned amid the dynamism of a globalized world.

Obviously the influence that living in the United States has on Latinos is crucial for the future of the nation and U.S. Catholicism. As David Rieff asked in a 2006 *New York Times Magazine* essay, "Is this [the growing Latino presence] a real turning point in the history of the American church that will lead to its enduring revival or, instead, only another cycle in that history?" He focused his attention primarily on the archdiocese of Los Angeles, its large immigrant population, and its clergy and then archbishop Cardinal Roger Mahony (who subsequently submitted his resignation as archbishop at the mandatory age of seventy-five). Rieff maintained that the stance of solidarity with immigrants that Mahony and many priests and other pastoral leaders in Los Angeles adopted bodes well for the present and immediate future of the U.S. Catholic Church. Nonetheless, fundamental questions remain. Will the national parish dynamic lead to the process of "integration through separation" as national parishes did for Italians and other European immigrants? And as more Latinas and Latinos have children and grandchildren in the United States, will their former immigrant Catholicism remain strong, or will they follow the trajectory of the descendants of European immigrants whose Catholic faith Rieff claims "eroded in the aftermath of Vatican II and assimilation"? Despite his hyperbolic claim that the faith of all European-descent Catholics has eroded, Rieff justifiably poses the competing scenarios in stark terms. He underscores the dilemma of the national parish dynamic, which is addressed in various ways throughout the remaining chapters of this volume: absent the potent combination of Catholic faith and ethnic solidarity that are intimately linked in the lives of many immigrants, will there be adequate structures and ministries to sustain the faith commitment among subsequent, more integrated generations?[38]

Pastoral and theological leaders like Eduardo Fernández, S.J., justifiably argue that unilateral approaches in Hispanic ministry are inadequate in this context, both those that solely emphasize rapid assimilation and exclusive English-language use and those that promote prolonged ethnic separatism and monolingual Spanish ministries. Focusing his analysis on the pastoral needs of ethnic Mexicans, Fernández counsels that "immigrant groups regularly need their own space" for worship and other gatherings. A pitfall to be avoided is equating unity with uniformity. In retrospect the incorporation of European-descent Catholics over three generations was prudent, even though many were "segregated" in national parishes. Their gradual integration allowed for the practice of their Catholic faith and for ethnic unity among Europeans to emerge in U.S. parishes. Today the too-frequent expectation that Hispanics, even recent immigrants, participate in English-language Masses and parish events for the sake of "unity" often provides a superficial harmony at best. In many cases it causes frustration, resentment, and Hispanics' choice to vote with their feet and abandon participation in Catholic parish life. At the same time, Fernández observes, "While recent adult immigrants have a sense of themselves in terms of identity and self-image, Mexican-American children and descendants of the first generation often do not" as they struggle with the reality of living between the Hispanic world of their parents and household and the U.S. world of their school and peers. Though "in many ways they [immigrants] are the ones who most need the help, more assimilated Mexican Americans cannot be ignored as they often suffer from more of an anthropological poverty, that is, one that does not allow them to love and embrace the [bicultural] person that God made them."[39]

Like Davíd Carrasco in his rejoinder to Samuel Huntington, beginning with the writings of Virgilio Elizondo U.S. Hispanic theologians and pastors have contended that those from Latin American and U.S. cultures not only coexist; they also clash, collaborate, and have the potential to mutually enrich one another. A native of San Antonio and a priest of the San Antonio archdiocese, Elizondo's experience of living between cultures in the Mexican-U.S. borderlands led him to explore the notion of *mestizaje*, the dynamic and often violent mixing of cultures, religious systems, and peoples. He asserts that his Mexican American people are *mestizos* born from two dramatic clashes: the sixteenth-century Spanish conquest of the indigenous peoples in the territories that became New Spain (and later Mexico) and the mid-nineteenth century U.S. conquest of what is now the Southwest. Elizondo rejects both wholesale assimilation and unyielding resistance to U.S. influences, claiming that Latinos shape and are shaped by the *segundo* (second) *mestizaje*, their encounter and clash with the pluralistic U.S. milieu and a majority-culture Catholicism steeped in European roots. Despite assimilatory pressures, he perceives in his people a mestizo identity that is neither fully Mexican nor North American, neither Spanish nor indigenous, but a dynamic mixture of all of these root cultures. He enjoins his fellow mestizos not to identify themselves in a negative way as "not Mexican" or "not American" but to claim the positive identity of mestizos, who have the advantage of benefiting from two (or more) cultures. The primary models he proposes for this creative synthesis are the Galilean Jesus and Mexico's Our Lady of Guadalupe, who unite diverse peoples and cultures in a mutually enriching manner. Elizondo recognizes that living between cultures is in fact often a painful experience that can easily become a source of confusion, rejection, and shame. Yet his bold vision has significantly shaped numerous Hispanic Catholics' attitudes toward authentic integration.[40]

The website for Hispanic affairs of the United States Conference of Catholic Bishops presents an outline on stages for the development of Hispanic ministry that embodies a theology of integration or, to put it in more ecclesial terminology, a theology of communion. Three major phases in this practical schema of nine steps or "stages" follow a "developmental sequence" for parishes, dioceses, and other church structures. The first phase, "strengthening the Catholic identity of the Hispanic faithful," responds to the gravitational pull of the national parish dynamic among newcomers. It encompasses "meet[ing] Hispanics where they're at," helping them feel at home, and working with them to cultivate leadership and ministries among those in their own group. Once this solid foundation of an ethnic faith community is established, the next phase, "fostering a sense of belonging in a new and diverse community," involves further leadership training, fostering relationships across cultural and ministerial groups, and, in the process, "open[ing] wide the doors" to Hispanic participation in communal decision-making processes. Ideally this transitional phase of mutual integration among partners, as opposed to the forced integration of underlings, leads to the final phase of "ownership and stewardship," which dawns when the former newcomers are enabled to become active participants who have a strong sense of belonging and responsibility for the good of the faith community as a whole. The final step of "full commitment to the life and mission" entails these now-incorporated members offering their talents, their financial support, and their service to those of all backgrounds in the community. While no distinct timeline is given for this sequence, the intent is clearly to progress at a measured pace, bearing in mind the admonition of Pope John Paul II, who "warn[ed] repeatedly against attempting to rush a process of assimilation or cultural adaptation in the name of unity, because the goal is the mutual enrichment of peoples, not their assimilation to one way of being human."[41]

Catholic leaders further declare that the integration of U.S.-born as well as immigrant Latinos is not merely a practical necessity, nor just a sociological process of intergroup relations, nor solely a matter of national security or identity as works like those of Samuel Huntington and Victor Davis Hanson might lead one to infer. Rather, for Catholics the incorporation of newcomers is a demand that Christian discipleship requires. Hispanic insights on a Catholic approach to integration contribute to ongoing efforts that span from the apostolic era to the present. According to the Acts of the Apostles, the very first Christians faced the controversy of whether and under what conditions to allow Gentiles into their originally Jewish Christian communities. For two thousand years Christians have faced similar challenges, from renowned missionary encounters such as those of Saints Cyril and Methodius among the Slavic peoples, Mateo Ricci and his Jesuit companions in China, and the Franciscan Fray Pedro de Gante in colonial Mexico, along with innumerable less known daily encounters and clashes around the globe among Christians of different backgrounds as well as those they have sought to evangelize. But the challenge is even more widespread in our own time, and particularly for a society and Catholic Church as racially and ethnically diverse as those in the United States. As the U.S. Catholic bishops put it in their 2000 pastoral letter *Welcoming the Stranger among Us: Unity in Diversity*, "The Church of the twenty-first century requires a profound conversion in spirit and in its institutions to reflect its own cultural pluralism, to address the needs of the whole

Catholic community, and to further a genuine communion and solidarity among the diverse members of the Body of Christ." Thus in Catholic theological understanding, the response to the Hispanic presence is not solely or even primarily about Hispanics, but about the Catholicity of the entire church, in the United States and beyond.[42]

The extent to which Catholics realize these lofty goals will continue to affect church and society. Intentionally or not, national parishes and their parochial schools were among the societal institutions that most effectively fostered the integration of European immigrants and their offspring. Similarly, parish ministries among Hispanics today have unintended consequences. Attitudes of forced assimilation can lead to frustration and thwart newcomers' desire to integrate. Yet church congregations and organizations remain a refuge for many émigrés and can help them and their children and grandchildren adapt to life in the United States. While across generations English language use and other influences of the U.S. milieu are inevitable, the relative success or failure of Latinos' incorporation into the U.S. Catholic Church enhances or inhibits that process. Within the Catholic fold itself, the progression from hospitality to homecoming, often ably met with national parishes for European immigrants, remains a daunting challenge that many Hispanic ministry leaders concur has only begun to be addressed. Like those European émigrés who sacrificed their time, energy, and scarce material resources to build and support national parishes, Latinos seek a sense of ownership in their parishes, apostolic movements, organizations, and the wider church. The issue is not only one of pastoral vision and strategy—which as delineated above are readily available—but more of implementation. Each local context requires creative, persistent action that enables parish and diocesan leaders to promote a sense of belonging and ownership among Latinas and Latinos as well as a growing unity between them and their fellow Catholics. As its leaders have articulated it, the task of Hispanic ministry is to multiply the structures and leaders who can enact this vision at all levels of the church and, in the process, sustain and strengthen the Catholic faith of Latinos as they become more deeply enmeshed in the U.S. cultural ethos and in the Catholic Church in the United States.

CHAPTER

# Hispanic Ministry

An overwhelming majority of the U.S. Catholic bishops voted to restructure their national operations at their annual fall meeting in 2006. With its central office in Washington, D.C., the United States Conference of Catholic Bishops (USCCB) is constituted of the bishops as members and at present a staff of more than 350 laity, clergy, and members of religious orders. The restructuring plan reduced the number of standing committees in the conference from thirty-six to sixteen (some struck committees became subcommittees), removed all sixteen ad hoc committees, eliminated sixty staff positions, and decreased by 16 percent the annual assessment of U.S. Catholic dioceses' revenues to support the work of the conference. It also called for greater collaboration among staff in USCCB departments and among committees, particularly in addressing five goals the bishops established as priorities for a three-year cycle beginning in 2008: the implementation of a pastoral initiative on marriage; faith formation focused on sacramental practice; priestly and religious vocations; life and dignity of the human person; and recognition of cultural diversity.[1]

Several bishops made pleas—a Catholic News Service reporter referred to some of their interventions as "strenuous objections"—for specific staff positions or committees not to be cut, but these proposed amendments were defeated. One of the few amendments that did pass concerned Hispanic ministry. Archbishop José Gomez of San Antonio (now the archbishop of Los Angeles) and emeritus Archbishop Joseph Fiorenza of the Galveston-Houston archdiocese objected that the priority of the "recognition of cultural diversity" did not sufficiently accentuate the urgency of ministries with the rapidly growing Hispanic population. Their entreaties led the bishops to restate their fifth priority goal as the promotion of "cultural diversity with a special emphasis on Hispanic ministry in the spirit of Encuentro 2000," a reference to an initiative Hispanic Catholics convoked with leaders from the diverse racial and ethnic groups in U.S. Catholicism that culminated in a national summit titled "Many Faces in God's House: A Catholic Vision for the Third Millennium."[2] Leaders of other groups, such as African Americans, have objected to the singling out of Hispanic ministry in the bishops' articulation of their goal. But a number of Latino leaders claim that Hispanic ministry—and some add ministries with other racial and ethnic groups—should be seen as a specific priority and not merely one among many.

Nonetheless, the USCCB restructuring encompassed the replacement of the Bishops' Committee on Hispanic Affairs with the Bishops' *Sub*committee on Hispanic Affairs, an administrative unit that has less clout within the bishops' conference. It also involved the subsuming of the national Secretariat for Hispanic Affairs into a new Secretariat of Cultural Diversity in the Church, as well as the early retirement of Ron Cruz, who had served as executive director of the Hispanic secretariat since 1991. The Secretariat of Cultural Diversity is intended to nurture church unity; integrate historically underrepresented groups more fully into the life and mission of the Catholic Church in the United States; and address the spiritual needs of Latinos, African Americans, Asians and Pacific Islanders, Native Americans, and migrants, refugees, and travelers.

A number of leaders in Hispanic ministry voiced their concern that with Hispanic Affairs no longer a freestanding secretariat, they lost both important national support for their efforts and the most prominent symbol of Hispanic visibility within U.S. Catholicism. With the backing of Archbishop Gomez and Bishop Jaime Soto, then serving in the diocese of Orange, California, and now the bishop of Sacramento, in August 2007 the National Catholic Council for Hispanic Ministry (NCCHM), an umbrella group of some sixty Hispanic Catholic organizations, convened a symposium of key Hispanic ministry leaders. Symposium participants sent a statement of concerns and commitments to the Bishops' Committee on Hispanic Affairs (which was still active until its final meeting in November 2007). The NCCHM statement thanked "the bishops who spoke out against the conference's decision to structurally subsume the Secretariat for Hispanic Affairs under a new Office for Cultural Diversity in the Church." It also cautioned that "the restructuring plan may negatively impact the pastoral care and leadership formation of Hispanics," whose growing numbers and "unique challenges and opportunities . . . require resources and institutional support that may be diluted by grouping Hispanic ministry alongside other ethnic and racial ministries." The statement bemoaned that the plan for the new Secretariat of Cultural Diversity in the Church "structurally divides the Church into two groups—

one for Catholics who are white and the other for Catholics who are not white according to the U.S. Census Bureau." It concluded with recommendations for addressing these concerns, including a request for the bishops to "clarify that the decision for a multicultural office in the USCCB is not meant to serve as 'the model' for Hispanic ministry at the diocesan and parish levels" and for the bishops to "evaluate and reassess the decision to cluster Hispanic ministry" with other groups "at the end of the three-year strategic plan." Despite their protests, the NCCHM leaders also pledged to support the bishops' five pastoral priorities.[3]

Subsequently the enactment of the restructuring encompassed the appointment of significant Hispanic leaders. The first executive director of the Secretariat of Cultural Diversity in the Church was Father Allan Figueroa Deck (2007–2011), whose appointment Hispanic ministry leaders warmly endorsed. To date the first two bishops to chair the new Bishops' Committee on Cultural Diversity in the Church have been Archbishop Gomez and Bishop Soto. The bishops' committee they chair is the largest in the history of the USCCB, save for the conference's general administrative committee. Both their committee and the new secretariat have reportedly had good initial success in collaborations with other secretariats, bishops' committees, and leaders within the bishops' conference to help address diversity concerns in a varied array of initiatives within the conference. Alejandro Aguilera-Titus, who had served as associate director of the Secretariat for Hispanic Affairs since 1996 and briefly as acting executive director after the retirement of Ron Cruz, provided leadership continuity and continues his work as assistant director of the Secretariat of Cultural Diversity in the Church and as the staff member responsible for Hispanic Affairs within the new secretariat.

Yet Hispanic Catholics who are familiar with the U.S. bishops' most recent official statement on Hispanic ministry, *Encuentro and Mission: A Renewed Pastoral Framework for Hispanic Ministry*, had good reason to wonder what had happened in the few short years since 2002 when the full body of bishops had approved that document. *Encuentro and Mission* expressed strong reservations about a growing "'multicultural' model that consolidates minorities under one office." According to the document, this model frequently "dilutes the identity and vision of Hispanic ministry and those of other ethnic ministries"; leads to "the reduction of resources and limited access to the bishop"; and excludes "Hispanic ministry staff from the decision-making process, particularly in the areas of budgets, plans, and programs specific to Hispanic ministry." While acknowledging that "we bishops are mindful of the cultural diversity of the Church," in *Encuentro and Mission* the prelates avowed that "the size and long-standing presence of the Hispanic population call for an assertive response by the Church to the challenge of ministering among Hispanic Catholics."[4]

The NCCHM symposium examined the changes within the USCCB in the larger context of shifting realities in church and society, developments in Hispanic ministry over recent decades, and "the current state of our ministry and its future direction." In an invited and subsequently published address to symposium participants, Archbishop Gomez commended the "many good things" and the "long list of accomplishments" in Hispanic ministry. He urged his audience "to continue our struggle" for immigrants and "for economic justice and better living and working conditions for our people." But he also noted that Hispanics have a higher rate of unwed mothers than any other group in the country, substantial dropout rates, a growing number who have switched from Catholicism to another religion or no religion at all, and that "for every 100 children born in our [Hispanic] community, another 23 are killed by abortion." Given these "signs of moral and spiritual poverty," Gomez said, "we [Hispanic ministry leaders] need to ask ourselves . . . why haven't our ministries made more of a difference in the lives of our people?" Other participants expressed concern that the changes at the USCCB and shrinking financial support diminished the capacity of ecclesial structures that are needed now more than ever for Hispanic ministry leaders to be agents of transformation in people's faith and lives.[5]

Hispanic ministry leaders have continued these conversations and debates since the NCCHM symposium, most prominently at three subsequent national events: a symposium that the Center for Applied Research in the Apostolate (CARA) at Georgetown University convened in 2008 on "Hispanic/Latino(a) Catholics in the United States," a 2009 symposium that the Boston College School of Theology and Ministry organized on the "Present and Future of Catholic Hispanic Ministry in the United States," and a 2010 congress that the NCCHM led titled "Rooted in Discipleship: *Enviados en misión.*" While the perspectives are varied, there is a common contention among Latino Catholic leaders that Hispanic ministry is at a crossroads, or, as Father Deck put it in his keynote address at the CARA symposium, a "roundabout," a metaphor that stresses how ministerial choices are often made between several rather than merely two options. Deck defines the current historical moment as one of momentous transition as the "European-American Catholic communities age and decline in numbers and as the Latino, Asian, African and African-American components rise in presence and influence in the church." Yet he also articulates a widespread concern among his fellow Hispanic ministry proponents: despite commendable efforts and commitments of resources and leadership, "precisely at a time when the Hispanic presence is reaching even higher levels of critical mass, the structures necessary to sustain and develop the church's response to these challenges and opportunities are relatively weak and even getting weaker." Deck contends that, along with ministries among youth, bolstering the structures that sustain Hispanic ministry is one of the two most urgent strategic goals for the vitality of Latino Catholicism.[6]

Understanding the evolution of Hispanic ministry and the theological insights its leaders have proposed to advance it are essential for assessing these current trends and debates and their significance for the Catholic Church in the United States. From the first Catholic subjects of Spain to arrive in territories now part of the United States until today, Hispanic ministry initiatives have sought in varying ways to evangelize and make a difference in people's lives. But the genesis of regional and national structures for Hispanic ministry did not emerge until the end of World War II. Increased activism during the civil rights movements of the 1960s, the reforms of Vatican II, the inspiration of developments in Latin America, and an expanding population with a growing number of Hispanic leaders extended U.S. Hispanic Catholic efforts for ecclesial and social reform. Subsequently a growing conservative political movement, the influential papacy of Pope John Paul II, and financial woes shaped ongoing developments in Hispanic ministry and its support structures. Current discussions occur as national and regional structures that developed since the late 1960s have waned, and Hispanic ministry proponents face challenging questions with regard to mechanisms for the advancement of Hispanic ministry and its relationship to the life and ministry of U.S. Catholicism as a whole.

Archbishop Robert Lucey of San Antonio led the first initiative among U.S. Catholic bishops to forge a coordinated national effort in Hispanic ministry with the founding of the Bishops' Committee for the Spanish Speaking in 1945. The motivations for this initiative included alarm over Protestant proselytizing efforts, the application of Catholic social teaching to ethnic Mexicans' situation, and a confidential U.S. government report during World War II alleging that the Catholic Church's neglect of ethnic Mexicans in the Southwest hindered the national war effort. Fourteen prelates founded the bishops' committee at a meeting in Oklahoma City. They initially agreed to collaborate on a ministerial program in four episcopal provinces of the Southwest: Los Angeles, Santa Fe, Denver, and San Antonio. With the support of annual funding from the American Board of Catholic Missions under the auspices of the U.S. bishops, Lucey and his collaborators established an Office for the Spanish Speaking to implement a plan that encompassed the construction of clinics, settlement houses, and catechetical centers in which an array of human services and instruction in the Catholic faith were available. The needs of migrant workers, whose poverty was among the worst in the region, were a particular focus. One of the most successful goals of the committee was to help establish diocesan Catholic councils for the Spanish speaking. The councils brought together key leaders, both Hispanics and their coreligionists, from diocesan office staffs and prominent Catholic organizations. Their purpose was to enhance ministries among Hispanics. By the early 1960s, diocesan councils had been established beyond the Southwest in places like Michigan, Ohio, and New York, and some seventy dioceses had liaisons to the Bishops' Committee for the Spanish Speaking.[7]

Archbishop Lucey headed the bishops' committee for more than two decades. Widely acclaimed as a tireless advocate for social action, labor unions, and civil rights, he shaped the Hispanic ministry vision of the committee and the diocesan councils toward the promotion of justice and Catholic faith as the intrinsically conjoined purpose of the Catholic Church's outreach to poor and working-class ethnic Mexicans. Lucey joined fellow prelates in the Southwest, like Archbishop John Cantwell of Los Angeles, to warn his fellow Catholic leaders about the Protestant "attack" on the Catholic Church, decrying that "the job for which these missionaries to the Latin Americans draw a salary is to make Protestants out of Catholics."[8] In response, the bishops recruited more priests, sisters, and lay leaders for the Spanish-speaking apostolate and fostered programs to train these apostolic workers in the Spanish language and Mexican culture. Catholic leaders increased social service outreach in part to counter similar Protestant efforts that attracted ethnic Mexicans to Protestant churches and ministries. Within his San Antonio jurisdiction, Lucey established the Confraternity of Christian Doctrine on an archdiocesan basis and promoted it as a means to form Catholics in their faith and help them defend it against proselytizers.

Lucey and his collaborators insisted that church teachings be put into actions that promoted human rights. A 1947 incident in Lucey's archdiocese demonstrates their conviction. The manager at a restaurant ordered three Mexican American women to sit in a designated section for Mexicans. Led by an executive board that consisted of two Euro-Americans and two Mexican Americans, including future eighteen-term U.S. Congressman Henry B. González, the Lay Council for the Spanish Speaking of the San Antonio archdiocese condemned this discriminatory action as "un-Christian" and "un-American." Whatever the immediate effect of a particular protest or action, such attempts to foster Hispanics' dignity and rights aligned the Catholic Church's ministry with a widening struggle for justice among Hispanics of various backgrounds over the first half of the twentieth century. Cuban and

Spanish cigar makers in Tampa fought to maintain their unions in the face of violent efforts to crush them. Members of the Porto Rican Brotherhood of America defended their people in instances like the release of four compatriots erroneously detained as aliens at Ellis Island. Mexican Americans established the League of United Latin American Citizens (LULAC), an organization that addressed issues such as school reform, increased Mexican American representation for juries and other public duties, and an end to discrimination.[9]

Subsequent events buttressed Latino struggles for justice even further. World War II was a watershed, as Hispanics increasingly argued that soldiers who fought tyranny abroad should not return to the prejudice they and their families often endured at home. Mexican American veterans formed the American G.I. Forum, which, while primarily intended to lobby for the rights of veterans, also promoted social and political reforms that benefited their fellow Mexican American citizens. Like the struggles of African Americans and other "minority" groups, Latino activism increased even more dramatically during the 1960s. Although Latino activism was most visible to the general public in the efforts of Chicano leaders César Chávez, Dolores Huerta, and the United Farm Workers (UFW), it was also evident in Puerto Rican–led organizations like the Young Lords and the Puerto Rican Forum, as well as predominantly Chicano groups such as the Mexican American Youth Organization, La Raza Unida Party, and the Crusade for Justice. Arguably the most renowned figure in Chicano history, César Chávez is also known for his Catholic faith, devotion, and enactment of Catholic social teaching. He chided fellow Chicano activists, many of whom viewed the Catholic Church as an oppressive institution and disregarded it as a potential ally in their struggles. Chávez averred, "There are hundreds of thousands of our people who desperately need some help from that powerful institution, the church, and we are foolish not to help them get it." He was not afraid to make demands of his church on behalf of struggling workers: "We ask the church to sacrifice with the people for social change, for justice, and for love of brother. We don't ask for words. We ask for deeds. We don't ask for paternalism. We ask for servanthood." Despite initial reluctance from Catholic bishops and priests, Chávez and his fellow union officials garnered support from church leaders, including backing for boycotts of grapes and lettuce that pressured growers to bargain in good faith with the UFW.[10]

The growing ferment for social change influenced Latino Catholic activism and directed its energies within the church itself. As Mexican American priest Virgilio Elizondo put it, Latino accusations that the Catholic Church had been negligent and even complicit in discrimination "forced me and many others to take a much deeper and more critical look at the inner functioning of our church." Father Ralph Ruiz, priest-director of the Inner City Apostolate for the San Antonio archdiocese, led other Chicano priests in the founding of PADRES (Padres Asociados por los Derechos Religiosos, Educativos, y Sociales, or Priests Associated for Religious, Educational, and Social Rights), the first association of Latino clergy in the United States. Spokesperson Father Henry Casso stated at the organization's initial press conference in 1969 that "one of the main reasons for the founding of the group . . . was the example set by young Mexican Americans on college campuses and the barrios." The following year Sister Gregoria Ortega, a Victoryknoll sister and community activist, and Sister Gloria Graciela Gallardo, a Holy Ghost sister who had worked as a catechist and community organizer, wrote a circular letter to their fellow Chicana women religious noting that "there are some of us who have tried to become more relevant to our people and because of this, find ourselves in 'trouble' with either our own congregation or other members of the hierarchy." Gallardo and Ortega led the effort to establish Las Hermanas (The Sisters). Echoing cries for equal representation in civil society, early Hermanas leaders pointed out that in 1970 approximately 27 percent of the U.S. Catholic population was Hispanic while less than 1 percent served in the U.S. episcopacy. At the same time, 17 percent of the U.S. Catholic population was Irish American while 56 percent of the Catholic bishops were of Irish descent. PADRES members also protested the lack of representation in the hierarchy and even announced the possibility of establishing a national Chicano church as a means to redress this inequality.[11]

The Second Vatican Council spurred Latino efforts in a number of ways. Like their coreligionists in the United States and beyond, Latinos sought to understand and enact the council's teachings in the context of their own situation. The council fathers' emphasis on the universal call to holiness is the foundation for the sense of vocation among many contemporary lay Catholics, including Hispanics. Vatican II's mandate for ecclesial renewal shaped Latino Catholic leaders and the changes they promoted in areas ranging from vernacular liturgy, to greater collegiality in ministry, to the need for church leaders indigenous to particular faith communities. The council's appeal for a return to the sources of faith was instrumental in the founding of U.S. Latino theology and in its emphasis on Hispanic faith expressions. Virgilio Elizondo, widely acclaimed as the founder of U.S. Latino theology, explicitly states that his efforts are a response to the Vatican II directive that "in each of the great socio-cultural regions, as they are called, theological investigation should be encouraged and the facts and words revealed by God, contained in sacred scripture, and explained by the fathers and magisterium of the church, submitted to a new examination in the light of the tradition of the universal church."[12]

Developments in Latin America also influenced Hispanic ministry proponents, most prominently the inspiration of Latin American liberation theology and the 1968 Latin American episcopal conference at Medellín, which addressed the continent's situation of poverty and suffering in light of the Vatican II renewal of the church. Latin American anthropologist Alfonso Gortaire, pastoral theologian Edgard Beltrán, and sociologist Manuel Velásquez facilitated a 1971 symposium that PADRES organized in San Antonio. Later that year, six members of PADRES and one from Las Hermanas participated in a program of pastoral training at the Instituto Pastoral Latino Americano (IPLA) in Quito, Ecuador. The following year PADRES member and Medellín attendee Virgilio Elizondo led the effort to found the Mexican American Cultural Center (MACC, now the Mexican American Catholic College) in San Antonio, a pastoral center like IPLA that combined lessons learned from Latin America with analyses of the U.S. Latino experience. Chilean émigré Mario Paredes, who served as director of the Northeast Hispanic Catholic Center in New York for twenty-five years after its founding in 1976, fostered links between the center and Catholic dioceses in Puerto Rico, the Dominican Republic, Mexico, Colombia, and other Latin American nations. Similarly, during his three decades as director of the Southeast Pastoral Institute (SEPI) in Miami after its establishment in 1978, Cuban exile Father Mario Vizcaíno, Sch.P., expanded Hispanic ministry in his region even as he forged relations with Spanish-speaking countries, especially through organizing an annual mission trip to the municipality of Macuspana in the state of Tabasco, Mexico. Prominent Latin American Catholics offered courses and presentations at these pastoral centers and at ecclesial gatherings in the United States, while key U.S. Hispanic leaders participated in Latin American church events and in training programs like those of IPLA, forging a vibrant exchange between Hispanic Catholic leadership in North and Latin America.[13]

More importantly, Hispanic Catholics in the United States probed their own distinctive experience, challenges, and faith. As MACC leaders put it, Hispanics were "well aware that we were not typical white Anglo-Saxon middle class North Americans but we also became critically conscious that we were not the same as Mexicans living in Mexico or Latin Americans in Latin America. We have a unique identity of our own, for we have maintained our language, religion, and many of our customs and traditions in an English-speaking environment."[14] The Hispanic pastoral institutes were centers for language and pastoral formation, Hispanic ministry and justice advocacy, and groundbreaking research and publications about Hispanic liturgy, faith expressions, history, and theology. They provided cultural and pastoral orientation to Latin American priests and religious who came to minister among U.S. Hispanic Catholics, an ecclesial service that honed analyses of the differences between the contexts of Latin America and the United States. The pastoral institutes' most decisive impact was on U.S. Hispanics themselves, who for the first time had institutions of their own to explore their heritage and the theological and pastoral implications of their experience as Latino Catholics living in the United States. Many participants at these pastoral institutes experienced a sense of self-discovery that enlivened their ministries among fellow Latinos and stirred their desire to learn more about themselves and their faith.

The various influences shaping Hispanic ministry leaders converged in the effort to establish the most significant national structure for Hispanics to voice their needs and concerns to the U.S. Catholic bishops. In 1971 Father Robert Stern, the director of the Spanish-Speaking Apostolate of the New York archdiocese, convened leaders in Hispanic ministry from his own archdiocese and the New England region to meet with Edgard Beltrán of the Latin American Episcopal Conference (CELAM) and develop a pastoral plan for their ministry among the Spanish speaking. During the course of their deliberations, Beltrán, who as executive secretary of the pastoral department of CELAM was part of the organizing group for the Medellín conference and a leader in implementing its conclusions in various Latin American countries, proposed that Hispanic Catholic leaders organize a national encounter to enhance pastoral planning in their apostolic endeavors. Beltrán's suggestion won unanimous support and the following month received further endorsement from more than one hundred Hispanic delegates to the National Congress of Religious Educators held in Miami. Father Stern and his counterpart in the Brooklyn diocese, Father John O'Brien, then gained the support of Pablo Sedillo, who had assumed the directorship of the bishops' Office for the Spanish Speaking in 1970 and overseen its move from Texas to the national offices of the bishops' conference in Washington, D.C., where it was renamed the Division for the Spanish Speaking. Sedillo in turn won the approval of Bishop Joseph Bernardin, the general secretary of the United States Catholic Conference (now the USCCB). Encarnación Padilla de Armas of the New York archdiocese chaired the planning committee for the 1972 Primer Encuentro Hispano de Pastoral (First Hispanic Pastoral Encounter), which brought together 250 leaders at Trinity College in Washington, D.C.[15]

The purpose of the Encuentro was "to develop a pastoral plan for the Hispanic American community." Organizers proposed to achieve this end through their collective effort "to analyze the present pastoral situation in the

Hispanic American community" and seek "solutions to the many problems that exist." Reflected in the Vatican II document *Gaudium et Spes* (The Church in the Modern World) and already influential in the Medellín conference and among Latin American pastoral leaders like Encuentro organizer Beltrán, this *ver-juzgar-actuar* (see-judge-act) approach was adopted as a standard methodology for the Encuentros and among many leaders in Hispanic ministry. The approach entails examining the conditions in which people live, discerning how those conditions reflect or contradict the will of God, and acting to transform their lives and surroundings accordingly. Since organizers sought a "participatory" style, the Encuentro was "organized around seven workshops which cover the essential elements of a pastoral plan." Because of the workshop format there were only three keynote addresses, that of CELAM representative Bishop Raúl Zambrano Camader of Facatativá, Colombia, on the theology of pastoral ministry; Virgilio Elizondo's presentation on pastoral planning for Hispanics; and the address of Bishop Patricio Flores, a PADRES member who two years previously had been ordained the first Mexican American bishop.[16]

Bishop Flores's talk, "The Church: Diocesan and National," captured the spirit of the event. He emphasized at the outset his "great love and dedication to the church," stating he wanted to be clear on that point, since he intended "to make some strong constructive criticisms of the North American Catholic Church." Bluntly comparing Hispanics' sense of rejection in the U.S. church to a daughter whose mother had failed to defend her from the attacks of a sexual predator within her own household, Flores said, "If the church wants to keep calling the Spanish-speaking 'her children' then the church must change attitudes and structures." He noted approvingly that with regard to abortion, "the position of the church has been firm against deprivation of life." But he also declared that church officials had too often chosen to "remain neutral" while Hispanics suffered oppression, discrimination, and attempts to dispossess them of their lands, their language, their cultures, and their faith expressions. He called for a greater acceptance of Hispanics among their coreligionists, for national parishes in locales where Hispanic Catholics "are not well received and where the people are entirely Spanish-speaking," and for diocesan commissions or pastoral teams that organize Hispanic ministry. On the regional level, he endorsed centers or pastoral institutes but warned against any presumption that a single program or approach could serve all the diverse needs in an entire section of the country. He disagreed with a PADRES resolution distributed to Encuentro participants that recommended a study of Hispanics forming a national church separate from the U.S. Catholic hierarchy. Flores deemed the likelihood of carrying out such a plan "impossible, or at least detrimental" and predicted that not all Hispanics would accept such an arrangement and "this would result in another division." Instead, he urged his fellow Hispanic leaders to work within existing structures and "speak out" for more Hispanic bishops, a national seminary for the Spanish speaking, and Hispanic appointments "in all departments of the structure of the North American church."[17]

Encuentro participants presented their blueprint for the enhancement of Hispanic ministry to the U.S. bishops' conference, which formed an Ad Hoc Committee for the Spanish Speaking to assess the seventy-eight Encuentro conclusions. Some of the Encuentro calls for change were outside the authority of the bishops, most notably the ordination of women as deacons and the ordination of "mature" married men to the priesthood. Other recommendations the members of the Ad Hoc Committee endorsed but deferred to local bishops and church authorities, such as the Encuentro participants' emphases on *comunidades de base* (base communities) and ethnic or national parishes as particularly effective structures for Hispanic ministry. But a number of the Encuentro conclusions won acceptance and gradual though uneven implementation, forming the foundation for the development of Hispanic ministry over the following decades. These included Hispanic leaders' requests for more diocesan offices for Hispanic ministry, Spanish-speaking personnel in church agencies, training in Hispanic cultures and the Spanish language for seminarians and priests, an increase in the number of married Hispanic deacons as a means to address the lack of Hispanic priests, religious education programs that engage Hispanics in their faith, Spanish sections of diocesan newspapers, Hispanic bishops, the elevation of the Hispanic office at the bishops' conference to the more influential level of a secretariat, and greater funding for Hispanic ministry.[18]

A number of the Encuentro conclusions mirrored strategies that the Bishops' Committee for the Spanish Speaking and their collaborators in the diocesan Catholic councils for the Spanish speaking had already articulated and begun to enact. Encuentro participants sought more resources and support for such strategies. Their first and most widespread additional demand was that "there must be greater participation of the Spanish-speaking in leadership and decision-making roles at all levels within the [North] American Church." This struggle for institutional access encompassed in the Encuentro conclusions reflects the demands Latinos made for equality in civic life during this same era. One Chicano priest lamented that "state and federal public institutions, with their affirmative action programs, are more open to the idea of equal employment opportunities and fighting discriminatory practices in hiring than the Catholic Church."[19] Vatican II, their contact with developments in Latin America, and their own pastoral and theological insights as Hispanic Catholics enabled them to integrate their struggles with their vocations as Catholics and church leaders. But the primary thrust of the First Encuentro was to apply strategies for social change to the task of church reform mandated in Vatican II. Drawing on Catholic social teachings and the experience many had in civil rights movements, Hispanic leaders contended that leadership parity, greater authority in decision making, and advocacy structures of their own were necessary to combat the inequality and discrimination they perceived within the U.S. Catholic Church. They insisted these changes were necessary to make the Church more faithful to its own mission and foundation in Christ. Over the following decades, Latino Catholics established national organizations to support and advocate for Hispanics in a wide range of church leadership positions, including liturgical ministers, pastoral musicians, youth and young adult ministers, catechists, seminarians, deacons, church historians, theologians, pastoral formation institute personnel, and diocesan directors of Hispanic ministry.

Several dioceses and at least four regions held their own Encuentros to replicate the process of the National Encuentro. In some cases convening these gatherings led to controversy, as in Denver when the criticisms of Euro-American Catholics prompted Archbishop James Casey to respond in the archdiocesan newspaper, "We were not besieged by the Chicano people nor were we forced in any way to have these two days of dialogue, but rather the Chicano people were there because we invited them to express openly their ideas, thoughts, and frustrations." Other gatherings had impressive results, most notably the Encuentro in the Northeast region. Archbishop Jean Jadot, the pope's apostolic delegate to the United States, along with five cardinals and ten other bishops, were among the 250 participants in this event that led to the establishment of the Northeast Hispanic Catholic Center. The most conspicuous national change following the First National Encuentro was the U.S. bishops' 1974 decision to grant the top administrative status of secretariat to the former Division for the Spanish Speaking. Pablo Sedillo engineered this development with the support of groups like PADRES and Las Hermanas to secure a more prominent national platform for Hispanic ministry under the auspices of the U.S. bishops.[20]

Hispanic ministry leaders energetically promoted initiatives to enact the Encuentro conclusions. Pastoral planning and action efforts among some of their fellow Catholic leaders complemented and buttressed these initiatives, such as the justice-oriented Call to Action Conference that U.S. bishops convened on the occasion of the national bicentennial, which drew significant participation from Las Hermanas, PADRES, and other Hispanic leaders. These developments encouraged Sedillo to press forward on the 1977 Second Encuentro. Its organizers titled it "Pueblo de Dios en Marcha" (People of God on the Journey). Sedillo and his enlarged staff of five formed the National Coordinating Committee for the Encuentro with representatives from Las Hermanas, PADRES, the Cursillo retreat movement, MACC, and six regions, as well as the special coordinator the Secretariat for Hispanic Affairs secured for organizing the Encuentro, Father Frank Ponce of San Diego. This team worked with the now more than one hundred diocesan directors of Hispanic ministry to select the Encuentro theme of evangelization and to conduct a national process of consultation that proceeded from small community gatherings to assemblies at the diocesan, regional, and finally the national level in Washington, D.C. Encuentro organizers reported that more than one hundred thousand people participated in the grassroots discussions, which surfaced the needs and aspirations of Hispanic Catholics that were then synthesized at the wider levels. The required criteria for delegates to the National Encuentro were participation in the grassroots consultation process and the endorsement of the Encuentro Coordinating Committee and one's local bishop.[21]

As with its predecessor, the vast majority of sessions at the Second Encuentro were interactive, with keynote presentations limited to those of Archbishop Robert Sánchez of Santa Fe, exiled Cuban bishop Eduardo Boza Masvidal, Bishop Patricio Flores of El Paso (who shortly thereafter became archbishop of San Antonio), and a brief opening radio address by Pope Paul VI. Encuentro delegates approved a final set of conclusions in broad areas related to the overall theme of evangelization: ministries, human rights, political responsibility, unity in pluralism, and integral education, by which delegates meant an education of the person in all aspects of life oriented toward "liberation" and "authentic human freedom." The presence of nearly 50 prelates, all 8 U.S. Hispanic bishops, some 600 delegates, an additional 600 observers, and an overall majority of laity signaled the advances in Hispanic ministry in the five years since the First Encuentro, with its lone Hispanic bishop, fewer than 10 other prelates, and 250 participants, nearly three-quarters of them priests and women religious.[22]

Logistics for such a large group brought various criticisms, most notably the adherence to parliamentary procedure, which many participants found confusing and not conducive to open discussion. A number of attendees were frustrated because they were not delegates and thus could not participate directly in final deliberations. Youth participants contested the lack of focus on younger Hispanics, successfully lobbied for an added workshop session on youth evangelization, and gained the inclusion of recommendations on Hispanic youth ministry in the Encuentro conclusions. Puerto Ricans objected with anger and hurt when organizers failed to include their homeland in a display of flags from Spanish-speaking countries. Mexican American leaders protested that despite their requests to have preparatory documents available in both Spanish and English, these materials and with few exceptions the Encuentro sessions were in monolingual Spanish, and thus "many of the Cubans and Puerto Ricans who spoke Spanish well dominated the meeting." Criticisms also addressed the content of the Encuentro conclusions, faulting them for perceived deficiencies like being inadequately representative of the poor and those who were not directly part of official ecclesial structures; too narrowly focused on Hispanic unity based on a relatively superficial understanding of culture; weak in social analysis; and, conversely, lacking sufficient attention to liturgy, catechesis, and spirituality due to a heavy concentration on political involvement and U.S intervention in Latin America.[23]

Archbishop Sánchez stated in his keynote address that "the First Encuentro succeeded in sensitizing the Church of our country to the presence of the Hispano," while the Second promised to achieve a similar purpose with regard to "our traditions of worship and our faith in God." He urged his fellow Hispanics to "continue to preserve the treasures of our heritage and the identity of our faith and culture," an admonition that Bishop Boza Masvidal echoed in his plea for Hispanics to "create unity in pluralism" and pursue "integration without assimilation" in U.S. church and society. Encuentro delegates stressed this point of view in various recommendations, among them their pledge to enhance the Catholic Church in the United States with their cultural values and popular faith expressions and their plea that "we urgently ask the Church *to take fully into account the Hispanic culture and the living reality of our people in evangelization*" (emphasis in original). The delegates recognized "the serious problems which exist among our [Hispanic] people due to the diversity of our histories and heritages" and urged church leaders to "keep in mind the sensitivities and historical circumstances of the different communities which compose the Hispanic mosaic in the United States, not focusing on the concrete experience of only one of these groups." Some Hispanic leaders lamented in response to the Encuentro that "although Spanish-speaking people often state that they do not want to assimilate into the United States society, their alternative has not yet become clearly defined." But the Encuentro accentuation of disdain for assimilation, and in its place a simultaneous fostering of Hispanic cultures along with participation in the wider church and society, articulated a widespread Hispanic Catholic conviction that profoundly influenced efforts in Hispanic ministry.[24]

Organizers regarded the process of the Second Encuentro as a historic moment in Hispanic contributions to U.S. Catholicism through the grassroots process that "signalled a change . . . from a Church of the masses to one made up of basic Christian communities; from a vertical Church to one of dialogue and communion firmly rooted in the Gospel." Although they did not define the term "basic Christian community" previously examined in the documents of Medellín, nor explicate which groups comprised such communities among U.S. Hispanic Catholics and where they were prevalent, they urged "that ordinaries, pastors and those responsible for the Hispanic apostolate accelerate the formation of these basic Christian communities" as a primary means to further the process of the Encuentro.[25] Certainly the most ambitious accomplishment of the Second Encuentro was the extensive consultation beginning in small community gatherings that made the process a learning experience for thousands of Hispanic Catholics and an opportunity for them to voice their concerns to their church leaders and coreligionists. Consequently, whereas the pastoral insights articulated in the First Encuentro were deepened rather than redirected in the Second Encuentro, the latter's conclusions had the weight of emerging from a process encompassing a wide group of grassroots Hispanic Catholics rather than the more elite leadership group of its predecessor.

Theologically, delegates of the Second Encuentro rooted their vision of Hispanic ministry in the call of all Catholics to evangelization articulated in Vatican II and, two years before the Encuentro, in Paul VI's apostolic exhortation *Evangelii Nuntiandi* (On Evangelization in the Modern World). In the first lines of the premier document of the Encuentro conclusions, they declared, "We understand evangelization to imply a continuous lifelong process in which a Christian makes an ever deepening effort to arrive at a personal and communal encounter with the messenger, Christ, and a total commitment to His message, the Gospel." The practice of daily conversion enables believers and their communities to witness to the Gospel in word, in a "life of service to one's neighbor," and in "the transformation of the world." Encuentro participants committed themselves to the life and task of evangelization. Through the strategies for Hispanic ministry outlined in the Encuentro conclusions, they also issued a call to conversion to their fellow U.S. Catholics, stating their desire for a church more deeply imbued with five core attributes: united in a collaborative approach to pastoral life, poor in spirit and equitable in its distribution of material resources, communitarian in its embrace of different cultures and leaders, missionary in its outreach to those who most need Christ's liberating message, and just in its mutual respect for all.[26]

Structures to implement the Encuentro conclusions continued to expand over the following decade. Regional offices, pastoral institutes, and other initiatives to coordinate Hispanic ministry emerged in various sections of the country, enabling the formation of a National Advisory Committee to the Secretariat for Hispanic Affairs composed of representatives from these groups and from national apostolic movements and organizations. These broader structures fostered increases in Hispanic ministry initiatives in dioceses and parishes. The growing contingent of Hispanic bishops supported these developments in their ministries as bishops and through pastoral statements such as one that the nation's eight Hispanic bishops released at the time of the 1977 Second Encuentro and another that the then fourteen Hispanic bishops issued four years later in conjunction with the 450th anniversary of the apparitions of Our Lady of Guadalupe in Mexico.[27]

Hispanic bishops paved the way for the full body of U.S. bishops to present their 1983 pastoral letter on Hispanic ministry, *The Hispanic Presence: Challenge and Commitment.* The letter reflected the Encuentro pastoral planning process of assessing the situation of Hispanics' lives, posing "urgent pastoral implications," and calling for action to address these implications. It also echoed many of the Encuentros' pastoral insights and commitments and introduced others, enumerating a broad range of "creative possibilities" in Hispanic ministry such as the renewal of preaching and increased Catholic educational opportunities for Hispanics. The pastoral letter expanded on the Encuentro treatment of previous topics such as *Comunidad Eclesial de Base* (Basic Ecclesial Community), which the bishops said "should be an expression of a Church that liberates from personal and structural sin; it should be a small community with personal relationships; it should form part of a process of integral evangelization; and it should be in communion with other levels of the Church." Acting on a proposal of the National Advisory Committee, the bishops invited "Hispanic peoples to raise their prophetic voices to us once again . . . in a *III Encuentro Nacional Hispano de Pastoral*" emulating the process of the Second Encuentro from the grass roots up to a national gathering the bishops would convoke in Washington, D.C., in 1985. Recognizing "that integral pastoral planning must avoid merely superficial adaptations of existing ministries," the bishops pledged, "We look forward to reviewing the conclusions of the *III Encuentro* as a basis for drafting a National Pastoral Plan for Hispanic Ministry to be considered in our general meeting at the earliest possible date after the *Encuentro*."[28]

Thus, from the start, the Third Encuentro had the distinction of being the first such event the U.S. bishops had themselves initiated and the only one that had as a specific purpose the bishops' promulgation of a National Pastoral Plan. National coordinator for the Encuentro, Father Juan Romero of Los Angeles; chairperson of the Encuentro executive committee, Sister Consuelo Tovar, D.C.; key leaders like Olga Villa Parra and Sister Dolorita Martínez, O.P.;

and an even wider array of representatives from Hispanic ministry initiatives than those involved in the Second Encuentro coordinating committee joined Sedillo in organizing the Third Encuentro. They determined to conduct a consultative process that addressed critiques of the Second Encuentro and was even more effective in reaching a diverse range of Hispanic Catholics to engage them in their faith, form leaders, and extend participation in the deliberations leading to the pastoral plan. The organizers coordinated the formation of mobile teams to approach people who were marginal to parish life, such as migrants and those who were inactive in the formal practice of their faith. They instituted quotas for laity, farmworkers and laborers, women, and youth in delegations selected to participate in the various phases of the Encuentro. As a result more than two-thirds of the 1,148 participants at the national Encuentro were laity, nearly half were women, and the number of economically disadvantaged was slightly less than the 20 percent goal the organizers had set. The only established quota not substantially met was that for young people between the ages of eighteen and twenty-five, who comprised less than 13 percent of the Encuentro assembly despite an initial goal of 20 percent. Nearly 80 percent of the participants had not been present for the Second Encuentro, and nearly 90 percent had not participated in the First Encuentro, indicating the success of efforts to engage new leaders and a broad spectrum of Hispanics. At the national gathering, delegates were divided into five large groups of approximately 230 persons each with smaller breakout groups of 45 and finally subgroups of 15, providing a structure that allowed for freer participation than the parliamentary procedure and delegate-observer distinction of the Second Encuentro. Organizers emphasized a "consensus" approach to deliberations, which they subsequently noted "was reached in practically all the decisions."[29]

Echoing the bishops' invitation that Hispanics "raise their prophetic voices," organizers chose "Pueblo Hispano: Voz Profética" (Hispanic People: Prophetic Voice) as the theme for the Third Encuentro. The first means of engaging this theme was the "ecclesial style of our Encuentro," which, according to the Encuentro conclusions, "following in the footsteps of Vatican II, [the 1979 Latin American bishops' conference at] Puebla, the magisterium of the popes, and especially of Jesus himself—makes an option for the poor, youth, women, for the rights of the unborn, the undocumented, farm workers, and all the marginalized in society." Though widely perceived as achieving a more ample participatory process than previous Encuentros, the Third Encuentro was not without its critics. When Encuentro organizers rejected a version of proposed conclusions on women, Las Hermanas leaders arranged a protest demonstration on the steps of the Shrine of the Immaculate Conception, where participants celebrated Mass during the Encuentro. In the end the final Encuentro document encompassed conclusions on women, although the wording was altered to remove an ambiguous passage that could imply a call for women's ordination.[30]

Building on the vision and conclusions of its predecessors, the Third Encuentro articulated sixty-eight commitments that would continue the Encuentro process in the areas of evangelization, integral education, social justice, youth, and leadership formation. One distinguishing feature of this Encuentro's conclusions was a more extensive and explicit analysis of the "reality" being addressed in each of these five major areas. The conclusions under the heading of social justice, for example, opened with an overview statement of this theme in the teachings of the Scriptures, Jesus, and the church, then proceeded to examine unjust situations in society, in the church, and in U.S. involvements in Latin America. Reflecting participants' intention to be agents of their own future, another distinguishing feature is that instead of calling on bishops and other leaders to take specific actions, the general pattern for articulating commitments in the five major areas was to begin with the words "We, as Hispanic people, commit ourselves to. . . ." Only in the follow-up section of the conclusions were specific charges addressed beyond the delegates to diocesan leaders, the National Secretariat for Hispanic Affairs, and bishops.

Father Vizcaíno of SEPI chaired the Encuentro writing committee that worked closely with the bishops' drafting subcommittee for the National Pastoral Plan for Hispanic Ministry, chaired by Bishop Ricardo Ramírez, C.S.B., of the diocese of Las Cruces, New Mexico. The full body of U.S. bishops discussed a draft of the plan at their 1986 national meeting, addressing concerns such as the prerogative of individual bishops to implement the plan according to local circumstances and the need to integrate Hispanics into the wider church while still respecting their distinctive traditions and backgrounds. At their 1987 annual meeting the National Conference of Catholic Bishops ratified the National Pastoral Plan, addressing it to Catholics in the United States. While explicitly rooted in the Third Encuentro and the bishops' pastoral letter on Hispanic ministry, the National Pastoral Plan endorsed principles and approaches for Hispanic ministry proposed since the First Encuentro and even before. The general objective of the plan was "to live and promote by means of a *Pastoral de Conjunto* a model of church that is: communitarian, evangelizing, and missionary; incarnate in the reality of the Hispanic people and open to the diversity of cultures; a promoter and example of justice; active in developing leadership through integral education; leaven for the Kingdom of God in society."[31] Specific objectives, programs, and projects, including the identification of a timeline and the responsible agents for their enactment, were presented under the general headings *pastoral de conjunto*, evangelization, missionary option, and formation, as well as for procedures to evaluate the implementation of the plan. In conjunction with their promulgation of the plan, the bishops' conference also established the Bishops' Committee on Hispanic Affairs, elevating what had been an ad hoc committee since the time of the First Encuentro to the highest level of standing committee within their national structure.

Several major categories of the plan mirrored those of the Third Encuentro. The most distinctive elaboration was the plan's treatment of *pastoral de conjunto*, a term identified in the Second Encuentro conclusions merely as "an integrated approach to pastoral work as explicated in the documents of Medellín" and mentioned only briefly in the Third Encuentro conclusions. *Pastoral de conjunto* is more clearly defined in the National Pastoral Plan as "the harmonious coordination of all the elements of the pastoral ministry" aimed at the goal of proclaiming "the Kingdom of God" and expressing "the essence and mission of the Church, which is to be and to make communion." Under this rubric of collaborative ministries aimed toward ultimate goals, the plan presented a series of initiatives to promote Hispanic pastoral planning, ministry, and leadership at all levels of the U.S. Catholic Church. On the other hand, whereas the Third Encuentro addressed youth, integral education, and social justice as distinct priorities, the National Pastoral Plan addressed these concerns more succinctly and within the context of other broad themes. The plan addressed obliquely, or not at all, some elements of the Encuentro conclusions such as the generational and societal difficulties Hispanic youth face as a result of living between cultures, the rights of workers and immigrants, and the contention that U.S. Catholics have not sufficiently practiced the social teachings of the church and in a number of cases are even guilty of discrimination against Hispanics within parishes and dioceses. As their titles indicate, on the whole the National Pastoral Plan focuses more on fostering effective Hispanic pastoral ministries, while the Third Encuentro accentuates its theme of prophetic voices or, as the concluding Encuentro document put it, enacting "a model of Church in which the prophetic dimension stands out."[32]

Divergent emphases in the final texts do not deter from the significance of the National Pastoral Plan as the U.S. bishops' endorsement of the Encuentro process and its intent, articulated at the First Encuentro in 1972, of enhancing Hispanic ministry through sounder pastoral planning, implementation, and allocation of resources. Yet even before the bishops voted on the plan, Hispanic leaders expressed doubts that it would achieve its potential. While over 90 percent of participants rated their overall experience of the Third Encuentro as "good" or "excellent," more than half of the same group rated the implementation of a pastoral plan for Hispanic ministry in their parish as "fair" or "poor" as compared to the Encuentro, while on the same scale more than 40 percent rated their diocese as "fair" or "poor."[33]

Concerns about a lack of funding further exacerbated Hispanic leaders' suspicions that even a national mandate from the U.S. bishops would not affect the desired level of increase in vital Hispanic ministries. The bishops' allocation of financial resources included Hispanic ministry budgets in a number of individual dioceses, the sustaining of the staff members and operation of the Secretariat for Hispanic Affairs, and funding for projects and organizations from units within the bishops' conference like the Campaign for Human Development (now the Catholic Campaign for Human Development) and the American Board of Catholic Missions. Yet, given the vast ministerial needs and the broad scope of the pastoral plan, some leaders pressed the bishops to designate specific further allotments for its implementation. Though the recently formed Bishops' Committee on Hispanic Affairs followed an established practice in appointing a handful of consultants of their own choosing to their National Advisory Council, that council's replacement of the National Advisory Committee led to frustration and accusations that the more representative committee was disbanded because its members disagreed with bishops about the funding of the pastoral plan.[34] Pablo Sedillo subsequently resigned from his directorship at the Secretariat for Hispanic Affairs. In one sense the U.S. bishops' promulgation of the National Pastoral Plan marked the culmination of the three Encuentros and the apex of official national support for Hispanic ministries, which had increased notably in many locales. But it also revealed that despite the high expectations the Encuentros inspired, they were not a panacea for swiftly realizing participants' dreams and visions for Hispanic ministry.

Developments in Hispanic ministry since the passage of the National Pastoral Plan reveal two simultaneous trends: while on the whole national and regional support structures have weakened over time, ministries at the local level have continued to expand. This growth reflects the achievement and ongoing influence of the Encuentros and efforts to promote Hispanic ministries dating back to Archbishop Lucey in the Southwest and Cardinal Spellman in New York. But it is also rooted in demographic shifts: since 1990 the increasing geographic dispersion of a growing Latino population across the United States has altered the landscape of Hispanic ministry. Immigrants from throughout Latin America comprise a major sector of new and expanding Hispanic communities, including émigré women religious and priests recruited to serve in U.S. parishes and dioceses, many of whom primarily serve their fellow Spanish-speaking immigrants. Numerous locales that previously had a relatively small or no conspicuous Hispanic presence now have significant Latino populations and an array of businesses, associations, and events that make their presence visible. The parishes and dioceses that have initiated Hispanic ministries over the past two decades are often responding to these Latino newcomers in their midst.

Shifting currents in the wider society and church further refashioned Hispanic ministry initiatives. They also explain in part the diminishment of regional and national support structures for Hispanic ministry. The U.S. social and political milieu has changed dramatically since the influential presidency of Ronald Reagan. Affirmative action backlash, criticisms of identity politics, and the introduction of terminology like "political correctness" into common parlance are elements of a more potent conservative ethos that contests "minority" demands for equal access to resources and representation in leadership positions. Although these societal trends do not determine the internal decisions that shape the Catholic Church, they influence the attitudes of Catholic laity and clergy toward ecclesial initiatives and structures intended, at least partially, to redress the neglect of Hispanics. Just as the climate of social change during the civil rights era buttressed the efforts of Hispanic Catholic leaders during the decade of the first Encuentros, more recent political debates have called into question the advisability of leadership quotas and separate institutional structures for historically underrepresented ethnic and racial groups.

A major influence within Catholicism was the papacy of Pope John Paul II, who inspired many Hispanic Catholic leaders with his charismatic leadership and his teachings, especially on evangelization and on the need for communion, solidarity, and the consciousness of a common destiny across the American hemisphere. His influence was evident in a 1995 event to commemorate the fiftieth anniversary of the establishment of a national Hispanic ministry office. The title of the event was "Convocation '95: The Hispanic Presence in the New Evangelization in the United States." The Bishops' Committee on Hispanic Affairs led this gathering of more than five hundred Hispanic ministry leaders, whose collective convocation statement of commitment was centered on John Paul's call for "a New Evangelization" and their pledge to "struggle against the culture of death denounced by our Holy Father Pope John Paul II, giving witness to the Gospel of life." John Paul's influence is also reflected in the bishops' *Encuentro and Mission* document issued on the fifteenth anniversary of the National Pastoral Plan. *Encuentro and Mission* instructed that the New Evangelization should become "integral to all the specific dimensions of the

Pastoral Plan" as a means "to reach out more effectively to inactive Hispanic Catholics and the unchurched."[35] The pope's popularity and pastoral solicitude for Hispanics were evident on his various visits to the United States, which stirred a number of Hispanic Catholics in their faith and service.

During his lengthy papacy John Paul's appointment of bishops and papal nuncios also steered Catholicism in the United States (and elsewhere) toward a greater respect for church authority. Various Hispanic ministry leaders have claimed that the Hispanic bishops appointed under John Paul tended to focus more on institutional loyalty than on the promotion of Hispanic ministry, which previous appointees like Archbishop Flores had championed. Though not explicitly opposed to demands like leadership parity between ethnic groups within the church—indeed, during John Paul's reign the number of Hispanic bishops more than quadrupled from eight to thirty-six—this focus was less conducive to the Encuentro approach of appealing to the U.S. bishops as a collective body to enhance Hispanic ministry through structural changes and the mobilization of resources. John Paul's desire to unify the church through its central authority raised the question of the purpose and jurisdiction of national bishops' conferences, organizations whose growing prominence after Vatican II led to ambiguity vis-à-vis their authority relative to that of the Vatican and that of a bishop in his own diocese. The pope's 1998 apostolic letter, *Apostolos Suos* (*On the Theological and Juridical Nature of Episcopal Conferences*), taught that a declaration of a bishops' conference is not binding on the faithful in their jurisdiction unless it receives the unanimous vote of the bishops in the conference—a rare occurrence in the United States with its diverse group of nearly three hundred active bishops—or, in the case of a majority but not a unanimous vote, Vatican approval of the declaration.[36] This teaching and debates about the role of national bishops' conferences increased the conviction that individual bishops were to take the lead in implementing initiatives like the National Pastoral Plan according to local needs and circumstances, a development that indirectly lessened the impact of national and regional church offices and structures such as the Encuentros and the Secretariat for Hispanic Affairs.

The crisis of clergy sex abuse and bishops' knowing transfer of offenders to new assignments also weakened Hispanic ministry. Expanding nationally from the epicenter of the Boston archdiocese beginning in 2002, the crisis affects Hispanics as it does other Catholics. Latino priests have been among the perpetrators of these crimes. The plaintiffs in lawsuits against various dioceses encompassed Latino victims, most prominently the 2007 settlement with approximately five hundred plaintiffs in Los Angeles. One Latino victim stated publicly that he had lost his faith and had strained relations with several practicing Catholics within his family because of his accusations against church officials. In a national radio interview after the settlement, he called for the resignation of Cardinal Roger Mahony and for a congressional hearing to investigate this "organization [the Catholic Church] that has protected, has shuffled, you know, pedophile men around the United States and internationally and has hidden, you know, the truth."[37] Hispanic ministry leaders note that besides the shameful effects on victims and their families, the crisis is yet another obstacle to nourishing the Hispanic presence in U.S. Catholicism. The decline in bishops' credibility weakens their moral authority and political clout on issues like immigration reform. Fearing that background checks would lead to governmental detection of their whereabouts, many undocumented Latinos dropped out of parish ministries when dioceses implemented screening procedures for church employees and volunteers. Moreover, estimates of settlements and awards to abuse victims now total more than $2 billion nationally. Coupled with major downturns in the U.S. economy in 2001 and again in 2008, this financial fallout was contiguous with the diminishment of fiscal resources church leaders allocated for national and regional Hispanic organizations, as well as for Hispanic ministries in many dioceses and parishes.

The repercussions of the sex-abuse crisis are part of the overriding cause in the decline of many support structures for Hispanic ministry: a lack of funding. For much of U.S. Catholic history the general expectation in a predominantly immigrant church was that each group was its own funder, drawing on fiscal and personnel resources that often included generous support from compatriots still in their homeland. But during the 1970s and 1980s many Hispanic organizations and regional offices received the bulk of their funding from bishops or the American Board of Catholic Missions. The lack of a self-sustaining fiscal model left a number of these groups at a loss when that core funding was curtailed or discontinued. Initiatives in Hispanic Catholic philanthropy are relatively sparse, among both the broad base of potential working-class donors and a growing number of professional and economically advancing Latinos. Strong leadership such as that of Sister María Elena González, R.S.M., provided relative stability within some organizations: with generous support from religious congregations, especially her own Sisters of Mercy community, during her tenure as president of MACC from 1993 to 2007 González led the effort to raise some $6 million and construct a new pastoral training facility. However, at MACC and elsewhere, such hard-won fiscal successes remain the exception rather than the rule.

Hispanic ministry advocates have rightly observed that the size of the Latino Catholic population is disproportionate to the resources dedicated to Hispanic ministry. The uneven distribution of fiscal resources within U.S. Catholicism has shaped the budget decisions of bishops and church administrators vis-à-vis those ministries. At the local level, many bishops and their advisers face the daunting challenge of continuing an array of institutions. Various difficulties complicate their efforts: rising maintenance costs for aging buildings, declining numbers of clergy, and an already depleted force of women religious, who in previous generations shouldered the burden of Catholic education, health care, and social services for a fraction of the salary costs now involved in such enterprises. In response, bishops across the country have established foundations and annual appeals to support underfunded ministries, including Hispanic ministries. Stewardship campaigns have increased Latino Catholic giving in a few locations. Some more prosperous parishes "twin" with poorer congregations in relationships that include sharing fiscal resources. The determination of bishops and the generosity of lay Catholics have garnered results. But such efforts inevitably face the challenge that donors are likely to give most generously for causes closer to home, a tendency that is evident nationwide in dioceses where new parishes and schools are constructed in more affluent suburban areas while their poorer inner-city counterparts are closed. The preference for local giving makes it more difficult for church officials to distribute resources across a diocese. It can also deter them from increasing the funding for initiatives like Hispanic ministry that are potentially controversial, especially if donors perceive support for such initiatives detracts from a ministry that impacts their family or parish.

Today even organizations with a track record for a relatively wider donor profile are undergoing financial duress. Allan Figueroa Deck led the effort to found the NCCHM in 1991 and served as its first executive director until 1997. Reportedly the "reasons [the founders] cited for forming the organization include[d] the bishops' refusal to fund implementation of the 1987 National Pastoral Plan for Hispanic Ministry." Expressing concern that "the voices of Hispanics are not heard in the public square nor even in the church councils to the extent their numbers merit," NCCHM leaders asserted that with the creation of their organization, "for the first time Hispanic Catholic organizations had a national umbrella organization independent of the bishops and seeking to serve as a bridge among 'secular' Hispanic leadership and the church-based leaders." Grants from outside of Catholic sources, especially from the Lilly Endowment and the Pew Charitable Trusts, were pivotal to NCCHM's successes, among them convening four national congresses of Hispanic leaders from church and society and serving as a clearinghouse and source of unity for national and regional organizations involved in Hispanic ministry. Yet, according to a 2008 NCCHM newsletter report, "because of the dire financial situation" the organization lacked an executive director and administrative assistant for the first time since its founding. The current president of the organization, Carmen Aguinaco, and its board of directors continue to promote NCCHM's reduced agenda through their volunteer efforts. Their dedication was the primary factor that enabled NCCHM to convene a national congress in 2010, a successful event despite the financial constraints its organizers faced.[38]

Insufficient funding led regional offices of Hispanic ministry created in the wake of the Second Encuentro of 1977 to close within a few years of the passage of the 1987 National Pastoral Plan. Now nearly all the offices are defunct or face financial constraints that significantly hamper their effectiveness. Funding is also alarmingly scarce for national Hispanic Catholic organizations. A 2009 study found that volunteers head half of the twenty-one national and regional Hispanic ministry organizations studied and that "*the* major challenge" in "virtually all" the organizations was the curtailment of their mission due to a lack of funding. The National Organization for Catechesis with Hispanics (NOCH), which served its members for more than three decades after its founding in 1976, has already disbanded, and a number of other organizations are in danger of doing so. Some "mainstream" national Catholic organizations have evidenced an encouraging desire to incorporate Hispanic leaders, such as the National Conference for Catechetical Leadership (NCCL) Forum on Catechesis with Hispanics, which Dennis Johnson Jr. and Alex Sandoval helped inaugurate to continue work initiated in NOCH. But such collaborations are by no means widespread. Hispanic leaders like Ken Johnson-Mondragón say that "an unintended consequence of the creation of national organizations for particular ethnic ministries has been that the national leaders of these cultural groups dedicate most of their available time and resources to their own organizations" and that consequently "very few" have worked systematically to "build bridges with the mainstream national organizations." The current malaise is unprecedented in the four decades since the establishment of the first national Hispanic Catholic organizations.[39]

Hispanic leaders' frustration at the subsuming of the Secretariat for Hispanic Affairs into the cultural diversity secretariat reflects their contention that, intentionally or not, the restructuring of this national body is emblematic of the general decline in the organizational infrastructure for Hispanic ministry. Allan Figueroa Deck launched an initiative to create a national conversation with experienced leaders in Hispanic ministry aimed at strengthening national and regional structures. One goal of this initiative is to raise funds or even create a national endowment to support those structures and to help cover costs for training Hispanic Catholic leaders. Deck's leadership as executive director of the Secretariat of Cultural Diversity in the Church, along with that of his colleague Alejandro Aguilera-Titus, the Hispanic prelates who have chaired the Bishops' Committee on Cultural Diversity in the Church, and the Bishops' Subcommittee of Hispanic Affairs have been assets for this effort. The recent symposiums at Georgetown University and Boston College—along with similar initiatives and programs at Catholic universities such as Barry in Miami, Loyola Marymount in Los Angeles, the University of San Diego, and Notre Dame, among others—suggest that another, but largely untapped, resource is greater collaboration with the nearly 250 Catholic institutions of higher education in the United States. The relatively sound fiscal health of these institutions as compared to that of national ministerial organizations and most dioceses make them potentially strategic partners. Foundations such as the Lilly Endowment and the Louisville Institute, their Catholic counterparts like Our Sunday Visitor Institute, and publishers like William H. Sadlier, Inc., have generously supported initiatives in Hispanic catechesis, evangelization, and ministry formation and could also be allies in efforts to rejuvenate support structures for Hispanic ministry. The promotion of Hispanic Catholic philanthropy remains a largely unmet challenge.

Barring an unexpected windfall, however, in all probability the weakening of the national and regional structures that Encuentro participants labored to construct appears to be irreversible, at least at funding levels that allow for paid directors and staffs in the various organizations and regions. Thus one challenge Hispanic ministry leaders face is to transcend the narrow parochialism of defending one's own organizational turf and engage in a frank discussion about which of the current structures are most essential for sustaining local ministries. Should the focus be on organizations with a renowned track record of success as a catalyst in a region, such as SEPI has been in the Southeast? Should priority be given to organizations with particularly vital links to local ministries, such as the National Catholic Association of Diocesan Directors for Hispanic Ministry (NCADDHM), whose members each have direct influence in the diocese where they serve? Should Latino leaders concentrate on working advantageously within existing "mainstream" organizations that have more stable funding mechanisms, as is the case with the NCCL Forum on Catechesis with Hispanics, endeavoring as newcomers in such organizations to advocate for Hispanic concerns while also fostering vital collaborative links? The three criteria implied in these queries strike this observer as sound priorities from which to begin a forthright conversation, if for no other reason than the strategic one of attracting financial support and maximizing the efficient use of limited resources. In any event, the extent to which

Hispanic ministry leaders address difficult questions and decisions such as these will largely determine the effectiveness of the support structures they are able to sustain into the future.

The contours of national and regional initiatives in Hispanic ministry emerged at the intersection of Latino Catholic faith convictions and their engagement of social change mechanisms that were prevalent in U.S. civil rights struggles. From the outset of the First Encuentro, the efforts of Hispanic ministry proponents reflected their concurrent—and at times conflicting—impulses to foster Latino advocacy structures within the church and to build common bonds of faith with their fellow Catholics. More recently, the Hispanics who played a leading role in Encuentro 2000 accentuated the latter impulse, organizing this national process and event, which, in the words of *Encuentro and Mission*, "marked the first time that the Church in the United States gathered to recognize, affirm, and celebrate the cultural and racial diversity of its members."[40] Conversely, other Hispanic ministry leaders opine that Encuentro 2000 inadvertently contributed to the waning of Hispanic ministry initiatives, as that Encuentro's accentuation of the rich cultural diversity in U.S. Catholicism buttressed a rationale for the consolidation of racial and ethnic ministry offices into multicultural ones. Even as Encuentro 2000 marks a high point of Hispanic Catholic attempts to foster ecclesial unity in diversity, such critiques reveal that the advocacy impulse among Hispanic ministry proponents is not quenched.

While retrospective analyses of the Encuentros must necessarily examine the documents and structural results they produced, it is important to remember that, like all such ecclesial meetings, first and foremost the Encuentros were events. No concluding document for such an event can fully capture the sense of solidarity among Hispanic leaders coming together nationally for the first time, the power of such an ambiance to enhance creativity of pastoral and theological vision, and the courage these gatherings gave participants to break silence and form a united front to confront their experiences of injustice. As Pablo Sedillo, a pivotal leader in all three Encuentros, put it: "Some people who came to the Encuentros drove all night to get there. I felt history was being played out before my eyes. People's hunger, listening to their hearts, their struggles, it enriched my life immensely and I think the lives of many others too." Arguably the most significant—though unquantifiable—legacy of the Encuentros is their part in forming several thousand leaders who have dedicated their energies, and even their life's work, to the advancement of Hispanic ministry. Edgard Beltrán attests that "while Medellín produced more influential documents, the excellence of the Encuentros was in their communal participatory process from the grass roots. This broad-based process instilled in people a consciousness of their Hispanic identity, a deeper integration into the life of the church, and an organization as a more united Hispanic Catholic community." Many leaders attest that the Encuentros are a primary focal point for the sense of common purpose based on a shared history—what *Encuentro and Mission* calls a communal *memoria histórica* (historical memory)—that has linked various Catholics from Mexican, Puerto Rican, Cuban, and other backgrounds in Hispanic Catholic initiatives and organizations.[41] The Encuentros were the symbolic center of a wide-ranging Hispanic ministry movement that shaped and was shaped by the Encuentros' own national gatherings and consultative processes.

Along with U.S. bishops' efforts spanning more than six decades, the Encuentros heightened recognition of and respect for the Hispanic presence in the U.S. Catholic Church, fostered apostolic zeal for Hispanic ministry, and advocated for the expansion of resources and personnel dedicated to that work. Most importantly, as leaders like Bishop Arturo Cepeda have noted, the Encuentros helped many Hispanics assume more fully "their mission within the Church in the United States."[42] In the latter regard, the Encuentros and the bishops' statements on Hispanic ministry are the most conspicuous means that Hispanics have engaged in conversations and debates about the renewal of Catholicism in the United States since Vatican II. Drawing on the teachings of Vatican II, the Latin American bishops in their conferences at Medellín and Puebla,[43] and the popes, particularly Paul VI and John Paul II, Hispanic Catholic leaders proposed core pastoral and theological precepts for the enhancement both of Hispanic ministry and of ecclesial life in U.S. Catholicism. Prominent among these precepts are respect for diverse languages, cultures, and faith traditions as part of the beauty of God's creation; the commitment to evangelization and justice as constitutive of the church's mission to proclaim Jesus Christ; the urgency to serve and foster leadership among marginal groups such as farmworkers, women, young people, and the wider Hispanic population; and the call to transform personal lives as well as cultures, society, and the internal dynamics of the church itself. Underlying these convictions is a core ecclesiology, an understanding of the Church, which the concluding document of the Third Encuentro deemed the body of Christ that "incarnates itself and wishes to journey together with the people in all their cultural, political, and religious reality." This perspective echoes the Vatican II statement that "The church . . . must implant itself among all these groups in the same way that Christ by his incarnation committed himself to the particular social and cultural circumstances of the women and men among whom he lived."[44] Underscoring the Church as a community charged to embody Christ's presence in the concrete circumstances of human life, the

Encuentro vision encapsulates the theological foundation that animated Hispanic ministry leaders in their collective efforts to transform U.S. Catholicism through their pastoral planning and action.

Yet constraints to the effectiveness of such initiatives—particularly the decline of civil rights forces that had given impetus and credibility to Hispanic ministry advocacy—are implicitly evident in the bishops' *Encuentro and Mission* document. The Bishops' Committee on Hispanic Affairs convened the 2001 National Symposium to Refocus Hispanic Ministry as a consultation to assist in preparing that document. Sixty symposium participants representing national and regional Hispanic Catholic organizations and various units of the USCCB identified ongoing challenges in Hispanic ministry that largely mirrored previous bishops' statements and conclusions from the Encuentros. Their conclusions encompassed the familiar litany of a lack of personnel and resources, limited access to leadership and decision-making positions, inadequate outreach to Latino youth, and proselytism. Symposium participants also addressed shifting realities like the growing complexity of the U.S. Hispanic population, particularly along generational lines. But most of the major concerns, and the urgency with which participants presented them, revealed that progress made on the agenda of the Encuentros and the National Pastoral Plan for Hispanic Ministry was far from comprehensive. Tellingly, one challenge participants identified was that "a survey of bishops and diocesan directors of Hispanic ministry showed that even though the [National] Pastoral Plan [for Hispanic Ministry] has existed since 1987, few ministers outside Hispanic ministry know about the plan, or they rarely conduct pastoral planning in collaboration with Hispanic ministry." Virgilio Elizondo succinctly expresses the overall assessment of many long-serving leaders regarding their efforts to foster Hispanic ministry in U.S. Catholicism: "When I look at all that has been accomplished since that First Encuentro, it is nothing short of a miracle. But when I look at all that remains to be done, it is scary."[45]

The pastoral outreach among Latinos today in dioceses, parishes, and apostolic movements extends the efforts of those who promoted Hispanic ministry during the Encuentro era. According to current USCCB statistics, more than 80 percent of the 195 dioceses in the United States have diocesan staff assigned to coordinate Hispanic ministry, though with varying degrees of time commitment ranging from part-time coordinators to full-time directors of Hispanic ministry. A 2002 CARA survey found that two strong emphases in these diocesan coordination efforts are leadership training for Hispanic ministries and collaboration with other diocesan offices, as well as with local Latino service agencies. More recently, through their NCADDHM organization diocesan directors have articulated to U.S. bishops their growing "concerns related to the closing of diocesan offices for Hispanic ministry or their placement under multicultural ministry offices" and their alarm "that while the Hispanic presence continues to grow and demands a more robust ministerial response, diocesan personnel and/or resources for Hispanic ministry are diminishing in a number of arch/dioceses." Diocesan directors note that their budgets are often among the first to be cut or eliminated when church officials restructure or downsize their operation. Hispanic leaders also decry what they perceive as a prevalent attitude that Hispanic ministry is "a specialized ministry separate from the mission of the diocese or the parish" and that Hispanic Catholics "are the exclusive responsibility of the [diocesan] office for Hispanic ministry."[46] Despite such deficiencies, diocesan-level Hispanic ministry is the most frequent at any structural level of the church. Given the even greater strains in national and regional organizations, today the center of gravity for Hispanic ministry initiatives is more focused on dioceses and their local faith communities than it has been since the First Encuentro. The leadership, close proximity to grassroots Latinos, and evangelizing potential of these communities make them the primary resources for the proximate future of Hispanic ministry.

CHAPTER

# Parishes and Apostolic Movements

**F**our years after Fidel Castro's 1959 rise to power in Cuba, Father Emilio Vallina and other Cuban exiles established the San Juan Bosco congregation at an abandoned car dealership in the Little Havana district of Miami. Vallina left Cuba when "Castro began persecuting the Church" and incited "mobs [who] came into the churches and beat up people and priests." In his native land, Father Vallina had celebrated Mass at the shrine of Jesús del Nazareno in Arroyo Arenas, a working-class Havana neighborhood. At San Juan Bosco he enshrined a replica of that very same Jesús del Nazareno statue donated by fellow exiles from Arroyo Arenas. He also oversaw the adornment of the church with other images popular among Cubans—St. Barbara, St. Lazarus, the Virgin of Regla, and the Cuban national patroness Nuestra Señora de la Caridad del Cobre—and he celebrated familiar religious feasts that made his new parish renowned as "a cathedral of Cuban traditions." Ministerial activities included outreach programs for the elderly, a credit union, and the Escuela Cívico Religioso (Civic Religious School), where Cuban children learned their ancestral language and heritage. San Juan Bosco also provided occasions for Cubans to "gather to ask of God what men have not been able to do—liberate their homeland," such as a memorial Mass that brought together veterans of the failed 1961 Bay of Pigs invasion and other exiles to pray for those who died in that attempt to overthrow Castro. Nicaraguans fleeing revolutionary violence in their homeland joined Cuban parishioners in noteworthy numbers during the 1980s. Hispanic émigrés from various other nations in Latin America have also joined the parish, which today remains a vibrant center of Hispanic, especially Cuban, Catholicism.[1]

Latinos' attraction to parishes like San Juan Bosco is mirrored in their enthusiasm for apostolic movements. Members of these groups engage in common prayer, faith formation, and evangelization activities, often in smaller-sized communities that foster a stronger sense of commitment and belonging than many large parish congregations. Though far more Catholics are attracted to evangelical and Pentecostal groups than vice versa, the dynamism of apostolic movements is illuminated in the non-Catholics who are drawn to participate in them. Puerto Rican Chicagoan Elisabeth Román "was raised in a strict Pentecostal household and indoctrinated from an early age about the evils of the Catholic Church." Faced with a personal crisis and lacking a spiritual home after a twenty-year hiatus from church attendance, she accepted a friend's invitation to a parish Mass imbued with the spirit of the Catholic Charismatic Renewal, an apostolic group centered on the gifts and the power of the Holy Spirit that seeks to renew Christian faith through community life, prayer, preaching, healing ministries, and evangelization. Román continued to worship at the Charismatic Mass each Sunday for three months. Impressed with the community's faith, her own sense of inner peace, and the fact that no one pressured her to become Catholic, she went through the process of being received into the Catholic Church, over the strong objections of her family members. To this day, at family gatherings Román is "lectured on how I have abandoned God for Catholicism, and should I die without repenting, my soul will be eternally condemned to hell." Yet she insists that "the spirited [Catholic Charismatic] church I encountered, and the one I have learned to love and serve, seems to be what many Latinos are seeking." Román concludes that "for Hispanics, who must live between two cultures, charismatic Catholicism can offer the best of both worlds: participation in the sacraments and a personal, livelier form of worship, which is at the heart of our religious experience."[2]

Surprisingly, the conclusions of the three National Hispanic Pastoral Encuentros say relatively little about local faith communities such as these. The Encuentros' strong emphasis on basic communities did not encompass a substantive analysis about how these small communities relate to parishes and apostolic movements. It is not even clear whether various passages in the Encuentro documents about basic communities were intended to include the growing number of small groups for prayer, faith formation, and apostolic endeavors like those of the Catholic Charismatic Renewal. Latin American theologians and pastoral leaders were emphatic that basic ecclesial communities are not another apostolic movement, but a structural unit of ecclesial life on par with the prevalent status of the parish in U.S. Catholicism. U.S. bishops echoed this perspective in their pastoral letter on Hispanic ministry, in which, citing a document of the Latin American bishops' conference, they acclaimed the basic communities as "the first and fundamental ecclesiastical nucleus" that had "appeared on the scene as a ray of hope in dealing with dehumanizing situations that can destroy people and weaken faith." But four years later the bishops' National Pastoral Plan for Hispanic Ministry included a slight but significant change in wording for what the bishops in this document called "small ecclesial communities."[3]

While the bishops never explicitly state the reason for this shift from the term "*basic* ecclesial communities" employed in their earlier pastoral letter, the change in language reflected concerns in the Vatican and elsewhere that these communities not be perceived as ecclesial expressions independent of or superseding hierarchical authority and parish and diocesan structures, nor as groups formed predominantly to foment political change through organizing exclusively the marginal persons from the "base" of society. Indeed, in a 1990 pastoral statement issued on the fifth anniversary of the Third Encuentro, the Bishops' Committee on Hispanic Affairs avowed that the value of small ecclesial communities "lies in the personal experience of the love of Christ that they can communicate. . . If understood and promoted this way, there is no need to fear that small communities would be at odds with the parish community, the diocese, and the universal Church." The committee subsequently prepared *A Guide for Bishops and Pastoral Leaders on Small Church Communities* to direct pastoral efforts toward "preserving and strengthening the Catholic identity of these communities."[4]

Promoters of basic ecclesial communities contended that fears of ecclesial divisiveness were largely unfounded and that the new terminology did not substantially alter the self-understanding of those involved with the communities. A few Hispanic ministry leaders made significant contributions to enacting the basic ecclesial community vision, such as Edgard Beltrán, who conducted numerous workshops to foster and nurture basic communities when he worked for the Secretariat for Hispanic Affairs during the 1970s. Subsequently Missionaries of Jesus sister Ninfa Garza led the effort to establish some five hundred communities modeled on the Latin American model in the diocese of Brownsville, Texas, while Brazilian priest José Marins and his team of collaborators conducted various workshops through the Mexican American Cultural Center in San Antonio aimed at expanding basic communities in the United States. Whatever one's conviction about the potential of the basic ecclesial communities to affect, as the English title of Brazilian Jesuit theologian Marcelo Azevedo's influential book on the subject put it, a fundamental restructuring and "a new way of being church," and despite the exceptional efforts of leaders like Beltrán, Garza, and Marins, a restructuring into basic ecclesial communities of this sort has never occurred massively in the U.S. Catholic Church.[5]

The U.S. bishops' National Pastoral Plan declared, "The Hispanic community recognizes that the parish is, ecclesiastically and historically speaking, the basic organizational unit of the Church in the United States, and it will continue to be so." Far from claiming basic communities as a means to restructure Catholic life, the bishops went on to add that "at the same time it is affirmed that conversion and a sense of being Church are often best lived out in smaller communities within the parish which are more personal and offer a greater sense of belonging." Thus they encouraged the development of the "many apostolic movements and church organizations [that] have traditionally served to unite our church people in small communities for various purposes." They further stated that small ecclesial communities are, in a definition that depicts them as strikingly similar to parish organizations and apostolic movements, "small groups organized for more intense personal and community relationships among the faithful and for a greater participation in the life and mission of the Church."[6]

Programs and projects outlined throughout the bishops' pastoral plan consistently presented recommendations to enhance and coordinate local Hispanic ministries. The bishops promoted a vision of the parish as a "community of communities," a unified network of apostolic movements and other small communal groups that fostered the faith and evangelization efforts of congregational members. They exhorted clergy and lay leaders to promote greater collaboration among the various apostolic movements as well as small ecclesial communities, implicitly recognizing that these groups sometimes operate in isolation or in competition with one another. They urged Hispanic ministry leaders to stimulate the evangelizing potential of these small groups, whose members often live and work in closest proximity to grassroots Hispanics. They charged diocesan personnel and pastoral institutes to form leaders for Hispanic ministry in all the structures of the local church, from diocesan initiatives to small ecclesial communities.[7]

The bishops underscore that the epicenter of Hispanic Catholicism and Hispanic Catholic ministries is the home and extended family, the apostolic movements along with other small ecclesial communities, and the parish. Nearly one-fourth of 18,280 Catholic parishes in the United States now have Hispanic ministries ranging from a weekly Mass in Spanish to a full program of outreach ministries for Latinos, a sizable figure though still disproportionate to the approximately 35 percent of the U.S. Catholic population that is Hispanic. From 1995 to 1998 Bernard Lee and William V. D'Antonio led a study of U.S. Catholics in small Christian communities and identified 7,500 such communities that were almost entirely Hispanic, about 20 percent of the total number they found in the United States. Given the lapse of more than a decade since this research, its overwhelming focus on Mexican Americans and not the other Hispanic groups, and the fact that various apostolic movements were not counted as constituting small Christian communities, it is safe to assume that the composite figure of Hispanic apostolic associations, prayer groups, and small communities is far greater today.[8] Understanding the challenges parishes and apostolic movements confront, the strengths and weaknesses of these local faith communities, and efforts to make them even more effective is a core lens for assessing the ways Hispanics, U.S. Catholicism, and wider trends in U.S. religion are reshaping one another.

Latinos and the leaders who work with them in grassroots Hispanic ministries face numerous difficulties. Most of these trials and temptations of daily life are familiar to anyone who has even passing contact or knowledge of many working-class Hispanic communities: lack of opportunity, low educational attainment, drug and alcohol abuse, violence, teenage pregnancy, poverty, undocumented status, inadequate health care, and a general strain on family cohesion and personal well-being, among others.[9] Looking inward to the vitality of their own faith communities, Hispanic ministry proponents have frequently lamented that the upsurge of religious traditions like Pentecostalism and evangelicalism provide the most momentous challenge. Preserving the faith of immigrants is one element of this challenge. At least as urgent is the need to invigorate faith among Latinos as they become more enmeshed in a pluralistic U.S. society with a range of religious options, including the choice for no religious affiliation.

The widely cited research of Andrew Greeley beginning in the late 1980s showed that at that time some sixty thousand Hispanics in the United States "defect[ed]" from their ancestral religion every year. Greeley's research and subsequent studies like the 2002 National Survey of Latinos and 2007 Pew Latino religion survey reveal that identification as Protestants varies across Hispanic groups, with Puerto Ricans, Salvadorans, and other Central Americans the most likely to identify as Protestants and ethnic Mexicans the least likely to do so. In a follow-up article a decade after his initial study, Greeley claimed that the overall situation had gotten even worse, noting that the annual loss of Latinos is one-half of 1 percent, although unfortunately he miscalculated the yearly exodus as the often-cited figure of six hundred thousand rather than the correct figure of sixty thousand based on the data he presented.[10]

Greeley's conclusion that the departure of Latinos is "the worst defection in the history of the Catholic Church in the United States" needs to be examined against the 2008 Pew Forum on Religion and Public Life survey and its findings that fully 10 percent of all U.S. residents were raised as Catholics but no longer describe themselves as Catholic, a loss of one-third of the Catholic faithful between childhood and adulthood. A CARA report confirmed that Euro-Americans accounted for 70 percent of those who self-identified as former Catholics on a 2003 survey, while Latinos accounted for only 20 percent, proportionately less than their percentage of the overall Catholic population. Most strikingly, the 2006 Faith Matters survey of Robert Putnam and David Campbell found that the defection rate among "Anglo" Catholics is double that of their Latino counterparts. Thus Hispanic patterns of affiliation are not an anomaly: they reflect the long-standing pluralism and voluntarism that are characteristic of religion in the United States as well as a widespread contemporary trend away from denominational loyalty and toward a religious culture of choice. Nonetheless, Greeley and subsequent researchers have rightly pointed to the departure of Latinos from Catholicism as a monumental pastoral predicament.[11]

Reflecting denominational shifts that are prevalent in Latin America and in other regions around the globe, the overwhelming majority of Latinos in the United States who leave Roman Catholicism for another faith tradition have embraced Protestantism in its Pentecostal and evangelical forms. Many observers subsume into a single "evangelical" category congregations ranging from churches that stringently discipline their membership to those that accentuate the "prosperity gospel" and its belief that God bountifully rewards the faithful with material blessings. A number of evangelical pastors disagree vehemently with the prosperity gospel. Some commentators have noted that it incited believers to take on risky loans in a blind leap of faith and thus helped fuel the housing and mortgage crisis beginning in 2008. Yet churches with prosperity gospel theologies, such as Casa del Padre in Charlottesville, Virginia, attract substantial Latino congregations. Hispanic Catholic ministry leaders contend that one group of Hispanics who are particularly prone to leave Catholicism for these churches are the gradually increasing number who have ascended to the middle class. According to these leaders, their fellow Hispanics find in such churches "justification and celebration of their upward mobility" and "personal therapies to deal with their family and work problems."[12]

The more prevalent immigrant, poor, and working-class Hispanics account for an even larger number of those who have become affiliated with Pentecostal and evangelical churches. Analyses of the causes for this trend are varied. Some immigrants are not even aware of denominational differences and fail to recognize they have begun to participate in a Protestant congregation. The disorienting effect of migration exacerbates the difficulty of elders handing down their faith tradition to their young and generally makes those of all ages more open to new religious experiences. It also makes the personal contact in relatively small Latino Pentecostal and evangelical faith communities more appealing. A 2002 report of the Program for the Analysis of Religion among Latinos (PARAL) showed that half of Latino Protestant congregations have fewer than one hundred members, and only 1 percent of them have more than a thousand members. Conversely, more than a third of Latino Catholic faith communities have more than a thousand parishioners and scarcely 5 percent number fewer than a hundred.[13] More intimate communities help facilitate the missionary zeal of Latino Pentecostals and evangelicals. Indeed, reinforcing evangelical objectives with the pragmatic reality of the need for worshipers and donations in typically small faith communities, the growth and even the ongoing existence of many such congregations can depend largely on the ability of the pastor and his or her collaborators to bring in new members. Newcomers are quickly encouraged to participate actively in the congregation and its missionary outreach. Preaching is not solely the role of the pastor: it is encouraged among all members of the congregation. Their door-to-door, person-to-person engagement and their pronounced clarity on teachings ranging from one's future in the afterlife to everyday moral codes have reordered many Latino lives. A number of Hispanics testify that in their new church God healed them from drug addiction, alcoholism, marital infidelity, depression, or other ailments.

Conversely, as Hispanic ministry leaders have noted, the Catholic Church is a hierarchical church with a long history and established institutions and structures in the United States that often put it in "business as usual" or "maintenance" mode, a state of affairs that a lack of priests and church finances usually exacerbates. While the average Latino Pentecostal or evangelical pastor expends significant time and energy trying to build an often fledgling congregation, the average Catholic pastor labors to simply keep up with the demands of his existing flock—or flocks, as an increasing number of priests are charged with more than one parish to shepherd. Lay Catholic evangelization efforts, which popes and other church leaders have consistently endorsed, are not as deep-rooted in the Catholic psyche and not as widespread among Latino Catholics as among Protestants. Movements like Misioneros de la Palabra de Dios (Missionaries of the Word of God) and websites like Católico defiende tu fe Cristiana (Catholic Defend Your Christian Faith) stress Catholic apologetics and attempt to protect Latino Catholics from proselytizing efforts. Nonetheless, many Hispanic ministry leaders bemoan that Protestant evangelizers "are eating us alive, simply because we don't know the bible and when they cite it to us, we get all confused and don't know how to respond, to defend our faith."[14]

Moreover, ecumenical and interfaith collaborations that increased notably in U.S. Catholicism after the Second Vatican Council are far more influential among Hispanic academic and ecclesial leaders than among grassroots believers. Latina and Latino theologians have displayed a marked ecumenical spirit in recent decades. The 2009 edited volume *Building Bridges, Doing Justice: Constructing a Latino/a Ecumenical Theology* stems from the 2007 annual meeting of the ecumenically conscious Academy of Catholic Hispanic Theologians of the United States and features paired articles from Protestant and Catholic theologians on topics such as revelation, grace and justification, and ecclesiology. It is part of an ongoing series of collaborations among Latino theologians of various denominations. Justo González, widely regarded as the premier Latino Protestant theologian, has noted that the common experiences of struggle for rights in U.S. society, second-class treatment within their respective denominations, and incorporation of Hispanic cultural expression into their faith have tended to distance Latino Christians from their non-Latino denominational coreligionists and to foster Hispanic ecumenical solidarity. Groups such as the Hispanic Summer Program and the Hispanic Theological Initiative Consortium are focused on graduate theological education and have sponsoring institutions from a variety of denominational backgrounds.[15]

Yet such efforts do not have sweeping influence at the grassroots pastoral level, where competition and even mutual condemnations are commonplace. Catholic leaders have characterized Pentecostals and evangelicals as anti-Catholic "sheep stealers"; labeled them with the pejorative term *sectas*, or "sects"; and accused them of being traitors to their Hispanic Catholic heritage and dividers of their families. Their adversaries often accuse Catholics of worshiping idols and images, fostering "Mariolatry" instead of faith in Jesus Christ, and relying on church tradition rather than the sole truth of the Bible. These taunts are not just hurled from the distance but increasingly become part of everyday life, even family gatherings, as the experience of Elisabeth Román reveals. While religious competition in the United States is widespread across many groups, the long-standing influence of Catholicism in Hispanic families, cultures, and identities often intensifies such exchanges among Latinos. A relative dearth of common initiatives among Latino Christian church leaders in local areas further exacerbates the estrangement. The 2002 PARAL report revealed that ecumenical ventures among Latino Christians in areas such as worship and social outreach transpire in well under 10 percent of Hispanic Catholic faith communities. As Catholic bishop Ricardo Ramírez has noted, Hispanic "Protestant and Roman Catholic leaders are never seen together, either praying, talking or working in united ministry. If the people see that it is all right to mix with one another, then they might follow our example."[16]

Latinos who join Protestant congregations often cite a direct and personal experience of God as their primary motive, such as 90 percent of the Pew Latino religion survey respondents who left Catholicism for another church. They tend to see themselves simply as Christians drawn to a deeper faith experience, not as "religious defectors." Thus they enlarge the spiritual seekers trend that scholars like Robert Wuthnow have noted mark the U.S. religious landscape. Yet the structures and character of the Protestant congregations that attract Latinos have striking parallels with effective ethnic Catholic parishes: they provide a strong sense of family and fellowship, indigenous Spanish-speaking pastors, an overwhelmingly predominant Hispanic membership, and worship services in which Latinos can pray and sing in their own language and cultural style. Enlivened worship is particularly important; more than 60 percent of formerly Catholic Latino evangelicals interviewed for the Pew survey found Catholic worship at Mass "unexciting," and more than a third of them said they switched denominations primarily because of this perceived deficiency.[17]

Thus the most effective elements of dynamic Hispanic Catholic, Pentecostal, and evangelical ministries are fundamentally the same: vibrant worship; a sense of community and belonging; and personal, affective appeal. This accounts in large part for the frequent—and in a sense ironic—antagonism between leaders of these groups, who simultaneously compete for adherents and imitate one another's best pastoral strategies. A key difference is the reticence of a number of U.S. Catholics and their leaders to foster Hispanic ethnic parishes and ministries. Moreover, among evangelicals and Pentecostals, more intimate-sized faith communities, strong congregational polity, and greater incentive for an individual pastor's initiative in a church assembly that is unapologetically Hispanic have made them far more successful in multiplying congregations and pastors with the passionate pastoral approach that attracts Latinos.

It is not clear how many Hispanic "converts" will persist in Pentecostal, evangelical, and other groups. Although the loss of Hispanic Catholics is well documented, analyses of Latino retention rates among these groups are relatively sparse. Some Latinos maintain dual or even multiple denominational attachments. Thus they may attend a Protestant congregation regularly for Sunday worship but celebrate baptisms, funerals, and other events in a Catholic parish. Other Latinos follow the path of numerous religious seekers in the United States: once they have abandoned the religious affiliation of their childhood, their propensity for changing congregations or denominations again increases. The PARAL report found that among lay church leaders who had switched denominations, 61 percent had done so more than once. And some Hispanics who leave the Catholic fold eventually return to it, such as San Antonio resident Mary Navarro Farr. After eight years in an evangelical church, Navarro Farr became upset with the anti-Catholicism in her congregation and was drawn back to a Catholic parish by "the treasure of the Eucharist, the maternal care of Our Lady of Guadalupe, and the music and sacred imagery" she remembered from her childhood. According to the 2000 Hispanic Churches in American Public Life (HCAPL) survey, however, although at the time of that study some seven hundred thousand Latinos in the United States had returned or converted to Catholicism, more than four times that number had left it. There is no sign that the Hispanic leakage from Catholic ranks will abate in the proximate future.[18]

By no means do all who leave Catholicism end up in Protestant congregations. The HCAPL survey revealed that 3 percent of U.S. Latinos belong to "alternative Christian" religions, most notably the Jehovah Witnesses and the Mormons, while another 1 percent are affiliated with a world religion other than Christianity. More significantly, the 2001 American Religious Identification Survey (ARIS) data revealed that the percentage of Hispanics in the United States who profess "no religion" doubled to 13 percent during the 1990s, a figure that parallels the percentage of "no religion" respondents in the general population. While other recent studies found a slightly lower percentage of "no religion" Latino respondents—in fact the 2008 ARIS study tabulated a slightly lower percentage of 12.4 percent—the upward trend in this statistic over recent decades is clear. Sociologists note the ambiguity of what they call the "nones" category, which can range from avowed atheists to those who believe a formal congregational membership is necessary to honestly identify a religious affiliation in response to a survey question. Though present surveys concur that the number of Latinos who profess to be atheist is minute, no study has yet provided a detailed breakdown of the reasoning among Hispanics who say they have no religious affiliation.[19]

ARIS researchers do show that in the U.S. context, "social trends such as greater suburbanization, more education, and increased Americanization" correlate to a rise in the number of religiously unaffiliated Latinos, as well as to increases in their religious switching. Another study of evangelicals and "apostasy" in Mexico found that nearly half the adults in the second generation after their parent(s) switched from Catholicism to evangelicalism no longer practiced that faith, with the clear majority of these stating their attendance in any religious denomination was less than once a month. Pentecostals evidenced "the highest drop-out rate." An extensive parallel survey of

U.S. Latinos remains an important area for further research, but this Mexican study is consistent with others that show once a person leaves a generationally established familial religion, the possibility of dropping out of formal religious association increases.[20]

All told, the current demographic state of Latino Catholics is, as PARAL founder Anthony Stevens-Arroyo has aptly called it, a "shrink-while-we're-growing" phenomenon: even as the percentage of Latinos who are Catholic decreases, in raw numbers and in percentage of the total Catholic population Latinos continue to increase. Overall the religious demographics of U.S. Latinos also reflect this phenomenon. Since 1990 the estimated number of Latinos who identify as Catholics has decreased roughly six or eight percentage points to somewhere between 60 to 70 percent, those who claim "no religion" increased by a similar amount to 8 to 13 percent, and Protestants remained roughly the same at about 20 to 23 percent, with a small percentage of Latino adherents to other religions. Yet all categories have increased in actual numbers as a result of Latino population growth fueled by ongoing immigration and especially relatively high birth rates.[21]

The media and public perception have tended to accentuate the significant number of Latino Catholics who switch to the practice of Pentecostal or evangelical faiths. Less frequent is awareness of recent studies that find a leveling off of the percentage of Latinos affiliated with these groups as they move further into generations beyond initial switching. Another underreported demographic trend is the growing number of Latinos who self-identify as not being part of any formal faith tradition. This trend is arguably the most significant for Latino leaders of all religious groups. Thus Hispanic Catholic ministry leaders face more than just the challenge of Protestant competition; they must also convince fellow Latinos who live in a culture of choice that Catholic faith is a viable, indeed in Catholics' view essential, life commitment. Without committed Latino Catholics and communities of faith, of course, Catholic influence on the many daily realities that affect Latino lives cannot be as effective as their urgency demands. Fostering adherence to Catholicism, both as an institutional affiliation and even more deeply as a faith that shapes one's life to the core, is therefore a fundamental—even if obvious—first order of priority for Hispanic ministry.

The conviction that the most effective way to address such challenges is through smaller groupings of Catholics committed to common formation and apostolic activities is not new. Spanish subjects established *cofradías* (literally "brotherhoods" or "sisterhoods") throughout Latin America during the colonial period. While one appealing aspect of these pious societies was the communal support networks the *cofradías* provided, their primary purpose was to promote the requirements that members observe Catholic codes of conduct, receive the sacraments worthily, practice specific devotions, and, in many cases, organize an annual celebration for a particular saint or feast day. Pious associations remained the most prevalent form of Latino small faith community well into the twentieth century. At San Fernando Cathedral in San Antonio, priests and brothers of the Claretian religious order were concerned that the cathedral's predominantly Mexican congregation suffered from "religious ignorance" and required "much attention" to keep them "constant in the practice of their religious duties; otherwise, Protestants who are zealous here will get them." Consequently they worked with a core group of lay leaders to establish nearly twenty pious societies that collectively spanned age cohorts in the parish from childhood to the elderly, providing the opportunity for their flock to engage in lifelong formation and intensified commitment to their faith. For ethnic Mexican Catholics, the Guadalupana groups dedicated to Our Lady of Guadalupe are among the most popular and enduring of these societies in San Antonio and various other locales. Latinos of other backgrounds supported their own associations, such as early 1960s Cuban exiles, whose strong tradition of involvement in the lay organizations of their homeland centered their faith practice more on smaller communal settings than on the largely parish-based Catholicism they encountered in Miami. Parishes like San Juan Bosco helped enable the transition to this predominantly congregational polity through parish-based sections of groups such as the Women of Catholic Action, the National Council of Our Lady of Charity, and the Christian Family Movement.[22]

Apostolic movements eclipsed pious societies as the primary small faith groups among both Latinos and non-Latinos during the second half of the twentieth century. For Hispanics, these new movements build on the strengths of their predecessors in their resonance with the devotional penchant of Latino Catholicism and their emphases on community and worthy reception of the sacraments. But they also reflect a more widespread and explicit stress among U.S. believers on a programmatic conversion to Christianity as an intentional way of life. In fostering intense religious experience, personal transformation, knowledge of one's faith, and fervor to evangelize others, apostolic movements are suited to the competitive religious environment of the United States and the pressures of modern urban life, including the unwieldy and oftentimes impersonal congregations in metropolitan areas.

The premier apostolic movement among Hispanics is the Cursillo de Cristiandad. Eduardo Bonnín and other Spanish laymen in Mallorca established the Cursillo in the wake of World War II. In 1957 two of their countrymen assigned to a Waco, Texas, military base collaborated with local priest Father

109

Gabriel Fernández to lead the first Cursillo weekend retreat in the United States. Within five years Cursillo weekends had spread to Puerto Ricans in New York, Cubans in Miami, and among ethnic Mexicans in various locales. By 1978 some thirty thousand Puerto Ricans in New York alone had participated in a Cursillo weekend, exerting an influence so great that one observer quipped, "In the Puerto Rican community to be a *cursillista* [a participant in the Cursillo movement] and a Catholic was almost one and the same." Seven years later a national survey of Latino Catholics found that more than one-fourth perceived the Cursillo as "very important" or "somewhat important" to their faith, ranking the Cursillo highest among thirteen choices of Catholic initiatives that influence them. Cursillo outranked other apostolic movements, the National Hispanic Pastoral Encuentros, the U.S. bishops' pastoral letter on Hispanic ministry, and even the Second Vatican Council. While the subsequent rise of other renewal movements moderated the centrality of Cursillo among Latino Catholics, a 1999 U.S. bishops' committee report found that still nearly 30 percent of the more than thirty-five hundred parishes engaged in Hispanic ministry at that time had Cursillo activities, a prevalence that the study indicated only the Catholic Charismatic Renewal had surpassed among apostolic movements. The 2002 PARAL report concurred with these findings.[23]

According to New York Hispanic ministry leader Father Robert Stern, the Cursillo is "a highly and tightly organized, three-day, study-retreat weekend with a strong emphasis on community experience." It presents to participants "a theological understanding of the sacramental life, Christian maturity, and the responsibilities of the lay person in the church." As a movement initially conducted in Spanish but later also in English to attract Hispanic (and non-Hispanic) leaders and participants across generations, the Cursillos have deepened the experience of God, faith, and active church leadership commitment of many relatively passive Sunday worshipers. The Cursillos have also had a significant impact on Hispanics who felt isolated or disaffected in their faith and parish life. In Stern's experience, "after attending a Cursillo, the average participant is enthused, highly motivated, and disposed to active involvement in the apostolate in his or her local parish."[24]

More concretely, the bulk of time on the highly structured Cursillo weekend is dedicated to a series of presentations called *rollos* on the fundamentals of Catholic faith such as grace, sacraments, the vocation of the lay person, and what cursillistas consider the three pillars for grace-filled Christian living: piety, study, and action. Lay leaders who previously "made" a Cursillo weekend give most of these talks, intermixing content on the topic with personal testimony that often includes how Cursillo has transformed them.

These powerful testimonies from participants' peers and the convention of holding separate weekend retreats for men and for women heighten the emotional impact of the Cursillo, providing an environment that, for men especially, enables them to overcome aversion to self-disclosure and "bar[e] their souls to other men." The experience of friendship and intense, close-knit community over the three days both enhances and is enhanced by the bonds created in such conversations, resulting in an unabashedly affective style to the Cursillo that is consistent with Hispanics' devotional traditions. Songs; prayers; chapel visits; Mass; and Catholic devotions such as Eucharistic adoration, the Way of the Cross, and the rosary (the latter sometimes prayed in the sacrificial posture of kneeling and outstretching one's arms in the form of a cross) give the weekend a deeply Catholic ambiance. Perhaps the most common participant testimony is that Cursillo enabled them to transcend faith as a mere custom or unconscious habit and enter into a deeper, more personal relationship with God in Christ. Many avow that the Cursillo experience brought them from being nominal Catholics to active participants in the church. A frequent highlight of the weekends is the reception of the sacrament of reconciliation or confession to a priest, which participants describe as an experience of healing, encounter with a merciful God, and a new beginning of life with Christ.[25]

The final talk of the Cursillo, called "The Fourth Day," challenges participants to live the message and the personal relationship with God they have received beyond the confines of the close fellowship experienced on the weekend. Participants are particularly encouraged to be active in inviting their family, friends, and coworkers to future Cursillo weekends and to participate in follow-up group reunion meetings called *ultreyas* at their local parish or diocesan Cursillo center. The commitment and spiritual growth of many is further enhanced through the invitation to be on a team that presents a subsequent Cursillo, a responsibility that includes weeks of planning and for most the preparation of a *rollo* through which they publicly witness to their faith. A number of cursillistas attest that as powerful as their initial weekend was in awakening their faith, participation on a Cursillo team solidified their faith commitment even more deeply. Some participate on a number of teams and support Cursillo in their parish or diocese through other means like *palanca*— prayers, sacrifices, and notes of encouragement offered for the spiritual benefit of those making a Cursillo. Past participants also attend the festive closing of subsequent Cursillo weekends, at which each new participant is invited to describe what the retreat experience meant to them.

Though in general the Cursillos received wide support from diocesan officials and pastors, some ministry leaders have criticized the movement. One charge is that the Cursillos can drain parishes of their most active and talented lay leaders, who prefer to work in the more satisfying ministries of the Cursillo than the everyday but necessary concerns of the parish. This critique reflects the emphasis on parishes and their parochial schools in U.S. Catholicism, which has led many pastors to value apostolic movements to the extent they support the structures of parish life. Pastors have also complained about a divisive spiritual elitism they perceive among some cursillistas, often evidenced in the claim that Cursillo is the best or only authentic way of relating to God. An even more fundamental critique is that the Cursillo merely succeeds in inciting an emotional conversion, not a deeper and more lasting conversion that encompasses the intellectual, moral, faith, *and* affective dimensions of the person. Critics argue that this defect leads many cursillistas to recurrently seek renewed emotional religious experiences through their Cursillo activities and, when those experiences are unavailable or no longer suffice, to fall away from their faith commitment.[26]

At the same time, it is difficult to overestimate the significance of the Cursillo, which revitalized the faith of numerous grassroots Catholics and their parish communities. Indeed, one is hard pressed to find a Latino Catholic leader, especially those active during the first fervor of the movement in the 1960s and 1970s, who has never had any involvement or contact with the Cursillo. In that sense it is not surprising that the Cursillo subsequently became less prominent in various locales; in a number of parishes a substantial majority of committed Latino Catholics had already been formed in the Cursillo experience and were now involved in other apostolic movements or activities. But even so, Cursillo remains an important and vibrant apostolic movement among many Latinos today, both those who are making their first Cursillo and those who continue to participate in *ultreya* groups, some of which have met regularly for decades. A number of bishops continue to appoint diocesan directors for Cursillo or even operate centers that advance Cursillo as a diocesan apostolate.

Several other Catholic apostolic movements have had noteworthy influence among Latinos from various national backgrounds. Founding national presidents Pat and Patty Crowley established the Christian Family Movement with other collaborators in 1949. It spread internationally, and in 1969 Gustavo and Isabel Erviti became the first presidents for the new Spanish-language Movimiento Familiar Cristiano in the United States. Like Cursillo, Marriage Encounter (Encuentro Matrimonial) originated in Spain. Father Gabriel Calvo was the key leader who organized the first Encounter weekend in 1958. Calvo and Maryknoll priest Donald Hessler promoted the initial Encounter weekends in the United States in 1966. The movement spread most rapidly among English-speaking Catholics, until the following decade when Roberto and Rosie Piña of San Antonio took the initiative to expand the Marriage Encounter among the Spanish-speaking. RENEW is the most widespread program in the United States centered on forming small communities to enable people and parish congregations to foster spiritual growth, integration of faith into daily life, and an evangelizing spirit. Established among Catholics in the Newark archdiocese in 1976, RENEW has grown into an international network with its materials translated into more than forty languages, including Spanish.[27]

The Lee and D'Antonio study of Catholics in small Christian communities provides a snapshot of Hispanic Catholic emphases on family and spiritual renewal in faith communities like those formed through RENEW, which their research found was one of the "most influential" movements in leading Latinos to become part of ongoing small communities. Most Hispanic small Christian communities meet weekly in private homes. More than 70 percent report having a woman as group leader, considerably more than their counterparts in Euro-American communities. The average membership size for Hispanic communities is twenty-five with nearly a fourth of community members under the age of seventeen, reflecting the tendency of Hispanics to participate as families as compared to the more adult-oriented groups researchers found among Euro-Americans. One Hispanic interviewee in the study commented, "We don't have family here. Our small Christian community is our family." Spiritual renewal is far more pronounced than social action. Less than a fifth of the groups said they regularly address political and social issues. The two most common activities, both present in well over 90 percent of the groups, were prayer and Bible study. Approximately 90 percent of community members said they were connected to a Catholic parish and participated in the Eucharist weekly, a startling figure when compared to the less than one-third who attend weekly Mass among the general Catholic population.[28]

The most widespread apostolic movement among Latino Catholics today is the Catholic Charismatic Renewal (CCR). English-speaking U.S. Catholics founded the CCR in 1967. The initially tepid response of some Vatican officials warmed with the supportive backing of popes Paul VI, John Paul II, and Benedict XVI, helping to spur the movement's growth to nearly 120 million participants worldwide by the early twenty-first century. More than 60 percent are Latin Americans, a number of whom brought the CCR spirit to the United States as immigrants and became leaders or founders of Charismatic groups in U.S. parishes. While a relatively small group of Hispanics participated as the movement expanded among English-speaking U.S.

Catholics during the early 1970s, rising immigration and the vibrancy of Spanish-language CCR groups later fueled their increased involvement. Hispanic leaders established the Comité Nacional de Servicio Hispano (CNSH) in 1990 to promote the CCR and coordinate activities among the growing number of active Hispanic Charismatics. The CNSH has three core commitments: to serve God in the Catholic Church and advance its mission of evangelization in the power of the Holy Spirit; to foment the experience of Pentecost as a grace of the Holy Spirit for the church; and to carry the fervor of the Charismatic Renewal to families, neighborhoods, parish communities, and all those who thirst for God. Structurally, the CNSH consists of a national coordinator, spiritual director, executive committee, and youth committee as well as representatives from eight regions spanning the United States and Canada. One of its major activities since its inception has been to conduct an annual leaders' meeting called the Encuentro Católico Carismático Latino de los Estados Unidos (Latino Catholic Charismatic Encounter of the United States), an initiative that provides opportunities for advanced training, networking, and greater cohesion among the national network of Latino CCR groups.[29]

The thousands of prayer groups that meet regularly in parishes or private homes are the most widespread manifestation of the CCR among Hispanics. Some clergy participate, but laity are the primary leaders in the vast majority of groups, which range in size from a handful to hundreds. The length of a meeting, order of service, and forms of prayer also vary and can encompass healing Masses, testimonies of God's action in people's lives, Marian devotion, prophetic utterances in which a participant speaks a word of admonition or encouragement in the name of God, teachings on CCR or other Catholic topics, Eucharistic adoration, periods of silent meditation, the ecstatic praise of speaking in tongues, spontaneous public prayer of praise and intercession, Bible reading, preaching, vibrant singing, and embodied worship such as hand clapping and raising one's arms in praise. A common experience of initiation is the baptism of the Holy Spirit, or "second baptism," which for many Catholics who received the sacrament of baptism as infants entails a renewed adult commitment to live their faith in the power of the Holy Spirit. Prayer group leaders usually present the Life in the Spirit seminar that prepares new CCR participants for this baptism. After what is often weeks of preparation, the baptism is celebrated with group members laying hands on the initiates and praying with them for the Holy Spirit to come upon them. Daily prayer, Bible study, parish involvement, witnessing to others, and inviting them to attend the prayer group are highly encouraged as some of the primary means to live as a Spirit-filled Catholic.

Surveys report a wide range of findings about the extent of Latino involvement in CCR groups. On the high end, the 2000 HCAPL survey estimated that 5.4 million Latinos in the United States self-identify as Catholic Charismatics, substantially more than the 3.8 million who self-identify as Pentecostals. The 1999 U.S. bishops' committee report found that the CCR is the most prevalent apostolic movement among Latinos, with well over one-third of parishes engaged in Hispanic ministry having CCR groups or activities, a finding confirmed in the 2002 PARAL report.[30] But even if every one of these CCR groups had five hundred Latino members—a conservative estimate—cumulatively they would still comprise less than a million Latino Charismatics. The wide discrepancy between these estimates and the HCAPL survey is not easily explicated, though one important factor is the statistical gap between members who are regularly active in CCR parish groups and the much larger group of those who in some way identify with the Catholic Charismatic Renewal. A number of Latinos participate at least occasionally in home-based CCR activities or larger events apart from the parish-based prayer groups counted in the bishops' report. In any case, a sizable number of Latinos in faith communities across the country participate in the CCR.

One of the most contested issues about the CCR is whether it is simply a form of "Catholic Pentecostalism." The 2007 Pew Latino religion survey asserted that "Renewalist Christianity" is one of the two major features of Latino religion in the United States and, more specifically, that "Hispanic Catholics practice a distinctive brand of Catholicism, one that incorporates many of the beliefs and behaviors most commonly associated with pentecostal or renewalist Christianity." Yet some of the specific findings presented to substantiate this claim are questionable or at least difficult to interpret. Fully 45 percent of all Latino Catholic respondents reported they had received the baptism of the Holy Spirit, the great majority saying they received it as an infant—a practice scarcely heard of, since this baptism almost universally necessitates a mature profession of faith—leading the researchers themselves to suggest that they were not sure if their respondents were speaking of the Catholic sacrament of baptism or the more Pentecostal-style baptism of the Holy Spirit. A fundamental question for the study was whether interviewees identified themselves as "charismatic"—54 percent of Latino Catholics responded affirmatively. But it is not clear what interviewees meant in affirming this self-identification. In response to another question, only 15 percent of self-professed charismatic Catholics said they participate in formal CCR organizations, while 7 percent of self-professed *non*-charismatic Catholics said they participate in such organizations.[31]

The authors of the study account for such findings with claims like the idea that even Latinos who do not self-identify as charismatic "are more likely than non-Latino Catholics to report having experienced or witnessed supernatural practices such as divine healings or revelations from God."[32] But Hispanics' belief in God's frequent intervention in everyday life and in faith healing practices like *curanderismo* have existed since long before the advent of the CCR and even before the Pentecostal spark was lit at the 1907 Azusa Street Revival. Though CCR practices like speaking in tongues clearly stem from Pentecostal origins, the premier sources for Latino Catholics' religious practices and beliefs are Catholic, especially Latino popular Catholicism and the widespread popularity of the Cursillo and other Catholic renewal movements. Of course the blending of religious traditions—which reflects a growing trend among U.S. believers of various backgrounds—is not a new propensity for Latinos, whose Latin American ancestors interwove elements of Iberian, Amerindian, and African religions. The pluralistic, competitive U.S. religious milieu enhances exchanges between Catholics and other religious groups in important ways ranging from prayer styles to doctrinal fidelity, from relations within families to those with church authorities. Countervailing influences of Latino Catholics include their strong belief in divine providence mirrored in the faith of their Pentecostal counterparts, the penchant for popular religious expressions that Latino Protestant theologians claim has shaped Pentecostal *coritos* (songs),[33] and the increasing enshrinement of Our Lady of Guadalupe images in Protestant congregations, including those of Pentecostals. Contentions of a unidirectional Pentecostal influence on Latino Catholics fail to account for these multiple and mutual influences that shape religious practices among Catholics and other religious groups in the United States.

Yet its exuberant style and especially its Pentecostal-related expressions have raised suspicions that the CCR is not essentially Catholic and poses a potential threat to the Catholic faithful. Some former CCR participants have in fact left the Catholic fold for Pentecostalism and in several cases become Pentecostal pastors, though Renewal leaders assert that this tendency was greater during the early years of the CCR than it is now. Another critique comes from social activist Catholics, who have bemoaned what they perceive as a common Pentecostal and CCR focus on prayer and personal conversion that excludes or even openly resists faith-based social involvement. Competition between apostolic movements can hinder the effectiveness of CCR and other groups. Infighting among CCR prayer group leaders themselves is not uncommon and at times is quite fierce. Leaders of parish or home groups often resent the loss of members to larger CCR organizations that attract followers in part through their mega-scale events and media-savvy outreach.

Still other objections mirror earlier critiques of apostolic movements like Cursillo. Latino pastoral leaders contend that the CCR can be a source of disunity when their members "adopt a quasi-sectarian attitude, focusing single-mindedly on their own activities and growth and neglecting the welfare of the parish" or, worse, "see themselves as holding the right way of being church," setting them against Latino Catholics in other movements or parish activities. A number of critics maintain that the CCR provides an affective spiritual solace but not an in-depth formation in Catholic faith. CCR leader Andrés Arango, the national coordinator of CNSH, concurs that some Latino CCR leaders lack adequate ministerial preparation. Many participate exclusively in CCR formation programs, despite CCR directors' admonitions that these programs complement rather than replace those of parishes and dioceses, further opening the door for potential misunderstanding and conflict. Arango attests that among groups clearly rooted in the CCR, "the biggest challenge we face is dealing with the issue of authority, especially leaders who want to be independent from any outside authority or influence," be it from diocesan or parish officials or from other CCR leaders like those of the CNSH.[34]

Though many have felt misunderstood or unappreciated, even among their fellow Hispanic Catholics, CCR leaders and prayer groups across the United States frequently express their allegiance to the traditions of the Catholic Church, its institutional leaders, and the overall well-being of their local parish. Leaders demonstrate their fidelity to church authority and doctrine in their citations of papal and other official teaching. When Catholics—including some Latinos—picketed Sunday Masses after the clergy sex-abuse scandal erupted in 2002, Hispanic prayer groups organized processions through downtown Los Angeles to show support for the church and for "those good priests who have left behind everything to serve the people." Many CCR leaders state explicitly that they incorporate traditional devotions like Eucharistic adoration and the rosary into their prayer meetings to enhance the Catholic allegiance and identity of participants. According to the Pew Latino religion survey, well over 80 percent of self-identified Latino Charismatics practice Marian devotion and believe in Catholic dogmas like the transubstantiation of the Eucharistic host and wine into the body and blood of Christ, slightly more than self-identified non-Charismatic Latinos. The same survey confirmed Latino Charismatics' emphasis on loyal participation in the life of the church, finding that nearly twice as many Hispanic CCR participants engage in parish ministries such as lector, choir, or parish council as compared to their non-Charismatic counterparts. Diocesan directors of Hispanic ministry confirm that "many Hispanics are energized and motivated to participate in the life of the parish by their activity in Charismatic Renewal and other prayer groups and in the different apostolic movements. They have a great thirst for knowledge of the Bible as well as for leadership formation." Pentecostal influences within the CCR are accompanied by these widespread attempts to accentuate Catholic ecclesial structures, teaching, and traditional devotions as constitutive influences among Latino participants in the Renewal.[35]

CCR leaders also acclaim the Renewal as providing a vital, Spirit-filled alternative to Pentecostal and other Protestant denominations. Arango points to the noteworthy successes of CCR groups in providing Hispanic immigrants a place to nurture their faith and develop their leadership within the U.S. Catholic Church, as well as forming bilingual leaders in the second and third generation who help revitalize the Catholic faith of both Latino and non-Latino youth alike. Father José Eugenio Hoyos directs the Hispanic apostolate for the diocese of Arlington, Virginia, where the Latino presence in the CCR has blossomed from some 150 in the late 1980s to an estimated 10,000–15,000 active participants in an array of home, parish, and diocesan-wide events. Hoyos considers Latino Charismatics the "engine of the Church" and attests that "a lot of [Latino] Pentecostals and other religions are coming back because of the charismatic renewal. . . . They can express themselves very freely and feel a closer belonging to the Church than before." Allan Figueroa Deck asserts that the CCR "is arguably the single most important factor in the new evangelization of Hispanics and in motivating new generations of them to serve in the church as lay ministers, deacons, priests and religious."[36]

Two major groups in Los Angeles reveal the CCR as a potentially viable—though at times contentious—means to foster Latino evangelization and Catholic allegiance. The origin of Southern California as a major regional hub of the CCR among Latinos dates back to 1972, when Catholic converts Marilynn and Glenn Kramar established their outreach efforts to Hispanics in the city. The Kramars then opened up the Charisma in Missions headquarters in East Los Angeles with the blessing of Cardinal Timothy Manning. Twenty-five years later their efforts had formed 220 active Spanish-speaking prayer groups of roughly 70 to 120 people each in the Los Angeles archdiocese alone. Their national ministry had reached an estimated more than one million Latinos. Marilynn Kramar, regarded by many as the "mother" of the CCR among Latinos in Southern California, continues to serve as the president of Charisma, which fosters CCR groups through leadership formation, youth encounters, book publications, audio and videotapes, preaching and healing ministries, and international conferences. Another Los Angeles–based organization, El Sembrador (The Sower), began when Noel Díaz, a parishioner at St. Thomas the Apostle parish in Los Angeles, "accepted the invitation [of Jesus Christ to work in his vineyard] and in 1984 began to assume the challenge of the new evangelization with a small group of people who met in a home within the parish." Though not formally linked with the national leadership structures of the CNSH, El Sembrador is clearly rooted in the CCR movement. From its origins as a home- and then parish-based prayer group, it has grown to international stature. Today the group's leaders conduct annual regional congresses and revivals for thousands of participants and provide a twenty-four-hour radio broadcast, as well as digital television programming that reaches from Canada to South America through their affiliate El Sembrador Nueva Evangelización.[37]

Cardinal Roger Mahony and other Los Angeles archdiocesan officials recognized the dynamism of these prayer groups and related ministries. But they became concerned that some CCR leaders form independent groups and maintain that the prime authority for their ministries is the voice of the Holy Spirit speaking to them, bypassing the official structures and approbation channels of the institutional church. For their part, leaders of Charisma in Missions accused Mahony of publicly supporting El Sembrador while distancing himself and the archdiocese from Marilynn Kramar out of fear that one day she might lead her devout Latino followers out of the church. One prayer group leader accused the archdiocese of employing a "divide and conquer strategy." Another leader commented, "It's so sad that [Charisma in Missions and El Sembrador] are fighting each other, instead of battling evil in the Latino community. The devil must be laughing at them." Though not always so vociferous, it is by no means infrequent that conflict and controversy accompany the powerful evangelistic forces of the CCR. Bishop Agustín Román aptly summarized the pastoral challenge and opportunity of such apostolic movements: "They are like a hurricane. They stir things up."[38]

Parishes remain the mainstay of Catholicism in the United States, particularly in comparison to Europe, where lay movements such as Opus Dei, Focolare, Communion and Liberation, and the Neocatechumenal Way emerged over the course of the twentieth century, gained support from popes John Paul II and Benedict XVI, and exerted influence in Europe and beyond. By one recent estimate nearly half the active Catholics in Spain relate to the church primarily through a movement rather than a parish. These developments have led to forecasts that movements like these, rather than parishes, are the wave of the future for Catholicism in Europe. Some Latinos are active in these same movements in the United States. Moreover, in various locales apostolic movements like Cursillo are administered at the diocesan rather than the parish level. Nonetheless, the current demographics of Hispanic involvement

119

indicate that the vital future of Hispanic ministry in parish-based U.S. Catholicism requires harnessing the energy of apostolic movements in parish life and fostering the ambiance and transforming experience of the movements in Hispanic congregations.[39]

A number of predominantly Hispanic parishes with active apostolic movements and small faith communities like San Juan Bosco meet this challenge admirably. One barometer of their effectiveness is that such parishes tend to address the funding difficulties that inhibit various Hispanic ministry efforts. The U.S. bishops' *Encuentro and Mission* acknowledges that "a significant number of Hispanic Catholics do not yet respond to the needs of the Church and its mission in proportion to what they possess." Yet the bishops agree with a number of Hispanic ministry leaders that, like European immigrants who built national parishes, Latinos are most generous in donating to church structures and leaders they perceive as being actively involved with them and their families and communities. A strong personal relationship with Hispanic donors is thus integral to enlisting their financial backing. Father Kenneth Davis, O.F.M. Conv., succinctly summarizes these dynamics: "Hispanics support religious institutions that support them." Davis sees this claim demonstrated among "Charismatics and Hispanic apostolic movements and religious rituals [that] never lack resources because Hispanics feel ownership." The tendencies of Hispanic donors can cause a conundrum for pastors and bishops: while many building projects in U.S. Catholicism are not begun until pledges or even sufficient cash is on hand to complete the work, Hispanic giving for such projects often increases only when construction has begun and they can see that their contributions are directed toward a worthwhile community endeavor. Pastors like Father Vallina have had great success in calling forth the stewardship of their parishioners, in Vallina's case even leading his San Juan Bosco parish community in the construction of a new church building during his tenure as pastor. But other pastors and parish staff have expressed frustration with Hispanic parish support, particularly when they perceive that Latinos give more generously to apostolic movements than to their parish.[40]

Like any parish, Hispanic faith communities are not without internal dissensions. Variations in pastoral style can be divisive, such as the Hispanic Catholic who is deeply committed to the sacraments and prayer life of the church and finds fault with others who emphasize the social justice implications of Catholic faith, or the Catholic who accentuates ongoing conversion and knowledge of the faith and objects to a parish in which sacraments and devotional exercises are dispensed with seemingly little catechesis. Generational differences, exclusive dedication to one's own prayer group or apostolic movement, and personality conflicts are some of the other frequent detriments to group cohesion in Hispanic parish communities.[41]

Gays and lesbians who perceive that the homophobic atmosphere they endure in their everyday existence also pervades in their church often feel particularly ostracized from parish life. Writer Richard Rodriguez articulates the inner conflict gay Catholics face: "The church that taught me to understand love, the church that taught me well to believe love breathes—also tells me it is not love I feel." Rodriguez attests that he "well understand[s] the wish to be quit of the church." But he confesses his reluctance—or, perhaps more accurately, inability—to abandon his Catholic roots. He also expresses admiration for the compassionate power of Catholic faith and ministries, in one moving passage presenting volunteers from the AIDS support group of Most Holy Redeemer parish in San Francisco as "the saints of this city." Fred Anthony Garza, the president of the local San Antonio chapter of the group DignityUSA, expressed similarly mixed sentiments when archdiocesan officials announced in 2010 they would end a Dignity-led Mass at St. Ann parish because it "continues to send conflicting messages about the church's official teaching concerning the proper celebration of the Eucharist and living an active homosexual lifestyle." Asked about the prohibition of the Mass, Garza responded, "It meant hurt. It means rejection." While archdiocesan leaders urged Dignity members to participate in parish Masses "as part of the broader Catholic community," Garza said the group was making plans to continue their worship "in a more welcoming environment."[42]

Consciously or not, tensions can also arise in faith communities where the dominant Hispanic group's concerns are taken to be those of all Latinos, whose diverse backgrounds and presence in the parish are consequently not adequately addressed or even acknowledged. Two-thirds of Latino faith communities studied in the 2002 PARAL report had members from two or more Hispanic groups, with Catholic faith communities more likely to be multi-Hispanic than those of Protestants. The study found greater collaboration and fewer instances of conflict between Hispanics of different backgrounds as compared to the interrelations between Hispanics and non-Hispanics. But it also found disagreements and strained relations among Latinos, a situation often related to the predominance of a group like ethnic Mexicans over other Hispanic groups in a single faith community.[43]

Parishes that are comprised of predominantly Latino congregants like San Juan Bosco are more the exception than the rule, a trend that is increasing. On the whole Catholic congregations are the most internally diverse of all Christian congregations in the United States and are becoming even more so due to the heterogeneity of the Catholic population, trends toward larger parishes, the geographic dispersion of Hispanics across the United States, and the growing Catholic population in the western region of the country, where churches of all groups tend to be more integrated. Michael Emerson's 2006 study on multiracial congregations in the United States found that despite the relative paucity of instances in which no single racial group comprises more than 80 percent of a congregation, the percentage of multiracial Catholic parishes is three times higher than that of Protestant congregations. Even Spanish-speaking newcomers are frequently in mixed parishes; the PARAL report stated that fully three-fourths of Spanish-language Latino faith communities share church facilities with coreligionists who worship in another language, usually English, with Latino Catholic faith communities more likely to do so than their Protestant counterparts. Nationally—and particularly outside of areas with more concentrated Hispanic populations such as the Southwest, Florida, New York, and Chicago—an increasingly frequent scenario in Catholic parishes is that Latinos are migrant newcomers in established, predominantly Euro-American congregations.[44]

Today the customary practice or stated norm in most dioceses is for integrated or multicultural parishes. However, as Ken Johnson-Mondragón has noted, in fact a number of such congregations could more accurately be deemed "Americanizing" parishes that promote the assimilation of newcomers or, conversely, "segmented" parishes in which two or more groups share the same church facilities but remain substantially isolated from one another. Brett Hoover, C.S.P., argues that naming such parishes "integrated" or "mixed" can tend to exaggerate the unity between groups or impose a predetermined prescription for rapid and often superficial acculturation in intergroup relations. At the same time, the designation "parallel congregations," a phrase synonymous with segmented parishes, is "a structurally accurate term that still fails to capture the explicit and implicit intercultural negotiations that characterize such communities." Hoover prefers the term "shared parish" in order to focus attention on "the intercultural dynamics of coexistence in such parishes."[45]

When a parish encompasses two or more language groups worshiping under the same roof, they often coexist in isolation or even in conflict. After more than half a century as a parishioner, one woman began to feel "my church isn't my church anymore" when the number of Hispanic parishioners increased. She claimed that most of the newcomers "can speak English," and she was frustrated that parish priests and staff were "enabling them" by offering Mass and other ministrations in Spanish. The sheer number of Latino newcomers can exacerbate tensions. When Hispanics attempt to make a parish feel more like home by placing one of their own sacred images in the worship space or scheduling a Spanish Mass in a "prime time" slot on Sunday morning, established parishioners frequently rebuff them with claims that "our ancestors built this church" or "we were here first." As one lay leader lamented, "I am discouraged by the fact that we, Hispanics, don't count here in this parish. We come to Mass in great numbers and our Masses are really filled with the spirit. But all the power is in the hands of a small group of [non-Hispanic] old-timers who contribute a lot of money to the Church." If Latinos respond with protest or complaint, their Euro-American coreligion-ists may perceive them as being unappreciative of the welcome offered to them. Like their non-Catholic neighbors, many European-descent Catholics presume that newcomers who do not adopt U.S. customs and speak English in public are ungrateful or even not qualified to remain in the United States. Critics also claim the practice of distinct language Masses creates "paral-lel parishes" that have virtually no relationship with one another, leading to fragmentation within the body of Christ. Leaders in Hispanic ministry like Father Chuck Dahm, O.P., counter that "the promotion of multicultural par-ishes is often little more than a veiled attempt to assimilate the minority culture into the dominant one."[46]

Increasing instances of church closings, such as in the Cleveland diocese, where church officials announced in 2009 the need to close nearly one-fourth of its 224 parishes, can further strain group relations, especially in cases where a predominantly Hispanic parish is abandoned and its congregants are asked to merge with a primarily Euro-American parish. Although finan-cial and personnel shortages often make such decisions impossible to avoid, original parishioners may resent newcomers' "intrusion" into the church they have built. Conversely, those who "lose" their church often feel betrayed at the loss of the parish home they and their loved ones helped develop. In turn, frustration with their perceived second-class status in their "new" parish and in the wider church is one factor that leads to Latino abandonment of parish involvement or even the Catholic faith.

Demographically the largest contingents in shared parishes are Latinos and Euro-Americans. But Hispanics also interact with African Americans in various Catholic congregations. In 1997 the Bishops' Committee on African American Catholics and the Bishops' Committee on Hispanic Affairs issued a joint statement to promote reconciliation and collaboration between their communities. The prelates noted that division and mistrust often mark Afri-can American and Latino intergroup relations, even though they have com-mon struggles with discrimination, poverty, and a lack of opportunity that could potentially unite them as allies. A particular challenge frequently oc-curs "when our people worship in the same parish and compete for liturgical resources." Concretely, the more prominent group in the parish tends to dominate the smaller group, efforts to celebrate joint liturgies are difficult because of differences in language and faith expressions, and both groups are prone to "negative forms of religious and ethnic pride" that deepen antagonisms. The bishops urged that parishioners strive to worship together in harmony, especially on major liturgical feasts that are prime occasions for the whole parish to gather. They also recommended that African Americans and Hispanics in shared parishes sustain systematic efforts to examine and appreciate each other's histories, faith experiences, music, art, and cultural heritage.[47]

A 2005 survey of the National Pastoral Life Center confirmed the difficulties in racially or ethnically mixed parishes; in response to the prompt "parishioners appreciate and encourage the multicultural diversity of our parish," pastoral leaders from 928 parishes rated their congregations exceedingly low—twenty-ninth out of thirty-two parish vitality indicators. John Andrews of the San Bernardino, California, diocese noted the need for a more concerted pastoral response to parishioners in communities undergoing an influx of newcomers: "Somebody who feels that way [uneasy about changing parish demographics] should not be ignored or dismissed. They should be ministered to." But he also added, "The church belongs to everyone who calls themselves a Catholic, and we need to pay attention to the needs of all people coming to the church." Through passive resistance or overt confrontation, it is not unusual for parishioners to criticize or flatly reject admonitions toward charity and "integration without assimilation," whether they emanate from their pastor, bishops, or the pope. When Bishop Edward Slattery of Tulsa held a 2006 meeting with parishioners who were angry with him for celebrating a confirmation service mostly in Spanish, he was stunned to hear that some practicing Catholics preferred no Masses in the diocese be conducted in Spanish. One man even offered to "drive a bus" to evict undocumented immigrants from the country.[48]

Pastoral leaders can easily feel conflicted in such situations, not wanting to antagonize the parties involved yet desiring to lead their flock to enact papal and episcopal pleas for unity rooted in Christ, not in cultural uniformity. Pastors are aware that offending the wrong parishioners may lead to a loss in donations needed to keep the parish viable for the good of all, but they also do not want financial matters to drive their decision between what is right and wrong. The strident emotions of ethnic tension can exact a strong toll on parish leadership. One pastor who asked to remain anonymous attested, "I am called to be a bridge builder between the groups in my parish. Unfortunately, bridges get walked on."

Such observations suggest that building unity within a diverse congregation is not merely a matter of tolerance or "celebrating differences," as is often imagined. Frequently at stake are the issues of how decisions are made and by whom, including the decision of marginal groups to vote with their feet when they perceive that existing ecclesial life is unwelcoming or irrelevant. Many of the difficulties in developing shared parishes stem from a lack of attention to power relations in parochial life and ministries, what Michael Emerson calls "the nightmare of misused power."[49] Intentionally or not, even many Euro-American Catholics who welcome their Hispanic sisters and brothers frequently embody the message that Latinos are guests and that Euro-American Catholics are the owners of the house. While hospitality and what many call "cultural sensitivity" are an essential first step in ministry with newcomers, often implicit is the notion that those in power will remain in power, although they may choose not to exercise it autocratically. At best, Hispanic traditions and religious expressions will be tolerated, but the established group will control and limit the conditions of this pluralism and diversity. It is as if Latinos are told, "Welcome to the home of God's family, but please don't touch the furniture without permission."

Hoover's research well illustrates the group dynamics in a shared parish.[50] He conducted a ten-month ethnographic study at a Midwest parish he gives the pseudonym All Saints, founded in 1860 and still the only Catholic church in a majority Protestant town. Waves of working-class Mexican immigrants arriving since around 1990 changed the demography of the small town considerably and led the parish staff to initiate Spanish-language ministries. At the time of Hoover's study a Euro-American priest served as pastor and a Mexican émigré priest as associate pastor. Hispanic Catholics had two Sunday Masses in Spanish, approximately twenty ministry programs, and an attendance that often exceeded five hundred at their most populous Mass, while Euro-American Catholics had three Sunday Masses in English, about thirty ministry programs, and a high Mass attendance of nearly four hundred. Yet an "environment of unequal power" in the parish reflected the lower social status of Mexican immigrants in the local populace: Euro-American Catholics held most positions on the parish council and the stewardship committee, had Masses in the earlier and generally more preferred time slots on Sunday morning, and the priest of their background was the pastor.

As was largely the case in the town around them, the parishioners of All Saints tended to operate "mostly separately but in parallel fashion." This was evident in important areas of parish life like the religious education programs. The English program addressed the need for Catholic "religious literacy" among young people, whose varied schedules and "multiple activities" required flexibility. The much larger Spanish program addressed the need of hundreds of baptized Catholic children who had not received the sacraments of first communion and confirmation. It required a more "comprehensive educational discipline" with a strict policy of children's attendance at catechism classes and Sunday Mass, parental involvement in bimonthly meetings, and weekly training sessions for catechists. Both the Euro-American pastor and religious education director initially objected to the potential divisiveness of establishing a Spanish-language religious education track, but they relented because of the large numbers and the obvious pastoral need. Recurrent tensions surfaced when Hispanic children began to transfer to the English-language program. The religious education director maintained that this was a natural and desirable adjustment to life in the United States, while the Mexican priest protested that children and their parents had made the switch to undermine his authority and avoid the more stringent requirements of the Spanish-language program.

Hoover found that despite good faith efforts on both sides, disagreements and ill feelings inevitably arose. Congested parking lots were one source of strain, as in a case when a Euro-American woman went with frustration to the Spanish-language religious education classes seeking someone who spoke English to help locate the person who had double-parked behind her car. Another Euro-American woman had scheduled a meeting to be held in the church basement but found that Hispanics had occupied the entire space. She stated that the fellow parishioners she approached responded "no English, no English" until finally she located one who translated her concern to the others. Though the people graciously accommodated her once they understood the situation, when she later recounted the incident to Hoover it still annoyed her that she had to ask for the meeting space to be relinquished: "You know, I've supported this parish for forty-some years, not tremendously financially, but I've been a big part of it, I've tried to put myself into it, and I should count for something."

Given language and cultural divides it is not surprising that "avoidance remained a common pattern" between Hispanics and Euro-Americans in the parish. Both Euro-American and Hispanic parishioners told Hoover that for Sunday Mass they intentionally parked in a place that reduced contact and potential conflict to a minimum. Some confessed that they left Mass quickly to avoid contact entirely with the incoming parishioners for the following Mass. When parish schoolteachers complained about disorder in their rooms after Spanish-language religious education classes conducted there, both the Mexican priest and the volunteer director of the Spanish religious education program were annoyed with what they considered picayune charges that sullied their community's reputation with Euro-American parishioners. They felt school personnel held the Hispanic community to an "unfair standard" and relentlessly asked "about the whereabouts of every pencil." Yet they did not generally voice their protests directly to the accusers, choosing instead to encourage the Spanish-speaking catechists to be diligent in keeping order and even keeping an extra supply of pencils to replace any missing ones proactively. Their simultaneous sentiments of "gratitude that the Euro-Americans had made space for them" and resentment over such conflicts typify the response of many Hispanics to shared parishes. Hoover concludes his frank assessment with the theological claim that the challenge for parishioners in shared settings is not to deny or minimize the significance of difficulties and conflicts but to "re-imagine intercultural negotiations not as tension-filled ordeals or necessary evils but rather as the ordinary work of the church as it enacts its unity on an everyday basis in a complex, culturally pluralistic ecclesiological context."

Intercultural encounters between Hispanics and their coreligionists in shared parishes alter the day-to-day congregational experience of numerous Catholics in the United States. Leaders of the Secretariat of Cultural Diversity in the Church estimate that approximately 30 percent of the parishes in the United States, more than five thousand in all, are shared parishes with significant contingents of at least two ethnic or racial groups. Spanish and English are by far the two most common languages in these parishes. While there are no detailed statistical studies of group relations in such parishes, ethnographic analyses like that of Hoover suggest that these intergroup dynamics are one of the most frequent sources of internal tension within U.S. Catholicism, in some locales even more divisive than the much-commented-upon disagreements between "conservative" and "progressive" Catholics. James Rutenbeck's 2009 film, *Scenes from a Parish*, explores communal dynamics in "a Catholic parish struggling to reconcile the ideals of faith with the cultural realities of a globalized United States." Filmed over a four-year period at St. Patrick parish in Lawrence, Massachusetts, the documentary examines the lives of new pastor Father Paul O'Brien, recent Hispanic arrivals to his parish, and established, predominantly Irish-descent parishioners. Some established congregants were "resentful of a new generation of immigrants," while others dedicated themselves to assisting new émigrés "but faced cultural entanglements that grew more complicated with the passage of time." Rutenbeck's series of vignettes on select parishioners demonstrates the various transformations that interethnic contact incited among them. He poignantly contends that "life at Saint Patrick's anticipates what lies ahead for all Americans: how [we] perceive each other, whether we choose to withdraw or whether we can forge community from disparate consistencies, are matters [of] consequence that will shape the future of our country." The provocative title of a *Boston Globe* film review of *Scenes from a Parish* encapsulates Hispanics' significance for numerous Catholic faith communities like St. Patrick: "In One Parish, the State of the Church."[51]

Hispanics' participation in parishes and apostolic movements is the way they most influence the internal dynamics of U.S. Catholicism. This is not surprising, since the congregation has long been the locus of religious life and experience in the United States and the general U.S. trend over recent decades has been away from denominational attachment. Commenting on the more than three hundred thousand local religious assemblies in the United States, a figure that ranks them as the most widespread institution in the country, sociologist of religion R. Stephen Warner succinctly summed up the status of the congregation as the "bedrock of the American religious system . . . an unofficial norm in American religious life." Scholars like Robert Wuthnow have examined how in recent decades the proliferation of small faith groups is "shaping American religion" in what could be regarded as an extension of the congregational impulse.[52] Many Catholics and those who observe the Roman Catholic Church recognize that it is a universal body with a centralized hierarchy overseeing everything from core beliefs to liturgical rubrics. Latin American immigrants tend to bring a strong tradition of home-based religion. But in the United States Catholicism and other religions have adapted to a religious milieu marked by a decidedly congregational polity.

Catholics who forge dynamic shared parishes broaden their potential for forming congregants in the intercultural relations increasingly encountered in church and society. One widely acclaimed parish is St. Camillus in Silver Spring, Maryland, where Sunday Masses are celebrated in English, Spanish, and French. The parish website prominently announces that it is "a Catholic multicultural parish" whose "community, composed of people from more than 100 countries, strives for unity while celebrating the diversity that is our strength and our challenge." A reflection in Spanish and English on the website attests that the St. Camillus parish community, like the patriarch Joseph's coat of many colors in the book of Genesis, is "woven into one body, the Body of Christ." Concrete implementation strategies range from incorporating the religious traditions and iconography of diverse groups into the community's worship life to fostering greater leadership parity among all. Parishioners like the Sabonis-Helf family became active at St. Camillus because they witnessed the concerted efforts to enact these ideals. The Sabonis-Helfs chose to live near the parish because they "had just returned from living overseas for many years and enjoying Catholic communities abroad, and were looking for a place that reminded us of the church universal, the church as a microcosm of the whole world." They were also drawn to St. Camillus's "social justice mission" enacted in numerous initiatives such as Habitat for Humanity efforts locally and abroad; the Gabriel Project to support women with unintended pregnancies as an alternative to abortion; a fair trade ministry that fosters just wages for "marginal farmers and trades people"; outreach to seniors and local residents needing material assistance; and ministries among recent immigrants, mostly from El Salvador and Guatemala, including English classes, legal assistance, a summer camp for young children, and advocacy for immigration reform.[53]

San Juan Bosco and other predominantly Hispanic parishes also exhibit the potential for vital parish life in U.S. Catholicism. Their most immediate influence is on their own congregants: émigrés seeking solace; the disquieted searching for peace and a deeper relationship with God; and families looking for guidance, healing, deeper faith, and a chance to serve a Godly purpose larger than themselves. The most active parishes extend their outreach beyond their faith community to the wider society. Paul Wilkes's study *Excellent Catholic Parishes* featured a parish exemplary in this regard, the largely ethnic Mexican St. Pius X congregation in El Paso. According to Wilkes, under the leadership of pastor Arturo Bañuelas and an energetic parish staff, over the past two decades St. Pius has creatively wedded "Hispanic values and faith with a Vatican II vision of a modern parish, infusing each with new meaning." The most distinctive feature of the parish is the ongoing formation and leadership of numerous lay Catholics, who conduct more than forty ministries in the parish, such as community organizing in poor neighborhoods, cancer ministry, evangelization retreats, HIV/AIDS outreach, assistance to children detained for crossing the U.S. border without papers, a Singles in Ministry group, mission outreach in Mexico and the United States, and much more. Frank Lopez, a graduate of the prestigious University of California at Berkeley Law School, exemplifies how parish life overflows into the surrounding community. He felt called through St. Pius to forego a more lucrative legal practice and serve among the indigent Mexican population of the El Paso–Juárez border. The son of working-class Mexican immigrants, he integrated his parents' lifelong example of treating fellow immigrants "with respect and dignity" with the vision in the documents of Vatican II, which enabled him to see "the 'why' behind the 'what' that I wanted to do." St. Pius is a school of formation for those seeking to live as active Catholics in the context of the U.S.-Mexican borderlands and bring their faith to bear on the world around them.[54]

Like parishes, apostolic movements like the CCR evidence the capacity for considerable impact. The CCR has influenced a number of parishes and dioceses, particularly in enlivening the faith and evangelization efforts of Latinas and Latinos. CCR leaders in the Galveston-Houston diocese (now archdiocese) established the Catholic Charismatic Center in 1972 with the support of Bishop John Morkovsky. Originally housed in an old high school, the dedication of an ample new building for the center in 1996 marked the solid foundation and expansion of the ministry, which encompasses Spanish-language evangelization, youth, and leadership formation components. For more than a decade Marina Carrion has been a paid staff member for the San Bernardino, California, diocese charged to oversee the CCR and link its members to parishes and diocesan formation programs. Her leadership has helped expand the number of Spanish-speaking prayer groups from 32 to 54, encompassing more than 60 percent of parishes and all regions within the diocese. She is pleased to report that various vocations to the priesthood have come from the CCR and that Hispanics involved in the CCR have increased their participation in parish ministries and in diocesan formation programs. Msgr. Joseph Malagreca, the spiritual director of CNSH, has been involved with the CCR among Latinos in his home diocese of Brooklyn since 1975 and has seen it expand from an initial 4 Hispanic prayer groups to a current total of 120. He estimates that one-third of Hispanic parishioners in his diocese are active CCR participants, who also comprise the majority of leaders in catechetical, evangelization, youth, liturgical, and other ministries. Nationally he points out that the most noteworthy features of the CCR are its evangelistic fervor and especially its distinctive capacity to draw Hispanic men and young people more deeply into their Catholic faith.[55]

Cursillo is the first and most significant apostolic movement to emerge out of Latino Catholicism and expand broadly to English-speaking Catholics and then to Protestants as well. Cursillista team members from previous Spanish-language weekends led the first English-language Cursillo at San Angelo, Texas, in 1961. By the following year cursillistas had conducted weekends in numerous cities such as San Francisco, Kansas City, Chicago, Detroit, Cincinnati, Newark, Brooklyn, Baltimore, and Boston. Over the ensuing two decades nearly every diocese in the United States introduced the Cursillo movement, affecting literally millions of Catholics from a variety of backgrounds. Consciously or not, as Cursillo spread a number of retreat programs that closely emulate its core dynamics appeared: Teens Encounter Christ (TEC); Search and its Spanish counterpart, *Búsqueda; Encuentros Juveniles;* Kairos; Christ Renews His Parish; and the Protestant Walk to Emmaus and youth-oriented Chrysalis retreats, among others. TEC, for example, began in 1965 with a "request from a local adult faith community" in the diocese of Lansing, Michigan, asking that Father Matthew Fedewa assist them "in creating a similar faith encounter for their youth as they had experienced in Catholic movements like Cursillo." The Cursillo-inspired retreat movements have mirrored their predecessor in their wide impact, as is evident in the claim of TEC leaders that since its establishment "hundreds of thousands of young people from multiple continents have encountered Christ through TEC." In both direct and indirect ways, the effects of Cursillo encompass the full range of these spiritual renewal movements. Religious studies scholar Kristy Nabhan-Warren rightly asserts that Spanish-speaking cursillistas were the "pioneers of what has become a widespread Christian retreat movement in the United States" and that in this way Hispanic Catholics have "made a deep impact" on North American Christianity.[56]

The growth of Pentecostal and evangelical religions among Latinos and the erosion of religious commitment in a secular culture of choice are momentous challenges for Catholic outreach ministries. Moreover, ongoing difficulties within apostolic movements and parishes often detract from their evangelizing potential. Yet even these struggles are an indicator of the Hispanic presence and influence within the faith communities of U.S. Catholicism. Hispanic influences at the local level have one driving force in common: leadership. From pastors to prayer group leaders, effective Latina and Latino leaders enhance the ministries of parishes and apostolic movements. Conversely, the absence of such leaders or the ineffectiveness of poorly formed or self-serving leaders can pose a major detriment to building vibrant faith communities. Thus future impact on church and society is contingent on identifying and preparing effective Hispanic ministry leaders. As budgets and available personnel in dioceses and parishes are stretched thin, Hispanic pastoral ministers face the core necessity of expanding the pool of trained leaders for the grassroots ministries that most directly impact the faith and everyday life of Latinos and their fellow U.S. residents.

# 5
## CHAPTER

# Leadership

More than a thousand devotees packed the backyard of Marian visionary Estela Ruiz in South Phoenix on the night of December 5, 1998. Ruiz had reportedly received some 277 public messages from Our Lady of the Americas over the previous decade. Several months earlier a vision had informed her that December 5 would be the last public message. The revelations to Ruiz paralleled those of other prominent Marian apparitions of the twentieth century, highlighting Mary's role as mother and intercessor, warnings about rampant evil in the world, and a call to prayer and conversion. Yet unlike contemporaneous apparitions of a more apocalyptic character, Ruiz testifies, "I don't think that the Blessed Mother is preaching or telling us about the end of the world. I think She's telling us about the beginning of beautiful things." The heart of Mary's last public message, which Ruiz read tearfully to her rapt listeners, was an admonition for "her 'soldiers' to fight her battles with their 'faith and sacramentals'" so that the "beautiful things" she had begun in them might continue to flourish.[1]

Estela Ruiz and her husband, Reyes, had experienced many of the Latino movements that arose during their lifetime. Both participated in Cursillo and in the Catholic Charismatic Renewal and its Life in the Spirit seminars. Reyes worked for a number of years with the Catholic diocese of Phoenix in their farmworker outreach ministries and participated in the processes of the National Hispanic Pastoral Encuentros. Estela was an activist in the Chicano movement, returned to college in her forties, campaigned for bilingual education and against a controversial state proposition to make English the official language in the state of Arizona, and became the administrator for bilingual programs in Phoenix's Murphy School District.

Estela confesses she was not always as active in her faith as her husband and that sometimes she resented his religious fervor. As is typical of conversion testimonies, she sees her life as radically different before and after her profound religious experience: she portrays herself before her Marian visions as a "lapsed Catholic," who "wasn't always there for my [six] children," and afterward as a Catholic evangelist called to imitate Mary through proclaiming her son, Jesus Christ, to her family, neighbors, and the wider society. In Estela's estimation, she is now simply the mother of an "average Hispanic family trying to make the world a better place for our children and grandchildren. We try to do what the Blessed Mother is calling us to do and we do everything we can to follow her."[2]

One of the most striking features of Estela Ruiz's visions is the outreach ministries that grew from them and eventually replaced them as the focal point of her and her collaborators' energies. The Ruiz family built a backyard shrine and hosted prayer meetings, including an annual retreat near the anniversary date of the first apparition, to spread Our Lady's messages. In 1993 they established Mary's Ministries, a group that forms Catholic evangelizers through intense weeklong faith courses. With the support of various priests, including several from Latin America and an international director of evangelization initiatives from the Vatican, these faith courses attracted numerous Mexican American participants from the Phoenix area and, later, Catholics from other U.S. cities, Mexico, Central and South America, Africa, and Western Europe as Mary's Ministries leaders internationalized their mission. Under the presidency of Estela and Reyes's son, Armando, who decided not to run for reelection as a state senator after a decade in public office in order to embark on his new venture, in 1995 the Ruiz collaborators founded ESPIRITU Community Development Corporation to advance housing, safety, employment, and other urban reforms in South Phoenix. One of their most ambitious projects is a charter school, which they named NFL-YET (National Football League Youth Education Town) Academy to honor a $1 million donation received from the proceeds of the 1996 Super Bowl game played in Tempe, Arizona. The state board of education has received various complaints about NFL-YET Academy centered on concerns such as nepotism and the violation of church-state separation: most prominent leaders of Mary's Ministries are employed at the school, Mary's Ministries receives some $400,000 annually for rental of the property on which it is located, and in turn it donates back $150,000 for "spiritual development" programs at the school. But NFL-YET Academy became the largest charter school in the state, had a regular waiting list of about one hundred students, and received wide acclaim for its bilingual approach to education, as evidenced in the honor of receiving a school visit and literary reading from renowned Chicana writer Sandra Cisneros. Estela and her family continued their various ministerial works even after her husband's painful death from bone cancer in 2003.[3]

Kristy Nabhan-Warren argues that the Catholicism of the Ruiz family "represents the next wave in American Catholicism—a religion that is lay-initiated and created, sculpted to fit the needs of people, even as it remains within the historical folds of the institutional church."[4] The Ruiz family intertwines social and religious forces often perceived to be at odds with one another: mystical visions and everyday lived faith, charismatic inspiration and institutional loyalty, traditional religion and social activism. Though Estela's Marian visions are distinctive religious experiences, the Ruizes share much in common with other pastoral leaders, such as their hunger for God, quest to live out their faith actively, and search for what that faith impels them to do. The Ruizes demonstrate that pastoral leaders are not limited to clergy nor to other designated ministers such as parish coordinators of worship, religious education, and youth outreach. They exemplify the claim of community organizers that "leader" is a relational word: to be a leader one must have the charisma to attract followers. They reveal Hispanics' desire not only to receive from the ministries of the church but also to shape the community of faith and its evangelizing work with their own leadership.

Engaging leaders from different ethnic groups to serve their own—and others— in ministries is a pastoral strategy as old as the Catholic Church itself. When Greeks in the early Christian community at Jerusalem complained that their widows received unequal treatment in the distribution of food as compared to their Hebrew counterparts, the twelve (Hebrew) apostles called seven Greeks to leadership as deacons charged with overseeing the daily allocations. According to the Acts of the Apostles, in the wake of this prudent decision "the word of God continued to spread, and the number of disciples in Jerusalem increased greatly" (Acts 6:7). Within U.S. Catholicism, historically the recruitment and formation of clergy and women religious native to various ethnic groups was, along with the national parishes and parochial schools they staffed, the most important pastoral strategy for serving European immigrants within a pluralistic church and society. Church leaders addressed the needs of Italian Catholics, for example, in large part through the enlistment of Italian priests and sisters such as the Scalabrinians, St. Frances Xavier Cabrini's Missionary Sisters of the Sacred Heart, and Italian diocesan clergy. The emergence of this indigenous leadership enabled other concerns to be addressed, such as participation in parish life, outreach to the unchurched, and cultural sensitivity in ministry. As Joseph Fitzpatrick has noted, European priests and sisters who rose from within their own immigrant groups were immensely important because they "knew the way their people felt, the sufferings they endured, the values they cherished, the practices that meant loyalty or generosity or devotion to the faith. They had a keen sense of the interests and needs of their people, not only religious and spiritual, but economic, social, and political."[5]

Thus it is not surprising that the most consistently articulated priority for enhancing Hispanic ministry—from the First Encuentro to the various U.S. bishops' statements— is the need for faith formation and for identifying and training leaders: laity, clergy, and religious. What the U.S. bishops stated in their 1983 pastoral letter on Hispanic ministry continues to hold true today: "The scarcity of Hispanic priests, religious sisters, brothers, and permanent deacons is one of the most serious problems facing the Church in the United States." In their National Pastoral Plan for Hispanic Ministry they bluntly reiterated the need: "There is a lack of pastoral ministers, which makes uncertain the survival of the Catholic faith among Hispanics." Fifteen years later they struck a similar tone of urgency in their *Encuentro and Mission* document: "An evangelizing catechesis and a solid formation are more necessary today than ever."[6] Examining the scope of Hispanic ministry leadership—bishops, priests, deacons, religious, and laity—and the approaches to Hispanic ministry they employ reveals vital resources and challenges for Catholicism in the United States.

Like groups from previous generations, such as the Germans and the Poles, proponents of Hispanic ministry have advocated for bishops of their own ethnic background. During a 1972 preparation meeting for the First National Encuentro, 159 Hispanic priests, sisters, and lay leaders in the New York archdiocese sent a letter to Cardinal Terence Cooke asking for greater Hispanic representation at the decision-making levels of the archdiocese, including the appointment of a Hispanic as an auxiliary bishop—that is, a bishop to assist the cardinal in his pastoral duties. Members of the PADRES and Las Hermanas organizations were at the forefront of similar initiatives, as in 1978 when PADRES' executive director, Brother Trinidad Sánchez, S.J., distributed a circular asking concerned parties to lobby church officials for the appointment of Hispanic bishops in dioceses with majority Hispanic Catholic populations. Though overt pressure tactics are rarely employed today, concern and speculation about the appointment of a Latino bishop in dioceses with significant Hispanic populations are common. At the time of this writing, there are thirty active Hispanic bishops in the United States, more than half of them immigrants. They account for less than 10 percent of active U.S. bishops. The fourteen Hispanics who are ordinaries, meaning they are the bishop in charge of a diocese, comprise about 7 percent of U.S. Catholic ordinaries and are all in dioceses located in the West or Southwest. Archbishop José Gomez of Los Angeles and Archbishop Gustavo Garcia-Siller, M.Sp.S., of San Antonio are the sole active Hispanic archbishops directly linked to the United States Conference of Catholic Bishops, though Archbishop Roberto González, O.F.M., a native of New Jersey and formerly the bishop of Corpus Christi, Texas, is archbishop of San Juan, Puerto Rico, a commonwealth associated with the United States but ecclesiastically part of the Latin American bishops' conference.[7]

One reason for the disproportionate number of Hispanic bishops to an overall Hispanic population that comprises 35 percent of U.S. Catholics is the scarcity of Latino priests, the candidate "pool" from which the pope and his advisers select bishops. Historically, various European ethnic groups suffered from a shortage of compatriot priests who identified with their customs, spoke their language, and represented their interests within the structures of U.S. Catholicism and the wider society. The diminishing numbers and aging of priests in the United States over the past forty years has been widely noted. Yet no past or present group has had such a dearth of clergy vocations relative to its size as do Latinos. USCCB figures reveal that Hispanics account for just over 6 percent of Catholic priests serving in the United States, approximately three thousand Hispanic priests in all, the vast majority of them foreign born. The ratio of Hispanic priests to Hispanic laity is approximately one to ten thousand, at least five times more lay persons per priest than the overall ratio for U.S. Catholics. Though on the whole Latino priests are younger than non-Latino priests, with more than half under age forty-five compared to only 15 percent of non-Latinos, the proportional need for Hispanic priests is still staggering. The shortage of Latino clergy is the most significant difference in the leadership of Hispanic Catholics as compared to European immigrants from previous eras. Given the strong foundation of U.S. Catholicism in the parish and in the authority of the pastor, within official church structures this shortage is also the most detrimental limitation to advancing ministries among Hispanics.[8]

Explanations for the lack of Hispanic vocations include kinship ties that deter prospective candidates from leaving the family circle, the requirement of mandatory celibacy, and particularly scant educational opportunities that leave many ill prepared for the ordination requirement of completing a master's degree. Bishop Daniel Flores of Detroit (now the bishop of Brownsville, Texas) contended in a 2008 presentation to his fellow Hispanic priests: "The difficulty we find in attracting vocations to the priesthood in contemporary U.S. culture is the same difficulty we find in preparing couples for matrimony: If the next generation does not understand or experience something of the generosity, the fidelity and commitment of Christ in their lives, the language we use to talk about a vocation to the priesthood, religious life or to the sacrament of matrimony does not get much beyond their ears." Flores noted challenges in both the U.S. Catholic Church's ministry among immigrant Hispanic families in which vocations could be nurtured and among second-generation Hispanics who grow up in the dual cultural milieus of their émigré families and the United States. The tensions, confusion, and lack of strong attachment to their Catholic faith traditions among many Hispanic young people detract from a personal relationship with Jesus Christ, without which "there is no Christian vocation of any kind." For the Hispanic young men who do sense a call to priesthood, further obstacles include an institutional culture in seminaries that often is not conducive to Hispanic emphasis on "personal contact and trust" and, for some, a lack of legal immigration status that in many dioceses precludes them from pursuing seminary studies. Flores called on his fellow priests to renew their dedication to youth ministries and to apostolic movements, the two primary places where Hispanic vocations to the priesthood are typically nurtured. He also urged them to be proactive about supporting Hispanic candidates for the priesthood at all stages of their preparation, from the application process to seminary formation and on through to ordination.[9]

Flores's vision of the pressing need to nurture vocational awareness in ministries with Hispanic families and young people is confirmed in studies of the Center for Applied Research in the Apostolate, which consistently show Latino Catholic males in the United States are less likely to have "considered becoming a priest or brother" than their non-Latino counterparts. In one sample the margin was more than three to one and merely 7 percent of Latino respondents said they had contemplated these vocations. CARA studies have also found that male Latino Catholics are less likely to have "ever known a Catholic priest on a personal basis, that is, outside formal interactions at church or school," inhibiting potential interest in the priesthood among many due to a lack of a clergy mentor or role model.[10]

The National Conference of Diocesan Vocation Directors (NCDVD) and the National Religious Vocation Conference (NRVC) have sought to enhance their members' Hispanic outreach through initiatives such as the NCDVD publication of its vocation discernment booklets in Spanish and the NRVC's *Encuentro Vocacional* online discernment tool. A number of dioceses have programs to help plant the seed of vocation among Hispanic and other young people, some concentrated on priesthood and religious life and others more broadly on the notion that adolescence and young adulthood are the time in one's life to be aware of a calling to these pathways or to the married or single life. One of the most long-standing programs is the Pilgrimage of Vocations in the archdiocese of Santa Fe. Father Michael O'Brien, pastor in Estancia, New Mexico, organized the first pilgrimage in 1973 with forty men who walked more than one hundred miles to the sanctuary of Chimayó. The pilgrimages have undergone various changes over the years, including the route and length of the journey, the participation of women, and the formation of separate pilgrimage groups to journey from different directions and converge on Chimayó for a culminating celebration of the Eucharist. Pilgrims are expected to prepare spiritually for their sacrificial walk. They elect to go on pilgrimage for reasons ranging from personal intentions, to seeking forgiveness, to gratitude, but most "especially for the increase of religious vocations." Great pride is taken in pilgrims who accept a calling to ordination or religious life, such as Father Joe Vigil, the first participant who became a priest, and Bishop Arturo Tafoya, the first priest participant to become a bishop.[11]

Other efforts have sought to make the seminary environment more viable for Latino candidates to the priesthood, as well as more equipped to prepare non-Hispanic clergy to serve Hispanic Catholics. In collaboration with their seminary directors, seminarians convene the Conference for Seminarians in Hispanic Ministry, typically an annual event, although its informal organizing structure results in an occasional hiatus. Originally a gathering for Hispanic seminarians in the Midwest that then regional Hispanic ministry director, Olga Villa Parra, established in collaboration with Father Vicente López, O. Carm., the conference is now a national event hosted at different seminaries on a rotating basis. The 2008 conference at Saint Paul Seminary in St. Paul, Minnesota, drew eighty participants, including Omar Guanchez, who commented on the need for learning about diverse Hispanic groups: "Even though I am from Venezuela and speak Spanish, Mexican culture is another culture. We speak the same language, but it doesn't mean we're the same." Conference organizer Jorge Canela said the gatherings are "a great opportunity for us Hispanics to get together, to worship together and build relationships between us." Reflecting on the predominance of Latino participants, he also expressed hope that non-Hispanic "seminarians can learn more about Hispanic ministry and not be afraid, but be open and continue learning from different cultures and traditions."[12]

One long-standing initiative is at St. Vincent de Paul Regional Seminary in Boynton Beach, Florida, which was founded in 1963 within the Miami diocese (later an archdiocese) and, responding to the significant influx of Cuban exiles, in 1971 began a bilingual program in English and Spanish. Though over the years some seminary leaders have been more successful than others in achieving their goal of enabling all St. Vincent priest graduates to be "functionally fluent in both languages," efforts in this regard remain ongoing. Several other seminaries have also sustained initiatives over decades, such as those at Assumption Seminary and the Oblate School of Theology in San Antonio and the Los Angeles archdiocesan seminary, St. John's, in Camarillo, California. Their Hispanic outreach is typified in the statement of purpose for the Oblate School of Theology, which avows: drawing on its "location and historical dedication to the Mexican-American presence in the Southwest, the learning, teaching, and research of the School pay particular attention to the diverse and rich Hispanic reality of the Americas."[13]

With the encouragement and support of several bishops from the United States, in 1989 Cardinal Norberto Rivera Carrera, the archbishop of Mexico City, launched the Seminario Hispano de Santa María de Guadalupe to form Hispanic seminarians from dioceses in the United States and Canada. Seminario leaders perceive their efforts as augmenting a "[North] American seminary system" that often "does not correspond to Hispanic culture." Perhaps anticipating protest about a seminary in Mexico preparing priests for U.S. dioceses, they state clearly their objective to "integrate Hispanics in the Catholic Church of the United States" and insist their mission is not to "form an 'Hispanic church' within the church of the United States, but to accept the reality that demands [Hispanics] be evangelized adequately in order that they continue to be Catholic." Liturgies at the Seminario are regularly celebrated in English, students read theological texts and English-language materials from the dioceses for which they are preparing for ordination, some do ministry field placements in English-speaking environments, and they receive instructional help to ensure that their use of English advances during their studies. But on the whole Spanish is still the predominant language; it is the native tongue of seminarians and faculty, the institution is located in Mexico City, and classes are largely taught in Spanish. The preponderance of Spanish is one factor in the relatively modest success of the Seminario. Others include the hesitancy of some U.S. bishops to accept immigrant seminary candidates who lack typical education prerequisites and the decision of other bishops to have their candidates study in U.S. seminaries. Though the Seminario has facilities for thirty-six students, only ten enrolled during the 2008–2009 academic year. Nonetheless, it provides an alternative formation process that several U.S. bishops have utilized, particularly for immigrant seminarians whose previous educational advancement does not align with the U.S. educational system.[14]

Ongoing efforts to increase Hispanic vocations to the priesthood—among both immigrants and the U.S. born—have produced some results. Hispanic priests serving in the Miami archdiocese number more than 80 and account for over 40 percent of the clergy there, reflecting the Cuban priests who remain from the exile groups of the 1960s and the generally higher education levels of Cuban Americans, but also in part the vocational efforts centered on St. Vincent de Paul Regional Seminary. In 2009 the archdiocese of San Antonio ordained its largest group of priests since 1930, more than half of them Hispanic. As of 2008 nine graduates of the Seminario Hispano were serving as priests in U.S. dioceses. Nationally, Hispanics comprised 12 percent of priests ordained in 2009, approximately 56 new Hispanic priests in all. Although this figure still places Latinos as the most underrepresented ethnic group relative to its total number of Catholics, it is also twice the overall percentage of Latino priests in the United States. Hispanic seminary enrollments for the 2008–2009 academic year were even higher, comprising 15 percent of the total number of major seminarians (those in the preparation stage immediately before ordination) and 20 percent of the total number at the earlier formation stage of college seminarians. If the recent seminarian retention rate of approximately 75 percent from entry to ordination holds true for Hispanics, the 465 current Hispanic seminarians would yield a number of newly ordained Hispanic priests similar to that of 2009 annually for the next five years.[15]

Demographics account in part for recent increases; the youthfulness of the Hispanic population provides disproportionate numbers of single persons eligible for Catholic religious vocations. Another factor is relatively larger numbers of immigrants, who historically have been a seedbed for priestly and religious vocations in U.S. Catholicism. One-fourth of the priests ordained in the United States in 2009 were foreign born, with the contingent of Mexican émigrés near the top of the list, second only to the Vietnamese. Collectively, Mexican and Colombian immigrants total half of the Hispanics ordained in the United States during 2009. The number of the foreign born among all new priests in the United States has been at least one-fourth the total for nearly every year over the past decade, and a similar number of foreign-born seminarians are currently preparing for ordination. Archbishop José Gomez avows that two core elements for advancing priestly vocations are the personal involvement of the local bishop with seminarians and sound formation programs that "give seminarians something solid they can hold onto," especially a growing number who seek a deeper truth and stability in their vocation "due to immigration or broken families."[16] Vocation initiatives of recent decades are consistent with these claims and present clear strategies for inviting and enabling both immigrant and U.S.-born Hispanics to pursue religious vocations: sustained outreach to youth groups and apostolic movements in which young Latinos are enlivening their faith commitment, broad initiatives in vocation ministry, priests' consistent encouragement and mentoring of seminary candidates, and formation programs that resonate with Hispanics.

Yet the shortfall of Latino clergy remains urgent. Recent increases in Hispanic priests and seminarians come far short of keeping pace with population growth, much less making up for the present low number of Hispanic priests, particularly the meager number of native-born Latino clergy who can accompany the expansive younger generations as they navigate their adaptation to life in the United States. For decades Euro-American as well as European émigré priests, many of them Irish, have served as pastors of congregations with predominant or significant Hispanic populations. The 2002 PARAL report on Latino congregational leadership illuminates the extent of their involvement. When asked to state their ethnicity independent of country of origin, one-fourth of the "heads" in a random sampling of nearly five hundred Hispanic Catholic faith communities self-identified as being of Hispanic background, the two largest groups being the 15 percent who said they were of Mexican heritage and the 4 percent who were Columbian. Another one-fourth of the respondents identified themselves as being of a European background other than Spanish, while 40 percent said they were U.S. American. Thus some two-thirds of those assigned to pastor these Hispanic communities—most of them priests—did not identify themselves as Latinos.[17]

Non-Latino priests are sometimes critiqued for shortcomings such as poor Spanish, a lack of charisma in their style of presiding at worship, inadequate appreciation of Hispanic devotional traditions, or merely translating English-language homilies verbatim into Spanish rather than preaching a message that specifically addresses a Spanish-speaking congregation. According to the 2007 Pew Latino religion survey, however, Hispanics are generally accepting of non-Latino clergy: 56 percent of Catholic respondents said they prefer Mass in Spanish, but three-quarters said it "doesn't matter" if the priest is Latino or not. While this statistic reflects a deferential attitude toward priests among a number of Hispanic Catholics, particularly among immigrants, it also suggests that many Hispanics have accepted as a status quo in U.S. Catholic parishes the scenario of non-Latino clergy serving them as pastors. Hispanics tend to place greater value on a priest's personal and pastoral leadership qualities than on his ethnic background.[18]

Permanent deacons are another major leadership group in Hispanic communities. Following a mandate of the Second Vatican Council, in 1967 Pope Paul VI restored the early Christian practice of the permanent diaconate as one of the Catholic Church's three "orders" or groups of ordained ministers, the other two being bishops and presbyters or priests. Whereas Catholic priests are ordained as transitional deacons and usually serve in that capacity for about a year as they prepare for their ordination to the priesthood, permanent deacons are men ordained to serve in the diaconate for the remainder of their lives. The vast majority of them are married and they promise not to remarry if they are widowed (or divorced) subsequent to their ordination. Most hold jobs apart from the church and serve without financial compensation in their parish and outreach ministries. U.S. bishops were among the first Catholic prelates to reinstitute the permanent diaconate, and the 16,380 permanent deacons in the United States today comprise well over 40 percent of the total in the world.[19]

The Asociación Nacional de Diáconos Hispanos (National Association of Hispanic Deacons), founded in 1984 with Deacon Benito Serenil as the group's first president, strives to address "the specific needs that confront the Hispanic Deacons" and "respond to those needs at all levels of ministry by continually assessing the experiences of the Hispanic Deacon, his family and his community." Diaconate preparation programs rarely require the pursuit of an academic degree, and more than a fifth of the 175 programs in the United States offer formation in both Spanish and English, making them accessible to a wider range of Hispanic candidates than seminaries. Currently Hispanics comprise 14 percent of the active permanent deacons nationally in the United States and 19 percent of those in formation programs for the diaconate. Given the minimum-age requirement of thirty-five for diaconate ordination and the youthfulness of the Latino population, these figures make the ratio of Hispanic permanent deacons to the Latino demographic eligible for this vocation more proportionate than any other officially authorized category of leaders. Indeed, the nearly 1,900 active Hispanic deacons is roughly two-thirds that of Latino priests, and their growing numbers are steadily decreasing that gap: during 2008–2009 some 440 Hispanics were deacon candidates, along with another 270 at the "aspirant" stage that precedes formal entry into the diaconate formation program.[20]

Their fellow Hispanic ministry leaders charge that some deacons have relatively weak theological knowledge and pastoral skills or focus their service too narrowly on one apostolic movement rather than the whole community. One of the primary criticisms of permanent deacons in general has been that they are overly clerical, more interested in vesting and being seen on the altar for Sunday Mass than in works of charity and service outside of communal worship. Yet, along with their non-Latino counterparts, a number of Hispanic deacons provide significant ministerial leadership, such as in adult catechesis; sacramental preparation; and outreach to families, youth, the infirmed, the elderly, and prisoners. Deacons' wives frequently accompany them in their apostolate, forming a team couple that can greatly enhance marriage and baptismal preparation, counseling, and outreach ministries. As ordained leaders commissioned to proclaim the Gospel and preach at Mass and to preside at baptisms, weddings, and funeral services, deacons are also important for the sacramental ministries they offer, particularly in parishes where the priest does not speak Spanish or can only read the prayers of the Mass. In many such instances regular worship in Spanish would be severely hampered—or completely absent—without the leadership of a Spanish-speaking deacon. Hispanic deacons, along with a few non-Hispanic deacons who speak Spanish, provide similarly crucial leadership in large congregations with a Spanish-speaking priest who cannot single-handedly administer a heavy volume of Spanish-language baptisms and other parish needs.

Hispanic women religious have been among the most vital Hispanic Catholic leaders, but, as with their non-Latina counterparts, aging and declining numbers have curtailed the breadth of their influence. Among all leadership categories the number of women religious in the United States has declined the most precipitously—more than 300 percent—since the end of the Second Vatican Council in 1965. More than 70 percent of women's religious communities have only one or two, if any, new members at any stage of the formation process, which extends from initial entry to final vows some five to nine years later. Women's orders affiliated with the Council of Major Superiors of Women Religious (CMSWR), a more traditional group as evidenced in emphases like wearing the religious habit, tend to have more members in formation than those affiliated with the Leadership Conference of Women Religious (LCWR): 28 percent of orders affiliated with CMSWR have more than ten members in formation as compared to only 1 percent of those affiliated with LCWR. A 2009 CARA study showed that among those who belong to religious orders—sisters as well as brothers and priests in orders like the Jesuits or Franciscans—Hispanics comprise only 3 percent of all members in final vows. While 21 percent of new members in formation are Hispanic, the raw number of new members is relatively meager, and since 1990 only half of the women who entered religious life have remained until their final vows. The study does not reveal how Hispanics are distributed between men's and women's communities nor between CMSWR and LCWR affiliates, but an even distribution would mean that nationally some 1,800 Latinas are fully professed members of women's religious communities and roughly 250 are now in formation, of which statistically 125 could be expected to eventually take final vows.[21]

As the number of religious and priests has decreased and the Catholic population has grown, increasingly the laity has assumed a number of leadership positions in Catholic institutions, such as those of principal in a Catholic school; pastoral associate working in collaboration with a pastor or in a parish with no resident priest; and parish director of catechesis, youth ministry, or liturgy. The U.S. bishops addressed this national trend in their 2005 document *Co-Workers in the Vineyard of the Lord: A Resource for Guiding the Development of Lay Ecclesial Ministry*. Articulating the Catholic belief that all the baptized are called to holiness and to participate in the Church's mission of transforming the world, the bishops distinguished the particular call of "lay ecclesial ministers" as embodying four characteristics: authorization of the hierarchy, leadership in a specific ministerial area, close mutual collaboration with ordained leaders, and preparation and formation appropriate to their pastoral responsibilities. *Co-Workers in the Vineyard* identifies lay ecclesial ministers as those who either work in paid positions or volunteer "at least twenty hours per week," most of them in parishes but others in settings such as schools, hospitals, and prisons.[22]

There are more parish-based lay ecclesial ministers in the United States than there are diocesan priests— more than 30,000 lay ecclesial ministers in all. Approximately 80 percent of them are women. More than 17,500 lay leaders are currently enrolled in formation programs for lay ecclesial ministry, five times the enrollment of U.S. seminarians. The late Msgr. Philip Murnion, founder of the National Pastoral Life Center, called the shift in recent decades from a male clergy to a significant lay, predominantly female leadership "a virtual revolution in parish ministry." Except for Mass and the sacraments, more and more primary leadership in parish services such as catechesis, sacramental preparation, and liturgy planning are in the hands of lay ecclesial ministers.[23]

Latinos account for only about 8 percent of lay ecclesial ministers but about a third of those who are currently enrolled in the formation programs for lay ecclesial ministry. The discrepancy in these figures is in part the result of a growing group of Latino lay leaders seeking formation. But it also reflects the gap between lay leaders who study in certification programs and those who study in more highly regarded academic degree programs; Hispanics comprise almost a fifth of those in the latter category but more than twice that percentage in the certification category. The simple reality in most U.S. Catholic parishes and dioceses is that lay leaders with master's degrees in theology or pastoral ministry, most of whom are Euro-American, are the first hired for paid ministry positions. Consciously or not, in various cases a degreed Euro-American is retained for a parish post like director of faith formation, and a Hispanic without a similar formal degree steps forward to do the same work in Spanish without pay, even when there are more Spanish speakers than English speakers participating in the parish programs. The influence of tight budgets on hiring poses a further challenge to increasing the disproportionate number of Hispanic lay ecclesial ministers. Moreover, the total number of more than 17,500 laity currently in formation programs comprise well over half the number of paid parish ecclesial ministers they might one day be called on to replace. Even if the quantity of lay ecclesial ministry positions grows, these demographics suggest that whether Hispanic or of another background, many if not most of those in formation will not be hired for a parish or diocesan staff. In raw numbers, currently some 1,200 Hispanics serve in lay ecclesial ministry positions, nearly that many are enrolled in degree programs, and more than 5,000 are in certification programs.[24]

*Encuentro and Mission* urged church ministers to engage another lay leadership group, "Hispanic professionals," with "a personal invitation" to enhance their "active participation in the life of the church" and their opportunities to "contribute their talent, time, and treasure." The National Catholic Council for Hispanic Ministry had already made some efforts to foster such engagement after its establishment in 1991. More recently, Mario Paredes, whose current position is presidential liaison for Roman Catholic ministry at the American Bible Society in New York, played the leading role in establishing the Catholic Association of Latino Leaders (CALL) in 2007. He served as the organization's first chairman with Archbishop José Gomez as episcopal moderator. CALL is an organization aimed at "Hispanics from varying business and professional backgrounds dedicated to transforming our own lives and communities according to the Gospel, and speaking out on social and faith issues important to both the Catholic Church and Latinos."[25] Still in its formative stages, it is not yet clear how broadly effective CALL will be in reaching Latino Catholic professionals. Unlike Hispanics who congregate at a Spanish Mass or other Spanish-language church groups, these professionals are not as easy to locate in a concentrated group. Often they do not live in predominantly Hispanic neighborhoods. The CALL initiative illuminates an often unrecognized and untapped lay leadership resource in the growing number of Hispanic Catholic professionals in business, politics, law, medicine, education, community organizing, the arts, the entertainment industry, and other fields.

Grassroots Hispanic Catholic lay leaders are the most abundant resource for Hispanic ministry. They do the bulk of everyday ministry as catechists, prayer group leaders, fund-raisers, community organizers, spiritual advisers, translators, immigrant advocates, and much more. They live and witness their faith in homes, neighborhoods, workplaces, and schools. The five thousand Hispanics who comprise 42 percent of those currently enrolled in certificate formation programs that qualify for lay ecclesial ministry make up the only leadership or formation category in which Hispanics have a higher ratio of participants than their proportion of the overall U.S. Catholic population. And these leaders are but a fraction of the Hispanics in the more numerous faith formation programs that are conducted in parishes, apostolic movements, and small Christian communities. Though such programs have varying degrees of effectiveness and links to diocesan structures and oversight, they are the primary means through which most adult Hispanic laity receive instruction and guidance to actively live their faith.

Of course, numbers alone do not provide a comprehensive analysis of Hispanic ministry leadership. Whatever one's position within the church, each leader operates from a vision for Hispanic ministry, a set of core perceptions and priorities, whether consciously articulated or not. Four approaches collectively map the most prevalent operative visions among current leaders. They are not mutually exclusive options. Rather, they reflect divergent, and at times conflicting, emphases. Though many pastoral leaders combine elements from two or more approaches, they tend to work within the general parameters of a single one. Both a leader's past experience and the needs of a particular Hispanic faith community he or she serves shape the preference of one approach over another. The four approaches evolved in historical experiences treated in the previous three chapters of this volume: the Hispanic ministry movement illuminated in the Encuentros, the national parish dynamic and the expansive Hispanic immigration of the past two decades, the push for unity and the rise of second- and subsequent-generation Latinos, and the upsurge of apostolic movements like the Cursillo and the CCR.

One ministerial approach is that of the *movimiento*, or organized movement. The advocates for Hispanic ministry who emphasize this approach helped create and develop its pastoral vision over decades, some of them serving as leaders from the time of the very first Encuentro in 1972 and even before. Members of this group have long struggled to make Hispanics visible within U.S. Catholicism and to make Hispanic leadership and ministry a priority, in many instances applying lessons learned in social movements and community organizing to foster Hispanic concerns within the U.S. Catholic Church. They tend to be deeply committed to justice issues in society and in the church, including the demand for leadership parity and Hispanic participation in ecclesial decision-making processes. Their experience tells them that, whether indirect or more overt, advocacy brings needed resources and attention to Hispanic ministry efforts. Since their vision of Hispanic ministry arose out of and shaped the National Hispanic Pastoral Encuentros as well as the National Pastoral Plan for Hispanic Ministry and other official statements of the U.S. bishops, movimiento leaders tend to see their approach as the most officially sanctioned, even normative. They are usually the most frustrated with recent transitions in the structures and general state of Hispanic ministry, changes that can appear to be a rejection or reversal of advances built on their own blood, sweat, and tears. For that same reason, a primary critique other Hispanic ministry leaders direct at those of the movimiento approach is that they are too focused on the past and on their own legacy, rather than on the changing social and ecclesial contexts shaping the ministry among new immigrants and other Hispanics today.

While they seek to uplift the leadership of grassroots Hispanics, members of the movimiento group often find the charismatic style of leadership in groups like Mary's Ministries too narrowly focused on personal salvation and affective religious experience. They also tend to be suspicious of multiculturalism; in theory they see it as an important goal for Hispanic ministry, but in practice they perceive that it often leads to superficial, even ideological, initiatives and structures that result in the co-optation of Hispanic ministry efforts. For this reason various movimiento-style leaders were among the most vocal critics of Encuentro 2000 as a step backward from hard-won gains in Hispanic ministry. They were also prominent among the leaders who reasserted the advocacy voice for Hispanic ministry at the 2001 National Symposium to Refocus Hispanic Ministry and protested the 2007 subsuming of the national Secretariat for Hispanic Affairs into a new Secretariat of Cultural Diversity in the Church. Although they recognize that new immigrants are a significant development and they tend to be staunch advocates of human rights for these immigrants, movimiento leaders take a longer view of Hispanic ministry, both its origins before the current immigration boom and its future into the generations of the U.S.-born children of immigrants. They disagree with depictions of Hispanics and Hispanic ministry as solely a phenomenon of recent émigrés.

According to the *Encuentro and Mission* document, these veteran leaders helped develop a *memoria histórica* that clarifies the "unique identity" and "unique history of Hispanic Catholics in the United States."[26] They remind their fellow leaders in ministry that conversations about the future must stand on a critical understanding of the past. Movimiento leaders can be found in various positions of influential leadership: directors of diocesan and regional offices, especially those for Hispanic ministry; heads of national organizations; and faculty members and administrators in pastoral centers and Catholic institutions of higher education. Non-Latinos are counted among their number, especially those who trained in Hispanic ministry programs or who learned the movimiento approach from mentors while serving in a predominantly Hispanic faith community. Many are lay leaders, but a number of religious, priests, permanent deacons, and some bishops also favor elements of this approach. Although they tend to be older, they have also influenced the vision of younger leaders, particularly those who serve as lay ecclesial ministers or have studied in the pastoral centers and graduate school theology and pastoral degree programs where many who advocate the movimiento approach serve as teachers and mentors.

New immigrants comprise another leadership group. Their primary reference point is the daily struggles for faith, survival, and dignity of the millions of émigrés who have arrived in the United States in recent decades. Many new immigrant leaders know little about historical developments such as the Encuentros and the rise of national Hispanic ministry organizations. They tend to equate Hispanic ministry with Spanish-language ministry, at times judging as deficient Latinos who speak Spanish poorly or do not know and strongly identify with their Hispanic cultural heritage. Some even presume that such Latinos fit better in "mainstream" parish structures and ministries, often with a pejorative sense that they have sold out their Latino birthright. Not surprisingly, distinctive emphases of this approach include émigrés' practice of Catholicism as learned in their homeland, retention of their language and culture, and struggle for dignity and rights in the United States. New immigrant leaders are the standard-bearers of the national parish dynamic; they foster worship communities and ecclesial initiatives that enable Spanish-speaking Catholics to sense that they belong to the church and that their commitment is needed.

Émigrés do not unilaterally adopt the new immigrant pastoral style, such as some newcomers who received ministerial training that emphasized the movimiento approach. Some non-Latinos also embrace the new immigrant ministerial vision as a means to reinforce Hispanics' Catholic faith and traditions. However, most proponents of this approach are themselves Spanish-speaking émigrés. Groups of émigré women religious have long served in the United States, such as the Carmelite Sisters of the Most Sacred Heart of Los Angeles, which Mother Maria Luisa Josefa established with fellow Mexican sisters while in exile at Los Angeles during Mexico's Cristero Rebellion. Today various congregations of immigrant Hispanic women religious have begun to associate more formally. One initiative is the Asociación de Congregaciones Religiosas Hispanas en Estados Unidos (Association of Hispanic Religious Congregations in the United States). The organization's leaders have already convened one national gathering to enhance the religious life and ministries of Hispanic sisters "sent to serve the [Hispanic] immigrant people in the United States." In 2010 they announced plans to convene a second such gathering. Hispanic permanent deacons also count a number of immigrants among their ranks, as is evident in their annual national conference, which is largely conducted in Spanish.[27] Latin American laity who arrive in the United States with professional credentials and leadership experience make important contributions to ministries directed at their fellow immigrants. Many grassroots lay émigrés support the new immigrant approach by gravitating toward leaders and faith communities that embody it. But the new immigrant leaders with the greatest collective influence are the more than 80 percent of Latino priests who are foreign born. Their presence as the primary pastoral leaders in many Hispanic faith communities gives them an influence beyond their numbers.

A 2008 CARA study revealed that Hispanics tend to be more satisfied with the ministries of international priests in their parishes than do non-Hispanic whites. But Dean Hoge and Aniedi Okure's study of international priests in the United States shows that, like other immigrant clergy, a number of Latinos who come with varying degrees of English-language ability and their most formative experiences in their countries of origin encounter various difficulties in their ministries. There is also a crucial difference: while many priests from places like India and Africa are asked to serve in predominantly English-speaking U.S. congregations, a number of Hispanic and Asian clergy work in their native tongue among fellow émigrés. Complaints against the former group tend to center on their ability to speak English and to adapt themselves to U.S. Catholics and parish life. A frequent criticism of immigrant Latino priests, on the other hand, is their propensity to serve predominantly Spanish-speaking flocks. One lay leader stated that serving one's own "should not be their sole focus. I don't think it's good for the church because it creates overly separate segments of the church. . . . it doesn't really foster diversity in a healthy sense. If I were a bishop, I would make it a requirement that the foreign priests are here to serve the whole community, not just their ethnic group." Some U.S. Hispanic leaders agree, noting that when priests do not learn English they fail "to reach English-speaking Hispanics and other members of the parish," often leading "to the segregation of Spanish-speaking Hispanics from the rest of the Church" and inadequate outreach to young U.S.-born Hispanics.[28]

Hispanic ministry leaders have also observed that "many Latin American priests bring models of pastoral work and understandings of church which may be at odds with the parish life and experience of U.S. Latinos. This difference can lead to priests taking insensitive positions toward the local populations." Insensitivity can range from disparaging the devotional traditions of a Hispanic group different from the priest's own, to abrasive criticism of the young, to an absolute authoritarianism. A frequent complaint is that a priest expects parishioners to adjust to his style of leadership and takes few if any steps to accommodate himself to those he is assigned to shepherd. The situation is particularly difficult when a new priest makes rapid changes in a parish community's worship, ministries, and leadership with little or no reference to those who have formed the community before he arrived. One parishioner in the Midwest reported: "When my friend and I went to the priest privately and with great respect to ask about all the changes he had made, he interrupted her and accused her of inciting the parish against him. When she tried to respond he said she was wasting his time. I was too shocked to say anything. I had never seen a priest act like that." According to one veteran pastor in California, in many cases a difference in perspective "starts with priests versus laity. But also sometimes it's the macho idea, of men kind of superior to the women, and the place of women is to be subservient." Hispanic lay leaders who have received ministerial formation lament that in various instances they are "marginalized or delegitimized by priests, who feel threatened or might not be willing to decentralize some of the pastoral work."[29]

Latin American clergy have their own critiques of Catholicism in the United States. Commenting on the bureaucratic ethos of the U.S. Catholic Church as compared to that of Latin America, one said, "I had to update my organizational skills tremendously" because "everything here is in a schedule." In the transition from his home diocese to his new ministry, he testified that "personally, I suffer a great deal, coming from a small place, very family-oriented, and in a kind of ministry that was nothing to do with administration but was in direct contact with the people." Latin American priests also bemoan what they perceive as unequal treatment compared to that of native-born U.S. priests, such as their sense of second-class status among fellow clergy in a diocese or in a parish under the control of a Euro-American pastor. Their outsider status and, for some, temporary condition as priests on loan from their home dioceses diminish their capacity to advocate for themselves and their Spanish-speaking flocks. One priest commented, "As a foreigner you know your voice is always somebody coming from outside. The pastor will say, 'That's good in your country, but here we are in America.'" Many newcomers are shocked at what they see in U.S. culture: "It's too much self-centered, and they forget the aspect of community. Sometimes the child has TV in his or her own room! . . . Whereas the other [Latin American] culture I have experienced, they take more time to serve, to give time to build community. American culture is more individualistic." Some Latin American priests have expressed their dislike for ministry among U.S.-born Latinos, such as one who complained that he was assigned to one of the "bad parishes" in "the dumps of the city" among "Puerto Ricans born in the USA" who "had a low level of education."[30]

Ongoing struggles and the need for support prompted Latino immigrant priests to take a lead role in the Asociación Nacional de Sacerdotes Hispanos (ANSH, the National Association of Hispanic Priests), established in 1989. Unlike PADRES, which Chicano priests founded two decades earlier, ANSH attracts a large—though not exclusive—émigré membership that conducts its affairs predominantly in Spanish. The group's first stated organizational objectives are to "foment unity, fraternity and support among Hispanic priests in the United States"; serve as the "official voice [to the USCCB] of the Hispanic priests who belong to the association"; and "support sacerdotal ministry and pastoral activities directed at the promotion and development of the Hispanic community."[31]

The long-standing practice in U.S. Catholicism of Irish, German, Polish, Italian, and other émigré pastors and women religious banding together and accompanying their compatriots continues in today's new immigrant leaders. Despite difficulties, these leaders—clerical, religious, and lay—are crucial for Catholic Church outreach to their fellow émigrés, who are among the most vulnerable members of U.S. society. New immigrant leaders provide Spanish-language ministries in prayer groups, youth outreach, and catechesis. Their familiarity with the religious traditions of their fellow immigrants vitalizes the worship and devotion in many Hispanic faith communities. They bring energy and spirit to parishes, apostolic movements, and the daily struggles of immigrants for dignity and survival. Immigrant Latino priests and permanent deacons help fill a desperate need for celebrating the Eucharist and other sacraments in Spanish. Their links to Latin America nurture the homeland ties that many immigrants seek, as well as the sense of hemispheric communion and mission that recent popes have encouraged: Pope John Paul II in his 1999 apostolic exhortation *Ecclesia in America* and Pope Benedict XVI in his opening address for the 2007 episcopal conference at Aparecida, Brazil.

Another leadership group is the integrationists. While Hispanic ministry leaders are nearly unanimous in affirming the importance of uniting Latinos with their fellow Catholics, proponents of this approach prioritize efforts to incorporate Latinos in church and society. The ministries of integrationists range from the Americanizing agenda that Hispanic ministry leaders have vilified to a process of incorporation that respects newcomers more adequately. Unlike movimiento and new immigrant leaders, most of whom identify with a particular vision for Hispanic ministry, integrationists do not necessarily consider themselves as engaging in Hispanic ministry. Some even reject as separatist the very notion of Hispanic ministry, claiming that the church has one ministry to all of its members. Others seem unaware that their vision for a united faith community can be a matter of controversy for Hispanics. Yet, intentionally or not, in its varied forms the integrationist approach has a wide influence on Latinos. A number of leaders who adopt this approach serve in parishes and dioceses where a significant Hispanic presence has blossomed during the past two decades, and where Latinos typically are newcomers in established Euro-American congregations. In various instances their ministerial vision clashes with that of new immigrant leaders who serve in the same faith community.

Integrationists avow that when it is enacted with mutual respect their approach embodies core theological concerns about ecclesial unity and the need to work together to foster the church's life and mission. They further argue that their approach provides the opportunity for Hispanics and their coreligionists of other backgrounds to learn from one another's traditions. A common faith and a diversity of adherents make the U.S. Catholic Church a privileged locale for teaching lessons sorely needed in the wider society about what Catholic bishops call "intercultural communication—sustained efforts, carried out by people of diverse cultures, to appreciate their differences, work out conflicts, and build on commonalities."[32] Proponents of the integrationist approach also attest that it is essential for the development of ministries to engage younger generations and other Latinos so that they can adapt to life in the United States with their Catholic faith intact. Most importantly, for integrationists, their approach is the best means for more established U.S. Catholics to embrace Hispanic newcomers with hospitality and ensure their equal treatment within the church.

Latino leaders are acutely aware that these high ideals are not fully realized in parishes and dioceses, where too often "integration" efforts do not encompass proportionate Hispanic participation in decision-making processes. They note that the greater sacrifice of adapting to others is usually expected of Hispanics, presumably because they are the newcomers, even though Euro-Americans tend to have resources, education, established membership in parishes, and legal status that more easily facilitate their adaptation to newcomers in their midst. Hispanic ministry leaders also insist on the pressing need for U.S. Catholics of all backgrounds to transcend forced assimilation and enact a common vision of authentic integration rooted in Catholic faith and teaching.

Yet many Hispanic leaders promote the integrationist vision as an important development, as is evident in the Latino initiative to convene Encuentro 2000 and the efforts of Hispanic leaders in the Secretariat of Cultural Diversity in the Church and the Bishops' Committee on Cultural Diversity in the Church. They urge their fellow Hispanic ministry leaders to perceive their pastoral responsibilities as extending to the whole church, even if primarily to Hispanics, and to build stronger collaborative relationships with African American, Asian American, and Native American leaders, not just the more dominant Euro-Americans. Bishops, pastors, and diocesan directors increasingly express the expectation that Hispanic ministry leaders serve as what *Encuentro and Mission* refers to as "*gente puente* (bridge-builders)—pioneers in opening doors to self and to others."[33] Among Latinos, many of these leaders are in the second and subsequent generations. They have noted the necessity for English-language Hispanic ministry, an outreach to those who linguistically fit into existing church ministries but culturally are seeking something that engages them and their integration process as Latinos in the United States. Hispanic ministry proponents see the formation of a large contingent of *gente puente*—leaders who can guide Hispanics to wed their Catholic faith, life experience in the United States, and Hispanic background—as a key leadership need for developing Hispanic ministry to the greater benefit of Hispanic Catholics and the wider church and society.

A fourth leadership approach is the charismatic style evident among the Ruizes and their collaborators. Its proponents place primary emphasis on the need for salvation through a personal relationship with Christ, growth in knowledge and living of the faith, and direct evangelization. Although a number of pastors and parochial and diocesan staff exhibit these same emphases in their ministries, charismatic leaders are typically more grassroots lay Catholics involved in prayer groups, a Catholic evangelization group like Mary's Ministries, or an apostolic movement. They initiate newcomers in their group through formation efforts like the Life in the Spirit seminars of the CCR. The relatively informal structures of such groups make them more attractive to undocumented immigrants, whose lack of legal status can make them reticent to participate in parishes and dioceses that have begun to require background checks on ministry leaders in response to the clergy sex-abuse crisis.

The relatively marginal ecclesial status of charismatic leaders fuels a concern among many of them that they be seen as faithfully Catholic. Usually they relate to clergy with a high degree of respect, even reverence, and they often crave clerical or other official approval of their activities. But at the same time, they can carry on without a priest's support and have demonstrated a high degree of resiliency when they meet clerical resistance, often based on a conviction that a "misguided" priest cannot contravene what God has ordered them to do. They tend to be less deferential to permanent deacons and lay Hispanic ministers, such as diocesan directors of Hispanic ministry, whose ecclesial posts and professional credentials are not seen as important as the authority of the priest. As one leader said, "For us the priest's word is what counts; the lay person, no matter how well prepared, has no credibility."[34]

Charismatic leaders express concern that the advocacy and programmatic pastoral planning of movimiento leaders can distance them from the everyday lives of believers and detract from the urgency of embracing salvation and preaching it to others. They are sympathetic with integrationists' plea for church unity but insist that the means to achieve it is personal transformation through Christ, as opposed to what they often perceive as human attempts to focus on language, ethnic identity, and the transformation of ecclesial group dynamics. They are not against societal integration but are quick to point out U.S. society's potentially corrupting influences, such as materialism, that can dissuade Catholics from the far more pressing need of assuring one's citizenship in heaven. A number of charismatic leaders are immigrants, and many resonate with the Spanish-language outreach ministries of their fellow émigrés. Yet they sometimes clash with new immigrant leaders whom they perceive as attempting to undermine charismatic fervor with an emphasis on traditional devotions and worship as the most authentic purveyors of Catholic faith.

Collectively the four ministerial approaches advance the aspirations of grassroots evangelization, integration, outreach to immigrants, and building stronger structural links between Hispanics and the U.S. Catholic Church. The approaches' different emphases, strengths, and limitations need not result in recurrent debates about which one is superior to the others. Indeed, given the wide diversity among Hispanic Catholics and their faith communities, each approach has substantial merit to address at least one segment of the population most effectively. Yet the most detrimental consequence of these four ministerial approaches is disagreements among leaders who mistrust or compete with those who espouse another approach.

The USCCB Hispanic Affairs website provides a schema of four stages in the development of diocesan Hispanic ministry, beginning with an outreach stage in which some parishes and groups initiate ministries with Hispanics, and culminating in a diocesan-wide stage in which all or the vast majority of parishes and diocesan offices are equipped to serve Hispanics as part of the regular ministries of the diocese.[35] Given the shortage of personnel and resources in many dioceses, the initial stage of strategically assigning effective priests, religious, and lay leaders to parishes and ministries that geographically access the greatest number of Hispanic Catholics is sage advice, as is the ongoing goal of striving toward the ideal of a comprehensive diocesan Hispanic ministry. The four approaches presented here further suggest that the strategic placement of trained Hispanic ministry leaders also entails considering the compatibility of a particular leader's ministerial vision with the needs of the faith community he or she will serve.

Implementing these approaches requires trained leaders for all the ministerial roles in the church. The shortage of Latino priests is a formidable drawback for Hispanic parish communities. Without priests access is curtailed to a central element of Catholic life: the sacraments, particularly the Eucharist. The vital ministries many Hispanic permanent deacons and their wives provide and their growing numbers suggest that enhancing their ministerial training and leadership will be all the more crucial, especially in parishes that need Spanish-speaking sacramental and pastoral care. Women religious and lay ecclesial ministers also help fill the parish ministerial gap, but only partially. The historical experience of priests and religious effectively enhancing ministry among their own ethnic group is a key motivation to foster Hispanic vocations for all of these leadership callings. But, barring an unexpected major shift in current trends, clergy and religious vocations will not "catch up" with population expansion anytime in the near future. Overall the demographic profile of leadership in Hispanic faith communities reveals three principal trends: a majority of non-Latinos serving as pastors, a preponderance of immigrants among Latino clergy, and a significant body of lay leaders who are hungry to receive faith formation and serve in ministry. These three groups exercise the widest influence in Hispanic faith communities, leading promoters of Hispanic ministries to urge that greater attention be given to their formation.

U.S. bishops have encouraged future priests to prepare for Hispanic ministry since the noteworthy post–World War II era efforts of Cardinal Francis Spellman in New York and Archbishop Robert Lucey in San Antonio. Father Kenneth Davis, who has led Hispanic ministry formation programs in three of the largest U.S. seminaries, maintains that seminary programs today should minimally require Spanish language skills; at least one required course in Hispanic Catholicism; opportunities for supervised ministry placements among Hispanics; and elective courses in topics such as worship, preaching, and youth and young adult ministry in Hispanic communities. His proposal is consistent with the bishops' *Encuentro and Mission* document, which directs that "seminarians must learn Spanish and become familiar with Hispanic culture. . . . This is no longer an option—it is a need."[36]

But for the most part Hispanic ministry formation is voluntary. The *Program of Priestly Formation* (*PPF*), the USCCB official instruction on seminaries, which is now in its fifth edition since the Second Vatican Council mandated seminary reform, states, "The study of the Spanish language and Hispanic cultures as well as other pastorally appropriate languages and cultures is essential for most dioceses and is strongly recommended for all seminarians." A growing emphasis on required subjects like philosophy in the latest edition of the *PPF*, however, often crowds Hispanic ministry preparation out of a seminarian's course of study. Thus the *PPF*'s tone of admonition, rather than the stronger language of *Encuentro and Mission*, reflects the overall trend in the forty-six major seminaries in the United States. Fewer than half of them have Hispanic immersion or Hispanic study programs. In most cases the program is optional, though sometimes a particular bishop will require his seminarians to participate. Other seminaries have courses in topics such as Hispanic ministry or multicultural ministry, and especially provision for students to study the Spanish language. On the whole, then, seminary preparation for ministering to Hispanics is more a matter of choice than the systematic inclusion into the core curriculum that Hispanic ministry advocates like Davis would prefer. Moreover, a number of seminaries have few or even no personnel who could encourage seminarians to select Hispanic ministry courses, such as regular faculty with expertise in Hispanic Catholicism, Latino faculty and administrators, or bilingual formation and spiritual directors who understand Latino cultures. Though somewhat dated and based solely on self-reporting, the most recent poll of priests ordained five years or less found that nearly two-thirds of them felt their seminary had prepared them "well" or "very well" for "working with multiple ethnic groups." Although this was a clear majority, it also ranked third to last on a list of thirteen elements of seminary formation the young priests were asked to rate.[37]

As with their seminary studies, further training in Hispanic cultures or the Spanish language is usually at the discretion of the individual priest after his ordination. A number of priests, along with women religious, deacons, and lay leaders, have endeavored to learn Spanish and Hispanic culture and religious traditions. Since the 1970s, training at pastoral centers like the Southeast Pastoral Institute in Miami and the Mexican American Cultural Center in San Antonio have formed clergy and other leaders in ministry specifically oriented toward the reality of Hispanics in the United States. More than three-quarters of the heads of Hispanic Catholic faith communities surveyed for the 2002 PARAL report said they knew about MACC, and fully 16 percent had trained or studied there. Other priests have attended intensive Spanish and cultural immersion programs such as those of the Seminario Hispano de Santa María de Guadalupe; the Maryknoll Language Institute in Cochabamba, Bolivia; and the various language schools in Cuernavaca, Mexico. After studying in the Curso de Hispanidad that the Legionaries of Christ conduct through their Sacerdos Institute and Universidad Anáhuac in Mexico City, Archbishop Allen H. Vigneron of Detroit said, "The information on Hispanic culture and religious experience were particularly useful. As I celebrate the Feast of Our Lady of Guadalupe this year I recognize that without my participation in the Curso de Hispanidad I would be at the periphery of this observance rather than at its heart, which is where I want to be."[38] Yet in most cases the ongoing formation that is typically required for priests, usually through annual workshops or study weeks, does not deal systematically with Hispanic ministry. A number of priests still have little formal linguistic or pastoral training to prepare them for ministry with their Hispanic parishioners.

Efforts to prepare Latino immigrant clergy for service in U.S. Catholic communities are also uneven. Hispanic ministry leaders like Father Davis maintain that "the Spanish language is a necessary but insufficient preparation for Hispanic ministry in the U.S.A. Neither returning missionaries from Latin America or even native Spanish speakers from those countries are sufficiently prepared for ministry to Hispanics in the U.S.A. solely because of their fluency in Spanish." Rather, they require training about "the very different pastoral realities between Mexican [and other Hispanic] families in the U.S.A. and those in Mexico [and Latin America] itself." Half of U.S. dioceses have orientation programs for émigré clergy. Other priests attend regional or national orientation programs such as the Maryknoll Cross-Cultural Services Acculturation Workshop in New York, the International Priest Internship at the Oblate School of Theology in San Antonio, or the Cultural Orientation Program for International Ministers at Loyola Marymount University in Los Angeles. Though some priests do not perceive a need to participate in such programs, since they bring the experience of serving Spanish-speaking communities from their native land, newcomer priests generally recommend such "acculturation training" as the best means to assist them with their ministries in the United States. Those who have participated are nearly unanimous that the orientation programs are "helpful." Yet only a third of immigrant priests participate in the programs when they first arrive in the United States, a fraction of the total that no doubt contributes to the difficulties some have encountered in adjusting to their new communities and ministries. Even more uncommon—in fact almost nonexistent—are coordinated efforts to prepare U.S. pastors or parishioners who receive immigrant priests in their parishes.[39]

The numerous lay Hispanics who desire to expand their faith formation and involvement in the church pose the most widespread challenge for Hispanic ministry leadership formation. In *Encuentro and Mission* the U.S. bishops stressed the need for institutional church commitment "to the academic and professional development of Hispanics" and particularly to "help Hispanic lay people attain degrees for church ministry." According to the bishops' document, the present low number of Hispanics enrolled in theology and pastoral leadership degree programs, the vast majority of which are at the master's level, is rooted in "a low educational attainment compared with other groups," limited resources dedicated to their education, and often "poor self-esteem." Immigrants who earned university degrees in their countries of origin frequently encounter difficulties in getting U.S. parishes, dioceses, and Catholic institutions of higher education to recognize their credentials. For those who prefer to study in Spanish, language is another obstacle: though about a fifth of the 273 lay ecclesial ministry formation programs in the United States offer instruction in Spanish, very few degree-granting programs do so.[40]

Financial considerations loom particularly large for lay leaders. Dioceses, religious communities, and sometimes in part candidates themselves pay as much as thirty or forty thousand dollars (or more) annually for a seminarian's education and living expenses. Conversely, funds for lay minister formation, particularly for degree programs with regular tuition costs, are comparatively sparse. Various dioceses and parishes help cover at least part of their lay leaders' formation costs. Some Catholic universities and seminaries offer scholarships or tuition reductions for lay ministry students. But a number of lay Catholics pay their own fees for formation programs, and they are nearly all responsible for their own living costs. Work and family responsibilities restrict their opportunities for study both financially and geographically. Along with a lack of qualifying credentials deemed acceptable in U.S. educational institutions, inadequate funding is the primary reason that the only accessible formation opportunity for many Hispanic laity is the diocesan or parish-based certification programs, or in some cases a program that a "mobile team" oversees in a diocese such as those of SEPI.

Initiatives to advance Hispanic participation in theology and pastoral ministry degree programs are ongoing. Father Mario Vizcaíno and his colleagues at SEPI established a Spanish-language program in collaboration with Barry University in Miami through which more than seventy leaders in Hispanic ministry have graduated with master's degrees since 1983.[41] In 2008 Arturo Chávez, president of the Mexican American Cultural Center, worked with the MACC board to rename it the Mexican American Catholic College and expand its mission to offer bilingual academic degrees in pastoral ministry. Their plan includes establishing accessible bachelor degree programs, which many Hispanic ministry leaders have averred are the most urgently needed but are difficult to implement because they typically require about three times the credit hours of a master's program. Several dioceses with certification programs renowned for preparing Hispanic pastoral leaders, such as the Tepeyac Institute in El Paso and the Ministry Formation Institute in San Bernardino, California, have teamed with the Loyola Institute for Ministry Extension Program at Loyola University in New Orleans to offer primarily English-language, distance-learning master's degrees. A few institutions of higher learning have onsite master's programs with Hispanic theology and ministry concentrations, such as those in the School of Theology and Ministry at Boston College and Catholic Theological Union in Chicago. Others, like the Institute for Hispanic/Latino Theology and Ministry at Barry and the Oblate School of Theology, have Doctor of Ministry programs with Hispanic concentrations. But as the leaders of these noteworthy efforts are quick to remark, they have scarcely begun to scratch the surface of the crying need to establish and enhance programs that are accessible to a broader range of Hispanic Catholics.

A number of Hispanic ministry leaders articulate a related challenge: discerning the content, approaches, and structures of ministry preparation programs, both for those pursuing academic degrees and for non-degree certifications. Many leaders avow that the programs should address the U.S. bishops' call in *Encuentro and Mission* to "incorporate Hispanic ministry, culture, and language" and "form ministers [who are] able to serve in a culturally diverse context." Hispanic leaders thus urge that formation program participants be provided with spiritual, pastoral, and human, as well as intellectual formation. Those who promote such concerns often accentuate what they call pastoral or practical theology, a term they use to connote the dynamic interaction between Catholic faith and the concrete circumstances in which pastoral leaders seek to live and proclaim it. Such an approach emphasizes intentional reflection on a faith community's everyday lived faith, including the historical, social, and cultural dynamics that shape their experience of God. Frequently, practitioners of this approach consciously proceed in a circular process from analyses of a faith community's situation, critical assessment in light of faith, ministerial action that seeks to transform the situation accordingly, and then a return to initiate these steps anew. But other church leaders, including a number of bishops, express concern that such an approach not detract from learning Catholic doctrine and teachings as the central priority for such programs. Both emphases can lead to extremes: reducing pastoral concerns to technique and sociological analysis, on the one hand, or presuming that accurate knowledge of church teaching is sufficient training for pastoral leaders, on the other. Hispanic ministry proponents contend that the result of either extreme is a false dichotomy between pastoral planning and sound doctrine. Thus, striking a balance between core content and forming participants in pastoral leadership skills is an ongoing challenge for ministry preparation programs.[42]

Hispanic ministry advocates further seek to ensure that Hispanics who complete certification programs proceed to active ministries. The Federación de Institutos Pastorales (FIP, the Federation of Pastoral Institutes), which Latino leaders founded in 1984 to develop Hispanic ministry formation efforts, established an accreditation process for formation programs in 2006 in part to enhance the credibility of non-degree certification programs with priests and other church personnel who hire and supervise lay ecclesial ministers. Some Hispanic ministry leaders argue that this effort will have only a minor influence, since it does not directly address the larger need of gaining program authorizations from the USCCB Commission on Certification and Accreditation, an official body of the bishops' conference. But all agree that recognition of credentials is a paramount concern. In the 2006 *Best Practices for Diocesan Ministry among Hispanics/Latinos* document, diocesan and regional directors of Hispanic ministry and members of the Bishops' Committee on Hispanic Affairs unanimously urged that "pastors recognize the [diocesan] formation program as a valuable resource to develop leadership within the parish" and help Hispanics who complete these programs transition to parish leadership responsibilities.[43]

Lay initiatives such as those of the Ruiz family and Mary's Ministries illustrate the most abundant resource Hispanics provide for Catholicism in the United States: an energetic leadership base. The large numbers of grassroots leaders and their extensive influence on friends, family, neighbors, and coworkers have attracted the attention of an increasing number of pastors, religious educators, and diocesan faith formation directors. A typical strategy that church personnel employ is to encourage key leaders' participation in an officially sanctioned program so that the faith formation they receive will filter down to members of their group or movement. In other instances, parish or diocesan staff members shape lay formation initiatives through their direct participation in them, as is the case with several priests in the Mary's Ministries faith courses. Consistent with the long-standing Catholic practice of fostering indigenous leaders for ministry among one's own group, some pastors address this formation challenge through periodically evaluating how their ministry activities engage new leaders. To cite one example, a program for baptismal preparation would be considered most effective if it not only provided engaging catechesis but also identified, called forth, and trained leaders to participate in giving that catechesis, particularly from among those who are natural leaders in their communities.

For many church officials, the fervent Hispanic Catholics in evangelization groups, apostolic movements, small faith communities, and youth ministries represent the organizational challenge of tapping into their leadership base and guiding it—some would say *controlling* it—so that it remains faithful to a canonical vision of the Catholic Church's teachings and mission. Hispanic ministry leaders contend that a particularly urgent challenge is to form their grassroots counterparts in a broad ecclesial vision that transcends the bounds of their own movement or group and diminishes competition between fellow leaders. Another frequent concern is that many charismatic leaders are overly focused on the pursuit of affective religious experience and ill equipped to deal with inevitable disappointments in their ministries and perceived defects in fellow church leaders, especially priests. These formidable challenges can detract from the dynamism of grassroots Hispanic leaders' evangelizing fervor and their contribution to the missionary outreach of U.S. Catholicism. The generally insufficient resources for Hispanic ministry heighten the significance of church personnel engaging these leaders who are a prime force for advancing Catholic faith in the ordinary circumstances of U.S. daily life.

CHAPTER

# Worship and Devotion

lvaro Dávila was surprised at his fellow parishioners, but more surprised at himself. Leaders at his parish, Nuestra Señora de la Merced (Our Lady of Mercy) in Chicago, had invited worshipers to wear the typical dress of their native countries to Sunday Mass. Back home in Guatemala, Dávila had been ashamed of the indigenous part of his heritage. He "learned to insult others by saying, 'You look like an Indian.'" After his parents labored to help him get an education, his mother had even encouraged him "not to say that she was my mother, so that I wouldn't feel tied to a 'peasant reality,' which in the capital city would only serve to make me part of a rejected heritage." In his younger days he had removed the photos of his father's ancestors from the wall of the family living room because he "was ashamed of them when my school friends came to visit me." To this day he can "remember the tears in my father's eyes" and he laments: "Every time I go home those pictures remind me of what I did."[1]

Now Dávila sat in a Chicago church amid a congregation proudly adorned with the indigenous colors and dress of their native lands. He wondered at his fellow Guatemalans especially, many of whom had fled as he did during the violent strife of the 1980s. Even the adults wore the special clothing, something he had never seen at home, where "the only time indigenous dress was allowed during the religious celebration of the town was for the festivals of the Virgin of Guadalupe, for which the boys and girls dressed as 'Little Indians,' but the adults never dressed up." Another bewildering thought followed: "My people, when they came to this country, brought with them those indigenous things that they had rejected for generations. It didn't matter how many rivers we had to cross; it didn't matter that we had never worn them; it didn't matter that we might never wear them." Looking at his own children beside him, he "trembled" to see them "dressed up like 'Tona,' the Indian woman who used to sell me corn drink every day." What was happening here? Why were people "celebrating what we had rejected our entire lives"?[2]

Dávila continued to ponder these questions while pursuing a master's degree at Chicago's Catholic Theological Union and in a series of pastoral leadership positions in Chicago. Eventually he returned to Guatemala to minister among those in his native land. His questions and his profound experience at Mass that Sunday taught him that "to be spiritual" involves getting "reconnected with my roots, with the source of my life." He calls this reconnection nothing less than a conversion, but not in the typical sense of leaving behind one's former self to become someone new. His transformation was just the opposite: it enabled him to embrace the beauty and dignity of his family, his ancestors, and of himself, even the indigenous part of him that he had been conditioned to conceal and despise. Dávila regards this "conversion to recognize ourselves as God made us" a life-altering enlightenment to see that no matter what rejection or shame we have experienced, each of us is a daughter or a son created in God's own image.[3]

Like Dávila, numerous Latino Catholics find deep meaning in the incorporation of their cultural expressions and faith traditions in celebrations of Catholic liturgy (the official prayer of the church like the seven sacraments), especially the Eucharist. Hispanics' feast days, saint images, artistic expressions, and penchant for processions are increasingly evident in U.S. Catholic parishes. As was the case for European Catholic immigrants of previous generations, Hispanics with roots in Latin America and the Caribbean also practice culturally inflected devotions, such as Puerto Rican veneration of their patron San Juan Bautista; Guatemalan faith in El Cristo Negro de Esquipulas (The Black Christ); and El Salvadoran dedication to Oscar Romero, the slain archbishop of San Salvador who is popularly acclaimed as a martyr and saint (and currently under official consideration in the Vatican for canonization). Other faith expressions abound among Hispanics, such as El Día de los Muertos (The Day of the Dead) and its communion with those who have gone before us; devotion to the Sacred Heart of Jesus; and the practice of keeping a home altar with images of Jesus, Mary, saints, and loved ones.

Latina and Latino Catholics have reflected on their faith for generations. But only over the past four decades have U.S. Hispanics produced a body of published theological literature and begun to exert a still evolving influence on theology departments, seminaries, and theological scholarship. These publications began with the groundbreaking work of Virgilio Elizondo, who wrote his first essay from a distinctly Mexican American perspective in 1972. By the end of the 1980s, the number of Hispanic Catholic theologians was sufficient for them to form their own professional association, the Academy of Catholic Hispanic Theologians of the United States (ACHTUS), which Arturo Bañuelas and Allan Figueroa Deck played the lead role in establishing. One of the most significant contributions ACHTUS members have made to theological investigations is their analyses of Latino faith traditions, which they have defended in response to pastoral ministers who indiscriminately criticize these practices and against theologians who overlook or explicitly dismiss them as a subject unworthy of scholarly examination. Theologians like Orlando Espín, the founding editor in 1993 of the ACHTUS *Journal of Hispanic/Latino Theology*, "insist that the people's faith be taken seriously as a true *locus theologicus* and not solely or mainly as a pastoral, catechetical problem." Elizondo asserts that the most important faith expressions for pastoral and theological analysis are those "celebrated voluntarily by the majority of the people, transmitted from generation to generation by the people themselves and which go on with the church, without it or even in spite of it." These foundational faith expressions are the everyday means through which people encounter God, whom they profess accompanies them during times of mourning and joy, rejection and welcome, hope and despair, death and life. Thus, according to Elizondo and his colleagues, these expressions are indeed a profound source for theological investigation, a window into the soul of Hispanic devotees that reveals significant insights about the horizon of their faith.[4]

Hispanics' dedication to their devotional traditions is so potent that it can lead to disagreement and conflict over their enactment. The most vociferous disagreements often involve practices like those of Santería that are partly rooted in African religions, or those based in indigenous religions like the healing practices of *curanderismo*. Both traditions are honored among a number of Hispanics, including those who self-identify as Catholics. But many pastoral leaders are suspicious of practices associated with these traditions or even condemn them as inimical to Catholic faith.[5]

A common occasion of disagreement in Catholic parishes is the *quinceañera*, a celebration that traditionally marks a young woman's maturation to adulthood. While for Hispanics the significance of this celebration can range from a means to honor family and cultural heritage, a rite of passage, a dedication of a young woman's life to her mother Mary of Guadalupe, or a festive gathering with friends and loved ones, many pastoral ministers perceive it primarily as an opportunity for evangelizing the young and enabling them to reaffirm their Catholic faith commitment. These divergent perspectives often lead to frustrations, as when pastoral ministers seek to restrain the banquet and dance that typically follow the church service or emphasize their evangelization approach with little regard for the family's "traditional" understandings of the event. The U.S. bishops responded to ongoing controversies through securing the 2007 Vatican approval of an official rite for quince-añera celebrations in the United States. Instructions for the rite direct that the young woman make an act of thanksgiving and of commitment to lead a Christian life before receiving a blessing from the priest at the end of Mass, or alternatively that the ritual be celebrated outside of the Mass. This direc-tive altered a previously common practice of celebrating the quinceañera rite in the midst of the Mass after the Scripture readings and homily, an order of service various pastoral leaders thought gave the mistaken impression that the quinceañera ritual has the same status as a sacrament rather than a ritual blessing. Yet tensions around this tradition remain, in some places so stridently that priests and other parish staff members outright refuse to celebrate quinceañeras.[6]

Such tensions reflect wider debates about the promotion of people's faith expressions, the relationship between popular piety and the liturgy, and the implementation of the liturgical renewal the Second Vatican Council man-dated. *Sacrosanctum Concilium* (Constitution on the Sacred Liturgy), the first document the bishops of Vatican II promulgated, strongly commends popular devotions, but enjoins that they be practiced "in accord with the sacred liturgy" and "lead the people to it." After the council, *Sacrosanctum Concilium*'s directive to foster as a primary goal the faithful's "full, conscious, and active participation" in the liturgy was the guiding principle for church leaders implementing the liturgical renewal. Hispanic ministry leaders and theologians promoted this as well as another principle rooted in *Sacrosanc-tum Concilium*, "liturgical inculturation," which Ansgar Chupungco, O.S.B., has defined as "the process whereby pertinent elements of a local culture are integrated into the texts, rites, symbols, and institutions employed by a local church for its worship." As *Sacrosanctum Concilium* itself avows, pas-toral leaders are to respect diverse people's wisdom and practices and even welcome them "into the liturgy itself, so long as they harmonize with its true and authentic spirit."[7]

Needless to say, *Sacrosanctum Concilium* and the liturgical renewal it initi-ated have received considerable attention among pastors, theologians, and church officials. Responding to one set of ongoing concerns, in 2001 the Vati-can Congregation for Divine Worship and the Discipline of the Sacraments issued a *Directory on Popular Piety and the Liturgy*. The document presents principles for the renewal of popular piety and an extensive set of guidelines for harmonizing popular piety with the liturgy. It also articulates various "fundamental presuppositions" to guide such efforts: "the superiority of the Liturgy in respect to other forms of cult; the dignity and legitimacy of popular piety; the pastoral need to avoid any opposition between the Liturgy and popular piety, [and] insurance that their various forms are not confused, so as to eschew the development of hybrid celebrations." Efforts to balance and implement these fundamental criteria in the concrete circumstances of local faith communities remain a source of pastoral concern and at times disagreement and dispute.[8]

Two devotional traditions widespread among all Latino groups have particular impact on worship and devotion in U.S. parishes: their dedication to the crucified Jesus and their devotion to his mother, Mary, the sorrowful mother who accompanies her son on the road to Calvary and who accompanies Latino faithful in images like the Cuban Nuestra Señora de la Caridad del Cobre and the Mexican Our Lady of Guadalupe. As Elizondo has attested, growing up as a Mexican American Catholic grounded his faith in these two celestial companions: Jesus of Nazareth, "suffering for us on the cross and with us in our struggles," and Our Lady of Guadalupe, "reigning majestically in the temple of our hearts while offering us all her love, defense, and protection."[9] Analyses of these core devotions reveal key elements of their faith that Hispanics bring to celebrations of the central act of Catholic worship: the Eucharist. Hispanic processions through city streets, feast days, efforts to enshrine holy images in churches, home and neighborhood devotions, participation in the Eucharist, and initiatives in liturgical renewal collectively alter the sacred landscape of numerous U.S. communities and the worship life of Catholic parishes.

Pastors and theologians like Elizondo have rightly deemed commemorations of Good Friday, the day Christ died, the Latino ritual "celebration *par excellence*."[10] The ritual of the *siete palabras*, or seven last words, of Christ is one popular tradition. Reflecting Hispanics' reverence for those who are dying and their tendency to cherish the final words their loved ones utter, this ritual includes a solemn proclamation of the seven statements Jesus made from the cross as remembered in the four canonical gospels. Each proclamation is accompanied with a sermon or some sort of meditation. Evening services can include traditions such as the *servicio del santo entierro*, or entombment of Jesus taken down from the cross, and the *pésame*, a wake service for Jesus with condolences offered to La Dolorosa, his sorrowful mother. Like other Catholics, Hispanics also participate in rites like the veneration of the cross, the gospel proclamation of the Lord's passion, and the Way of the Cross, which traces the way of Jesus from his trial to his crucifixion and placement in the tomb.

Latinos' widespread participation and leadership efforts to organize Way of the Cross rituals comprise their most conspicuous influence on Good Friday worship. These rituals have been prominent in Latin America for centuries and continue throughout the Spanish-speaking world in places like the Iztapalapa section of Mexico City, where devotees organize "the biggest and most ambitious annual passion play in the world today."[11] In many U.S. Hispanic faith communities this devotion encompasses a public reenactment of Jesus's trial, carrying of his cross, encounter with his sorrowing mother, and crucifixion, or simply an outdoor Way of the Cross procession. The rituals usually involve hundreds, if not thousands, of participants processing through neighborhoods and city streets.

Many Latino participants pray the Way of the Cross primarily as a plea for forgiveness. One of the traditional hymns Latinos sing during Way of the Cross processions, "Perdona a Tu Pueblo" (Forgive Us, Your People), confesses "we recognize our sin, which you have pardoned many times, forgive us Lord." The song verses meditate on the extent of Jesus's sacrifice for us—his "cruel wounds," "inhuman scourging," and the "thorns that pierced him"—and stir confidence that his "affectionate mercy" will grant pardon to the sinner. Ernest Muniz is a parishioner at San Antonio's San Fernando Cathedral who for more than a decade portrayed a Roman soldier in the annual Way of the Cross procession through the city's downtown corridor. He avows, "The experience becomes so real to me that I feel as if I'm right there with Jesus, a Roman soldier whipping him and kicking him." After participating in Jesus's crucifixion, Muniz sheds his costume, and "I go into the church, where I pray a lot and ask forgiveness" for his part in the suffering of Jesus.[12]

Participants are also drawn to what they describe as a personal encounter with Christ that they experience in these rituals. An opening meditation for the San Fernando Way of the Cross captures the desire to grow in faith:

> Jesus invites you and I to "come and follow me." It is easy to follow him along the lakes and fields of Galilee, but it becomes more difficult as he enters Jerusalem, and most difficult as he walks under the weight of the cross unto Calvary. Yet he still invites you and me to come and follow along his very own footsteps. Let us accept his invitation together that we might continue to grow in the appreciation of his love for us.

After participating in the Way of the Cross in Chicago's Pilsen neighborhood through "pouring rain and cutting wind," Emily Carrasquillo attested, "To me, this is the best thing that I can do. It's an act of faith because Jesus died for me and sacrificed his life for me." On that same occasion, Cardinal Francis George, O.M.I., of Chicago avowed that the significance of this faith event is that "the people who are walking along are reliving those mysteries [of Christ's passion and death] in their hearts."[13]

Large crowds and the public location of the devotion often draw media coverage, which in a number of instances has focused on the rituals' embodied messages of protest against violence and injustice. The opening line of a *Milwaukee Journal Sentinel* report observed: "The symbolism was blinding as an actor playing Jesus Christ was handed over to be crucified during a Good Friday re-enactment on the same [St. Anthony] church steps where a teenage boy was shot to death last month." This report went on to state that the ritual's "prayers and readings drew a line from the suffering and death of Christ 2,000 years ago to the social ills that plague this poor neighborhood today."[14]

Outrage at social injustice was the genesis of the annual Way of the Cross in the Pilsen neighborhood. On Christmas Eve 1976, ten children and two mothers died in a fire that swept through an apartment building two blocks from St. Vitus parish. Because they did not understand Spanish, Chicago firefighters who responded to this emergency were unaware that these victims were trapped inside the burning building. In a public meeting held after the tragedy, parishioners from St. Vitus and other Pilsen parishes argued that these deaths resulted from a lack of Spanish-speaking firefighters, as well as absentee landlords, overcrowded housing, and city neglect of public services. The following Good Friday they began their annual Way of the Cross as an expression of faith intended to draw the community together in a collective act of solidarity, remember their lost loved ones, and connect their deaths and the plight of the Pilsen neighborhood with the unjust crucifixion of Jesus. To this day the annual procession links the Way of the Cross with "community problems such as housing, crowded schools, immigration and gang violence." In the words of Father James Colleran, who was the pastor of St. Vitus in the year of the first Pilsen Way of the Cross, "the important thing is to relate the stations to what is happening in the community."[15]

Alyshia Gálvez's study of Mexican immigrants in New York examines El Viacrucis del Inmigrante (The Way of the Cross of the Immigrant) conducted through the financial district of Manhattan. The organizers for this Way of the Cross are the leaders of Asociación Tepeyac de New York, an umbrella organization of parish Guadalupe societies that a Mexican Jesuit brother, Joel Magallán, took the lead to establish in 1997 with pastors who had growing numbers of Mexican émigré parishioners. Undocumented Mexican immigrants are the primary organizers and participants in the procession. The links between Jesus's suffering and that of the undocumented are repeatedly underscored: the procession begins at the offices of the U.S. Citizenship and Immigration Services, Roman soldiers order Jesus to carry his cross with the command "*¡Camina, camina ilegal!*" (Walk, walk illegal!), and the prayer booklet for the event says it is dedicated "in memory of those migrants who have fallen in the struggle to survive with greater dignity, outside of their land, far from their families." Meditations for the traditional fourteen Stations of the Cross expound on the agony of Jesus and the undocumented, such as the second station, which compares Jesus's bearing his cross and suffering undeservedly to the immigrants' cross of separation from their families resulting from circumstances of poverty beyond their control.[16]

Some critics have bemoaned the potential for false hope or fatalism among participants in such devotions, echoing the observation of Catherine Bell that often in rituals "temporary inversions or suspensions of the usual order of social relations dramatically acknowledge that order as normative." Organizers of El Viacrucis del Inmigrante have no illusion that their annual prayers and protests will dramatically alter U.S. immigration policy, but of course they cannot control the expectations for social change that might arise among participants in these rituals. Pilsen Way of the Cross devotees won a small victory when their protests convinced the Chicago Park District to abandon a plan to flatten the park hill where annually they stage the crucifixion. But a few years later Park District officials had the hill flattened. Today devotees are struggling against gentrification in the Pilsen neighborhood, even along the very route of the Good Friday procession.[17]

In other instances, Latino devotees have successfully contested local officials' decrees that thwart their desire to enact the Way of the Cross publicly. When town leaders of Cicero, a western suburb of Chicago, denied a permit for the annual procession of St. Anthony of Padua parish, Gaudencio Gutiérrez, an eighteen-year old Mexican immigrant who was one of nearly sixty parishioners organizing the live Way of the Cross, protested the cancellation and declared he would "take part in it anyway." Associate pastor Father Marco Mercado threatened, "If we have to be arrested, I think we will. . . . we have the right to express our faith." Town officials based their decision on a new city ordinance enacted to prohibit the Ku Klux Klan from holding a parade. Cicero board president Betty Loren-Maltese accused pastor James Kastigar of "run[ning] to the media" and declared, "I think it's just appalling, especially for a priest." She even warned that the parish's "not-for-profit status" was "in jeopardy." Public pressure and the negotiation of Chicago archdiocesan attorneys eventually led to an eleventh-hour agreement. Devotees prayed the Way of the Cross with what they estimated to be "twice the normal 1,200 participants." They also expressed their ongoing disgust over the controversy, altering the words of the traditional Spanish song "forgive your people" to "forgive your town."[18]

Some Latinos have contested what they believe is an overly politicized approach to the Way of the Cross. Wayne Ashley's study of Good Friday rituals at St. Brigid's parish on Manhattan's Lower East Side revealed significant tensions between activist Euro-American priests and their Puerto Rican parishioners. Congregants objected to the clergy's overt political messages linked to Christ's way to Calvary, such as in 1991 when one station presented before a Mobil gas station included the prayer reflection: "This latest venture [the first Gulf War] was undertaken so that we might have inexpensive gasoline to fuel an important American idol, the automobile. . . . Lord, have mercy on us!" One woman said such antiwar sentiment had driven many people from the church, especially those who had family and friends in the military. Conversely, she noted that at her hometown parish in Puerto Rico: "They put a big tree in the plaza, and they put the names of all the people that gone to the Gulf, and light candles. And nobody died from my town. They came home safe. That's what we wanted in the church, but he [the priest] wouldn't." Another parishioner assessed the situation more comprehensively: "We Puerto Ricans have real religion. We do not involve politics with religion. . . . He [the priest] talks a lot about politics. We want to hear religion."[19]

Other Hispanic leaders counter that their Good Friday traditions are not merely political protests intended to effect social change, but rather holy events that enable them to endure present hardships with faith and encourage them to struggle for the transformation of their personal and collective lives. Karen Mary Davalos's study of Pilsen's Way of the Cross encompassed conversations with leaders like Claudia, one of the event's first coordinators, who considers this public ritual to be "the real way of praying," because it is "the opportunity to reflect and analyze how we are living and the things we have to [do] in order to have a better life." For many participants, the ritual mediates an encounter with God that transcends limiting distinctions like those between religious experience and political activism, our "secular" age and the "sacred" time of Jesus, Chicago and Jerusalem, Pilsen and Calvary Hill. Another Pilsen leader, Patricia, summed up the power of the event to unite current struggles with those of Jesus: "Christ suffered way back two thousand years ago, but he's still suffering now. His people are suffering. We're lamenting and wailing. And also we are a joyful people at the same time. . . . So this is not a story, this is not a fairy tale. It happened, and it's happening now."[20]

Pastors and liturgists have asserted that Hispanics' focus on Christ's passion can diminish the centrality of the resurrection for Christian faith. Many note the typically smaller attendance among Hispanics at the Easter Vigil or Easter Sunday Masses as compared to their participation in the processions and rituals of Good Friday. Consequently, these pastoral leaders seek to curb, reorient, or reinterpret Hispanic prayer on Good Friday and encourage greater participation at Easter services. Hispanic ministry leaders rejoin that Easter celebrations among European-descent Catholics tend to exhibit the "crown without the cross," the triumphalist distortion of celebrating Christ's victory and salvation without confronting the suffering of Good Friday and the need for continuous conversion. They further contend that it is pastoral hypocrisy to take away Latinos' symbols of a suffering Christ without struggling to eliminate the root causes of personal and collective tribulations that make those symbols so meaningful. Hispanic theologians like Espín add that Latino devotions to the crucified Christ are "not a direct or indirect denial of the Resurrection," since "the crucified and dying Jesus [is] always addressed as eternally living."[21] While church teaching dictates that Christ's death and resurrection are intrinsically related and merit complementary emphasis in Catholic faith and worship, disagreements continue about the best means to ritually mediate this balanced approach in parish worship.

Internal discord among Way of the Cross organizers themselves takes various forms. A number of disagreements concern the proper way to conduct the ritual, often with divergent perspectives based on how leaders remember the worship practices from past years, their childhood or, for immigrants, from their place of origin. Some disputes center on interpretation, such as a controversy with the Pilsen Way of the Cross regarding the age of the woman chosen to enact the part of Mary. Early organizers had chosen young women, teenagers or at most in their early twenties, based on the scriptural witness that Mary was a young maiden (Luke 1:26–27). But mothers involved in later processions successfully argued that this was not correct, since Mary would have aged by the time the adult Jesus was put to death. Applying Mary's grief to that of mothers who had lost sons to drugs and violence, communal leader Patricia (previously cited) posed the question that settled the argument: "What did she look like when the sword pierced her heart when she saw her son die? What do women look like when their sons die?"[22]

Patricia's identification with Mary reveals a core intuition of Latinas and Latinos about Good Friday: their prayers and faith expressions are not just about Jesus but his mother, Mary, too and, even more, about the mutual love of mother and son they believe death cannot break. The concluding verse of "Perdona a Tu Pueblo" reminds those who sing it that "from the cross you [Jesus] gave us your mother." After the crucifixion, traditionally at three o'clock in the afternoon, Mary's presence becomes even more prominent as devotees turn their attention to the sorrowful mother who mourns her son and lays him to rest in the tomb. Although the official Roman Catholic liturgy for Good Friday has no sustained prayerful remembrance of Jesus's burial or of Mary on that fateful night, Hispanic faith expressions relive these events of the Lord's passion. In some places an evening candlelight procession accompanies Mary and the crucified body of her son through the streets around the church. The *pésame* (condolence) given to Mary often encompass moving testimonies of mothers and other community members who have lost loved ones and ritually conjoin their sorrow to Mary's. Good Friday connects devotees with Jesus's sacrifice for them, but also with Mary's agony of witnessing her son's passion, with her strength as a woman of faith, and with her maternal love for her son and all her children.

The love of Mary is also honored in Hispanics' veneration of the respective Marian patronesses from their countries of origin. As Espín has noted, among Latinas and Latinos "it is difficult to find, besides the crucified Christ, another more powerful religious symbol" than Mary. At least ten national and regional images adorn a chapel at the Misión Católica de Nuestra Señora de las Americas near Atlanta, including Our Lady of Charity from Cuba, Our Lady of Guadalupe and Our Lady of San Juan de los Lagos from Mexico, Our Lady of Altagracia (Highest Grace) from the Dominican Republic, Our Lady of Copacabana from Bolivia, Our Lady of Suyapa from Honduras, and Our Lady of Peace from El Salvador. Hispanic pastoral leaders have promoted Catholic unity by encouraging Latinos and others to appreciate each other's Marian traditions, an initiative enacted in some parishes through a devotional display or procession of parishioners' varied Marian images on a feast day dedicated to Mary, such as the Immaculate Conception or the Assumption.[23]

Every Spanish-speaking country in Latin America and the Caribbean, along with Portuguese-speaking Brazil, has a national Marian patroness. The Dominican Republic's Our Lady of Altagracia is recognized as "the first evangelizer of the Americas," since she is associated with the first place Spanish Catholics sought to spread their faith in the New World. Our Lady of Copacabana is esteemed both as patroness of Bolivia and as the "Queen of the Incas" among Quechua and Aymara indigenous peoples. Like the famous Marian shrine at Lourdes in France, various prominent Latin American images are associated with the Immaculate Conception, such as Our Lady of the Miracles of Caacupé of Paraguay, Our Lady of Aparecida of Brazil, and Nicaragua's Our Lady of the Immaculate Conception of El Viejo.[24]

Nuestra Señora de la Caridad del Cobre's rise to prominence in Cuba illustrates the evolution of a Marian image from a local to a national patroness. The devotion emerged during the early seventeenth century in the mining settlement of El Cobre near the southeast coast of Cuba. The Spanish Crown confiscated the mines and the administration of slaves who worked them in 1670, changes the now "royal slaves" supported because they afforded the slaves greater autonomy in local affairs and in their everyday lives. Royal slave

Juan Moreno later gave the first documented testimony on the origins of the devotion. His 1687 account stated that around 1612 he and two Indian brothers, Rodrigo and Juan Joyos (spelled "Hoyos" in contemporary accounts), found the image with the inscription "I am the Virgin of Charity" in the Bay of Nipe. Devotees deemed the image to be miraculous because it was found floating in the water but not wet; mysterious lights led authorities to understand Our Lady of Charity wanted to be enshrined near the mines where the slaves worked; and soon her faithful attributed many wonders to her intercession. Various factors led to the ongoing expansion of the devotion to Our Lady of Charity: reports of miracles and shrine supporters' promotion of their occurrence, a consequent increase in donations that helped expand facilities and ritual celebrations, the fervor of El Cobre royal slaves who grounded their claims to dignity and self-determination in their patroness, the pastoral efforts of chaplains assigned to the sanctuary, and priests' writings that codified the cult and enhanced its ecclesiastical legitimacy. In 1756 Cuban bishop Pedro Agustín Morell de Santa Cruz observed that "the sanctuary of El Cobre is the richest, most frequented, and most devout on the Island, and the Lady of Charity the most miraculous of all those venerated [in Cuba]."[25]

Her fame now solidified and still growing, it is not surprising that when Cuban soldiers fought for independence from Spain in the Ten Years' War of 1868–1878 and the victorious conflict of 1895–1898, they sought her protection, referring to her as "*la Virgen Mambisa*" (the Revolutionary Virgin). Veterans of the latter struggle gathered at a 1915 reunion in El Cobre to celebrate Our Lady of Charity's September 8 feast day and "prostrate themselves before her altar" in thanksgiving for her protection. They petitioned Pope Benedict XV to officially name her the patroness of Cuba, which he did the following year. Devotion to Our Lady of Charity in the United States continues to invoke her protection of Cuba, as is evident in feast-day celebrations and in the Caridad del Cobre shrine that Cuban exiles established in Miami. Like other sacred sites, devotees offer personal prayers to their patroness: Thomas Tweed's study of the shrine revealed that three primary categories of intercessory petition are for healing, help in conception and childbirth, and marriage and family needs. But the most conspicuous collective meaning is exile faith and nationalism. José Martí, the father of Cuban independence, and Father Félix Varela, a revered priest and early Cuban nationalist, are prominently enshrined. So is the Cuban flag. A striking mural that exile Teok Carrasco created places Our Lady of Charity at the center of Cuban history, from colonial settlement, to the winning of independence, down to the current painful exile. Rituals at the shrine include rites of "consecration to the Virgin of children born in exile," prayer and festive gatherings designated for those with origins in specified provinces and municipalities of Cuba, and a popular weekend Mass that is broadcast to Cuba through the federally funded Radio Martí network. One female devotee succinctly summed up the central focus of Cuban exile devotion: "The Virgin is the patroness of Cuba, and above all we want to petition her to make Cuba free."[26]

Devotion to Our Lady of Guadalupe has also developed over centuries, including its expansion to what is now the United States beginning in the Spanish colonial era. Guadalupan devotees acclaim the Nahuatl-language *Nican mopohua* (a title derived from the document's first words, "here is recounted") as the foundational text of the Guadalupe tradition. The text narrates the well-known tale of the tender encounters between Guadalupe and the indigenous neophyte Juan Diego, whom Pope John Paul II canonized a saint in 2002. Guadalupe's first words to him were "dignified Juan, dignified Juan Diego." She sent him to request that Juan de Zumárraga, the first bishop of Mexico, build a temple in her honor at Tepeyac (in present-day Mexico City), where she would "show and give to all people all my love, my compassion, my help, and my protection." In one of the most moving passages of the apparitions narrative, he returned to her from an unsuccessful interview with the bishop and asked that she send another messenger, "who is respected and esteemed," because he judged himself too incapable and unworthy. Her response was tender but firm: "Know well in your heart that there are not a few of my servants and messengers to whom I could give the mandate of taking my thought and my word so that my will may be accomplished. But it is absolutely necessary that you personally go and speak about this, and that precisely through your mediation and help my wish and my desire be realized." Her words to Juan Diego in a later encounter when he was troubled about the illness of his uncle, Juan Bernardino, are the most quoted among contemporary devotees: "Do not let your countenance and heart be troubled; do not fear that sickness or any other sickness or anxiety. Am I not here, your mother?" Juan Diego's faithfulness to Guadalupe's bidding was eventually rewarded. After several interviews the bishop came to believe when Juan Diego presented him exquisite flowers that were out of season and the image of Guadalupe miraculously appeared on the humble *indio*'s *tilma* (cloak).[27]

Dramatic reenactments of the apparitions narrative are one of the most common ritual practices at parish celebrations of Guadalupe's December 12 feast day. Like Juan Diego, numerous Hispanic devotees have stinging memories of being ignored or rejected. They have met polite disdain or outright hostility in their dealings with sales clerks, bosses, coworkers, teachers, police officers, health care providers, social workers, government employees, professional colleagues, and even from fellow Catholic parishioners and leaders. Like Juan Diego, many are tempted to internalize the cumulative effects of such incidents and perceive themselves as inferior. Thus it is not surprising that devotees resonate with the liturgical drama of the lowly Juan Diego's rejection, his encounter with a loving mother, his calling to be Guadalupe's chosen messenger, his unwavering faith, and his final vindication as an unexpected hero. Devotees ardently attest that Guadalupe uplifts and strengthens them as she did Juan Diego. Thus they confess that the Guadalupe narrative is true: it reveals the deep truth of their human dignity and exposes the lie of social inequalities and experiences that diminish their fundamental sense of worth.[28]

The most widespread parish devotional tradition for the Guadalupe feast is *las mañanitas* (literally "morning songs"), a tribute offered before daybreak that often leads into the celebration of Mass for her feast. Devotees' offerings of flowers express their love and thanks to their mother. Other devotions accompany the song tributes, such as prayer of the rosary, Scripture readings, and testimonies or meditations about Guadalupe. The sentiment of joyful veneration resounds in the song offerings like the beginning and ending of the traditional hymn "Buenos Días, Paloma Blanca" (Good Morning, White Dove): "Buenos días, Paloma Blanca, hoy te vengo a saludar.... Recibe estas mañanitas, de mi humilde corazón" (Good morning, White Dove, today I come to greet you.... Receive these *mañanitas* from my humble heart). Most of Guadalupe's faithful know these songs by heart and internalize their collective emphases on thanking her; seeking her blessing and protection; and acclaiming her motherhood, purity, miraculous apparitions to Juan Diego, and providential connection to Mexicans and the Mexican nation.[29]

Devotees such as Esperanza Gama attest that the primary relationship between Guadalupe and her faithful is "a strong mother who takes care of her children." Her fellow Chicago resident Catalina Andrade agrees: "For me and all Mexicans, she is our mother.... Talk to her. She listens." Her children's most fundamental belief about her is that she never abandons them. As Mary Esther Bernal of San Antonio put it, "She is love, but first and foremost she is hope in all that we face." Similar convictions are illuminated in a *mañanitas* meditation of Socorro Durán, director of Hispanic ministry at St. Leander parish in the diocese of Oakland, who grew up across the street from the Guadalupe basilica in Mexico City before migrating to California. Durán told her listeners, "Hope is very important, especially when people are discouraged by sickness, poverty, lack of a job, lack of schooling for their children, the insecurity of being undocumented, and on and on." She reminded them that their times are "not that different" from Mexico at the time of Juan Diego or the time of Jesus two thousand years ago: "They didn't have many reasons to hope either." But just as Christ's birth and Juan Diego's encounter with Guadalupe were both "a sudden, unexpected event which then and now brings hope and expectation to us," so too the Guadalupe feast "renews hope in our wilting spirits."[30]

Some Guadalupe celebrations explicitly accentuate the link between Guadalupe and social concerns. One homilist for a Guadalupe feast-day Mass in San Antonio emphatically challenged devotees with the message, "We cannot love Our Lady of Guadalupe unless we love *el pobre* [the poor one] Juan Diego with the commitment of our lives." Leaders at the Jesuit-run Dolores Mission in East Los Angeles have invited guests from their parish Guadalupano Shelter to enact the apparitions drama, underscoring their homeless guests' dignity as children of Guadalupe and as the Juan Diegos who struggle in today's world. Asociación Tepeyac de New York organizes an annual Carrera Internacional de la Antorcha Guadalupana (International Guadalupan Torch Run), in which over a two-month period runners relay a torch nearly three thousand miles from the Basilica of Our Lady of Guadalupe in Mexico City; up Mexico's eastern seaboard; across the U.S. border at Brownsville, Texas; through communities in the southern United States; past the White House; and then to New York City, where it arrives at St. Patrick's Cathedral for the Guadalupe feast celebration. Runners wear shirts declaring themselves "*mensajeros de un pueblo dividido por la frontera*" (messengers of a people divided by the border). Many runners participate "out of devotional impulse" with little "awareness of or interest in the political goals" of drawing attention to immigration reform, and some critics have objected to what they perceive as the political use of Guadalupe. But leaders like María Zúñiga, the first female *capitana* (captain) for the torch run, attest, "We go out to take her message like the Indian Juan Diego did. . . . [We] struggle in search of a more just and dignified life, where we can walk together as a great human community."[31]

The fervor of Guadalupan devotion has fueled various controversies over representations of her image, as in 1998 when parents were outraged that Santa Fe elementary school principal Bobbie Gutiérrez banned on school property "any outerwear that is deemed gang-related, for example, Our Lady of Guadalupe shirts." Though local law enforcement officers supported the principal, Santa Fe archbishop Michael Sheehan summarized the opposing view of Guadalupe devotees, who convinced Gutiérrez to rescind her policy: "Mary is Our Lady of Peace, not Our Lady of the Gang, and I think we shouldn't allow gang members or anyone else to take away the symbols that are sacred. I don't think this sacred image, which is so important to Catholics, should be discouraged because a few people abuse it." Three years later, grassroots devotees and church leaders protested an exhibit in Santa Fe that included Alma López's digital artwork "Our Lady" depicting Guadalupe in floral garlands with her legs and midsection exposed. Though art museum officials did not acquiesce to demands that López's art be removed, as Linda Hall has averred, "The perception of her [Guadalupe's] strength was part of what made the conflict about how that [power] should be accessed so heated." Disagreements about representation also transpire in parishes like Our Lady of Guadalupe in Denver, where in 2009 pastor Father Benito Hernandez had a wall constructed in front of a mural depicting Guadalupe's appearance to Juan Diego because it "detracted from the central focus of the holy presence of the Blessed Sacrament." Parishioners protested that "Our Lady of Guadalupe [had been] crudely hidden behind a white wall" and their "inspiring source of devotion, pride and faith" removed, but to no avail.[32]

Mexican dedication to the Guadalupe image can also lead to ethnic rivalry within parishes. As the Mexican population in New York tripled during the 1990s, newcomers to Our Lady of Mercy parish in the Bronx worked with their pastor to create an outdoor Guadalupe shrine. Established Puerto Rican parishioners sarcastically asked the priest: "Why don't you name the church the Virgin of Guadalupe?" At St. Cecilia parish in East Harlem, another dynamic unfolded. When Mexican émigrés enshrined a Guadalupe image in a niche within the church, they stimulated what their pastor regarded as a "renewed interest in patron saints" among fellow parishioners who pressed for equally prominent public displays of their own celestial patrons: for blacks, the mulatto St. Martin de Porres; Puerto Ricans, Nuestra Señora de la Divina Providencia; Ecuadorans, the Virgin of Cisne; and Filipinos, their customary regal-looking child Jesus. Pastoral leaders from less populous Hispanic groups, like Colombian émigré Fanny Tabares, are keenly aware of intra-Hispanic relations in such communities. Tabares notes that many South American immigrants teach their children the Spanish language and encourage their children to have a healthy pride in "their culture, their ancestors, their social and religious customs." However, she also observes that South Americans in the United States are "a minority group within the Hispanic community" who make great sacrifices to "accept as their own customs which, though Hispanic, originated in countries not their own." Many participate in the religious traditions of other Hispanic groups, especially the predominant Guadalupe feast, and can be chagrined at the comparatively tepid appreciation for Catholic feasts from their own countries of origin, such as the Peruvian feast of El Señor de los Milagros (The Lord of Miracles), the Colombian Our Lady of Chiquinquira, the Venezuelan Our Lady of Coromoto, and the Argentinian Our Lady of Lujan.[33]

Some Latinos complain that "pastors have sought to eliminate the practices of popular devotion" because they allegedly detract from "true" evangelization, or pastors have stated that these practices "should only be used as a stepping stone to greater faith maturity and then dropped." Hispanic ministry proponents argue that such approaches usually "alienate Latinos from the church." Conversely, pastors and liturgists have bemoaned that Marian and other "popular devotions are nothing more than 'a Catholicism of a day' . . . stressing great but isolated moments of fervor, yet failing to translate into deep and lasting spiritual transformation and sustained participation in the life of the church." One priest with half a century of experience in Hispanic ministry asserted that many devotees seem "locked into" their "attraction to the Virgin [of Guadalupe] as a source of favors" and pay scant attention to living out the discipleship and evangelization that church leaders proclaim as Guadalupe's call to her faithful. Other pastoral leaders note that although most devotees are familiar with the Catholic belief that Mary is not God but an intercessor before God, in practice many turn to her as a mother who herself wields divine power. They cite comments they have heard from Hispanic devotees, such as "[We] always pray to Mary, because we go to the mother to get what we want from the father" or "It is easier to go to Mary, because she is a woman." As Elizabeth Johnson has shown, these perspectives have a long history among Roman Catholics of various backgrounds. For various pastors, such understandings raise concerns not only about putting the human Mary in the place of God, but also about distorted images of God as a stern father who lacks compassion and, indeed, of a dysfunctional celestial family in which one needs maternal intervention to cajole unpredictable paternal authority.[34]

One of the most frequent sources of disagreement and misunderstanding related to parish Guadalupe celebrations occurs in years when her feast falls on a Sunday. Catholic liturgical norms state that Sunday Mass has precedence over feast days—in this case the Mass for the third Sunday of Advent, the liturgical season that precedes Christmas. When this happened at St. Leander parish near Oakland several years ago, the parish liturgy director declared that no Mass for Guadalupe could be celebrated. Devotees were distraught and bewildered. How could a parish that called itself Catholic fail to offer their celestial mother proper veneration on her feast day? After some confusion and consternation, the pastoral staff agreed to a compromise. A Mass in honor of Guadalupe would be celebrated at 5:00 a.m., early enough so as not to upset the regular Sunday Mass schedule. Pastoral leaders reasoned, "How many would come at such an early hour anyway?" To their amazement, despite the cold and dark winter morning, by the time the Mass began a standing-room-only assembly had gathered. Similar scenarios play out around the country whenever Guadalupe's feast falls on a Sunday, with pastors and liturgy coordinators either permitting or disallowing Mass for the feast, or reaching a compromise for a celebration that either is subsumed into the designated Sunday Advent liturgy or does not interfere with the regular Sunday schedule.[35]

Proponents of Hispanic ministry have sought to articulate why traditions like Guadalupe are of such importance and, more generally, to foster greater understanding about Hispanic faith expressions and to promote the liturgical renewal that Vatican II mandated. Pastoral institutes like the Mexican American Cultural Center began Hispanic liturgical renewal initiatives in the early 1970s through efforts to examine Hispanic faith traditions theologically and pastorally, organize formation programs for worship leaders in Hispanic communities, and develop resource materials like bilingual ritual books for celebrating the sacraments. The Northeast Hispanic Catholic Center accomplished the formidable task of preparing and publishing for U.S. Hispanic communities a three-volume Spanish-language lectionary, the liturgical book with the assigned Scripture readings for celebrations of the Eucharist. But the national organization whose leaders have focused their primary attention on shaping the liturgical renewal among Hispanics is the Instituto de Liturgia Hispana (now the Instituto Nacional Hispano de Liturgia). Hispanic leaders established the Instituto in 1979 "to study, develop, and promote the liturgical life of the Hispanic communities in the United States" and to foster "the inculturation of liturgical celebrations in order to help the meaningful and complete participation of the total assembly."[36]

Currently the Instituto Nacional Hispano de Liturgia faces the same severe funding challenges that have beset national Hispanic Catholic ministry groups across the country. Yet its leaders strive to build on a record of service developed over three decades. They have convened national conferences, published widely on topics related to Hispanic liturgy, and coordinated liturgy planning for national events such as the 1985 Third Hispanic Pastoral Encuentro. They have also served as advisers and members of national liturgical commissions and ably assisted the national Bishops' Committee on the Liturgy (now the Committee on Divine Worship) in the Spanish translation of official liturgical texts, especially through the efforts and expertise of Instituto leader Rosa María Icaza, C.C.V.I. Collaboration with the Bishops' Committee on the Liturgy was solidified in 1982 with the establishment of a subcommittee on Hispanic liturgy. Through this structure bishops and Instituto members were instrumental in initiatives such as Vatican recognition of Spanish as a liturgical language in the United States, the adoption for U.S. parishes of the Spanish-language sacramentary book that priests use to preside at the Eucharist throughout the Spanish-speaking world, and the elevation of annual Guadalupe celebrations from the official rank of "memorial" to "feast" in the United States, effectively making it obligatory in U.S. parishes.[37]

One concern of Instituto Nacional Hispano de Liturgia and other Hispanic ministry leaders is the efforts in some faith communities to celebrate bilingual or multilingual liturgies, which generally they support as long as they do not replace Masses in Spanish. Leaders like current Instituto president, Father Juan Sosa, are adamant that such celebrations not become occasions "in which the groups are represented by token improvisations with a sprinkling of cultural symbols." Rather, in the words of Mark Francis, C.S.V., worship leaders need to bear in mind that "the primary purpose of multicultural liturgy is not to celebrate cultural diversity" but "to help each member of the assembly participate fully, actively and consciously in the liturgy." Recommendations typically offered to enact this vision include celebrating these liturgies only on select feast days, such as Pentecost, or a Marian feast like the Assumption; making the words of the prayers and Scripture readings as accessible to as many in the congregation as possible; avoiding excessive translated duplication of spoken words through skillful use of language and printed worship aids; and paying special attention to nonverbal communications like art, environment, symbol, gesture, and prayerful silence. Hispanic pastoral musicians have joined their fellow ministers from other backgrounds in preparing multicultural choirs and composing bilingual or multilingual music to enhance such liturgical celebrations.[38]

The overriding parish liturgical concern of Hispanic ministry leaders has been the expansion of Sunday Masses in the Spanish language or in a worship style that resonates with Hispanics. A 1982 Instituto Nacional Hispano de Liturgia survey found that a wide cross-section of Latino Catholic parishioners "almost unanimously . . . made liturgical music their first priority" for renewing the liturgy. Hispanic pastoral musicians have sought to enhance Eucharistic celebrations through their sung prayer leadership and their composition of numerous hymns, antiphons, and psalm responses in rhythms ranging from those of the Caribbean to those of Mexico and the Southwest United States. They have also convened various Hispanic Pastoral Musicians Conferences like those organized biennially under the auspices of the Southwest Liturgical Conference. The growing repertoire of Hispanic liturgical music is published in several collections from U.S. Catholic presses such as *Flor y Canto* and *Cantos del Pueblo de Dios*. Both of these anthologies contain hundreds of selections and are in a second edition with Oregon Catholic Press and World Library Publications, respectively.[39]

Many immigrants are moved when they hear songs in U.S. parishes that they recognize from their home country. Some selections have been widely sung across Hispanic groups in the United States, such as the "Ofertorio Nicaragüense" that accompanies the preparation of the gifts of bread and wine, or the "offertory" part of the Mass. The song refrain echoes the prayer the priest says during the preparation rite as well as that rite's deeper significance: "Te ofrecemos Padre nuestro, con el vino y con el pan, nuestras penas y alegrías, el trabajo, nuestro afán" (We offer you, our Father, with the wine and bread, our joys and pains, [our] work, our zeal). Then the verses integrate Hispanic cultural sensibilities with the liturgical action, such as the first verse, which unites agrarian and biblical imagery; the custom to *persignarse* (make the sign of the cross) and honor the cross in daily life; a strong communitarian ethic; and a Catholic understanding of communion as becoming the Body of Christ: "Como el trigo de los campos, bajo el signo de la cruz, se transformen nuestras vidas en el cuerpo de Jesús" (Like the wheat of the fields, under the sign of the cross, transform our lives into the body of Jesus). Similarly, hymns composed for the Mass as part of the Vatican II liturgical renewal express Catholic Eucharistic spirituality in Hispanic idiom. "Un Pueblo que Camina" (A People That Journey), another song widely employed among diverse Hispanic groups, announces a sense of the Eucharist as the prophetic fiesta of a people who struggle but simultaneously celebrate a joyful foretaste of their ultimate destiny with God: "Somos un pueblo que camina, y juntos caminando podremos alcanzar otra ciudad que no se acaba, sin penas ni tristezas: ciudad de eternidad" (We are a people who journey, and walking together we can reach another city that doesn't end, one without pain or sadness: the eternal city).[40]

Like their fellow Catholics, when the Eucharist was shifted to vernacular languages after Vatican II and lay ministerial roles in worship developed, Hispanics fostered the liturgical renewal by preparing themselves to assume roles such as lectors who proclaim the Scripture readings, Eucharistic ministers who distribute the consecrated bread and wine to the faithful, and hospitality ministers who greet worshipers as they arrive at church. Many of the first Hispanic liturgical ministers came from apostolic movements like Cursillo, while others had experience as prayer leaders in home-based religious traditions. Informal mentoring networks enabled a number of parishioners to sense a call to liturgical ministries and gave them the confidence to respond to it. Pastoral institutes such as the Mexican American Cultural Center, the Northeast Hispanic Catholic Center, and the Southeast Pastoral Institute were among the first to offer Hispanics formation for these ministries. Various dioceses and parishes also initiated their own programs. A number of

Hispanic permanent deacons felt called to their vocation after first serving in a lay leadership role in worship.[41]

Among Hispanics, the efforts to foster these developments are especially significant in the many worship communities that do not have a Latino priest, as often it has been the liturgical ministers and deacons who are the first Hispanics seen serving in public leadership roles at Mass. Consciously or not, for Hispanics and other Catholics, lay leadership provided an alternative understanding of the Eucharist from the liturgy they had experienced in the pre-Vatican II era. Seeing "one's own" proclaim the Scriptures, approach the altar with the priest during the communion rite, or minister the body and blood of Christ were changes that extended to lay people functions that were previously reserved to the clergy and, for many, transformed their understanding about their access to the holy within the most revered Catholic sacrament. Because liturgy shapes the collective imagination of worshipers, Hispanic ministry leaders have called for the inclusion of the various Hispanic ethnic groups, women, and those of lower socioeconomic rank in liturgical ministries. They do so out of concern that the symbolic meaning of those leading the community in worship might unconsciously embody an elitist ethos contrary to the spirit of the Eucharist as a gathering of all God's family.

Priests like Kenneth Davis and Jorge Presmanes, O.P., have endeavored to enhance preaching and presiding in Hispanic Eucharistic assemblies through their writings, teaching, and conference presentations. They give particular attention to clergy who are not of Hispanic background. Many seminarians and priests receive training that highlights faithful adherence to the Roman Ritual, at times excluding or even objecting to attempts to link the Roman liturgy to the traditions of a local faith community. Conversely, Davis and Presmanes counsel concerted efforts among their fellow priests to know their parishioners' backgrounds, strive to link the Scriptures and the prayer of the Eucharist to their faith expressions and daily struggles, and thus nurture active participation in the liturgy and in liturgical ministries. When most people in a community come from cultures and speak a language other than the priest's own, Davis and Presmanes contend, it is particularly important to learn key worship elements from one's congregants such as "what ambience is most welcoming, which symbols are most powerful, and when people are most likely to respond to prayer." It is equally important to develop preaching that "names *la gracia* (the grace) and denounces *la desgracia* [tragedy or 'the lack of grace']" in a way that concretely incarnates the Word of God in worshipers' everyday lives.[42]

The experience of Alvaro Dávila illustrates a fundamental concern among Instituto and other Hispanic leaders: building a strong relationship between the Eucharist and Hispanic cultural and faith expressions. Hispanic preachers have addressed this concern on occasions like the Guadalupe feast. Often they link the Eucharist, the assigned Scripture texts for the feast, and the narrative of Guadalupe's encounters with Juan Diego. In one homily, Allan Figueroa Deck observed that the relation between Guadalupe and her faithful "is sometimes simply that of a loving mother who literally lavishes care and concern on her needy children." He maintained that this is only half the meaning of Guadalupe, since "the story of Tepeyac," like Gospel readings officially approved for the Guadalupe feast such as the angel's annunciation to Mary (Luke 1:26–38) and Mary's visitation to her kinswoman Elizabeth (Luke 1:39–47), "graphically portrays the central role of love and service in our Christian lives." Exhorting his listeners to put into action their gratitude for the gift of God's love offered in their mother Guadalupe and in the Eucharist, he concluded, "Seized and saturated by such love, what will be our response to others, especially those most in need?" In another homily, Virgilio Elizondo relates the dynamics of conversion, the transformation of life and heart that the Gospels, the Eucharist, and the Guadalupe encounter mutually incite. He asks for the vision and strength so that he and his faith community can evangelize and draw others to Guadalupe's "holy mountain and through [her] to the great banquet table of our Lord Jesus Christ."[43]

Hispanic worship leaders have also sought to incorporate communal faith expressions into the Eucharist. In some communities a modified celebration of the *posada* (literally "dwelling" or "shelter") opens the Christmas Eve Mass. Posada is a home or neighborhood tradition in which participants accompany with a candlelight procession the pregnant Mary and her husband, Joseph, on their way to Bethlehem. On Christmas Eve, Mary and Joseph are welcomed at the parish church, where they lead the entrance procession to the vigil Mass accompanied with the singing of the traditional posada pilgrimage song. A number of pastors and liturgical ministers have prohibited, attempted to curtail, or simply never initiated such intermingling of devotional traditions with Eucharistic celebrations, often out of concern that the centrality of the official Eucharistic rite not be in any way diminished. Proponents of the practice contend that faith expressions like the posada are enriched and their relationship to the Eucharist strengthened when they are incorporated with due preparation and care. They further avow that, in the words of Juan Sosa, these expressions "can enhance our Eucharistic celebrations and engage the assembly into a deeper celebration of the Paschal Mystery [Christ's passion, death, and resurrection]." In the case of the posada and the Christmas liturgy, both the rebuff of the holy pilgrims Mary and Joseph at Bethlehem and Christ's birth in a lowly manger mutually reveal that God esteems those whom this world disdains or ignores. Practitioners of the posada present the dramatic proclamation of the welcome that worshipers are called upon to offer the pilgrims Mary and Joseph, embodying the call of the Christmas liturgy that believers welcome Christ and let him be born anew in their hearts.[44]

More fundamentally, Hispanic leaders contend that Latino faith expressions mediate a communitarian understanding of the human person that shapes Latinos' lives, faith, and, consciously or not, their modes of participation in the Eucharist. In the face of emphases on the autonomous individual in modern cultures, which clearly influence Hispanics as well as others, the tendency of Hispanic devotees to accentuate relationships like those between Jesus and Mary presents an alternative vision of what fundamentally constitutes our humanity. Theologian Ada María Isasi-Díaz asserts that, for Hispanics, "community is not something added on, but a web of relationships constitutive of who we are." Roberto Goizueta concurs, avowing that Latinos tend to derive their sense of identity more from "the community [that] forms and shapes" them than from their life as "autonomous individuals." Numerous Spanish-language *dichos* (sayings or proverbs) underscore the conviction that a person is profoundly shaped and known through his or her relationships, such as the popular expression "dime con quién andas y te diré quién eres" (tell me with whom you walk and I will tell you who you are). As one Hispanic woman parishioner observed: "For the Hispanic, we cannot know someone without knowing their family. The first question we ask when we meet someone is 'Where are you from? Who is your family?' "[45]

The communitarian dimension is evident in Hispanic Good Friday rituals, for which markers of individuality and worldly success and achievement are not what matter, since the terrible destiny of Jesus and Mary on this day are already known in advance. Like the expression of condolence Hispanics frequently offer at a wake service or funeral to those who have lost a loved one—"te acompaño en los sentimientos" (I accompany you in your sentiments)—what matters on Good Friday is faithful accompaniment. Mary and Jesus walk together in their hour of gravest need while participants ritually imitate what mother and son did at the first Way of the Cross in Jerusalem. Walking with Jesus and Mary, devotees are more intimately joined to the familial circle of their mother-son bond. All of this culminates in what Goizueta deems an embodied "theology of accompaniment": Hispanic devotees accompany Jesus and Mary in prayer, particularly in the dark hours of Good Friday, with unwavering confidence that Jesus and Mary will also accompany them in their struggles.[46]

Similarly, Miguel Díaz contends that "in her accompaniment of U.S. Hispanic communities . . . Mary provides a central locus from which to construct

U.S. Hispanic theological anthropologies"—that is, religious understandings of what it means to be human. Exploring the tradition of Our Lady of Charity, Díaz highlights that her accompaniment of the slaves at El Cobre assured them that their humanity was not defined by their state of bondage, but by their dignity as the children of so blessed a mother. Likewise, Goizueta says, "Guadalupe does not merely 'appear' to Juan Diego; she invites him into a profound relationship, in and through which he experiences his own humanity." Her love transforms Juan Diego from his self-abasement—the debilitating internalization of the Spanish conquerors' presumption that the natives were inferior or even subhuman—to a healthy embrace of divine love and the mission of living for God and others. Thus "a central theme of the [Guadalupe apparitions] narrative is the affirmation of community . . . as the birthplace of authentic human personhood and freedom."[47]

James Empereur, S.J., and Eduardo Fernández explore the implications of this communitarian dimension for Eucharistic celebrations in their study of Hispanic faith expressions and the sacraments. They conclude that "among the various gifts that the Hispanics bring to the larger church" and its worship, one of the foremost is the rootedness of their daily life and devotion in "relationality" and a "communal sacramental world." At the core of this symbolic world is the confident assurance that heavenly beings are family members whose presence is, in the words of Raúl Gómez, S.D.S., "immanently accessible." According to Hispanic ministry leaders and theologians who present this view, Hispanics' sense of a profound interconnectedness between family members who span heaven and earth—saints and ancestors of the past, those who walk together in present struggles, future generations to come, and the eternal God who is over all—forges a spirituality that is conducive to celebrating the Eucharist as a communion between God and all of humankind.[48]

Empirical analyses confirm that familial and communal networks are comparatively strong among Hispanic Catholics. According to the authors of *Young Adult Catholics: Religion in the Culture of Choice*, relative to their non-Latino counterparts, young Hispanic Catholics are more likely to live close to their family's home after high school, even when level of education is controlled to account for discrepancies in economic opportunity and mobility. Young Latinos are also more than twice as likely to marry a fellow Catholic and to participate in a parish where at least three of their five closest friends are members. Robert Putnam and David Campbell's 2006 Faith Matters survey shows that among married adults three times as many Latino as compared to "Anglo" Catholics have a Catholic spouse. The survey results also rank Latino Catholics as the group with the highest rate of "religious homogeneity of their family, friends, and neighbors," more than double the rate of

"Anglo" Catholics. Whatever the extent that the limits of Hispanic integration account for such homogeneity, these data demonstrate communal dynamics that are consistent with the relational emphasis in Hispanic cultures.[49]

Yet the central place of the communal that Hispanic theologians and pastoral leaders so eloquently articulate is evident to varying degrees in parishes. Indeed, among Hispanics the cultural emphasis on the relational by no means transfers automatically into a deep commitment to parish as faith community. Often even more intensely than their fellow Catholics, Latinos gravitate toward parishes with a strong spirit of community. But individualism, religious indifference, the preoccupations of everyday life, or non-church relational networks can diminish this gravitational pull. San Antonio parish leader Zulema Escamilla Galindo attests to the anguish of parents and grandparents who, like elders of other groups, perceive such tendencies as particularly acute among their young. Galindo urges her grandchildren and other young people to participate in their parish community and in Hispanic faith expressions, because "we need these traditions to evangelize our children. . . . We've got to give our *jóvenes* [young people] something that can guide them." Lynette DeJesús Sáenz adds that in her experience as a parish youth minister, she has "repeatedly heard stories from heart-broken Hispanic parents whose children refused to participate in the youth ministry programs, and in some cases even to come to church."[50]

Various obstacles impede the full participation in parish worship among Hispanic young people and adults alike. Rosa María Icaza regrets that many Hispanics do not partake fully in the Eucharist. A number do not come forward to receive communion, sometimes because church law prohibits them for reasons like being married outside the church's sacramental system. But in other cases it is because of a misunderstanding of humility "as an exaggerated sense of 'unworthiness.'" Icaza further avers that the affective and engaged religious experiences of Hispanic faith traditions can lead devotees to feel alienated in celebrations of the Eucharist, particularly when the presiding priest and liturgical ministers lead prayer in a rigid or formulaic fashion. Arturo Pérez-Rodríguez adds that merely superficial efforts to engage Hispanics are also inadequate: "Speaking Spanish, singing with a guitar, and throwing a serape on an altar do not make Hispanic worship." These critiques are consistent with the concern various Hispanic ministry leaders have expressed about the insufficient number of priests whose ministries as prayer leaders and preachers "imbue [the celebration of the Eucharist] with the deep spirituality and joy that characterize Hispanic Catholicism."[51]

Latino worship and devotion reflect a divergent emphasis for implementing the liturgical renewal that Vatican II mandated. Following the council the predominant approach to the renewal accentuated the core Conciliar principle of full participation, often enacted in the United States through emphases on the gathered assembly and the Word of God as integral elements of the Mass and other sacraments, vernacular celebration in which the priest and congregation pray in a dialogical format, and the removal of most imagery to focus attention on the altar and on the ambo, or pulpit, from which the Scriptures are proclaimed. More recently, various Catholics have sought to restore what they perceive as a loss of reverence in parish liturgies since the Second Vatican Council, echoing a concern among a number of church leaders, including Pope Benedict XVI. Those acting on this concern in the United States perceive that their efforts are buttressed in Vatican directives such as those concerning bodily posture at key moments of the Eucharist like the reception of communion. They also find support in new Vatican-mandated translations of Mass prayers "marked by a heightened style of English speech and a grammatical structure that closely follows the [original] Latin text."[52]

Hispanic ministry leaders, on the other hand, have promoted additional means for fostering active participation in the liturgy. They emphasize that the Second Vatican Council also fostered culturally conditioned expressions of faith like those Latinos practice. The lament of Juan Sosa echoes that of many Latino Catholics: "The Council especially attempted to thwart efforts to do without all these [popular] devotions and to reduce them exclusively to the liturgy. Yet unfortunately this became the attitude and the actions of many church leaders." Moreover, while many Euro-American liturgical leaders have underscored the council's emphasis on the "noble simplicity" of the Roman rite, Latinos insist that this does not deter from the character of the Eucharist as a celebration, a joyful and festive prayer gathering of the church on its pilgrim way to God. Latinos' viewpoints are reflected in the U.S. bishops' teaching on liturgy in *Encuentro and Mission*. This document encapsulates Hispanics' insistence on the need to foster liturgies in which worshipers "experience a true spirit of community." It also calls on prayer leaders to ensure "all are invited to share ways of prayer that reflect their different cultural values and traditions" and are able to appropriately "incorporate popular faith expressions . . . into liturgical celebrations."[53]

As with most aspects of U.S. Catholicism, the more dominant Euro-American influence has overshadowed that of Hispanics in official liturgical renewal. English-speaking Catholics developed a liturgical movement well before the Second Vatican Council and led the enactment of the council's directives in the United States.[54] Hispanics were latecomers to these efforts, with no national organization dedicated specifically to liturgical renewal until sixteen years after the promulgation of *Sacrosanctum Concilium*. Even then Latinos had far fewer resources and less access to key leadership positions. Moreover, most Hispanic leaders during the pivotal decades of renewal after the council focused on what they believed were more fundamental concerns of bolstering ministerial leadership and outreach among Hispanics, as is illuminated in the relatively scant treatment of liturgy in the conclusions of the three National Hispanic Pastoral Encuentros.

Yet the expanding contact of non-Latinos with Hispanic traditions has increased the influence of those traditions in U.S. parishes. Parishioners and their leaders have responded to Hispanics' devotional images and faith expressions in ways ranging from prohibiting or restricting them, engaging them as a means to promote causes of justice, seeing them as an inducement to recover their own ethnic Catholic traditions, or incorporating them into celebrations of the Eucharist. A number of non-Latino Catholics have embraced traditions like Guadalupan devotion and through contact with Hispanics have been inspired to increase their practice of Marian piety. St. Mark the Evangelist parish in San Antonio exemplifies these developments. It is one of an increasing number of primarily Euro-American parishes with growing Hispanic membership that prominently celebrate the Guadalupe feast. Within a few years of beginning this annual celebration, St. Mark's parish Guadalupana Society grew from 12 mostly Hispanic members to nearly 140, both men and women, nearly half of them European Americans.[55]

Hispanic public rituals also draw reactions and participation from non-Hispanics on the streets of a number of U.S. cities and towns. Passersby occasionally gawk at public Way of the Cross processions, and some of them annoy devotees in New York and other locales when they "don't even bother" to make way for the procession or "turn down their music." A few onlookers hurl insults. On the other hand, curiosity, the devotional ambiance of the events, decisions to conduct some rituals bilingually, and non-Hispanics' personal involvement with Hispanic communities have attracted an increasingly diverse array of participants. Even non-Catholics join in Hispanic public rituals like those for Good Friday. After the San Fernando Cathedral Way of the Cross in San Antonio, Baptist minister Buckner Fanning attested, "When I walked behind Jesus on the Way of the Cross I wondered what I would have done had I been there. The people of San Fernando drew me into the passion and put me right there with Jesus." Hispanic leaders contend that their practices provide a viable model for public worship in a society that often accents individual spiritual quests and the "privatization" of religion that scholars like Stephen Carter have noted. As Virgilio Elizondo put it: "Latinos' love for public ritual is a contribution we make to American society. I think there is a hunger for it in American life. It lets you enter into the power of a collective experience."[56]

An insufficient number of clergy and liturgical leaders who actively promote Latinos' Good Friday, Marian, and other religious traditions keep Hispanic impact on communal prayer in U.S. parishes and their environs from being even greater. However, the geographic dispersion of the Hispanic population over the past two decades has expanded Latino influence. For good or for ill, even conflicts and debates about Hispanic traditions and liturgical participation reveal that Latinos shape parish worship and public ritual in significant ways. Hispanics' ritual and devotional proclivities and their promotion of a liturgical renewal that engages their faith expressions currently comprise one of the fundamental dynamics in the prayer life of numerous Catholic parishes in the United States. Moreover, these dynamics and the ways pastoral leaders and parishioners welcome, refine, or resist them transform Eucharistic celebrations that are at the heart of Catholic faith and worship.

# 7
CHAPTER

# Public Catholicism

eacon Carlos Valdéz was angry. Gang member intimidation of seventh and eighth graders on the school playground of his parish, Ascension Catholic Church on the north side of Minneapolis, was so intense that the school principal had begun to patrol the schoolyard with a baseball bat. Frustrated at the lack of police response to the principal's pleas for help, in 1996 Valdéz enlisted the support of the Joint Ministry Project (JMP), a local faith-based community organization that addresses urban issues. Armed with training in community organizing from JMP and professional organizers from the Gamaliel Foundation who work with it, Valdéz and other parish leaders gathered six hundred people and demanded that the police chief and mayor increase patrols to deter gang recruitment. While city officials initially refused to negotiate, the media coverage that local organizers fostered soon shamed them into action. The following week "Safe Teams" comprised of civilians and police patrolled the schoolyard and adjacent neighborhood every afternoon. Gang members fled.[1]

Elated with their success, Valdéz and his fellow parishioners concluded that these events represented far more than just winning back their schoolyard. More importantly, they had learned that they could exercise collective power for the good of their community. As Deacon Valdéz summed up his own transformation after the victory, "I feel alive, and I'm being called by God to organize in my community, the Latino community." Valdéz later played a leading role in founding Sagrado Corazón (Sacred Heart) parish. Hundreds of Latino Catholics from this congregation have received leadership training in faith-based community organizing. Along with numerous other small victories stemming from this organizing effort, Latino leaders created a Mercado Central business cooperative, raised $3 million for the cooperative's forty small businesses, and compelled immigration officials to process applications in a more efficient and accessible manner.

The various successes of Deacon Valdéz and his collaborators—political victories, community improvement, leadership training, organization building, and establishing a needed Hispanic parish—provide evidence that Catholicism in the public sphere is not limited to lobbying efforts. Indeed, Catholic influence in explicitly political arenas is intrinsically linked to the daily pastoral life of the church, without which efforts ranging from grassroots organizing to bishops' pronouncements would be severely hampered. Understood in its broadest sense, the Hispanic presence in "public Catholicism" today is greater than in any past era although by some measures like influential leadership positions, it is still disproportionate to that of non-Hispanics. Latinos participate and provide leadership in the expansive networks of Catholic educational, health care, and social service institutions through which the U.S. Catholic Church influences daily lives and the broader society. Hispanic Catholics also sustain organizations such as Hispanic ministry associations, pastoral training centers, parishes, and apostolic movements. They operate Spanish-language initiatives in radio, television, Internet, and print media, such as the dedicated work of Carmen Aguinaci at Claretion Publications in Chicago and the editorial leadership of Victor Alemán with *Vida Nueva*, an award-winning Catholic newspaper in the archdiocese of Los Angeles. Rituals enacted in neighborhoods and city streets, yard shrines, prayer gatherings in homes, and the evangelizing activities of grassroots Hispanics are all further examples of public acts rooted in Catholic faith. While this chapter focuses primarily on public Catholicism in the narrower sense of involvement in the political structures and decision-making processes at federal, state, and local levels, much of this volume examines the diverse ways Hispanic Catholics bring their faith to bear in local communities and collectively in society at large.

Hispanics have long engaged as Catholics in U.S. political life. After members of the anti-Catholic, anti-immigrant Know Nothing Party gained control of the San Antonio mayoral office and city council in 1854, citizens of Mexican descent organized to oppose them. They accused Know Nothings of desiring to make them "political slaves" solely because they chose "to worship God according to the dictates of our conscience and the ritual of our ancestors." Local political leader José Antonio Navarro wrote an open letter that was read publicly and published in both the English and Spanish press. Navarro reminded his audience that his people's Hispanic-Mexican ancestors founded their city and that one of their first community initiatives was to build the parish of San Fernando in which they worshiped God. Citing Know Nothing anti-Catholic attitudes, he also proclaimed that "the Mexico-Texans are Catholics, and should be proud of the faith of their ancestors, and defend it inch by inch against such infamous aggressors." Ethnic Mexicans joined forces with fellow Catholics and other allies to defeat their Know Nothing opponents in the next election cycle.[2]

Hispanic Catholics who are concerned for the well-being of immigrant and working-class families face new challenges today, such as more stringent legal restrictions on immigration, the many repercussions of a consequent "illegal" status for millions, the availability of abortion and its influence in the lives of Hispanic women and their families and friends, and a strident contingent of antigovernment and antitax forces that affects health, education, and social welfare policies. At the same time, Hispanic Catholics have more resources at their disposal than the electoral franchise with which Navarro and his contemporaries combated the Know Nothings. For four decades the U.S. bishops have given critical support to faith-based community organizing efforts, which Hispanic Catholics have helped shape in significant ways. Labor organizing and unions have also facilitated Latino Catholics' struggles to improve their lot in life and that of their families. A much larger Latino population has gained greater attention from bishops and other U.S. Catholics, most notably on the immigration issue, and increased the importance of Hispanic votes in local, state, and even national elections. Latino Catholics extend their church's impact in electoral politics, the immigration debate, local communities, and increasingly in regional and national initiatives to shape public policy.

The national growth of faith-based community organizations like the Joint Ministry Project encompasses a number of Latino Catholics along with people of other religious, racial, and ethnic backgrounds. Though somewhat dated, the most recent statistical survey on these organizations, the 1999 Interfaith Funders study, identified 133 of them in the United States with an office and at least one full-time staff person. Most of the 133 organizations are associated with one of four major organizing networks. The oldest and largest of these networks is the Industrial Areas Foundation (IAF), which Saul Alinsky founded in 1940. Like the IAF, the Gamaliel Foundation is also based in Chicago, while the PICO National Network (formerly the Pacific Institute for Community Organizations, or PICO) has its headquarters in Oakland and the Direct Action Research and Training Center is based in Miami. Each network contractually provides professional organizers and leadership training to local organizations. The organizations set their own action agenda. They have addressed a wide range of concerns, the four most common reported in the Interfaith Funders study being issues about public schools, the economy, policing, and housing. Other issues subsequently rose to the fore such as health care, foreclosures, finance reform, and youth violence. Collectively, the 133 faith-based community organizations link 3,500 congregations plus 500 other institutions such as public schools and labor union locals. The congregations engaged in the organizations encompass between one and three million members and are in nearly all major urban areas and many secondary cites across the nation. While no subsequent study has provided as detailed a portrait of faith-based community organizations, more recent analyses reveal that the number of organizations has increased at least 20 percent and they exist in nearly every state.[3]

According to the Interfaith Funders study, Latinos comprise a majority in 21 percent of the congregations in faith-based community organizations. This figure surpasses their overall percentage of the U.S. population, though it is less than the percentage of majority African American and majority Euro-American congregations in the organizations, both of which are slightly more than one-third. Since the non-Catholic congregations—most of them mainline Protestant or predominantly black churches—tend to be smaller than the average Catholic parish, in all probability the overall percentage of Hispanics affiliated with faith-based organizing is even higher. There is considerable regional variation in Latino participation; in cities and regions with large Latino populations such as Los Angeles, Chicago, Denver, Phoenix, San Antonio, El Paso, and the Rio Grande Valley, Latino participation and leadership is the most conspicuous. About one-third of the majority Latino congregations in faith-based organizing are predominantly composed of immigrants, a number that reflects not only émigrés' strong desire to participate but also the important inducement of citizenship that abets the greater participation of native-born Latinos. Hispanics account for 21 percent of the board members in faith-based community organizations and for more than 16 percent of some 550 paid professional organizers. Compared to women's involvement more generally, the considerable number of Latinas among congregational leaders in faith-based organizations is not unusual. More striking is the statistic that more than half of the Hispanic organizers are women, a significant percentage in an historically male-dominated field where women "have confronted the same kinds of challenges as women in other professions." Latinas and Latinos still lag behind in their attainment of supervisory positions in the four major organizational networks, though several have advanced to key leadership positions, such as Mary Gonzáles and Juan Soto in the Gamaliel Foundation; Ernie Cortés and Elizabeth Valdez in the IAF; and Denise Collazo, Gina Martinez, and José Carrasco in PICO.[4]

The first predominantly Hispanic faith-based community organization, San Antonio's Communities Organized for Public Service (COPS), is a prime example of Latino Catholics' leadership in this type of civic engagement.

Beginning in 1973 IAF organizer Ernie Cortés worked with lay leaders like founding president, Andrés Sarabia, and priests such as Edmundo Rodríguez, Albert Benavides, David García, and Bishop Patricio Flores to establish COPS among ethnic Mexican Catholic parishes in the working-class neighborhoods of the city's west side. Their first major issue was the horrendous drainage and frequent flooding in their neighborhoods, which had resulted in school closings, accidents, damaged homes, impassable roads, bridge collapses, the closing of business establishments, and even deaths. When COPS members discovered that many drainage projects had actually been authorized in bond issues approved as far back as 1945, they filled city hall during a council meeting to voice their outrage. Stunned by the crowd and the overwhelming evidence presented, Mayor Charles Becker ordered the city manager to devise a drainage project implementation plan. COPS then took the lead in the passage of a $46.8 million bond issue for fifteen west-side drainage projects. Led primarily by Latina leaders such as Beatrice Gallego, Carmen Badillo, Beatrice Cortés, Sonia Hernández, Patricia Ozuna, and Virginia Ramírez, the organization won expansive infrastructure improvements for primarily low-income and working-class neighborhoods, as well as significant advances on community issues like education reform, job training, economic development, and a living wage. More importantly, COPS transformed its members and refashioned what one COPS observer called the "formerly Anglo-controlled politics in San Antonio." As members themselves attest: "The most positive change has been in the attitude of our people. Twenty-five years ago, we couldn't imagine that a city council member would attend our meetings, now we know that with the power of educated, organized people, anything is possible."[5]

Arguably the greatest influence Latinos have exerted on faith-based organizing is their role in transforming Saul Alinsky's organizing model to root it more deeply in local congregations and the faith convictions of their members. In his study of IAF organizations in Texas, Mark Warren concluded, "While Alinsky took a rather utilitarian view of churches as repositories of money and people to be mobilized, the modern IAF developed a close collaboration with people of faith, fusing religious traditions and power politics into a theology of organizing." COPS was the first such initiative to forge a new pathway in congregation-based organizing. As Richard Wood has asserted in his extensive studies of these organizations, the evolution of COPS "became the foundational experience leading to the elaboration of the faith-based model of organizing." Under the innovative guidance of Cortés, COPS leaders learned Alinsky's tools of analysis, strategies, and tactics as they confronted an entrenched political and business establishment that sought first to thwart them and then to limit their nascent organization's influence. But as Hispanic Catholics, COPS leaders also infused Alinsky's style of organizing with their own religious convictions and those of their core members: parishioners who perceived their activism as an extension of their commitment to God, church, family, and neighborhood. Inez Ramírez summarizes the perspective of many COPS leaders on their collective purpose: "This is not merely politics we are engaged in, but correcting injustice, which is God's work and the mission of the church. There is more to our spirituality than just going to Mass on Sundays. Our spirituality embodies a deep concern for the physical well-being of every individual."[6]

The COPS approach of building a community organization on the foundation of congregations and faith-based leaders has been adapted and further developed in various forms throughout the national networks of community organizations. Wood's research on religion, race, and organizing asserts that the faith base enables many community organizations to develop an ethos of "ethical democracy," a mutual engagement of faith and nonpartisan participation in the democratic process. The faith dimension is evident in the prayer, songs, preaching, and religious symbols that are frequently part of the public and internal events of faith-based community organizations. It is illuminated in the "moral vision" of "how society ought to be" that enlivens and lends credibility to an organization's attempts to lobby for its public policy proposals. Leadership training sessions include resources like the Bible, Catholic social encyclicals, and the pastoral letters of the U.S. Catholic bishops. Studying the specific visions of Latino leaders in faith-based activism, Catherine Wilson echoed the contention that their "interpretation of the Christian narrative" shapes the religious identity and political activism of their respective organizations. Some faith-based organizations have even taken on the role of parish development, engaging in activities such as identifying and training new leaders, building congregational unity around common goals and needs, expanding church outreach and ministries, attracting more active members, and enhancing stewardship and church finances. A number of Catholic leaders, such as Lupita Mendiola and Father Bart Flaat of the predominantly Hispanic St. Joseph the Worker Church in McAllen, Texas, credit community organizing with revitalizing the faith in their parish. They attest that a community organizing effort transformed their parish from a languishing congregation where "pews were nearly empty" to an active community of three thousand families.[7]

Scholars and other observers contend that the influence of faith convictions is also evident in comparisons between explicitly faith-based organizations and community organizations that do not work primarily with congregations, as was the case with the Association of Community Organizations for Reform Now (ACORN) network, which received intense public criticism during the course of the 2008 presidential elections and is now defunct. Heidi Swarts's comparative analysis showed the greater capacity of faith-based organizations to unite people across class, race, and political divides through a conscious effort to build on participants' faith and their desire to act on it collectively for community improvement. Faith-based organizations also deliberate more about the degree to which they should incorporate what Swarts called the well-known "boisterous confrontational protests" of ACORN. Such differences in organizational culture are consistent with the analyses of scholars who critically consider the personal testimonies of leaders in faith-based community organizations. One Latina organizer for the PICO network attested that, although public exchanges with political figures can be tense, "we have to respect their dignity, and I think that comes from the faith base." A Catholic parish leader who spoke about the direction faith gives to community organizing said, "When we organize, people really do feel like they are opening up and letting God work through them." She added: "It sounds simple to say that your faith makes a difference, but I think that's one way you hang onto hope. . . . Somehow I do, and it's not because I think that things are going to get better fast. It's because I think there's God."[8]

U.S. Catholic bishops and other religious leaders have provided seed money to help launch faith-based community organizing projects. They have assisted fledgling organizations toward their financial goal of being self-sustaining, which successful organizations accomplish primarily through the annual dues of their member congregations. Addressing concerns made painfully evident through the civil rights movement and the rage and despair of poor urban African Americans, in 1969 Catholic bishops founded the Catholic Campaign for Human Development (CCHD, formerly the Campaign for Human Development) to "address the root causes of poverty in America through promotion and support of community-controlled, self-help organizations and through transformative education." Since its inception CCHD has consistently supported faith-based community organizations. Indeed, the Interfaith Funders study revealed that CCHD provided more funding for faith-based community organizations than all other religious givers combined, with CCHD support totaling 16 percent of all funding for faith-based community organizations nationwide. In recent years about one-third of national CCHD funding has gone to such organizations, approximately $3 million annually.[9]

CCHD support for community organizing has drawn sharp criticism from some Catholics. In 2008 the bishops' CCHD subcommittee was the first prominent national group to discontinue funding of ACORN, because of its leaders' "lack of financial transparency, organizational performance, and questions surrounding political partisanship." Yet in the wake of the national controversy surrounding ACORN, various critics formed the Reform CCHD Now coalition and called for a boycott of the annual national CCHD collection in November 2009. They expressed concern that CCHD funds "have gone and continue to go to corrupt and partisan political groups, and even groups which sometimes work against the Church."[10]

CCHD leaders issued a series of rejoinders "for the record," including the public release of a report from Bishop Roger Morin to the bishops' CCHD subcommittee, which he served as chair. Morin summarized the mission of the CCHD; its procedures, including the practice of funding only applications that have approval of the local diocesan bishop; its faithful adherence to Catholic teaching; and its accomplishments in putting that teaching into action. While acknowledging the concerns of those who raised questions about CCHD as a means to strengthen it, he bemoaned those "few with their own ideological or political agendas" who "spread outrageous claims that the bishops are funding abortion, attacks on the family, and other untruths." Morin encouraged and applauded his fellow bishops for steadfastly backing CCHD in the face of such allegations. Factoring in the effect of a concurrent downturn in the economy, the influence of protests on the 2009 annual CCHD collection appears to have been modest. During the first half of 2010, bishops from 10 of the 195 U.S. Catholic dioceses elected to suspend or discontinue their remittance to the national office of the annual CCHD collection in their diocese. Some cited criticisms of CCHD administration, others a desire to channel the collection funds to meet critical local needs in a strapped economy. At the time of this writing, the decided majority of bishops have persisted in their support of CCHD, though protests against it are ongoing. Bishop Morin's report alluded to the importance of the bishops' resolve for Latino and other working-class U.S. residents, noting that CCHD continues to help "thousands of low-income families improve their lives and communities, to seek justice, and to defend their dignity."[11]

Faith-based community organizations face various challenges beyond the potential loss of funding sources. Pastors like Father Chuck Dahm, who served for two decades at St. Pius V parish in Chicago's Pilsen neighborhood, warn that community organizing efforts can have negative effects when they are not directed wisely. These effects include depleting leaders for needed parish ministries, an elitist and narrow focus on social change that divides one group of parishioners from others, and the misguided conviction that the end of promoting a just cause justifies employing whatever means are necessary to achieve it. Barriers to enlisting congregations as organizational members include uneasiness with ecumenical or interfaith alliances, with mixing faith and politics, and with public attempts to hold elected officials accountable for their actions. Yet another limitation is the lack of collaboration between faith-based organizations in the four major networks, even in instances where organizations aligned with separate networks are working in the same region or locale. Wood and other observers are clear that there is also a need for ongoing vigilance to preserve the faith base to community organizing initiatives, as opposed to a merely instrumental engagement of religion to "provide a perception of legitimacy, access to social capital, and some organizational and financial resources to sustain political engagement."[12]

The greatest political challenge to continued progress on the impressive track record of faith-based community organizations is the transition from organizations focused explicitly on local concerns to statewide and even national coalitions that shape the wider public policy decisions affecting local communities. As Wood has put the question starkly: "When so much of the decision-making that determines the quality of life for poor, working-class and middle-class Americans occurs 'over the heads' of local political leaders, how influential can locally rooted social movements be?" Are faith-based community organizations "relegated to fiddling on the margins of social policy—perhaps extracting minor concessions, but powerless to affect the decisions of national political elites whose policies determine the availability of societal resources, or the state-level elites who distribute those resources?" Beginning with the Texas IAF Network in 1983—another "first" in faith-based organizing which Hispanic Catholics played a prominent role in enacting—organization leaders have sought to address these questions through establishing various state, regional, and even national initiatives within their respective networks. Since its first public policy advocacy efforts in 1997, for example, PICO California has taken a lead role in securing the allocation of more than 13 billion dollars in state funds to various education and health initiatives. Subsequently, the PICO National Network emerged as an alliance among the now fifty PICO organizations across seventeen states. Their involvement in national debates on issues like comprehensive immigration reform and health care—clearly policy concerns that will influence most or all locales where faith-based community organizations are active—exemplifies the need for organization leaders to forge coalitions among their own networks and with other allies if they are to have an impact in the wider arenas of the U.S. democratic system. Leaders in a number of faith-based organizations are concerned that campaigns in these broader arenas might detract from further advancements on their proven track records in local initiatives. PICO organizer Gina Martinez succinctly summarizes the challenge: "Ideally, we want to integrate the national, state, and federated work all fully into our local work.... I don't think we're there yet, but that's our goal."[13]

The most noteworthy instance of how the expanding Latino presence has shaped the public policy positions of the U.S. Catholic Church is the bishops' growing public solidarity with immigrants. A number of historical events have fueled debates about Hispanic immigration to the United States: the massive and often illegal deportations of Mexican residents during the Depression years of the 1930s and "Operation Wetback" during the 1950s; the Bracero program, which brought in some five million guest workers between 1942 and 1964; Operation Peter Pan and other efforts to assist Cuban exiles fleeing the socialist revolution in their homeland; the major national immigration legislation of 1965 and 1986; the Central American civil wars and the Sanctuary Movement of the 1980s; the influence of NAFTA (North American Free Trade Agreement) and other international trade agreements on immigrant flows; anti-immigrant backlash like the 1994 passage of Proposition 187 in California; the notorious 2000 custody battle for Elián González after his mother drowned in her attempt to flee Cuba with him; and the current immigration debates in Congress and the nation. Catholic bishops have increasingly defended Hispanic immigrants, from their lackluster response during the Depression-era deportations to their noteworthy advocacy on behalf of immigrants in their 2003 joint pastoral letter with the bishops of Mexico, their subsequent Justice for Immigrants campaign, and their ongoing lobbying efforts for comprehensive immigration reform.[14]

The 2003 pastoral letter illuminates developments in the bishops' approach to immigration since their response to the Bracero program a half century earlier. Archbishop Robert Lucey, chair of the Bishops' Committee for the Spanish Speaking, was the foremost Catholic episcopal spokesperson on the Bracero issue. Reflective of views held among his contemporary Catholic clergy in Hispanic ministry, organizations like the League of United Latin American Citizens and the American G.I. Forum, and labor activists like Ernesto Galarza, Lucey charged that farm owners lobbied heavily for guest worker contracts in order to undercut the salaries and rights of Mexican Americans and other U.S. citizen workers. Thus he urged that Congress enact legislation to "control the traffic in 'wetbacks'" and even to allow U.S. immigration officials greater latitude to search for undocumented workers on farms. While Lucey recognized the plight and pastoral needs of immigrants, until Congress abolished it in 1964 he consistently cast the Bracero program as primarily a controversy over workers' as opposed to immigrants' rights. In contrast, the 2003 pastoral letter *Strangers No Longer: Together on the Journey of Hope*, the first such collaborative effort between the bishops of Mexico and the United States, examines migration as a hemispheric and global phenomenon and as a long-standing concern in the Bible and in Catholic social teaching. That teaching undergirds the vision the bishops articulate for the church's multi-faceted pastoral response to contemporary migrants. It is also the foundation for the broad range of public policy recommendations they make in major areas of concern: addressing the root causes of migration, protection of family unity, the process of legalization, just treatment for both permanent and temporary immigrant workers, and humane enforcement policies.[15]

The most renowned Catholic spokesperson in recent immigration debates is Cardinal Roger Mahony of Los Angeles, who is affectionately known among Latino immigrants as "Cardenal Rogelio" and acclaimed as their most relentless episcopal defender. Hispanic Catholic leaders have also long been advocates for their immigrant sisters and brothers. Father Luis Olivares, C.M.F., is recognized as a champion of immigrants, especially for his 1986 declaration of Our Lady of the Angels parish in Los Angeles as a sanctuary for Central American refugees. That same year bishops Agustín Román and Enrique San Pedro, S.J., issued a pastoral statement calling attention to the plight of their fellow Cuban exiles who languished in federal prisons, most of whom had arrived in the massive 1980 exodus from the port of Mariel. The prelates called for "an end to the inhumane situation of uncertainty and indefinite incarceration" of the mentally ill, prisoners found to be unjustly convicted in Cuban courts, and those who had served sentences and were now at an impasse because U.S. immigration law required their deportation but the Cuban government would not receive them. The following year, when Cuban prisoners rioted after U.S. authorities negotiated a return of some detainees to Cuba, Bishop Román played a crucial role in convincing the prisoners to release their hostages and lay down their arms in return for a government promise to adjudicate their cases individually. Bishop Gabino Zavala's public advocacy for immigrant rights encompasses a 1994 speech to the Los Angeles County School Board urging the rejection of California's Proposition 187, a controversial ballot initiative to deny government services to the undocumented, which voters approved but a federal court later declared unconstitutional. Zavala denounced Proposition 187 as a contradiction to the U.S. creed, a defilement of the nation's immigrant heritage, and a transgression of "the law of God."[16]

Archbishop José Gomez gave a 2008 speech that explained the faith and moral convictions of many Catholic leaders about contemporary immigration furor in the United States. Gomez asserted that immigration is "one of the critical challenges the church faces in our hemisphere" and "the greatest civil rights test of our generation." He professed that "in Catholic teaching the right to migrate is among the most basic human rights," one "very close to the right to life . . . because God has created the good things of this world to be shared by all men and women—not just a privileged few." While recognizing government's right to regulate immigration, Gomez reminded his audience that "the church also insists that no country can deny this basic human right [to migrate] out of exaggerated fears or selfishness." He articulated the tragic human cost of negative responses to immigrants among U.S. citizens: it "is bad for the soul of America. And it's bad for the souls of Americans. There is too much anger. Too much resentment. Too much fear. Too much hate." Noting that the lack of comprehensive immigration reform at the federal level had led to at least two hundred new laws in more than forty states during each of the previous two years, Gomez called for "a moratorium on new state and local legislation," which too often is "so clearly vindictive, so obviously meant to injure and intimidate" that it creates new problems without resolving existing ones. For similar reasons, he urged "an end to federal worksite enforcement raids." "Most troubling" to Gomez as a pastor "is that these deportations are breaking up families," since "a fundamental dimension of Catholic social teaching on immigration is that our policies should be aimed at reuniting and strengthening families—not tearing them apart." He called on church leaders to be instruments of reconciliation, not excusing those who entered the country illegally, but seeking "more suitable penalties" for them, such as "intensive, long-term community service," as a "far more constructive solution than deportation." His concluding appeal was for Catholics to be faithful to Christ: "We will change the hearts and minds of our countrymen on this issue only if we ourselves become living examples of the Gospel we proclaim."[17]

Dioceses, religious communities, and the national bishops' conference sustain numerous immigrant outreach efforts, most notably the bishops' Migration and Refugee Services office and the Catholic Legal Immigration Network (CLINIC), a network of nearly three hundred field offices in forty-eight states whose mission is "to enhance and expand delivery of legal services to indigent and low-income immigrants principally through diocesan immigration programs and to meet the immigration needs identified by the Catholic Church in the United States." The bishops also address immigration legislatively at the state level, an arena of increasing importance as the "New Federalism" that has emerged under presidential administrations dating back to Richard Nixon places more governance responsibilities on state officials. State Catholic conferences give the U.S. Catholic Church an organizational strength in state-level politics that is matched among few other national institutional bodies. Two-thirds of states and the District of Columbia have a state conference. For most, the state's bishops serve as the board of directors, though nearly a dozen have members besides bishops, and all employ staffs that carry out daily operations. State Catholic conferences across the country have issued numerous statements on immigration that reinforce the bishops' principles and policy positions, both in states with large Hispanic populations and in those with growing numbers of Latinos, such as Washington, Nebraska, Indiana, Ohio, Kentucky, Georgia, Virginia, and Connecticut. A Maryland bishops' 2007 statement, "Where All Find a Home: A Catholic Response to Immigration," presents a typical admonition, urging that "as Catholics, we must move past divisions and remain focused on the dignity of the human person and the welfare of families." The Maryland Catholic Conference posts further resources on its website and also advocates for specific policy decisions regarding émigrés, such as the Conference's unsuccessful support for state legislation to allow undocumented residents to obtain a driver's license. Collaboration between Catholic leaders reinforces a number of state and local efforts, as in 2010 when Bishop John Wester, chairman of the USCCB Committee on Migration, expressed the strong support of the USCCB for the Arizona Catholic bishops' opposition to a new state law criminalizing undocumented immigrants and those who assist them.[18]

Even those who criticize the bishops' immigration stance acknowledge their collective resolve on the issue, though some question the prelates' motives. The late Father Richard John Neuhaus, founding editor of the journal *First Things*, attested in its editorial pages that "immigrants continue to be a revivifying force in our national life" and that "the largest immigrant group, the Hispanics, is in fact many distinct groups, almost all of whom enthusiastically embrace the chance to enter into the mainstream American experience." But in a subsequent editorial he quipped, "On immigration the U.S. bishops take pretty much the position of the *Wall Street Journal*, which, only half tongue in cheek, calls for a constitutional amendment abolishing national borders." He concluded: "The Catholic Church is the largest, and possibly the most effective, pro-immigration organization in the country. This has everything to do with strategic and pastoral planning, reflecting the fact that Latinos constitute" a growing number of U.S. Catholics, bolstering the bishops' conviction "that a generous immigration policy is good for poor people seeking opportunity, good for America, and good for the Catholic Church."[19]

A sizable group of U.S. Catholics disagree with all or at least significant parts of the bishops' stance on immigration. Many contend that border enforcement is a necessary first step before the consideration of any other measures, especially proposals like those of the bishops for comprehensive immigration reform. Some Catholic political officials and activists have taken the lead in enacting laws aimed at inducing the departure of undocumented immigrants. Several detractors are so incensed at the bishops' teaching and advocacy that they have left the church, such as Californian Raymond Herrera, who avows, "A church that rails on behalf of the criminal [undocumented] elements in our society is a church that's un-American and against the rule of law. They [the bishops] should be ashamed of themselves."[20]

On the other hand, a number of Catholics promote education on the church's immigration teaching and on policy debates, seek to focus attention on the human struggles and life stories of immigrants, and engage in conversation about responding in faith. A 2008 forum on immigration organized by the social justice ministry leaders of three New Jersey parishes is but one example of local efforts. Numerous Catholic pastors, activists, and scholars have also endeavored to enhance the church's immigration work, such as Father Daniel Groody, C.S.C. His writings, presentations, and video productions on the theology of migration and on the perilous experience of border crossing and life as an undocumented immigrant have engaged substantial audiences among Catholics and their fellow citizens. Catholic institutions have launched initiatives like the Theology of Migration project, which research centers at Fairfield University and Georgetown University, CLINIC, and other partners organized to address a range of topics centered on "immigration as an issue for those of the Catholic faith."[21]

Numerous grassroots Latinos have advocated publicly for the rights of émigrés and for immigration reform. In the wake of massive pro-immigrant rallies across the nation that rancorous immigration debates incited during spring 2006, the Pew Latino religion survey found that slightly over a fourth of Latino Catholics said their congregation had participated in an immigrant rights protest or boycott during the previous twelve months, a substantially higher percentage than mainline Latino Protestants and more than double that of Latino evangelicals. Reflecting in part the higher percentage of immigrant Latinos who are Catholics, Hispanic Catholics were also more likely than Protestants to have personally participated in an immigrant rights demonstration and to report that their parish clergy had spoken out on immigration. Father Claudio Díaz, director of Hispanic ministry for the archdiocese of Chicago, commented on this feverish activity—rallies, protests, voter registration drives, and public prayer—among Latino and other area Catholics: "It's been like a jolt of energy to really have a group of people be updated, get informed, be organized."[22]

Grassroots Latinos have also participated in and helped lead efforts to defend the rights of immigrant workers. Their activism is timely, since long-standing Catholic involvement in labor struggles has been less frequent in recent decades as more U.S. Catholics exited the working class, organized labor faced mounting challenges, and Catholics' public activism addressed a growing range of issues and concerns. Many United Farm Worker members are Latino Catholic émigrés. The immigrant activism of the UFW is exemplified in its AgJOBS legislative proposal to grant undocumented farmworkers currently in the United States the possibility of gaining legal status. Numerous Hispanic Catholic immigrants are among the more than two hundred thousand janitors in the Justice for Janitors campaigns, which since 1985 have been organized in cities across the United States and Canada under the auspices of the Service Employees International Union. They have gained concessions like better wages, improved working conditions, health insurance, and full-time employment. Émigrés are also a leading group in Hotel Employees and Restaurant Employees. One member is José, a dishwasher at a luxury hotel in Santa Monica, California, who attested he faced intimidation from hotel managers but persevered with the union "after consulting with a priest." He gained a pay increase of nearly $2.50 an hour and was delighted that his new hourly wage of $8.91 enabled him to feed his family without "handouts." Testifying to his experience before an interfaith group of clergy, José declared, "Pope John Paul II said the church should support workers and the union." He urged his listeners to follow John Paul's counsel and example.[23]

The most widespread form of Catholic public presence on immigration is the numerous outreach efforts in local faith communities. Many parishes are a "safe haven" for immigrants, such as St. Pius V in Chicago, where an impressive array of ministries enable émigré parishioners to learn and act on their faith and provide for one another's everyday needs, such as food, shelter, clothing, parenting skills, family counseling, refuge from spousal abuse, employment, safe neighborhoods, English language classes, and legal defense. When federal authorities raided the Agriprocessors factory in Postville, Iowa, on May 12, 2008, and arrested nearly four hundred undocumented workers, most of them Guatemalan and Mexican men, their wives and children fled to St. Bridget's parish. Parish life coordinator Sister Mary McCauley, B.V.M., pastor emeritus Father Paul Ouderkirk, and lay Catholics, many the descendants of earlier Irish and Norwegian immigrants, served food to the frightened families, compiled a list of the detained workers, and stood watch at the church door. Immigration officials placed electronic homing devices on the ankles of about forty mothers they had detained and allowed them to reunite with their children, but the other workers faced deportation. Father Ouderkirk mourned on behalf of all, saying the raid "ripped the heart out of the community and out of the parish. Probably every child I baptized has been affected. To see them stunned is beyond belief." Irma López, who was arrested along with her husband, Marcelo, but released to care for their two-year-old daughter, said, "I came to the church because I feel safe there, I feel secure. I feel protected. I feel at peace." A *New York Times* reporter concluded that "the only redemptive thing that can be said, perhaps, is that in the crisis of Postville . . . the beacon of the Roman Catholic Church to immigrants has rarely shone more brilliantly."[24]

Latino Catholic public officials tend to take a pro-immigrant stance, but no major study has examined the extent to which their faith and official Catholic teachings influence them. According to statistics of the National Association of Latino Elected and Appointed Officials (NALEO), as of 2007 a total of 5,129 Latino elected officials served in forty-three states, mostly in the Southwest. There are about ten times as many Democrats as Republicans in partisan elected posts. NALEO statistics do not reveal how the number of Latino officeholders compares to that of other groups, but a 2000 study showed that Latinos held less than 1 percent of all elected offices. While Hispanics constitute more than 15 percent of the U.S. population, at the time of this writing they comprise less than 5 percent of the representatives in the two houses of the U.S. Congress. Many Latino officials at least come from Catholic backgrounds, such as the first Hispanic Supreme Court justice, Sonia Sotomayor, whose widowed Puerto Rican mother sacrificed greatly to send her to Catholic schools in New York. According to an administration official's comment at the time of her nomination for the Supreme Court, "Judge Sotomayor was raised as a Catholic and attends church for family celebrations and other important events."[25] A few public figures have strong links to the institutions and mission of the U.S. Catholic Church, such as Miguel Díaz, a Cuban who in 2009 became the first Hispanic to serve as U.S. ambassador to the Vatican. Díaz is a Catholic systematic theologian who at the time of his appointment was a professor of theology at St. John's University and the College of Saint Benedict in Minnesota. Previously he had taught theology at four other Catholic institutions of higher education: Barry University in Miami; St. Vincent de Paul Regional Seminary in Boynton Beach, Florida; the University of Dayton; and the University of Notre Dame.

Generally Latinos tend to follow the pattern of most elected officials and mirror the proclivities of their constituents. Thus one of the most prominent recent instances of a Latino officeholder making public policy more consistent with Catholic teaching is not surprising: according to opinion polls Democratic governor Bill Richardson's 2009 decision to sign into law a repeal of the death penalty in New Mexico reflected the view of the majority in his state. In his remarks at the signing of the repeal bill, Richardson avowed that "throughout my adult life, I have been a firm believer in the death penalty as a just punishment—in very rare instances." But, he concluded, "the potential for wrongful conviction and, God forbid, execution of an innocent person stands as anathema to our very sensibilities as human beings. That is why I'm signing this bill into law." Archbishop Michael Sheehan of Santa Fe later accompanied Richardson to the Vatican, where the governor received personal greetings from Pope Benedict XVI and a silver olive branch from the Community of Sant'Egidio, a lay group whose various activities include a worldwide campaign against capital punishment. On that occasion Richardson noted the influence of "the archbishop and the Catholic Church" on his decision to change his stance and on the views about the death penalty among the citizenry in New Mexico. Archbishop Sheehan expressed his contentment that "we were able to help him understand our opposition to the death penalty and he did indeed change his view and signed the law." In light of Richardson's legislative support of abortion and stem cell research, Sheehan also pledged to continue promoting the church's teaching on the full range of "political issues that have a moral implication."[26]

Some Latino elected officials publicly acclaim their Catholic faith as a central influence in their lives and careers, such as former Florida senator Mel Martinez, who also served as secretary of Housing and Urban Development under President George W. Bush and as chairman of the Republican National Committee. Melquiades Rafael Martinez was born in Cuba, where he attended Sagrado Corazón de Jesús elementary school, attended daily Mass, served as an altar boy, and was formed in a "strong Catholic faith" that became "a source of strength throughout my life." At age fifteen his parents sent him into exile as part of Operation Peter Pan, a program of the U.S. government and the Catholic Church in Miami to relocate Cuban children fleeing the Castro regime in their homeland. Martinez credits his faith with enabling him to endure four painful years of separation from his parents while he matured to young adulthood in a new land, as well as with guiding him through his subsequent education, marriage and family life, death of loved ones, and career as a lawyer and in politics. Like any political figure, Martinez has faults and critics, some of whom undoubtedly see his Catholic faith betrayed in his actions; they have accused him of negative campaigning, failure to comply with campaign finance laws, and of course disagreed with some of his legislative stances. His positions on issues such as abortion and same-sex marriage reflect the teachings of the Catholic Church, though they are also consistent with his Republican Party affiliation and constituents. Yet other public positions are not, most notably his change of perspective on immigration; in 2006 Martinez cosponsored a Senate bill on comprehensive immigration reform that reflected various concerns of Catholic immigrants and their bishops, even though many of his own party members derided the unsuccessful legislation as "amnesty" and criticized Martinez for supporting it.[27]

Candidates pay increasing attention to the most widespread form of Latino political participation: voting. From presidential to local campaigns, many are prepared to offer at least a few lines of their stump speeches in Spanish. The combined Republican and Democrat Spanish-language advertising budgets tripled between the general elections of 2000 and 2004. During the 2008 campaign, Barack Obama alone spent $20 million to reach Spanish-speaking voters, more than the cumulative total for both presidential candidates in the 2004 election. Spanish-language media are attractive in part because they enable candidates and political parties to target Latino audiences without offending their base of white non-Hispanic voters. Linguistic segmentation leads major party candidates to fashion a "parallel presidential campaign." At the height of the 2008 race one reporter wrote, "The millions of Hispanic voters who read, watch and listen to media in Spanish have been gathering impressions that often differ in content and tone from those being communicated to the rest of the country in English. Ads and coverage have focused on family, jobs, health care, education, relations with Latin America and, of course, immigration." Latino activists feed the frenzy to gain Latino votes, as they are quick to remind candidates and party leaders that the Hispanic population is densest in high-prize electoral states like California, New York, Texas, and Florida.[28]

The growing Latino electorate has been the subject of much debate. When George W. Bush won a higher percentage of Hispanic votes than any modern Republican presidential candidate in his 2004 reelection, political pundits and strategists made controversial predictions about Republican voter realignment among Latinos. Dick Morris's bold assertion three days after the election exemplifies such claims: "The biggest reason for Bush's victory was that he finally cracked the Democratic stranglehold on the Hispanic vote." Though John Kerry won a majority of Hispanic votes, Morris based his contention on estimates that Latinos' increased support for Bush since the 2000 campaign accounted for more than three-fourths of the president's 3.1 percent margin of victory in the 2004 popular vote. According to Morris, Bush's popularity with Latinos was rooted in a platform consistent with their preferences on core issues, as he held firmly to his party's stands on "values" concerns like abortion and same-sex marriage but reversed his party's typical positions on issues such as bilingual education, English-only policies, and immigration reform. Arguing for potentially "enormous" future consequences stemming from Bush's electoral success, Morris's Republican loyalties were evident in his conclusion that "Bush may have begun to crack the unholy triple alliance of blacks, Hispanics and single women that anchors the political base of the Democratic Party."[29]

Four years later, Martin Kettle, associate editor of the British newspaper *The Guardian*, made similarly dramatic proclamations about Latino voters in the wake of their electoral support of Barack Obama. Noting that African American votes for Obama represented a relatively modest boost, given the long-standing African American electoral loyalty to Democratic candidates, Kettle opined that "the big racial game-changer in the voting patterns on Tuesday was not among white or black either. It was among the Hispanic vote." He contended that the two-thirds of Latino voters who cast their ballots for Obama raised his margin of victory among Latinos twenty-five percentage points above that of John Kerry's far narrower Latino majority in the previous election. Kettle concluded that the 2008 election was "a signal about the kind of American political map that will take shape later in the 21st century, as Hispanic voters come to outnumber all others. It is very bad long-term news for the Republicans, whose immigration policies are costing them dear."[30]

The post-election enthusiasm of both Kettle and Morris overstated the case. In a thorough review of voter polls for the 2004 election, scholars David Leal, Matt Barreto, Jongho Lee, and Rodolfo de la Garza pointed out the range of findings in these polls and questioned the claim that Bush received 45 percent of the Latino vote, the figure both Morris and Kettle presumed, estimating that 39 percent is a more likely figure. Even sources that concluded a mid-forties percentage for Bush, such as the National Election Pool, found that Latinos only cast approximately 8 percent of the votes, not 12 percent as Morris claimed. Given the general consensus that Bush received 35 percent of the Latino vote in 2000, these figures reveal a slimmer increase in Latino support between the two campaigns. Moreover, taking a longer view, Leal and his colleagues noted that Ronald Reagan won 37 percent of the Latino vote in 1984, but in the following three presidential elections Republican candidates received 32, 28, and 21 percent, respectively. Even when Ross Perot's 1992 and 1996 third-party candidacies are taken into account, these decreases temper predictions of Latino voter realignment, since it is at least as plausible to conclude that, like Reagan's, Bush's success among Latino voters reflected his own popularity with them. The longer view also suggests that the 31 percent of Latinos who voted for John McCain in 2008 does not represent an irreversible trend of weaker electoral support for Republican presidential candidates.[31]

The impact of Latino voters is greater, of course, in the states where they are most populous. Their influence is most frequently noteworthy in local, congressional, and some state elections. But in presidential elections Latino votes are not yet as significant as some observers contend. In California, New York, and Texas the victorious presidential candidate's margin of victory ranged from nine to twenty-seven percentage points in both the 2004 and 2008 presidential elections: Bush and McCain carried Texas while Kerry and Obama won in California and New York. These comfortable margins in states where collectively the majority of Latino voters reside mitigate claims of a critical Latino swing vote in presidential elections (and potentially reduce Latinos' incentive to vote in elections that pollsters declare are predetermined in advance).[32]

On the other hand, in the 2004 swing states of Florida and New Mexico, a higher percentage of Latinos voted for the victorious Bush than his national average among their counterparts. Exit polls in both states showed that Bush received nearly the same percentage of votes from whites that he had in 2000. But he received seven percentage points more from Hispanic voters in Florida and twelve percentage points more from Hispanics in New Mexico, along with six percentage points more in Florida from African Americans (whose population in New Mexico is too low for a statistical calculation from exit polls). Four years later Obama won in these two states. The percentage of whites voting for the Democratic and Republican candidates was once again virtually the same, whereas Obama's results were thirteen percentage points higher than Kerry's among Latino voters in each state and ten percentage points higher among African American voters in Florida. Moreover, the overall percentage of Hispanics among the electorate increased nine percentage points to 41 percent of all votes cast in New Mexico, raising Obama's number of Hispanic votes there even higher. In Florida, Obama was the first Democratic presidential candidate to win a clear majority of Latino votes since at least 1988, the year of the first exit poll conducted there (in the 1996 and 2000 elections, Bill Clinton and Al Gore came close enough that their margin of defeat was within the exit poll's statistical margin of error). Obama's Florida victory stemmed from his success among younger Cuban American voters and among the growing population of Hispanics in Florida who are not of Cuban background.[33]

Of course, in close races—Bush's 2004 margin of victory was five percentage points in Florida and only one in New Mexico, whereas Obama's margin in Florida was only three percentage points—the importance of every grouping of voters is magnified. As Leal and his colleagues soberly conclude, though Hispanic votes are as important as any others in such elections, there is not sufficient evidence to deem Latinos "the decisive factor." Yet Latino voters are increasingly significant for candidates in states such as Florida,

New Mexico, Nevada, and Colorado, all of which have a growing Latino electorate and went to Obama in 2008 after Bush had won them in 2004. Thus it is not surprising that from the 2004 to the 2008 elections the "battleground" states of New Mexico, Colorado, and Nevada were the three states with the largest increases in the Latino percentage of the voters who cast ballots. Rodolfo de la Garza argues that asking if Latino voters were decisive in such election results is not the sole or even the most important question to investigate. Rather, he proposes that analysts focus greater attention on Latinos' participation in voter coalitions that unite diverse constituencies to affect electoral outcomes.[34]

Relatively low voter registration and turnout have inhibited Latinos from playing an even greater role in elections. When the late Willie Velásquez founded the acclaimed Southwest Voter Registration and Education Project (SWVREP) in 1974, there were about 2.4 million registered Latino voters, a number that increased nearly fivefold to 11.6 million by 2008. Pundits cite such increases as evidence that the Latino electoral "sleeping giant" is awakening, but the upsurge is not as dramatic when seen in comparative perspective. Though the overall Latino population is now greater than that of African Americans, many Latinos are not eligible to vote, because they are not citizens or are younger than the legal voting age. According to SWVREP statistics, for the 2008 general elections eligible African American voters outnumbered Latinos by five million. About 70 percent of both eligible black and white voters registered, while less than 60 percent of eligible Latinos did so. Most importantly, less than half of eligible Latino voters cast ballots, while nearly two-thirds of black and white eligible voters did.[35]

Overall the electoral significance of Latinos is growing steadily, but not as exponentially as some commentators suggest. One religious influence on their electoral participation is the denominational switching of recent decades, which has produced a discernible shift in their preference of political party. Though survey results differ on partisan allegiance percentages, Latino Protestants and especially evangelicals are more disposed to the Republican Party than their Catholic counterparts. Four recent surveys concur that although the affiliation of Latino evangelicals is roughly split among the two major parties, Latino Catholics favor the Democrats by a margin of three or even four to one. The only major exception to this pattern is Cuban Catholics, particularly the elder generation, among whom the inverse is true: nearly three times as many are Republicans, a pattern generally attributed to their higher socioeconomic status and a conservatism born of their painful experience of exile in the wake of the socialist revolution Fidel Castro led in their homeland. The 2004 presidential election reflected these preferences.

Political scientist John Green's analysis shows that despite Bush's relatively strong appeal to Latinos, the Catholics among them voted for Kerry by about a two-to-one margin, while well over half of Latino Protestants cast their ballots for Bush. A pre-election poll showed fully 80 percent of Cubans intended to vote for Bush, but since they comprised only about 6 percent of the Latino electorate overall, Kerry's majority among Latino Catholics was still substantial. No exit poll analysis has yet examined Latino voting patterns along lines of religious affiliation for the 2008 presidential elections, though pre-election surveys showed that Obama's appeal to Latinos would result in gains across denominations and win him a majority from both Latino Protestant and Catholic voters. But the surveys also demonstrated the continuing significance of denominational allegiance, revealing that Obama's margin of support among Latino Catholics was more than double that among their Protestant counterparts.[36]

Another distinction across denominations is Latino Protestants' somewhat greater tendency for electoral political involvement. According to the 2000 Hispanic Churches in American Public Life survey, Hispanic Protestant churches and religious organizations had higher levels of involvement than their Catholic counterparts in conducting voter registration efforts, providing rides to the polls on Election Day, handing out campaign materials, and asking people to support a particular political candidate. Mainline Protestant Latinos drove this statistical trend, with higher levels for all activities than both Latino evangelicals and Latino Pentecostals. Lead researcher Gastón Espinosa noted demographic characteristics that contributed to these differences, such as the lower income and education levels and higher number of immigrants among Latino Catholics, all factors that across ethnic groups tend to decrease these types of political involvement. Another contributing factor is the conviction among many Catholics that faith should enter into the public arena in nonpartisan ways. Indeed, consistent with Hispanic Catholics' higher levels of participation in pro-immigrant protests, the sole indicator on the HCAPL survey in which Hispanic Catholics rated higher than Protestants was their involvement in "advocat[ing] on behalf of a specific ballot issue, proposition or referendum." The parental portion of the 2002–2003 survey for the National Study of Youth and Religion confirmed these differences in the political involvement of Hispanic Protestants and Catholics.[37]

A common perception is that Latinos tend to hold more "conservative" views on life and reproductive issues and on same-sex marriage while also endorsing social, economic, and immigration reforms that are generally considered liberal. Selective attention to such tendencies has led partisans to claim both that Latinos are "natural Republicans" and that they are "natural Democrats." Hispanic ministry leaders have maintained that in fact Latino Catholic views bridge the typical divides of contemporary U.S. politics and reflect Catholic teachings on a range of issues. The more than five hundred Hispanic ministry leaders who participated in "Convocation '95: The Hispanic Presence in the New Evangelization in the United States" underscored these contentions in their collective statement of commitment. Pledging themselves to join Pope John Paul II and their bishops to "defend the value of each human life from the first moment of conception to natural death," they expounded on concerns entailed in this commitment that span the typical priority issues of both political conservatives and liberals, such as abortion, capital punishment, euthanasia, drugs, the arms trade, poverty, women's and workers' rights, discrimination against immigrants, health care, education, domestic violence, the dignity of the family, and respect for the elderly. Hispanics also contest—or even reproach as hypocritical—the views of fellow Catholics who do not conform to the positions of their bishops across the divides of U.S. politics. As one undocumented Catholic mother put it, "They say our children in the womb are 'innocent life,' but the day the children are born they call them 'illegals' who have no rights and should 'go home' [to their mothers' country of origin]."[38]

Yet the assertions from Hispanic leaders do not reflect the views of all their Latino counterparts. Though no study has correlated Hispanic beliefs on core issues with their degrees of church involvement, a commonsense assumption is that Latinos tend to mirror the statistical data showing that Catholics who practice their faith through regular participation in parish life and worship are more likely to uphold positions consistent with official teaching. Even on a supposedly "Hispanic" issue such as immigration, though a clear majority of Latinos join the U.S. Catholic bishops in favoring comprehensive reform, a notable minority are concerned that new immigrants depress wages, take jobs that otherwise would go to native workers, are a financial burden on taxpayers, or increase crime. Among Hispanic participants in the HCAPL survey, both Catholic and Protestant, one-third did not think undocumented immigrants should be eligible for government assistance such as Medicaid or welfare benefits. One-fifth said that not even churches or religious leaders should assist the undocumented.[39]

Other surveys challenge the presumption that Latinos staunchly support the pronouncements of church officials on public policies about legalized abortion and gay marriage. The 2002 National Survey of Latinos found that Latino Catholics, evangelicals, and even Latinos with no religious affiliation are much less accepting of abortion than their white counterparts. But subsequent studies like those of the Pew Research Center found that, while the majority of Hispanic Catholics oppose abortion and same-sex marriage and are more likely to do so than non-Latino Catholics, the margins of difference are only 9 and 4 percent, respectively. The 2010 Associated Press–Univision Poll revealed a generation and language gap on Latino acceptance of legalized abortion and same-sex marriage: those under thirty and those who speak mainly English tend to be more accepting of both. Similarly, a 2009 Pew Hispanic Center study on young Latinos found the percentage of those who believe abortion should be legal more than doubles to 58 percent from the first to the third generation. The study also showed a parallel, though less precipitous, rise in the percentage of those who support gay marriage. While collectively the range of findings in existing surveys are not amenable to precise statistical conclusions, at the very least they call into question the assertion that Latino Catholics are considerably more apt to uphold church teachings on these issues than non-Latino Catholics. Indeed, studies of young Latinos indicate that acclimatization to the U.S. milieu correlates with weakened adherence to various positions consistent with official Catholic teachings. Moreover, the statistical data that show more Latino Catholics consent to these teachings than their non-Latino coreligionists by no means eradicate the concern of Hispanic ministry leaders who are alarmed at the number of Latinos who do not concur.[40]

Some Catholic leaders have defined "nonnegotiable" moral issues such as abortion, stem cell research, and same-sex marriage as the determinative criteria for Catholic voters. Nonetheless, like other Catholics, many Latinos give more decisive weight to issues they believe affect them and their families most immediately and, strategically, the concerns they believe a particular candidate is most likely to address with effective actions and not merely with words. For many Hispanics, such issues include education, health care, immigration, and, most prominently in recent elections, jobs and the economy. In 2004 the economy ranked as the most influential concern among nearly 60 percent of Latino Catholic voters, the highest percentage among all religious groups except black Protestants. For the 2008 election, the economy continued to be the paramount concern; according to the exit poll survey of the William C. Velasquez Institute, once again nearly 60 percent of all Latino voters said the economy and jobs was the issue that "mattered most" in their voting choice for the presidential election. No other issue "mattered most" for even 10 percent of Latinos polled, with the next two most important issues being the Iraq War policy and abortion, which respectively received top priority among 9 and 7 percent of Latino voters. While the large number of working-class Latinos do not tend to have the same lens on the economy as more affluent voters—to use the language of the 2008 presidential campaigns, these Hispanics' focus is more on jobs and Main Street than on investments and Wall Street—their strong focus on economic issues reflected a concern widespread among many in the broader electorate.[41]

The Democratic preference among Latino Catholics has a noteworthy impact on the overall profile of Catholic voters. It offsets gains Republicans have made in recent decades among white non-Latino Catholics, who are now nearly evenly split between the two major parties. This upward trend is rooted in Republicans' stances on issues like abortion and an approach to lessening taxation and government increasingly favored among a Catholic population that has risen economically since World War II. While the most crucial factors for enlarged Latino electoral influence are voter registration, participation, and strategic collaboration in effective coalitions, convictions on social and moral issues and trends in denominational affiliation shape the interplay between Latino voters and those who crave their electoral support. Republicans' demonstrated potential for gaining votes drives their ongoing attempts to reach Latinos, especially among evangelicals and traditional Catholics who seem more amenable to their message. The Republicans' past success has alerted many Democrats to the fact that they cannot take Latino voters for granted, in terms of neither turnout nor party loyalty. Hispanics' expanding numbers and willingness to cross party lines in a particular election further instigate competition for their votes. Nonetheless, Latino Catholics' economic concerns, resonance with Catholic teachings about immigration and the social order, and perception that Democrats represent them best on bread-and-butter issues generally overshadow the attraction of some Latinos to Republicans' moral traditionalism. These trends will continue to shape overall Catholic voting patterns for the foreseeable future.

For the most part, Hispanic ministry leaders have not attempted to sway Latino Catholics' electoral decisions toward particular candidates or political parties, nor to influence Hispanic Catholic public officials in a partisan manner. But they have advocated for legislation consistent with Catholic teachings on issues pertaining to life and human dignity, as Archbishop Sheehan's attempts to sway Governor Richardson illustrate. Six bishops who met with Hispanic and other congressional representatives from both major political parties in September 2009 illuminate the potential for nonpartisan Latino Catholic initiatives that span the typical divides of U.S. politics. The delegation consisted of Archbishop José Gomez of San Antonio (currently archbishop of Los Angeles); Bishop James Tamayo of Laredo; Bishop Ricardo Ramírez of Las Cruces, New Mexico; Bishop Jaime Soto of Sacramento; Bishop Carlos Sevilla, S.J., of Yakima, Washington; and auxiliary bishop

Edgar Da Cunha, S.D.V., of Newark. Among the issues they discussed were health care, housing, poverty, immigration, and education. They expressed their concern that looming health care legislation could fund abortions and might weaken conscience protections for medical professionals. Addressing the raging national debate on the issue, the bishops declared that the failure of Congress to enact comprehensive immigration reform exacerbated harsh attitudes toward émigrés in proposed health care legislation, leading some critics so far as to suggest that undocumented immigrants should not even be permitted to purchase their own insurance plans. In a press conference following their meetings, Bishop Soto said the bishops find such proposals "foolish and short-sighted," an instance of "runaway anti-immigrant rhetoric" that detracts from the necessary "commonsense approach" to health care reform. The bishops urged the representatives to enact comprehensive immigration reform as well as health care reforms that encompass immigrants and citizens alike—in Archbishop Gomez's words, a reform that "offers a universal plan in which everyone is able to participate and that would provide care from conception to natural death."[42]

Hispanic efforts have had greater resonance within the U.S. Catholic Church than in instigating federal legislation on issues like comprehensive immigration reform, which, at the time of this writing, remains an unattained goal for bishops, Latino faithful, and faith-based community organizers and activists. The presence and activism of Hispanics have elicited debates about immigration among their coreligionists, but they have also incited fellow Catholics to advance immigrant initiatives in education, advocacy, and especially pastoral care. Among Catholic bishops, immigration is the social issue that draws the most consistent public response across regions and theological perspectives, complementing the bishops' more frequently noted stance on the right to life. The bishops' collective stance on immigration perceptibly supports the contention that the Catholic defense of life extends, in the words of many Catholic leaders, across the lifespan from "conception to natural death." Immigration is also the issue that has most prompted Latino Catholic leaders to publicly address the link between faith and politics, as they have sought to integrate Catholic teaching with the complex challenge of formulating just and effective immigration policies. Latinos shape the immigration debate and public Catholic witness through their ongoing attempts to convince their fellow U.S. residents that immigration is not merely an ethnic Hispanic nor solely a legal or a U.S. issue, but a human and, for them and their coreligionists, ultimately a profoundly Catholic issue.

Current efforts to expand the reach of faith-based community organizations into regional and national initiatives demonstrate how far these organizations

have come since the first Hispanic-led attempt to amplify the faith foundation of the locally focused Alinsky organizing model. Leaders in community
organizations contest the presumption that voting is the sole means for ordinary U.S. citizens to participate in a democracy. They stress that what voters
do after an election to shape governmental budgets and policy decisions is
an even more important means of exercising political responsibility. Unlike
social service efforts such as food banks and soup kitchens, faith-based community organizations focus on active citizenship rather than temporary assistance. Unlike groups like the religious right that generally promote a fixed
moral agenda through national and state lobbying efforts, these organizations
are mediating institutions that help working-class and other congregational
members participate more effectively in U.S. democratic society. The organizations offer an inherent critique of a political culture with limited nonpartisan
alternatives for acting on one's faith in the political arena. In the U.S. Catholic
Church, faith-based organizations have enabled numerous Latinos and their
fellow parishioners to affect the policy decisions and social conditions that
influence their lives.

Yet the vitality of these organizations is an ongoing concern. Activist
priests worry that younger clergy are not as engaged in organizing efforts as
their elders. Parishioners who are too involved with other activities or too ap-
athetic can have a negative effect. Moreover, pundits and even some pastors
have conspicuously argued that church support of organizing is an improper
conjoining of religion and politics. The most ardent critics have claimed that
such efforts are inimical to the gospel of Jesus Christ and have called on Christians to boycott churches where preachers speak of "social justice." Current
controversies about the Catholic Campaign for Human Development are the
most noteworthy instance of such debates within the U.S. Catholic Church.
These debates pit Catholics who see the benefits of faith-based organizing in
their own lives and parishes against their coreligionists who fear the political involvements entailed in such efforts can taint the moral witness of the
church. It is not yet clear if the bishops' long-standing support of CCHD will
continue to hold firm in the face of this pressure. Nor is it clear how or if the
U.S. Catholic Church would replace CCHD with a similar national initiative
to promote justice, which church leaders insist is the foundation for works of
charity. Pope Benedict XVI noted the relationship between the two in his 2009
encyclical *Caritas in veritate*, avowing that the charity of gratuitously giving
beyond what is required presumes ongoing efforts to ensure that members of
a society receive at minimum the basic necessities and dignity they are justly
"due" as human beings.[43] Whatever course of action the bishops take, the
CCHD controversy is arguably the clearest instance in U.S. Catholicism today

in which they are challenged to choose between the aspirations of working-class Catholics like many Latinos and the activism of other Catholics who are at best uneasy with church-supported organizing efforts to foster justice through grassroots political participation.

While media attention and even Catholics themselves often accentuate church leaders' pronouncements as the core component of Catholic public witness, Hispanic ministry concerns underscore the urgency of complementing such pronouncements with pastoral efforts to confront the struggles of daily existence. The experience of unintended pregnancy illustrates the need for these complementary approaches. A Guttmacher Institute study showed that in 2004 the abortion ratio for Hispanic women was twenty-two abortions per one hundred pregnancies, more than non-Hispanic white women's ratio of fifteen abortions per one hundred pregnancies, though less than the African American ratio of forty-two per one hundred pregnancies. While the Hispanic abortion rate decreased 20 percent from 1994 to 2004, approximately twenty-eight of every one thousand Latina women between the ages of fifteen and forty-four had an abortion in 2004. No national study has examined the abortion rates for Hispanic Catholic women, but with the preponderance of Catholics in the overall population, clearly many Catholics are among those who have had abortions. These substantial figures underlie the very personal and often familial saga of unintended pregnancy that touches the lives of many Hispanics, in a number of cases exacerbated by poverty, already large families, a lack of health care, or the possibility of a teenage mother dropping out of school. Unintended pregnancies frequently affect a woman's family and friends, whether these companions offer her assistance and support or become instigators of shame and humiliation. Proclamations of the resolute Catholic teaching about the need to protect the life of the unborn, which are obviously transgressed in such abortion rates, need to be complemented with even more widespread ministries in response to the various pressures that lead to decisions for abortion, particularly among the most vulnerable who face unintended pregnancy with little or no support.[44]

The growing Hispanic presence makes the ramifications of moral and social issues more imminent in numerous parishes. Employment, workers' rights, education, affordable health care, unintended pregnancy, the dignity of immigrants, pressures on family unity, violence both in the streets and in homes, and men who abuse and abandon women to face pregnancy alone are but some of the critical pastoral concerns Catholic ministry leaders face. In this context, Catholic teachings such as those on justice and civic responsibility are more salient when embodied in local organizing initiatives that enable grassroots people to address community concerns and participate in the decision-making processes affecting them and their families. Similarly, official declarations of solidarity with groups such as immigrants, women, and the unborn are strengthened or weakened in the treatment that émigrés and those with unintended pregnancies receive in parishes. Arguably the most significant contribution Latino Catholics make to public Catholicism is the various ways they reveal that the sometimes-harsh realities of everyday pastoral work are the ordinary means through which the church lives out its mission to transform lives, communities, and society.

CHAPTER

## Passing on the Faith

tudents in the theology classes I have offered in San Antonio; Los Angeles; and South Bend, Indiana, have taught me much about young Hispanics' aspirations and struggles for faith and identity. One young woman sent me an email that included the following comments:

> I had a few thoughts about some of the topics we discussed in class today. I didn't want to mention them in class just because I hadn't quite worked them out in my head....
>
> Immigrants come to the United States not because they want to, but because they have to. The only thing they truly know and have is the Catholic Church, those that have been Catholic their whole lives I mean. From day to day they face various forms of oppression and racism and sometimes they have absolutely no one to turn to but the Church.
>
> Now, what if all their children see is that suffering? What if, day after day, they only witnessed their parents turning to God or Mary in all their trials, praying the rosary every day, asking patron saints to intercede, struggling in life for some hope or reward that only comes from being faithful? On a personal level I am one of those Hispanics. I can't go to Mass without feeling like I have to suffer. I only know the suffering Jesus because that is how I experienced him with my mother. So now I feel that the Church, moreover, Christianity has nothing to offer me even though I know it does and I would like it to, but my experience and identity as a Catholic is wrapped up in suffering.
>
> The Church was there for my mom in her sufferings and I felt it and I loved it for that. It became a part of me, but that isn't my experience

of life anymore. I have learned that I don't have to suffer through everything. I have the resources to fight oppression.

While her mother or Hispanic pastoral leaders might well respond that
faith itself is a resource to confront suffering and oppression, this daughter's
perception of differences between her experience of Catholicism and that
of her mother encapsulates the particular challenge of passing on the faith
among numerous Hispanics: approaches that engage one generation, particularly first-generation immigrants, can easily be less resonant—even coun-
terproductive—with that generation's children. A number of young Latinas
and Latinos perceive their elders' faith as too entwined with suffering, too
connected to a bygone immigrant homeland, too focused on strict obedience
to authority, too simplistic to address the realities of contemporary life, or
simply irrelevant to the concerns of a new generation. Even Hispanics like my
student who "love" the church out of gratitude for the faith nurtured in them
and their parents, acknowledge that "it became a part of me," and say they
would like to be more involved today often struggle to do so. Others scarcely
exert such a struggle, if at all.

Passing on the faith is a concern among every religious group, as is evident
in the wide attention given to studies of faith among the young, such as Robert Wuthnow's *After the Baby Boomers: How Twenty- and Thirty-Somethings
Are Shaping the Future of American Religion* and James Heft's *Passing on the
Faith: Transforming Traditions for the Next Generation of Jews, Christians, and
Muslims.* Colleen Carroll's *The New Faithful: Why Young Adults Are Embracing
Christian Orthodoxy* highlights young Catholics who are committed to knowing Catholic doctrine, living Catholic morality, respecting church authorities,
and participating in the sacraments and traditional devotions. But Christian
Smith and Melinda Lundquist Denton's *Soul Searching: The Religious and Spiritual Lives of American Teenagers* concludes that Catholics "stand out among
the U.S. Christian teenagers as consistently scoring lower on most measures
of religiosity." The authors attribute these differences primarily to loosened
faith commitment accompanying many Catholic parents' upward mobility,
especially the Euro-Americans, who collectively have advanced more than
any other group. Another key factor is a weaker U.S. Catholic institutional
commitment of paid personnel and fiscal resources for youth ministry as
compared to that of their Protestant counterparts. In the follow-up study
of Christian Smith and Patricia Snell that reexamined these teen interviewees as eighteen-to-twenty-three-year-old emerging adults, one-fourth of the
original Catholic respondents no longer identified themselves as Catholics.
The authors of *Young Adult Catholics: Religion in the Culture of Choice* found

that "for many young adults, Catholic identity is weak, focused outside the institutional church, and only moderately central to their lives." These authors conclude that this is a "portentous" state of affairs and that "[U.S.] Catholicism's institutional vitality, public witness, and capacity to retain its young are in jeopardy."[1]

Smith's acclaimed National Study of Youth and Religion (NSYR) and other surveys reveal that Hispanic young people participate in Sunday worship and Catholic devotional practices as least as regularly as their Euro-American peers, though like most young people their level of participation is relatively low compared to other age groups. As with their non-Latino counterparts, studies of self-reported religious affiliation also indicate that the U.S. Catholic Church faces an immense pastoral challenge of declining allegiance across Hispanic generations. The 2000 Hispanic Churches in American Public Life survey showed that the self-reported Catholic affiliation of U.S. Latinos drops from 74 percent among the first generation to 62 percent among the third generation. Subsequent studies by the Center for Applied Research in the Apostolate, the American Religious Identification Survey researchers, the Pew Hispanic Center, and the Associated Press-Univision concur with the HCAPL findings and conclude that adoption of the English language correlates closely with decreased Catholic affiliation. Thus the key factor in generational transition for Latinos is the increasing numbers of those born in the United States who speak English and, presumably, become more enmeshed in the U.S. social milieu. Ken Johnson-Mondragón, director of research and publications for the national Latino Catholic youth and young adult ministry organization Instituto Fe y Vida (Institute for Faith and Life), provides analysis based on the NSYR that is consistent with these findings. He asserts that "the large gap between the 74% of Spanish-dominant teens who are Catholic and the 57% of English-dominant Hispanic teens who are Catholic indicates that more acculturated Hispanics are more likely to be Protestant and less likely to be Catholic." These figures also reflect the growing number of Hispanics who reply "no religion" to survey questions about religious affiliation.[2]

No factor affects efforts to form young Hispanics in the Catholic faith more than the dynamics of generational transition, through which most Hispanics pass amid the accompanying process of adapting to life in the United States as immigrants or as the children of immigrants. Estimates from Instituto Fe y Vida for 2007 approximated that among the nine million Hispanic Catholics between the ages of thirteen and twenty-nine, 45 percent were immigrants, 32 percent the children of immigrants, and 23 percent the children of U.S.-born parents. Tomorrow's Hispanic teens and young adults—those currently twelve years old or younger—encompass a far greater ratio of second- and subsequent-generation children. These current trends illuminate the staggering demographic reality of generational transition: over the next three decades the number of third-generation Latinos will triple, the second generation will double, and the overall percentage (though not necessarily the raw numbers) of first-generation immigrants will decline.[3]

Clearly, Hispanic young people are crucial for the present and the future of U.S. Catholicism. The catechesis of young Latinos today will influence the shape of vocations to the priesthood, religious life, and lay ecclesial ministry tomorrow. It will significantly determine whether Catholic pews are full, half full, or empty. According to the research of Robert Putnam and David Campbell, Latinos already comprise two-thirds of Catholics under the age of thirty-five who attend church regularly. Moreover, collectively, young Latinos are a vital population for the future of the United States. One-fifth of schoolchildren and one-fourth of newborns in the United States are Hispanic. Generation gaps are noteworthy not only within families but also among Hispanic and Euro-American state populations. One of the widest gaps is in Arizona, where Hispanics comprise 30 percent of the population; 83 percent of Arizona residents over sixty-five years of age are white, while only 43 percent of those under eighteen are. Wide age gaps like this reveal the significance of young Latinos for the future of the U.S. economy, as well as the potential for conflicting views between Latino young and Euro-American elder populations on issues such as proportionate funding for social security, health care, welfare assistance, and public schools. The 2009 Pew Hispanic Center study on young Latinos coming of age in the United States summarizes the demographic ascent of Hispanics, who comprise "the youngest minority group in the United States." Pew researchers avow that "never before in this country's history has a minority ethnic group made up so large a share of the youngest Americans."[4]

Catholic bishops and other leaders do not see Latino teens and young adults merely as a pastoral predicament or problem, but as "a source of energy and renewal for the Church." The faith commitment and evangelizing potential of young Hispanics were clearly evident in the First National Encuentro for Hispanic Youth and Young Adult Ministry, a landmark 2006 event that the National Catholic Network de Pastoral Juvenil Hispana–La Red (literally "the net") convoked in collaboration with the Secretariat for Hispanic Affairs, the Bishops' Committee on Hispanic Affairs, and other supporters. An estimated 40,000 young people and ministry leaders participated in the parish, diocesan, and regional Encuentros that culminated in a national gathering at the University of Notre Dame in South Bend, Indiana, with 1,680 Latino youth delegates and 250 leaders who accompany young Hispanics in ministry. The commitment of young Latinos was evident in the sacrifices they made to participate in the National Encuentro. Many traveled overnight on buses and vans, paid part or all of their own costs related to the conference, or worked long overtime hours to make up for missed days at work. The concluding Encuentro document presents participants' vision for ministry and evangelization among the young and attests that "the new life young Hispanics are giving to our Church comes from the apostolic zeal of *jóvenes* who, having made Jesus the center of their lives, dedicate hours and hours to sharing and increasing the faith with other young people."[5]

Yet in their *Encuentro and Mission* document the U.S. bishops avow that youth ministry in parishes "does not, for the most part, reach Hispanic young people" and that "U.S.-born Hispanic teenagers are the largest segment of Hispanic young people—and the least served." In a 1999 survey U.S. bishops self-ranked youth programs as the least effective aspect of Hispanic ministry in their dioceses, with only 7 percent rating these programs highly. In their 2005 statement *Renewing Our Commitment to Catholic Elementary and Secondary Schools in the Third Millennium* the bishops further avowed that Catholic schools "must reflect this reality [of the expanding Hispanic presence] and reach out and welcome Hispanics." Young Latino Catholics are a significant and potentially transformative force in U.S. Catholicism and the wider society, but there are considerable obstacles to that force being actualized. The central challenge for Catholics is passing on the faith, which they endeavor to do in families, youth and young adult groups, retreat and apostolic movements, catechetical programs, Catholic schools, and campus ministry. Analyses of generational transition among Latinos, efforts to develop ministerial and educational initiatives that engage young Hispanics, and the current state of those initiatives are crucial for understanding the present and future contours among this pivotal segment of the U.S. Catholic population.[6]

Children with at least one immigrant parent comprise a majority among young Hispanics today. They are on the front lines of the everyday realities that émigrés face, one of which is periods of family separation. Many fathers and an increasing number of mothers initially leave their children behind with friends or relatives when they cross the border to earn needed wages, or they send the young back home for a time so that their children can improve their Spanish, learn from the cultural ways of the homeland, or escape what their parents perceive as the bad influences of growing up in the United States. As many as 85 percent of immigrant Hispanic teenagers have lived apart from one or both parents for a time span of at least six months. Periods of separation result in predictable tensions, as many children feel abandoned, even if they recognize their parents' sacrifice to provide for them, and parents are befuddled with feelings of guilt, loneliness, and at times anger that their children are upset about the separation rather than grateful for their elders' hard work. The longer the separation, the more painful these tensions can become. For some, faith strengthens perseverance and family ties. Contact with extended family, especially grandmothers, often has a strong influence. One Latina interviewed for the *Young Adult Catholics* study related that she and her siblings spent summers in Mexico, where their grandmother took them to daily Mass, led them in the rosary, and provided "the only formal religious education training we had." Yet, for many parents, irregular contact with their children is an obstacle to the transmission of core values like religion.[7]

Transnational movement has created a number of "mixed status" families, with some children born in the United States, and thus legally U.S. citizens, and others born away, who usually share the immigrant status of their parents. As many as three-quarters of undocumented families, nearly 2.3 million of them, have at least one child who is a U.S. citizen. Some critics derogatorily label such children "anchor babies" intended to be a means to gain legal status for their parents and other loved ones. Immigrant defenders retort that the time lapse before newborns reach the age when they can sponsor immigrants and the length of the legalization process inhibit the vast majority from securing citizenship for their parents. In any event, mixed status can wreak havoc on family relations. One Ecuadoran couple in New York separated from each other after years of longing for home and struggling with the loss of family, friends, and professional careers they had enjoyed there. Their older daughter achieved high grades in school but because of her undocumented status struggled in her efforts to attend college and pursue her chosen accounting career. Meanwhile her younger, U.S.-born brother seemingly squandered his privilege of citizenship with his lack of motivation. At one point he even shocked the family by declaring he would like to move back to Ecuador. His sister's affection for him is tinged with frustration and resentment. Their father closely monitors his schoolwork to goad him on to success. Their mother expresses the sacrificial resignation of numerous immigrants: "My hopes are dead. Right now we're just focused on the education of the children and their future. Let them reach their goals and have their dreams." Amid relentless work schedules, worries, and hardships, apparently neither parent devoted extensive time to nurturing their faith or passing it on to their children.[8]

Even when families remain physically intact, parents face considerable difficulties in transmitting their values and faith. As the title of the 2009 Pew

Hispanic Center study put it, the daily existence of numerous young Latinos occurs at the intersection "between two worlds"—those of the United States and those of their family's Hispanic origin. One young Latina complained that her parents guarded her zealously but never taught her "anything having to do with sexuality." Her experience in the world of young people in the United States led her to conclude that "sending a girl out without a clue is more dangerous than sending her out alone." Nancy Foner's research on intergenerational relations in immigrant families shows that these families confront strains and conflicts over concerns such as discipline and respect, expectations regarding sexual relations, disproportionately restrictive regulation of daughters, and the role reversals rooted in Spanish-speaking parents' dependence on their children to translate for them in mercantile or other transactions. Experienced Hispanic youth ministry leader Carlos Carrillo adds that communication between many immigrant parents and their offspring suffers from inadequate proficiency in each other's primary language and from the elders' lack of knowledge about growing up in the United States. Conversely, many children of immigrants do not have extensive experience living in their parents' country of origin. Consequently, they tend to judge their elders' values and standard of living based on what they hear in the media and from their peers. Although the younger age cohort of any religious group is susceptible to veer from the faith tradition in which they were raised, in this context immigrant parents' Catholic faith can appear to their U.S.-born or U.S.-reared children as one more antiquated tradition from their native land.[9]

Generational divides are so noteworthy that various scholars have identified what they deem the "immigrant paradox." Despite lower levels of education, employment opportunities, access to health care and social services, and, for many, the daily complications of undocumented status, a range of survey results show that Hispanic immigrants tend "to be healthier than their U.S.-born children, have lower divorce rates, experience fewer mental or emotional problems, have lower rates of incarceration and otherwise outdo the second generation on a variety of measures of well-being." A 2009 conference at Brown University bore the telling title "The Immigrant Paradox in Education and Behavior: Is Becoming American a Developmental Risk?" The Pew Hispanic Center study found that second-generation Latino youth are more than twice as likely as their first-generation counterparts to have engaged during the previous year in each of three risky behaviors examined: carrying a weapon, involvement in a fight, and being threatened with a weapon. Hispanic youth born in the United States are more than twice as likely as young immigrant Latinos to have a friend or relative who is a former or current gang member, a trend particularly prevalent among the young of ethnic Mexican background. The U.S. born also have a higher rate of incarceration. According to the Pew researchers, religious practice is a key explanatory factor for the immigrant paradox. Participation in religion correlates inversely with risky behaviors, so when the more widespread religious participation of Hispanic émigré youth is "taken into account, the 'risky behavior gap' between young immigrants and their native-born peers narrows or disappears."[10]

Risky behaviors reflect in part negative experiences and low expectations. The Pew study found that native-born Latino youth report more experiences of racial or ethnic discrimination directly affecting them, their families, or close friends than do their immigrant counterparts. While indicators such as high school dropout and poverty rates decline noticeably from the immigrant to the second generation, they then increase slightly with the third generation, leading various scholars to express "skepticism that the children and grandchildren of today's Hispanic immigrants will enjoy the same upward mobility experienced by the offspring of European immigrants in previous centuries." Alejandro Portes, a sociologist with expertise in acculturation among the children of immigrants in the United States, notes that although most of them "are doing well," a "sizable minority" are caught in a pattern of "downward assimilation." A number of scholars and activists concur that what is often viewed as a failure to assimilate is in fact "assimilation to the wrong things: crime, drugs and self-fulfilling prophecies of racial defeat." One nineteen-year-old daughter of El Salvadoran émigrés was caught in a descending spiral of risky behaviors in an ill-fated attempt to gain approval and respect from her peers. She lives in the suburbs of Washington, D.C., one of numerous suburban areas nationwide that are ill prepared to deal with growing poor and working-class immigrant populations more typically associated with urban cores. Her father expressed gratitude and admiration for the United States, attesting, "You can achieve what you want here." But his daughter, though admitting to her own faults and destructive behaviors, revealed a sense of futility in her rationale that "if you're Hispanic, people already expect you to steal, to fight, to be rude, to be ghetto. If everyone thinks wrong of you, eventually you're going to start thinking wrong about yourself."[11]

Johnson-Mondragón provides an insightful categorization of Hispanic young people. The categories he distinguishes range broadly from Spanish-speaking immigrant workers, to bilingual "identity seekers" negotiating between cultures, to English-dominant speakers who have sought or achieved a level of mainstream status and identification. As is generally the case with such schemas, a number of young Hispanics have characteristics of two or even more categories. Nonetheless, Johnson-Mondragón's analysis provides a helpful template for assessing present and future efforts to hand down the faith to young Latino Catholics as they mature to adulthood in the United States.[12]

The first category of young Hispanics that he identifies, immigrant workers, came to the United States after age fifteen—that is, after the age at which they might have received some of their education in English-speaking U.S. classrooms. According to Johnson-Mondragón, they comprise some 25 to 45 percent of young Hispanic Catholics. They tend to have lesser economic means and formal education; prefer to speak in Spanish; and work in a number of service sector, agricultural, and manual labor occupations within the U.S. economy. Their concerns and daily labor schedules are vastly different from those of students and young professionals of a similar age. The conclusions of the First National Encuentro for Hispanic Youth and Young Adult Ministry attest that their plight is often one of great suffering: loneliness at being far from family and home, experiences of marginalization and discrimination, a living environment marred with violence and temptations to addiction.[13] Though generally industrious and focused on supporting their families back home and building a brighter future, isolation and the drudgery of their labors exacerbate instances of binge drinking, drug use, and unintended pregnancy. The majority of immigrant workers are from Mexico. About half are undocumented. Some immigrated with their families. Many others live in the United States apart from their families back home, leading them to engage Catholic parishes and apostolic movements as means to build networks of friendships and faith.

The faith experience of many immigrant workers is rooted in Latin American ministries with young people that are generally called *pastoral juvenil.* Latin American pastoral juvenil groups and apostolic movements have formed a number of young people in their faith and shape immigrants' desire to encounter or create similar ministries in the United States. Delegations of bishops and youth ministry leaders from the United States have participated in Latin American Encuentros of Directors of Pastoral Juvenil for more than two decades. Two of the leading centers promoting Hispanic youth and young adult ministry in the United States—Instituto Fe y Vida in Stockton, California, and the Southeast Pastoral Institute in Miami—are members of the Latin American Network of Institutes and National and Regional Centers for Pastoral Juvenil. Latin American links were evident in the participation of a delegation from the Latin American Episcopal Conference at the First National Encuentro for Hispanic Youth and Young Adult Ministry and in the enthusiastic response of the Latino youth listeners to the keynote address of Cardinal Óscar Rodríguez Maradiaga of Tegucigalpa, Honduras. Even the terminology and understanding of youth as a life stage reflect Latin American influence. Whereas in U.S. Catholicism teens and young adults eighteen and older are typically in separate groups, many Spanish-language ministries reflect the perspective of Hispanic cultures in which "*jóven*" refers to single persons between the ages of sixteen and thirty, but not those of a similar age who are married with family responsibilities and thus perceived to be at a different state in life. Catholic leaders' response to clergy sex abuse has led to alterations in this arrangement in various locales, with a *pastoral con adolescentes* (adolescent pastoral ministry) for teens employed to separate minors from those who have reached the legal age of adulthood. But in other U.S. parishes and dioceses the Latin American understandings of "jóven" and "pastoral juvenil" continue to be prevalent.[14]

Among their young Hispanic peers, immigrant workers are statistically more likely to practice traditional Hispanic devotions and retain a Catholic affiliation, though some are attracted to Spanish-language Protestant youth groups and congregations. Their willingness to work at almost any job is parallel to the energetic desire many of them bring to Spanish-language youth ministries. In a number of instances these youth establish prayer, retreat, liturgical choir, and fellowship groups on their own, though the support and backing of a priest or parish are usually desired and sought. Immigrant youth tend to lack leadership and faith formation, but many anxiously pursue opportunities to receive them when available, even amid strenuous work schedules that sap their time and energy. The U.S. bishops note in *Encuentro and Mission* that some pastoral leaders perceive these youth initiatives as separatist, and thus "there is resistance to accepting, affirming, and supporting" them even though they help "fill the void" of outreach to Spanish-speaking young people. Johnson-Mondragón bemoans such "misguided pastoral convictions" among diocesan personnel, pastors, and youth ministers who fail to guide and support pastoral juvenil or even "shut the ministry down or prevent its inception in the parish or diocese." Nonetheless, as with Hispanic ministry in general, ministries that engage predominantly immigrant youth in a language and style that is familiar tend to draw the most dynamic results of any initiatives among young Latinos. The delegates of the First National Encuentro for Hispanic Youth and Young Adult Ministry agreed that Spanish-language pastoral juvenil groups and *grupos de oración* (prayer groups) "are the two most prevalent models [ for ministry among Hispanic young people] in the country."[15]

Mainstream movers are at the other end of the spectrum in terms of their knowledge of the English language and their acclimatization to life in the United States. They comprise a smaller group that Johnson-Mondragón estimates to be about 15 to 25 percent of young Latinos. The overwhelming majority are U.S. citizens, the children or grandchildren of immigrants. Most speak English and little or no Spanish, though many who do speak Spanish gain sufficient fluency to employ the language advantageously in their profession. A more privileged family background, parental sacrifice, personal initiative, or the benefit of a mentor or quality education enable them to achieve an educational level and socioeconomic status that enhances their advancement in U.S. society. Some later give back to their Hispanic community in professional work, service, or philanthropy. Others see their Latino counterparts as lacking initiative or as barriers in their own pathway to success. Some even dissociate themselves from what they think of as the lowly status of being Hispanic, or they criticize Hispanic cultures and communities as inhibiting the progress of Latinos. These attitudes can shape their views of Catholicism, especially if they view the religious practices of Hispanic Catholics as vestiges of an outmoded immigrant heritage. Mainstream movers with these perceptions are more susceptible to joining Protestant churches or not practicing any religion. Like their counterparts of other ethnic and racial groups, their busy lives, professional success, and focus on other concerns can also tempt them to drift away from practicing their faith.

Mainstream movers who are involved in Catholic youth ministries tend to fit more easily into English-speaking parish youth and young adult groups and outreach in Catholic schools, campus ministry, and youth retreats like Teens Encounter Christ and Kairos. Like other young Catholics, many mainstream movers are inspired to deepen their faith through involvement with faith-based efforts to serve the needy, protect the environment, and create a more just world. Two pastoral statements of the U.S. bishops published in 1997, *Renewing the Vision: A Framework for Catholic Youth Ministry* and *Sons and Daughters of the Light: A Pastoral Plan for Ministry with Young Adults*, addressed Catholic ministries among teens and a growing constellation of young adult ministry initiatives directed at those in their late teens, twenties, and thirties. A young Catholic named Linda from Arizona illustrates the influence these ministries can have. Raised in the Mexican traditions of her mother and neighborhood, her faith was later nurtured in the Newman Center campus ministry at Northern Arizona University, the challenge of Christian community living she experienced in a period of faith-based service with the Jesuit Volunteer Corps, and the young adult Theology on Tap discussion groups she subsequently encountered in New York. These ministries both provoked and guided her faith development during the years after she left home. Committed Catholics like Linda can be valuable *gente puente*, leaders who are able to build bridges between Hispanics and people of other backgrounds.[16]

Johnson-Mondragón's third category, identity seekers, comprise some 25 to 45 percent of young Latinos. They are similar to mainstream movers in terms of generation, but they tend to struggle more with being caught between the homeland of their elders' often nostalgic views and the new home of the land in which they were raised. Perceiving themselves to be neither fully a part of the Hispanic immigrants' world nor that of the U.S. cultural mainstream, their primary quest is for identity and self-esteem. Many are at least functionally bilingual, though they tend to speak English among their peers. The sting of prejudice and their often being educated in public schools with high dropout rates stifle the energies of self-initiative and advancement. When they don't receive support and guidance to motivate themselves, they can easily become busy seeking immediate gratification in activities like playing video games, watching television or movies, chatting online, gossiping, listening to music, or dancing. A downward cycle of boredom, blaming society or themselves for their sense that their lives are not progressing, and little hope for setting and realizing personal goals can eventually lead to more destructive behaviors, such as drinking, drug use, and sexual promiscuity.

English-language parish youth ministry and Spanish-language pastoral juvenil potentially can address the longing to belong that these young people confront in their daily existence, depending on the availability of a welcoming group and the young person's capacity to speak the language in which its gatherings are conducted. But many don't encounter such a group or fail to participate because they feel they are being judged or that they don't belong. Those who do participate are typically most attracted because they identify with a group's leaders and members as companions in their search for identity and a sense of dignity and worth. Some young Latinos switch religious affiliation when they encounter such companions in a group that is evangelical, Pentecostal, or of another religious group. Hispanic ministry leaders and young Hispanics themselves have initiated efforts to address their bicultural situation. Their efforts range from their insistence that fellow delegates address Hispanic youth ministry at the 1977 Second Hispanic Pastoral Encuentro to bilingual programs like RESPETO: A Curriculum for Latino Youth Leadership Formation, which Arturo and Mary Baez-Chávez developed at the Mexican American Cultural Center in San Antonio. Yet, as the U.S. bishops confirm in *Encuentro and Mission*, one of the most "vital" needs in Hispanic ministry remains "to develop ministerial models that respond to the specific needs and aspirations of U.S.-born Hispanic youth."[17]

Johnson-Mondragón's final category, gang members and high-risk youth, tend to be born in the United States or have come here at a young age. The Pew Hispanic Center study found that 3 percent of young Latinos self-report that they are now or used to be gang members, and nearly 3 percent of Hispanics between the ages of sixteen and twenty-five were incarcerated during 2008, in both cases nearly all of them young men. Estimates based on the National Youth Gang Survey are even higher, showing that approximately 7 percent of Hispanic males and 0.5 percent of Hispanic females in the fifteen-to-twenty-four age range were active gang members in 2008.[18] These figures represent a considerable number of lives adversely influenced: young Hispanics, their families, neighbors, and the victims of their criminal acts. Yet the vast majority of Latino youth are neither in jail or gang members, a number of them despite ample temptations and pressures to choose these pathways. They are often given less media coverage than images of Latino youth and gangs, violent crime, and a host of other ills. When one adds the Latino young who are at high risk for possible drug abuse, violence, or other criminal activity, Johnson-Mondragón estimates they are still the smallest group among his four categories but nonetheless comprise a tragic and unacceptable ratio of around 10 to 15 percent of young Hispanics. The common denominators among most of them are that they were raised in poverty, lack formal education, are exposed to various negative role models and destructive peer pressures, and are prone to a level of hopelessness or anomie that enhances the possibility they will turn to gangs, drugs, and other unsocial behavior.

Parishes, dioceses, and pastoral institutes have scarcely begun to address Latino youth in this situation. Father Greg Boyle and his Jesuit confreres at Dolores Mission in East Los Angeles began a ministry among Latino gang members with the establishment of their Jobs for a Future initiative in 1988. Under Boyle's leadership, their efforts evolved beyond the parish into Homeboy Industries, a nationally renowned effort to offer young people a way out of gangs and accompany them as they transition to new lives.[19] In Los Angeles and other cities, former gang members and prisoners who have had profound faith conversion experiences are the most effective ministers to high-risk Latino youth and those who are already caught in the web of criminal and gang activity. For Latino and other young people involved in this destructive cycle, outreach drawing them into a radical religious conversion is one of the few available forms of intervention that might allow them to avoid incarceration, or even to live until their thirtieth birthday. Yet such efforts are sporadic, as are leaders prepared to enact them and church resources to support their ministries. In numerous places these ministries are simply nonexistent.

Johnson-Mondragón concludes that the lack of ministries tailored to the range of life situations among Latino youth is a major detriment to nurturing their Catholic faith and practice. Leaders of Hispanic youth and young adult ministry concur in their First National Encuentro document that "diverse pastoral responses are needed" to engage Hispanic youth, because they comprise a widely diverse population and "no single model works for everyone." Yet the Encuentro delegates and the U.S. bishops' *Encuentro and Mission* document note that "generally speaking, the majority of parish youth ministry programs serve a population that is mostly European white, mainstream, middle-class, and English-speaking" and, conversely, do not reach many young Hispanics because of differences in cultural, educational, and economic backgrounds. NSYR data confirm that Hispanic involvement in the average U.S. parish youth group is greater as family income increases and is notably higher for English-dominant Latinos. In Johnson-Mondragón's terminology, present ministries tend to resonate more with the demographic minority of Hispanic mainstream movers than with the other three categories of young Hispanics.[20]

Consequently, Hispanic youth and young adult ministry proponents contend that pastoral outreach to Latino young people often necessitates forming two or more groups to engage the diverse young people in a parish. They contest charges that such an approach is divisive. As Instituto Fe y Vida director Carmen Cervantes avows, "A real division of the church occurs when" young Hispanics "are not offered pastoral care and religious formation in an appropriate sociocultural context for them, and they end up either being unchurched or seeking an ecclesial community elsewhere." One California teen expressed the dismay of his peers after their pastor merged a Latino and "mainstream" youth group and the vast majority of Hispanics ceased participating: "I have to suffer in this brown skin all day at school, and you want me to feel the same way at church?" Cervantes voices the plea of a number of her colleagues in urging their fellow pastoral leaders to adopt a "community of communities" approach to youth and young adult ministry. Their conviction is that two or more small youth faith communities in a parish can address diverse needs while still joining together occasionally for worship and other common activities, much the same way that distinct parish groups perform particular functions but still unite for Sunday Eucharist and parish-wide events. The bottom line to a community-of-communities approach is that "if done well, [it] creates spaces for diverse groups to participate in the life of the parish by overcoming the cultural and socioeconomic differences that usually lead to alienation and separation."[21]

Various efforts already exist to address the faith formation needs of young Latinos. A number of Hispanic youth themselves, along with their adult supervisors, have initiated and sustained ministries, often in locations where the structures of U.S. Catholic parishes and dioceses do not engage Hispanic young people effectively. The scores of apostolic movements and youth groups that participated in the diocesan and regional gatherings of the First National Encuentro for Hispanic Youth and Young Adult Ministry reveal the wide range of these ministries. Entities represented in the Encuentro process included those with a presence among the young in various regions and dioceses such as the Catholic Charismatic Renewal, Jóvenes para Cristo, and Cursillo, as well as numerous groups distinctive to particular locales such as Cristo y Yo (Christ and I), Ministerio Alianza Nueva (New Covenant Ministry), and Youth to Youth.[22]

Young Hispanics' persistence and desire to serve is illustrated in the experience of a male immigrant who settled in Chicago and says, "When I arrived I looked for a youth group like the one I belonged to in Guatemala, but I couldn't find one. I became part of an adult group in my parish, but I was the youngest and they didn't understand me." Next he tried a CCR prayer group in another parish, but he didn't "feel comfortable praying like that." At yet another parish he encountered an English-speaking youth group for teens, but didn't feel at home there either, because he was the oldest participant in the group, English was the dominant language, and "no one understood me." After four years of searching, he finally "found a small community of *jóvenes* my age." The faith and community he encountered in that group led him to pursue formation as a leader for pastoral juvenil. His sojourn to find a spiritual home in a faith group stirred what he describes as a vocation: "I feel that God is calling me to not allow other *jóvenes* to go around lost and disoriented without finding a community that supports them and helps them to live their faith."[23]

Hispanic ministry leaders and organizations have supported young people in their efforts. Since first inaugurating a course on Pastoral Juvenil Hispana in 1980, SEPI has created no fewer than eight formation programs in collaboration with leaders for ministries with Hispanic youth. In the Northeast, Father Juan Díaz Vilar, S.J., authored various publications that address issues young Hispanics face in daily life. Hispanic leaders worked with the De La Salle Christian Brothers and their Saint Mary's Press in Winona, Minnesota, to establish the Hispanic Publishing Project under the general editorship of Carmen Cervantes in 1988. They have produced a number of bilingual studies and resources for Hispanic youth and young adult ministry, including the multivolume Prophets of Hope collection, the first articulation of a common theological and pastoral vision for that ministry. These studies led to the founding of Instituto Fe y Vida in 1994, which Cervantes has served as director since its inception and the De La Salle Christian Brothers have generously supported. Fe y Vida is the institute that has most advanced ministry with young Hispanics through its national leadership training programs for young Latinos and those who work with them, its development of ministerial resources, and the research of its National Research and Resource Center for Hispanic Youth and Young Adult Ministry.[24]

The work of Instituto Fe y Vida complements that of the National Catholic Network de Pastoral Juvenil Hispana–La Red, which Latino young people established in 1997. Under the leadership of organization president Rey Malavé and his successors, Jesús Ábrego, Elizabeth Torres, and Marilyn Santos, La Red convoked the important 2006 First National Encuentro for Hispanic Youth and Young Adult Ministry and is now engaged in efforts to implement its conclusions. La Red initiatives focus on promoting formation and leadership among young Hispanics as well as developing pastoral models, practices, strategies, and resources that enable them to live as active disciples.[25]

Catechetical ministries comprise another constellation of efforts for passing on the faith to young Latinos. The most long-standing of such ministries among Hispanics themselves are those of numerous grandmothers, parents, other family members, and catechists. Often they have catechized the young in the traditional manner referred to as *doctrina* that centers on memorizing prayers and core Catholic doctrines. A number of Hispanic catechetical leaders helped expand *doctrina* with new insights and approaches, such as the Missionary Catechists of Divine Providence, the members of the National Organization for Catechesis with Hispanics, and, more recently, the National Conference for Catechetical Leadership Forum on Catechesis with Hispanics.[26]

In the United States no Hispanic has been more influential in catechetical ministries than Sister Maria de la Cruz Aymes, S.H., who first served as a catechist in her Mexican homeland during the religious persecutions of the Cristero Rebellion. She came to the United States in 1938 to enter religious life with the Society of Helpers because church-state conflicts had resulted in the closure of formation programs in Mexico. After completing her training, she created the On Our Way catechetical series for grades one through six with the editorial assistance of renowned catechetical expert Johannes Hofinger, S.J. In accord with a core principle of the worldwide Roman Catholic catechetical movement, the series engaged Scripture, liturgy, and daily life experience along with doctrine as the primary sources for a comprehensive faith formation. The William H. Sadlier Company published the series beginning in 1957. Parishes and dioceses throughout the country adopted the series for their catechetical programs. It was translated into more than a dozen languages for use around the globe. Over the following half century Aymes authored or coauthored more than one hundred curricular texts for religious education, along with an influential program for forming Hispanic catechists titled Fe y Cultura. She also took the lead in establishing and enacting the Sin Fronteras catechetical guidelines for evangelization and religious education among Latino migrants in eighteen dioceses on both sides of the Mexico-U.S. border.[27]

Contemporary grassroots Hispanic catechists in the United States make significant contributions of their time, talent, and faith to children and young people. Some are immigrants like Clemencia Calderon. After raising ten children, she longed to continue serving the young, so she prepared to become a catechist at her parish in Chicago. She was unsure of herself at first but gradually became more confident in her ability to pass on her faith and has even given presentations to large assemblies of children and their parents. Other catechists are U.S. born or raised, such as another Chicago resident, Patricia Hernandez, who became a catechist during her high school and college years. Her motivation was "to give something back to my community" and to recapture her strong childhood faith that had begun to wane. Like numerous catechists, she discovered that in seeking to deepen the faith of others she became more committed herself: "I had thought I was going to enrich the lives of children as their catechist, but instead they taught me about faith." Numerous catechists like these serve in relative anonymity, but the mission of the U.S. Catholic Church would be impoverished without them.[28]

A 2008 national consultation convened under the auspices of the Secretariat of Cultural Diversity in the Church at the United States Conference of Catholic Bishops provided insights for ongoing efforts to enhance faith formation among Hispanics. Participants gave high priority to models of family catechesis that engage parents in the religious formation of their children, enlisting parental involvement not only in their children's preparation for sacraments like first communion but also in their year-to-year formation in faith. Recognizing the different experiences of immigrant and subsequent-generation Hispanics as well as the diverse backgrounds among Latinos, consultants advocated for the use of multiple languages or bilingual catechesis as needed in particular parish communities. They also called for flexibility in adapting catechetical approaches and texts to address local circumstances, such as accessible publications written by and for U.S. Hispanics that engage the best theological, biblical, pastoral, and doctrinal sources. A particular challenge noted was for parish and diocesan leaders to work more closely with apostolic movements, which form numerous Hispanics in their faith and provide many leaders who are eager to share their faith as catechists. Consistent with the style of these movements, consultants emphasized small communal gatherings and a strong evangelization witness as elements of faith formation that are generally effective with Hispanics. Finally, consultants noted the urgency of greater collaboration in U.S. Catholicism between Hispanic Catholic organizations and leaders, parishes, dioceses, pastoral institutes, institutions of higher education, and Catholic publishers to continuously expand and improve initiatives in catechesis with Hispanics.[29]

Efforts to increase Catholic parochial and high school education among Hispanics are also ongoing. They are significant both for faith formation and because, as a 2009 report avowed, disadvantaged students like poor or working-class Latinos "benefit the most from access to a Catholic education." Leaders at St. Ignatius Martyr elementary school in Austin increased enrollment 35 percent in a single year after energetically inviting groups of Hispanic and other parents to information sessions. By convincing their pastor to drop the higher out-of-parish tuition rate, they alleviated some neighboring pastors' fears that their parishioners would change parishes to get the cheaper rate if they sent their children to St. Ignatius. The new spirit of cooperation enabled school personnel to recruit students during and after Sunday Masses at neighboring parishes, contributing significantly to their enrollment success. At Immaculate Conception parish in Chicago, pastor Michael Enright followed a familiar pattern in U.S. Catholic education: he invited women religious from the background of his parishioners, the Daughters of Mary of Guadalupe from Mexico, to help staff the school. Along with Dominican sister colleagues, lay teachers, and a parish commitment to tithing, the Daughters have played a key role in extending the impact of Immaculate Conception parish school among Hispanic families. Voucher and tax credit programs have enabled Catholic schools in several states to expand their outreach to Latinos, most notably St. Anthony School in Milwaukee. Benefiting from the nation's oldest voucher system and a school administration that sets high student performance expectations, St. Anthony expanded its facilities to serve more than one thousand Latino children and has become the largest Catholic elementary school in the United States.[30]

Other efforts are wider in scope than individual parishes and schools. In many dioceses bishops and educational leaders have conducted campaigns to build endowments for school tuition scholarships, such as the Catholic Education Foundation in Los Angeles, the Seeds of Hope Charitable Trust in Denver, and the Big Shoulders Fund in Chicago. Jesuits, Christian Brothers, and lay colleagues have built a national network of Cristo Rey high schools and NativityMiguel middle schools for students from predominantly poor and working-class families, a total of eighty-eight schools with over nine thousand students, nearly half of them Hispanic. Collaborators at the University of Notre Dame established the Alliance for Catholic Education (ACE) in 1994.

ACE teachers are recent college graduates who serve in under-resourced Catholic schools for two years, live in community with fellow ACE teachers, receive spiritual formation, and earn a master's degree in education through summer and distance learning courses. Since its inception ACE leaders have undertaken a number of related educational initiatives and grown the organization to its current contingent of nearly two hundred teachers annually serving Catholic parochial and high schools in more than thirty locations across the United States, including a number of predominantly Hispanic communities. Notre Dame is one of fourteen Catholic universities with programs similar to ACE. Together they have formed the University Consortium on Catholic Education to enhance their efforts. The School of Education at Loyola Marymount University in Los Angeles is another leading institution in Catholic school and Hispanic outreach efforts, with initiatives like Leadership in Equity, Advocacy, and Diversity and the Catholic Higher Education Collaborative that build collaboration between Catholic institutions of higher education and Catholic schools.[31]

The 2009 report of the Notre Dame Task Force on the Participation of Latino Children and Families in Catholic Schools presented a strategy to double the percentage and triple the number of Hispanic students in Catholic parochial and high schools to one million by the year 2020. This report explicates the "Catholic school advantage," an array of educational benefits that sociological studies demonstrate are widespread among students in Catholic schools. Numerous Latino students attend "heavily segregated" public schools in inner cities that "tend to be the most underfunded, with few advanced courses and the most low-level technical courses." Thus it is not surprising that Latino students in Catholic schools are 42 percent more likely to graduate from high school and two and a half times more likely to graduate from college than their public school counterparts. Among low-income Hispanics and other minority groups in Los Angeles, 98 percent receiving a Catholic education graduate from high school in four years, while only 66 percent of those in public schools do. Various studies reveal other positive attributes: as compared to their public school peers Catholic school graduates are more likely to vote, engage in civic affairs, tolerate diverse views, and even earn higher wages. Pope Benedict XVI implicitly highlighted such benefits in his 2008 address to U.S. Catholic educators. He urged his listeners to foster Catholic education because it forms young people in faith and "in turn nurtures the soul of a nation."[32]

Not surprisingly, the obstacle Hispanic Catholic parents reported most prominently to focus groups of the Notre Dame Task Force is their inability to afford tuition costs. But the simple economics of tuition are not the sum total of the complex challenge of enrolling more Latinos in Catholic schools. Task Force members estimate that Catholic schools have more than 691,000 empty seats and that the dioceses with the greatest numbers of empty seats also have large Latino populations: New York, Philadelphia, Chicago, and Los Angeles. The opportunity is to match families who desire Catholic education with schools that need students by using innovative strategies like "fair-share" tuition, charging on a sliding scale based on ability to pay so that empty seats are filled. Barriers to recruitment of Latino students include insufficient direct marketing outreach, even sparser efforts to disseminate school information in Spanish, Latin American perceptions that Catholic schools are institutions strictly for the elite, and relatively few Hispanic teachers and Spanish-speaking personnel on school staffs, a lack that is particularly detrimental in communities with immigrant parents. The Task Force report addresses such obstacles through a number of specific recommendations for action from Latino families and from leaders of Latino communities, the church, schools, the public sphere, and higher education.[33]

Addressing Hispanic access to higher education, Bishop Patricio Flores (now emeritus archbishop) of San Antonio founded the Hispanic Scholarship Fund, an independent organization that since 1976 has granted almost $300 million in scholarships to nearly one hundred thousand college students. Two-thirds of them were the first members of their family to receive a college education. There are no Hispanic institutions parallel to historically black colleges and universities like Xavier University in New Orleans, but in 2008 the Association of Catholic Colleges and Universities (ACCU) listed 10 Catholic institutions of higher education with at least one-fourth Hispanic enrollment. Three of these are majority Hispanic, all located in San Antonio: Our Lady of the Lake University, St. Mary's University, and the University of the Incarnate Word. A growing number of the nearly 250 Catholic institutions of higher education in the United States have initiatives to recruit and retain Latino students. DePaul University in Chicago has the distinction of being ranked in the top ten of the "Diverse Student Population" category for six consecutive years in the *Princeton Review* annual survey of the best U.S. colleges and universities. At a time when the pursuit of higher academic rankings consumes the energies of many institutions, DePaul leaders consciously seek to continue the legacy of Catholic higher education offering access to immigrant and working-class students. The entering class for the 2009–2010 academic year illustrates their priorities: more than a third of new students came from families in which neither parent holds a college degree. Latinos comprised 18 percent of the incoming class.[34]

Nonetheless, the considerable efforts to address the challenge of passing on the faith to Hispanic young people pale in comparison to the need. Tuition costs and selective admissions standards tend to diminish the accessibility of Catholic colleges and universities for many Hispanic and other working-class and even middle-income Catholics. Moreover, there are only eleven two-year Catholic colleges in the United States, and cumulatively their enrollment is just over five thousand, while nationally 40 percent of Latino college students attend two-year institutions. In many instances bishops and dioceses are hard pressed to even assign campus ministers to community colleges with a large number of Hispanic Catholic students. According to a 2005 CARA report, students at as many as 70 percent of the 4,453 degree-granting institutions of higher education in the United States have little or no access to Catholic campus ministry. An earlier CARA report found that less than 10 percent of the students participating in Catholic campus ministries were Hispanic. Neither the ACCU nor any other organization has yet adopted a strategic plan to enhance young Hispanic Catholics' access, success, and faith formation as students in undergraduate or graduate higher education.[35]

Catholic parochial and high schools enroll only 3 percent of Hispanic Catholic children and teens, a paltry figure compared to the heyday of these institutions during the 1950s, when nearly half of Catholic elementary school students and a fourth of Catholic high school students were enrolled in Catholic schools. Members of the Notre Dame Task Force on the Participation of Latino Children and Families in Catholic Schools accentuated the immensity of the need for increasing Catholic education among Hispanics in the final lines of their report: "for all the concerns that do and will emerge surrounding the challenges we recognize and embrace, is it possible that our greatest concern should be this: Have we aimed too low?" Yet currently the number of Catholic schools is decreasing: in the first decade of the new millennium, fourteen hundred U.S. Catholic schools closed, nearly one-fifth of those operative in the year 2000, and their overall enrollment declined by half a million. The declining number of women and men religious who teach in these schools since the 1960s has necessitated raising tuition costs to pay the typically higher salaries of lay faculty members. Many Catholic schools that in the past served primarily students from working-class families now have majority contingents from the middle or upper classes. Archbishop Timothy Dolan of New York forewarns that "failure to include the expanding Hispanic population in Catholic education would be a huge generational mistake." Cardinal Francis George of Chicago echoes his concern and further attests, "The sad truth is that Catholic schools in urban contexts are in decline just when they are most needed for this generation."[36]

Even if the Notre Dame Task Force and its collaborators exceed their goal of doubling the percentage of Hispanics enrolled in Catholic schools, the vast majority of Hispanic children, teens, and young adults will not receive faith formation in these institutions, amplifying the vital importance of catechetical efforts among Latinos. No national survey has examined the current state of catechesis among Hispanics, though there is no question that thousands of Hispanic catechists serve in parishes and dioceses and that the number of young Hispanic Catholics who participate in religious education programs is significant. So, too, is the number of those who fail to participate. Martha Nuñez, who directs a Spanish-language Bible institute for the Los Angeles archdiocese, reports that in Los Angeles alone several hundred Hispanics complete their training and are commissioned as catechists each year. The archdiocese forms new catechists through initiatives such as their catechist formation programs offered in both Spanish and English and their annual multilingual Religious Education Congress, the largest event of its kind in the United States. Nuñez also attests that approximately one hundred thousand Hispanic children are baptized in the archdiocese each year, presenting parishes with numerous new members and the accompanying opportunity and challenge to assist parents in evangelizing them and forming them in the Catholic faith.[37]

Like Catholics of other backgrounds, many Hispanics do not send their children to parish catechetical programs. Most are accustomed to the practice of sending their children for first communion classes after they have reached the age of seven or eight. A significant but lesser number have their children prepared for the sacrament of confirmation, usually received during the teenage years. But participation in religious education not directly related to sacramental preparation is less frequent. Thus the need to train more catechists, provide engaging catechetical programs, and encourage parents and their children to participate in them is a fundamental challenge for any Hispanic ministry effort in U.S. parishes and dioceses. Funding and personnel for such efforts are a widespread and frequently only partially addressed concern. In various parishes the annual budget provides a Catholic school subsidy and a disproportionately lower allocation for the larger number of public school students whom the parish religious education programs are expected to catechize.

Relatively low participation rates in youth groups are another frequent detriment to evangelizing young Latinos. Hispanic youth leaders decry what they deem a weak "missionary" dimension to Catholicism in the United States. Citing her own experience as a youth minister and NSYR data that show Protestant congregational outreach to inactive teens surpasses that of

Catholic parishes, Lynette DeJesús Sáenz notes, "It is very rare for leaders to go searching for the 'lost' adolescents in the community unless their parents actively request the help." Indeed, in many ministries young people are taught to be wary of the potentially negative influences of peers who are not actively living their faith commitment. Consciously or not, their youth group and their Catholic faith are seen not as a catalyst to evangelize their peers but as "a safeguard against the moral pitfalls of adolescence." Sáenz recognizes that young people need maturity and preparation to serve as peer "missionaries." Most will be able to take on evangelization efforts only gradually. But Sáenz insists that outreach to young people "on the margins of social and congregational life" is nothing less than "the gospel call." Hispanic youth delegates at their First National Encuentro proclaimed that this approach is especially imperative for young Latinos today. According to their Encuentro conclusions, conditions like peer pressure, the influence of the media, poverty, loneliness, discrimination, the particular difficulties of generational transition for the children of immigrants, and the number of young émigrés who come to the United States without their families "call for missionary action by active *jóvenes* to their own generation."[38]

Thus Hispanic ministry advocates declare that at all levels of U.S. Catholicism there is a dire need for a more robust institutional response to expand the leadership base of both Latinos and non-Latinos who engage the growing numbers of Hispanic young people. In particular, Latinos remind their fellow pastoral leaders that youth who have been on the margins of social and ecclesial life themselves, have struggled with generational transition, or have simply experienced being a young Hispanic in the United States are often the best witnesses to others in similar circumstances. An overview of "best practices" in the First National Encuentro for Hispanic Youth and Young Adult Ministry conclusions accentuates the strong focus on Latino leadership formation in the initiatives of Cervantes, Johnson-Mondragón, and their colleagues at Instituto Fe y Vida; those of their counterparts at SEPI; and various others in dioceses, parishes, youth retreats, and apostolic movements.[39]

Sociological data underscore the urgent pleas of Hispanic ministry leaders. The consistent presence of a parish staff member with a regular and sustained commitment to youth has a substantial bearing on Hispanic involvement in youth ministries: Hispanics are four times less likely than their Euro-American counterparts to persevere in a youth group for two years if the leader is a volunteer rather than a paid pastoral minister. Utilizing NSYR data to explore well over a dozen factors that shape Latino youth participation, Johnson-Mondragón concludes that "having a paid parish youth minister is the strongest predictor of youth group involvement for Hispanic Catholic teens." Similarly, a "most effective structure" for enhancing pastoral juvenil in parishes and apostolic movements is hiring a diocesan staff member to coordinate these ministries. Yet Hispanic teens are more likely than Euro-Americans to not have a paid youth minister at their parish, as are participants in pastoral juvenil as compared to their counterparts in English-speaking young adult ministry. Moreover, a 2002 study of the National Federation for Catholic Youth Ministry found that only about 5 percent of youth ministers surveyed were Hispanic. It also showed that the ministerial skill in which youth ministers felt least competent was "responding to the needs of youth from different cultures" and that "courses in various cultural backgrounds" were among the offerings most frequently omitted in the dioceses, pastoral institutes, and Catholic institutions of higher learning where many of them receive their pastoral leadership formation.[40]

Furthermore, the status of the National Catholic Network de Pastoral Juvenil Hispana–La Red as a volunteer organization with no paid staff inhibits progress on its daunting but crucial ministerial agenda. Johnson-Mondragón notes that La Red's mission encompasses half of young Catholics, but the bulk of resources for youth ministry in U.S. Catholicism support parish programs in which Hispanics "are significantly less involved." Thus Johnson-Mondragón and other Hispanic ministry leaders call for "greater institutional and philanthropic support for its [La Red's] ministry."[41]

The immense challenges for passing on the faith to young Latinos parallel the weak religious institutional commitment among U.S. youth more generally. In his widely cited studies, Christian Smith refers to the religious outlook typical among U.S. teenagers as "moralistic therapeutic deism," a generalized belief in a God who created the world, wants people to be fair and good, promises heaven to those who are, and helps solve the problems of humans in lives that have as a primary purpose "to be happy and to feel good about oneself." The lack of institutional church commitment implied in such an understanding is consistent with Robert Wuthnow's findings about young adults, who "in the late 1990s were significantly less likely to attend church regularly than young adults in the early 1970s were." Wuthnow observes that social trends shape this shift in church attendance significantly, most notably marriage patterns; while the percentage of young married persons who attend church regularly has remained stable over time, the growing number of people in their twenties and thirties who are not married coincides with the diminishment of their generation's current church attendance.[42]

Many critiques of religious education in contemporary U.S. Catholicism mirror these larger trends. Various commentators have focused on younger Catholics' lack of knowledge and commitment to core Catholic doctrines, teachings, and practices. They note young Catholics' spirit of service, but often with the accompanying contention that these efforts reflect generous humanitarianism more than a grounded vision of lived Catholic faith. The diminishment of a pervasive Catholic subculture, especially among Euro-Americans, and the decreasing percentage of Catholic children who have attended parochial schools over the past half century exacerbate the urgent need for today's parents and religious educators to transmit the faith to new generations. Bishop Ricardo Ramírez sums up the pastoral urgency of evangelizing the young: "What will the church be like 50 or 100 years from now? . . . The way the church will be then depends on what we do now."[43]

The transition from immigrant to U.S.-born or U.S.-reared generations is at the heart of the evangelization challenge among Latinos. As they begin to surpass their parents' and grandparents' often limited formal education, young Latinos need catechesis that engages their minds as well as their hearts. In many instances the faith of their elders does not adequately address the complex reality of the world in which young people live. Consequently, they need formation in Catholic faith and teachings that both addresses that reality and builds on their elders' religious traditions. When Catholic families, parishes, schools, and youth ministries do not provide formation that takes into account young Latinos' background and life situation, they are more likely to become adherents of moralistic therapeutic deism, participants in Pentecostal or evangelical churches, or progressively detached from any religious practice or tradition.

What will it take to awaken the Catholic faith of young Hispanics? Collectively, the variety of efforts and pastoral recommendations to foster Hispanic youth and young adult ministries, catechesis, parents' efforts to form their children in faith, and participation in Catholic education demonstrate the need for a response parallel in scope to the building up of Catholic schools in the nineteenth and twentieth centuries. While sometimes denoted as a national school system, Catholic schools in fact emerged as a diverse array of local institutions with a variety of administrative structures, instructional approaches, and ethnic populations. Their commonality was the broad mission of education and Catholic faith formation. Catholic schools continue to be a vital resource to prepare new leaders for church and society. But from a purely demographic perspective, today the greater need among young Latinos is for catechetical programs, youth and young adult ministries, and outreach to the vast majority who are being educated in public institutions or are already in the workforce. In Johnson-Mondragón's terminology, ministerial outreach is needed for the full range of Hispanic young people, not just the mainstream movers who are disproportionately represented in Catholic schools and English-language parish youth groups. Current efforts to nurture faith among young Latinos range from those in families, like that of my student's mother presented at the outset of this chapter, to national initiatives such as those of Instituto Fe y Vida, La Red, and the Notre Dame Task Force. These largely nascent ecclesial outreach efforts are not yet generally perceived as a communal attempt to address the massive transition of second- and subsequent-generation Hispanics into church and society. Like the expansion of Catholic schools in previous eras, the capacity of U.S. Catholic leaders and Latinos themselves to meet the current challenge hinges not only on the effectiveness of particular initiatives but also on a more widespread conviction that passing on the faith to young Latinos is an urgent priority for the entire U.S. Catholic Church.

# Transformation in America's Largest Church

atinos present a distinct agenda of core concerns within U.S. Catholicism. In the half century since the Second Vatican Council, many Euro-American Catholics have emphasized concerns such as liturgical reform, the role of the laity, dissent or obedience to sexual ethics and other church teaching, the proper exercise of authority, and the question of who is called to ordination. The focus on these issues has produced debates along a liberal-conservative continuum, at times so stridently that they are deemed the "Catholic culture wars." Conversely, Latinos have been more inclined to accentuate concerns such as funding for Hispanic ministry offices, youth initiatives, outreach efforts, and leadership training and formation programs, as well as an increase in Spanish Masses, Hispanic bishops, celebrations of feast days that are part of their Hispanic traditions, efforts to promote immigration reform, and culturally sensitive formation programs for seminarians and other ecclesial leaders. Although these efforts encompass attempts at reform in areas such as liturgy and participation in church leadership, they are primarily intended to equip the church to serve and accompany its Latino members in their faith and daily struggles. In a word, whereas Hispanic Catholic leaders frequently perceive the U.S. Catholic Church as a significant institution that could do much to uplift their suffering sisters and brothers, Catholic leaders of European descent tend to be more concerned with issues of authority and the adaptation of the church to the U.S. milieu or, conversely, with the alarming worry that U.S. Catholics already embrace societal norms far more than they do fundamental Catholic teachings. Former *New York Times* religion reporter Peter Steinfels observes that distinctive Hispanic concerns are increasingly prominent at the foundational level of Catholic parish life: "The Latino Catholics who constitute the majority of my fellow parishioners at the Church of the Ascension on 107th Street in

Manhattan . . . don't know or follow many of the concerns that upset Catholics like me. They have other problems. And they are likely the typical Catholics of the future."[1]

The concerns of Hispanics reveal that in addition to the widely discussed split between the right and the left, another prominent divergence in U.S. Catholicism is one along class and cultural lines. At the heart of the various topics addressed in this book are the interactions between predominantly working-class Hispanics, a number of them immigrant newcomers, and their more established coreligionists. From perspectives on the Catholic past, to current ecclesial life, to faith formation for the Catholic adults of tomorrow, Hispanics' viewpoints are more akin to those of European immigrants of yesteryear than to present-day Euro-Americans. But Latinos are not merely a reminder that the bedrock of the U.S. Catholic Church was immigrants and their children and grandchildren. Rather, they are a rapidly expanding group that advances their cultural and working-class perceptions in a church whose membership is still largely Euro-American and middle class, and whose leadership is overwhelmingly so. While Latinos are the mainstay of the "new immigrant church," as David Badillo has rightly referred to them, in large part they are also, as Joseph Fitzpatrick even more aptly put it, the "Hispanic poor in a middle-class church."[2] The seismic demographic shift summarized in this turn of phrase underlies Hispanic perspectives and modes of participation that are altering the landscape of U.S. Catholicism. These changes and the immense and often competing ministerial challenges they produce will intensify over the coming decades as the transition from a Euro-American to a majority Hispanic church continues to unfold.

Hispanic ministerial initiatives do not negate the importance of other Catholics' efforts to enliven their faith, the church, and its public witness. Moreover, struggles with poverty, discrimination, and other hardships do not inherently make people virtuous, nor do middle-class material comforts categorically diminish one's sense of a need for God and faith. Catholics of all backgrounds and income levels endure the trials and tribulations of life, including the economic woes that have devastated many who previously worked for years in successful careers. Some Hispanics are in the middle or even upper class, and many aspire to this higher status. Nonetheless, the attempts of a predominantly working-class Hispanic Catholic populace to celebrate their faith and bring it to bear on the everyday realities of their lives transforms U.S. Catholic parishes, apostolic movements, leadership, ministries, worship, voting patterns, social activism, and much more.

Latinos have much to offer U.S. Catholicism. Their youthfulness is a source of revitalization for Catholic faith communities. Their leadership has extended Catholic involvement in faith-based community organizing and activist efforts that expand grassroots participation in civil society. Their ritual and devotional traditions incite embodied prayer and faith. Their desire for faith formation and to serve in ministries provides a new cadre of pastoral leaders. Their promotion of apostolic movements and small faith communities established the influential three-day Christian retreat movement in North America and continues to enliven groups like Cursillo and especially the CCR. Their ministerial initiatives and their life struggles have inspired Latinos and non-Latinos alike in their faith and service. Their historical and contemporary links with Latin America are a vital connection to the most populous Catholic region in the world and enhance the prospects for greater solidarity and common purpose among Catholics across the American hemisphere. The U.S. bishops noted in their 1983 pastoral letter on Hispanic ministry that Latinos accentuate salutary values such as respect for the dignity of each person, profound love for family life, a deep sense of community, an appreciation of life as a precious gift from God, and pervasive and authentic devotion to Mary, the mother of God. Echoing their pastoral letter, in their 2002 *Encuentro and Mission* document the bishops stated, "Hispanic Catholics are a blessing from God and a prophetic presence that has transformed many dioceses and parishes into more welcoming, vibrant, and evangelizing faith communities."[3]

Hispanics can also receive much from their participation in the U.S. Catholic Church. Historically, reform measures that Euro-Americans advanced in U.S. Catholicism after the Second Vatican Council buttressed Latino efforts to foster greater leadership parity and more systematic pastoral planning processes in parishes and dioceses. Today Catholicism's considerable array of ethnic and racial groups invites Latinos and their coreligionists to seek a unity rooted in faith that can be a countersign to human divisions in society and even in churches. Collaboration with other Catholics who are not from the majority culture is another possible source of enrichment, particularly with African Americans, who have many social and ecclesial concerns similar to those of Hispanics. A strong emphasis in the United States on the congregation encourages Latinos to strengthen their cultural and familial Catholic traditions with a deeper commitment to the parish community, especially the sacraments that are at the heart of Catholic life and faith. Many parishes continue to serve as familiar places that mediate adjustment to life in the wider society. Established Catholics' knowledge of U.S. educational, economic, social, and political institutions can be invaluable for Latino newcomers. Influential Catholic leaders and organizations provide critical support on concerns ranging from immigration, to unintended pregnancy, to faith-based organizing, to general familial well-being. Catholic schools are among the most effective pathways for Latino young people to receive faith formation and a brighter future. Religious education and leadership formation programs in U.S. Catholicism provide opportunities for Latino Catholics to expand their knowledge of their faith and live it as catechists, youth ministers, deacons, and more.

Yet various factors inhibit mutual enrichment between Hispanics and their fellow Catholics. Ethnic tensions and suspicions between English- and Spanish-speaking parishioners pose barriers to parish community life. Generational differences between the youthful Hispanic population and generally older Euro-Americans often add to these tensions. So too can cultural differences, anti-immigrant attitudes, and disagreements about what constitutes authentic integration in shared parishes. Latinos often hold fewer leadership positions and exert less influence over the decisions that affect parish life. Collectively, these conditions lead a number of Latinos to participate sparingly in parishes, if at all. On the other hand, as more parishes have significant or majority Hispanic congregations, some other Catholics feel overtaken and leave a parish where they had been active or even abandon their practice of Catholicism. The lure of Pentecostal and evangelical religions also diminish the numbers of Catholic adherents. Secular forces detract from religious practice among Latinos and their coreligionists. A privatized approach to religion among many U.S. believers can dilute the communitarian dimension of Hispanic faith and worship. The repercussions of the clergy sex-abuse crisis weaken the credibility of the church and its bishops, negatively impacting their influence on issues like immigration and a host of other concerns. Lawsuits add to the financial fallout from a depleted economy that lessens resources for ministerial initiatives. The ritual and devotional traditions that Latinos seek to foster in parish communities are at odds with some pastoral leaders' more narrow emphases on official rites and rubrics. Catholic education is financially inaccessible for large numbers of Hispanics. Comparatively low levels of Hispanic vocations to the priesthood, particularly among U.S.-born Hispanics, impede Latino access to ecclesial decision-making processes as well as their contributions as pastors. A relative lack of higher education and the preference that lay ecclesial ministers have academic degrees further hinder Latino leadership contributions.

The late Cardinal Avery Dulles, S.J., pointed to two scenarios for potential Latino influence on the U.S. Catholic Church and the wider society. Dulles avowed that "the immigration flows from culturally Catholic areas such as Latin America . . . have the potential for increasing the church's influence on American culture." Yet he also noted, "The prognosis is uncertain," since "there is a serious danger that this Hispanic American population, intent upon success in American terms, will forget or repudiate its own roots and adopt the prevailing American values of individualism, professionalism, and worldly success."[4] Dulles's frank assessment identifies the single most important issue that undergirds the contours of Hispanic impact within the U.S. context: Latinos' critical engagement as Catholics of the wider societal and cultural milieu. Yet his assessment also presents starkly dichotomous alternatives. Implicit in his claims is the contention that Hispanics should shun the Americanization process that numerous European Catholics underwent before them. The "American values" he cites are acutely negative. Such values are best resisted through cleaving closely to the Catholic faith and church and adopting a countercultural stance to the prevailing culture. Failure to do so leads almost inevitably to capitulation to powerful secular forces.

Hispanic ministry leaders have paralleled Dulles's viewpoint in their insistent pleas that Latinos retain their Hispanic cultural values, their faith expressions, and their Spanish-language ability. Many have particularly urged their fellow pastoral ministers to not merely tolerate Hispanic religious traditions, but to appropriately foster them as dynamic expressions of Catholic faith. Latino leaders have promoted Sunday Masses in Spanish or with a Hispanic liturgical style, prominent celebrations of Hispanic feasts and devotional traditions, predominantly Hispanic parishes and apostolic movements, prayer groups, pastoral juvenil, and other ministries consistent with the national parish dynamic. These ministries have regularly been the most effective in energizing the participation and commitment of Hispanics. Ongoing support and development of such ministries is indispensable for the future of U.S. Catholicism. Without them an even larger number of Hispanics will drift away from their practice of the Catholic faith; moreover, the distinctive contribution of Hispanic Catholic faith expressions and cultural values might be seriously debilitated. For various Hispanic ministry advocates, a nagging preoccupation is that Latinos will advance in numbers and in church leadership positions but in the process will lose the traditions that ground Latino Catholicism as they know it.

However, resistance to the majority culture is not sufficient. Indeed, in the extreme a countercultural stance is naïve. The potent effects of modern and secular cultures cannot be nullified with a mere act of will. For good or for ill, with each passing generation numerous Hispanics become more enmeshed in the ambiance and dispositions prevalent in the U.S. milieu. The core challenge of passing on the faith to Hispanic young people today, particularly those who were born or raised in the United States, underscores the necessity of faith formation that enables Catholics to engage the surrounding culture with critical discernment. Many Hispanic ministry leaders are concerned that a growing number of young Latinos have not experienced the Hispanic religious traditions that formed their elders in faith. Yet a capacity to credibly address with Catholic faith the situations and issues in contemporary life—education, career, childrearing, gender, homosexual unions, welfare and health care reform, to name but a few—is a necessary complement to rootedness in one's Hispanic Catholic heritage. The most urgent need is for apostolic movements, religious education experiences, pastoral leaders, and mentors that both build on familial and ethnic traditions and form Latinos in a faith that is an intentional way of life. In the final analysis, the transformative potential of the growing Hispanic Catholic presence hinges primarily on the extent to which they and their coreligionists address this challenge.

Hispanic ministry proponents have noted for decades that the historic transformation of the U.S. Catholic Church vis-à-vis its Latino members is a difficult and uneven process. Archbishop Patricio Flores exhorted his fellow participants at the 1977 Second Hispanic Pastoral Encuentro: "I must warn you that the great temptation which abides in all painful struggles is that of becoming disenchanted. . . . We cannot allow ourselves the luxury of despairing." He noted the "incredible impact" Latinos had already made in church and society and likened what is needed today to Jesus's call to his followers during a storm at sea. Flores's proclamation provides a fitting final thought for the Hispanic ministry leaders examined in this volume who seek to mutually enrich Latino Catholics, their church, and society: "'Let us not falter,' the Lord told his apostles when they struggled against the winds. He tells us now that we are in mid-sea, 'Courage, do not be afraid. It is I!'"[5]

# NOTES

## Preface

[1] Navarro-Rivera, Kosmin, and Keysar, *U.S. Latino Religious Identification,* 22; Johnson-Mondragón, "Socioreligious Demographics," 19; Putnam and Campbell, *American Grace,* 17, 299.

[2] Kosmin and Keysar, *American Religious Identification Survey 2008,* Summary Report, Part IIIC–Geography, table 12; Odem, "Our Lady of Guadalupe," 50; National Conference of Catholic Bishops (hereafter, NCCB; now United States Conference of Catholic Bishops)/Bishops' Committee on Hispanic Affairs (hereafter, BCHA), *Hispanic Ministry,* appendix C.

[3] De la Torre and Espinosa, *Rethinking Latino(a) Religion;* Díaz-Stevens and Stevens-Arroyo, *Recognizing the Latino Resurgence;* Badillo, *Latinos and the Church;* Monroe, *États-Unis;* León, *La Llorona's Children;* Díaz-Stevens, *Oxcart Catholicism;* Poyo, *Cuban Catholics.*

[4] S. Pitti, *Devil in Silicon Valley,* esp. 6–7; R. Gutiérrez, "Hispanic Identities."

## Chapter 1. Remapping American Catholicism

[1] Primary sources and a fuller account of the incidents recorded in this and the following paragraph are in Matovina, "Lay Initiatives in Worship," 108–11; Wright, "Father Refugio de la Garza," 83, 96–97n50.

[2] Tweed, *Retelling U.S. Religious History;* Brekus, *Religious History of American Women.* See also the book series edited by Kaufmann, *American Catholic Identities;* and by Silk, *Religion by Region.*

[3] Sandoval, *Fronteras;* Sandoval, *On the Move; U.S. Catholic Historian* 28. Documentary histories of U.S. Hispanic Catholicism with reprinted and annotated primary sources are in Stevens-Arroyo, *Prophets Denied Honor;* Matovina and Poyo, *¡Presente!*

251

[4] O'Toole, *Faithful*, 100, 226, chap. 6, "The Church in the Twenty-first Century."

[5] Hennesey, *American Catholics*; J. Dolan, *American Catholic Experience*, 125, 417; C. Morris, *American Catholic*, 431; Fisher, *Communion of Immigrants*.

[6] Varacalli, *Catholic Experience in America*, xx, 23–24, part 2, "Catholicism and Civilization in the United States: A Chronological Overview."

[7] See, e.g., Baxter, "Writing History"; Portier, "Americanism and Inculturation"; D'Agostino, *Rome in America*.

[8] J. Dolan and Deck, *Hispanic Catholic Culture*, 440; A. Taylor, *American Colonies*.

[9] Texas State Historical Association, "First Thanksgiving?"; El Paso Mission Trail Association, Inc., "First Documented Thanksgiving Was Held 23 Years before the Pilgrims' Celebration." Press release. 3 April 1995. (Copy in possession of author.)

[10] Baylies, *Narrative of Wool's Campaign*, 11.

[11] Sagarena, "Building California's Past," 432–34; Jackson, *Ramona: A Story*. The quotation is cited from Sagarena, originally in Helen Hunt Jackson, "Father Junípero and His Work (pt. 2)," *Century Magazine* 26 (June 1883): 201.

[12] Matovina, "Beyond the Missions."

[13] Reséndez, *Land So Strange*.

[14] The best overview of Spanish settlement in what is now the Southwest United States is Weber, *Spanish Frontier in North America*.

[15] Weber, *What Caused the Pueblo Revolt?*

[16] César, "Recollections of My Youth," 13.

[17] Hinojosa, "Friars and Indians"; Hinojosa and Fox, "Indians and Their Culture."

[18] "Eulalia Pérez: Una vieja y sus recuerdos," in Sánchez, Pita, and Reyes, *Nineteenth-Century Californio Testimonials*, 32–44.

[19] Cruz, *Let There Be Towns*, 111, 124–25.

[20] R. Gutiérrez, "El Santuario de Chimayó."

[21] Wright, "How Many Are 'A Few'?"

[22] M. Taylor, "Cura de la Frontera."

[23] Manuel Antonio García del Valle, Good Friday sermon, 20 April 1821, in Steele, *New Mexican Spanish Religious Oratory*, 19–39.

[24] M. Carroll, *Penitente Brotherhood*, 41, chap. 2, "The Golden Age That Wasn't: Hispano Piety before 1800."

[25] Handlin, *Uprooted*, 3.

[26] Seguín, *Personal Memoirs*, iv; De la Guerra, Speech to the California legislature, 19.

[27] Romero, "Begetting the Mexican American"; Acuña, *Occupied America*, 118–21; Matovina, *Tejano Religion and Ethnicity*, 51–52, 68.

[28] Engh, *Frontier Faiths*, 189–90; *San Antonio Ledger*, 10 July 1851.

[29] Engh, "From *Frontera* Faith," 90–95. The quoted passages are from *Constitutiones... Synodo Dioecesana Prima* (San Francisco: Vicente Torras, 1862), 26.

[30] Colton, *Three Years in California*, 224; Steele, *New Mexican Spanish Religious Oratory*, 94. One of the earliest and most infamous depictions of the Penitentes was Lummis, *Land of Poco Tiempo*, 79–108.

[31] Lawrence, Introduction, xviii–xix; Prescott, *History of the Conquest*; Franchot, *Roads to Rome*, 38–62.

[32] Cather, *Death Comes for the Archbishop*, 141. I am indebted to Roberto Lint Sagarena for his insightful work on *Death Comes for the Archbishop* and its role in shaping the historiography of the Southwest and perceptions of the region's Mexican inhabitants.

[33] "Willa Cather," 30; Williams, "Willa Cather's Masterpiece," 491–92.

[34] Weber, *On the Edge of Empire*, 78; Wright, "Local Church Emergence," 44; Hinojosa, "Enduring Hispanic Faith Communities"; Hennesey, *American Catholics*, 21, 137–38, 140–41.

[35] Quoted correspondence is from the transcription in Thompson, *El Gran Capitán, José de la Guerra*, 219–25.

[36] Montejano, *Anglos and Mexicans*, 34; Dysart, "Mexican Women in San Antonio," 370.

[37] Camarillo, *Chicanos in a Changing Society*; Griswold del Castillo, *Los Angeles Barrio*; Matovina, *Tejano Religion and Ethnicity*, 49–82.

[38] Steele, *New Mexican Spanish Religious Oratory*, 148–59.

[39] Pitt, *Decline of the Californios*, 33–35; Acuña, *Occupied America*, 43–47, 124–25; J. Navarro, *Defending Mexican Valor*, 19–20.

[40] Juárez, "La iglesia Católica y el Chicano," 230–32. For the conflict between Martínez and Lamy, see, e.g., Romero with Sandoval, *Reluctant Dawn*; Angélico Chávez, *But Time and Chance*.

[41] Odin to Étienne, 729; Odin to Anthony Blanc, 12 December 1852, Catholic Archives of Texas, Austin; Burns, "Mexican Catholic Community," 134–35; Engh, *Frontier Faiths*, chap. 7, "Soldiers of Christ, Angels of Mercy"; McKevitt, *Brokers of Culture*, chap. 8, "'The Darkest Part of the U.S.A.': The Southwest."

[42] J. Espinosa, "Origins of the Penitentes"; Pulido, *Sacred World*.

[43] Ronstadt, *Borderman*, 92; Matovina, *Guadalupe and Her Faithful*, chap. 3, "Defender of *Dignidad*, 1836–1900."

[44] Salvatore Personè, Letter of March 1875, as cited in Stoller and Steele, *Diary of the Jesuit Residence*, 185–86; R. Green, *Memoirs of Mary A. Maverick*, 53–54; Odin to Étienne; Domenech, *Missionary Adventures*, 357–59.

[45] *Los Angeles Star*, 22 August 1857.

[46] Jaramillo, *Shadows of the Past*, 85–86.

[47] Díaz-Stevens, "Saving Grace."

[48] Granjon, *Along the Rio Grande*, 39.

[49] Zangwill, *Melting-Pot*, 37; Gleason, "American Identity and Americanization," 31–34.

[50] Boorstin qtd. in Ellis, *American Catholicism*, ix, 129; C. Morris, *American Catholic*, 431.

[51] "Denies Catholics Oppose Separation"; Sorensen, *Kennedy*, 194; A. Smith, "Catholic and Patriotic"; Kennedy, Speech to the Greater Houston Ministerial Association; Shannon, *American Irish*, 393.

[52] D. Gutiérrez, *Walls and Mirrors*, chap. 2, "Economic Development and Immigration"; Poyo, *With All, and for the Good of All*; L. Pérez, "Cuban Catholics," 158–73.

[53] Spaniards and Hispanic Americans of San Francisco, *Lo que puede y necesita la raza española en San Francisco* (circular letter printed in San Francisco), 1871, copy in Bancroft Library, University of California, Berkeley; *A History of St. Mary Star of the Sea Catholic Church: The Oldest Roman Catholic Parish in the Diocese of Miami* (Key West: n.p., 1996); "Chronicles of the Sisters of the Holy Names of Jesus and Mary—Key West, Florida" (typescript), n.d., records of the Sisters of the Holy Names of Jesus and Mary, Albany, New York.

[54] Travieso, *El Padre Varela*; Varela, *Letters to Elpidio*; Navia, *Apostle for the Immigrants*.

[55] M. Gonzales, *Mexican Revolution*; D. Gutiérrez, *Walls and Mirrors*; Treviño, *Church in the Barrio*; E. Hernández, Burwell, and Smith, "Study of Hispanic Catholics," 112.

[56] Fitzpatrick, *Puerto Rican Americans*, 10, 17, 33–36; Díaz-Stevens, *Oxcart Catholicism*; Vidal, "Citizens Yet Strangers"; E. Hernández, Burwell, and Smith, "Study of Hispanic Catholics," 112.

[57] Poyo, *Cuban Catholics*, 50–84; L. Pérez, "Cuban Catholics," 189–207.

[58] Reimers, *Still the Golden Door*; M. C. García, *Seeking Refuge*; Torres-Saillant and Hernández, *Dominican Americans*; Tabares, "Pastoral Care."

[59] Düssel, *Church in Latin America*,; Peterson and Vásquez, *Latin American Religions*; Díaz-Stevens, *Oxcart Catholicism*, 52–59.

[60] Archdiocese of Newark, *Presencia Nueva*, 158–63.

[61] J. Dolan and Hinojosa, *Mexican Americans*, 74, 163, 248, 266, 281–82; Engh, "From the City of Angels"; Díaz-Stevens, *Oxcart Catholicism*; Vidal, "Citizens Yet Strangers," chap. 6, "Implementing the Vision"; De Luna, *"Evangelizadoras del barrio."*

[62] Poyo, *Cuban Catholics*, 11–32.

[63] Ibid., 93–96, 102–103.

[64] J. Hernández, "ACU."

[65] Tweed, *Our Lady of the Exile*, chap. 1, "The Virgin's Exile: The Cuban Patroness and the Diaspora in Miami."

[66] J. Hernández, "ACU," 104; *Alerta* (Miami), 1 September 1972; Poyo, *Cuban Catholics*, 190–99.

[67] Deck, *Second Wave*, 1.

[68] John Paul II, "Do Not Leave to the Poor"; John Paul II, *Ecclesia in America*, no. 5 (emphasis in original).

[69] Greer, *Mohawk Saint*. On the history of African American Catholics, see C. Davis, *History of Black Catholics*; C. Davis and Phelps, *"Stamped with the Image."*

[70] Jones, *Pierre Toussaint*; C. Davis, *Henriette Delille*; Costello, *Black Elk*. On the history of Native American Catholics, see Vecsey, *American Indian Catholics*; Archambault, Thiel, and Vecsey, *Crossing of Two Roads*.

[71] Murillo, "Tamales on the Fourth of July"; Amor en Acción, http://www.amore naccion.com. See also Badillo, *Latinos and the Church*, 125–41; R. Smith, *Mexican New York*, esp. chap. 7, "'Padre Jesús, Protect Me': Adolescence, Religion, and Social Location."

[72] Matovina, "Sacred Place and Collective Memory," 50.

# Chapter 2. Integration

[1] *America* 12 (17 October–19 December 1914): 7, 66.

[2] Ibid., 19 December 1914, 246; Vecoli, "Prelates and Peasants," 243–44.

[3] Shaughnessy, *Has the Immigrant Kept the Faith?*

[4] Huntington, *Who Are We?*, esp. chap. 9, "Mexican Immigration and Hispanization," 256, 324; Hanson, *Mexifornia*, 147–48.

[5] G. Rodriguez, *Mongrels, Bastards, Orphans,* chap. 8, "The Chicano Movement," 211–12, 229–30.

[6] Arlene Dávila, *Latino Spin*, 3.

[7] Massey, review of Huntington, *Who Are We?*, 544; Chavez, *The Latino Threat*; Carrasco, "Borderlands and the 'Biblical Hurricane,'" 354. See also Telles, "Mexican Americans"; Hayes-Bautista, *La Nueva California*.

[8] NCCB, *National Pastoral Plan*, no. 4; United States Conference of Catholic Bishops (hereafter, USCCB; formerly National Conference of Catholic Bishops), *Encuentro and Mission*, no. 60.

[9] NCCB/BCHA, *Hispanic Ministry*, On-Site Interview section, no. 2.

[10] Tomasi, *Piety and Power*.

[11] Ibid., 105.

[12] Ibid., 140.

[13] Cardinal Francis Spellman, "Dedication," in Ferrée, Illich, and Fitzpatrick, *Spiritual Care*, 7; Summary of the conference, in Ferrée, Illich, and Fitzpatrick, *Spiritual Care*, sec. 1, pp. 6–7.

[14] Fitzpatrick, "Sociological Aspects of Migration"; Summary of the conference, in Ferrée, Illich, and Fitzpatrick, *Spiritual Care*, sec. 1, p. 7. See also Fitzpatrick, *Stranger Is Our Own*, esp. chap. 14, "The Role of the Parish in the Spiritual Care of Puerto Ricans."

[15] Bardeck, "Problems of Religious Practice"; Vidal, "Citizens Yet Strangers," 137–38.

[16] Encarnación Padilla de Armas et al., Report of Some Catholic Women on the Religious Condition of Puerto Rican Immigrants in New York City, 1951 (copy in possession of author).

[17] Stern, "Evolution of Hispanic Ministry," 2:309, 313; Cooke, Archdiocese of Chicago [Report]; Vidal, "Citizens Yet Strangers," 129–33.

[18] Vidal, "Citizens Yet Strangers," 87; Deck, "At the Crossroads," 13; Fitzpatrick, "No Place to Grieve." See also Deck, *Second Wave*, 58–63.

[19] USCCB, "Hispanic Ministry at a Glance"; Instituto Fe y Vida, "Fast Facts."

[20] Dahm, *Parish Ministry*, 63.

[21] Pew Hispanic Center and Pew Forum on Religion and Public Life (hereafter, PHC/PFRPL), *Changing Faiths*, 48, 50, 55.

[22] NCCB, *Hispanic Presence: Challenge*, no. 5. The sixteen documents of Vatican II are available in various English translations, including Abbott, *Documents of Vatican II*.

[23] Fraga et al., *Latino Lives*, 73–74; Duarte, "Negotiation of Ethnicity."

[24] Fitzpatrick, "Hispanic Poor." Cited statistics are from a presentation of Luis Lugo, "Latinos and the Future of Catholicism in the United States," Georgetown University, October 2008, based on findings of the Pew Forum on Religion and Public Life, *U.S. Religious Landscape Survey*.

[25] NCCB, *National Pastoral Plan*, no. 37.

[26] Vecoli, "Prelates and Peasants," 268; T. Smith, "Religion and Ethnicity," 1156, 1181.

[27] Duncan and Trejo, "Who Remains Mexican?," 311.

[28] Alba and Nee, *Remaking the American Mainstream*, chap. 4, "Was Assimilation Contingent on Specific Historical Conditions?," chap. 6, "Evidence of Contemporary Assimilation," 144, 273.

[29] Johnson-Mondragón, *Welcoming Hispanic Youth*, 2–3; Johnson-Mondragón, "Socioreligious Demographics," 24; Fraga et al., *Latino Lives*, 140.

[30] Quiñones Martínez, Presentation, 77.

[31] Anita Jones interview with Mrs. Mesa, 25 July 1928, Chicago and Calumet Areas, Field Notes, Paul Schuster Taylor Papers, BANC MSS 84/38c, carton 11, folder 34, page 262, Bancroft Library, University of California, Berkeley; "Styles of Catholic Living: Gloria." In Doyle et al., *Hispanics in New York*, 1:153–56.

[32] Badillo, *Latinos and the Church*, 151; D'Antonio et al., *American Catholics Today*, 165–71; Marta Vargas, interview by author, 9 August 2007.

[33] Fraga et al., *Latino Lives*, 45; G. Rodriguez, *Mongrels, Bastards, Orphans*, xv; Alba and Nee, *Remaking the American Mainstream*, 226–27. An early and influential analysis of structural assimilation, or intermingling between groups at the level of primary social relationships like intermarriage, is in Gordon, *Assimilation in American Life*.

[34] Telles and Ortiz, *Generations of Exclusion*, 9; Goldstein and Suro, "Journey in Stages"; Fraga et al., *Latino Lives*, 52; Pew Hispanic Center, *Between Two Worlds*, 21.

[35] Grebler, Moore, and Guzmán, *Mexican American People*; Telles and Ortiz, *Generations of Exclusion*, 264–65.

[36] Hayes-Bautista, *La Nueva California*, 111–13.

[37] Conversations with Edward Gutierrez, 2008–2010 (quoted with permission).

[38] Rieff, "Nuevo Catholics," 43.

[39] Fernández, *Mexican-American Catholics*, 118, 124.

[40] Elizondo, *Galilean Journey*; Elizondo, *Future Is Mestizo*; Elizondo, *Guadalupe*; N. Medina, *Mestizaje*.

[41] Aguilera-Titus, *Weaving Together*; final quote as cited in USCCB, *Welcoming the Stranger*, 33.

[42] USCCB, *Welcoming the Stranger*, 30.

# Chapter 3. Hispanic Ministry

[1] Filteau, "Bishops Downsize." For an overview of the five priorities and the goals and objectives the bishops established for each, see USCCB Priorities, http://www.usccb .org/priorities.

[2] Filteau, "Bishops Downsize."

[3] National Catholic Council for Hispanic Ministry, "Response to the USCCB." The reader should know that I was an invited consultant to this symposium as well as to the two subsequent symposiums mentioned below. To honor confidentiality, I have confined myself in this presentation to quoting from the official consensus statement of the symposium participants, the texts of published addresses, and general summaries of perspectives expressed among participants.

[4] USCCB, *Encuentro and Mission*, no. 69.

[5] National Catholic Council for Hispanic Ministry, "Response to the USCCB," 486; J. Gomez, "Encounter with Christ," 479. The abortion statistic Archbishop Gomez cited is from Strauss et al., *Abortion Surveillance*.

[6] Deck, "Hispanic Ministry: New Realities," 406, 408; Ospino, *Hispanic Ministry*; J. Gomez, "Evangelization, Education."

[7] Sandoval, "Organization of a Hispanic Church," 133–35; M. T. García, *Católicos*, 113–19.

[8] Lucey, "'Christianizing' Mexican Catholics," 541.

[9] Lay Council for the Spanish Speaking, Archdiocese of San Antonio, Letter of support for the affidavit of Henrietta A. Castillo, 28 February 1947, in Perales, *Are We Good Neighbors?* 150; Ingalls, *Urban Vigilantes*; Sánchez Korrol, *From Colonia to Community*, 147–53; Márquez, *LULAC*.

[10] Allsup, *American G.I. Forum*; Stevens-Arroyo, *Prophets Denied Honor*, 98, 277; Rosales, *Chicano!*; César Chávez, Speech on the Mexican American and the Church, March 1968, in Matovina and Poyo, *¡Presente!*, 206–209.

[11] Elizondo, *Future Is Mestizo*, 38; *San Antonio Light*, 10 October 1969; Gregoria Ortega and Gloria Graciela Gallardo to Mexican American Sisters, 20 October 1970; Carmelita Espinoza and María de Jesús Ybarra, *La historia de las Hermanas* (n.p.: privately printed, 1978), 6; Alberto Carillo, Presentation to the PADRES national congress, October 1971, in Matovina and Poyo, *¡Presente!*, 212–16; L. Medina, *Las Hermanas*; R. Martínez, *PADRES*. Primary documents of Las Hermanas are in the archives at Our Lady of the Lake University in San Antonio.

[12] Vatican II, *Ad Gentes*, no. 22. For an overview of the influence of Vatican II on Elizondo, see Elizondo, *Virgilio Elizondo*.

[13] "Origin and Development of PADRES," in PADRES national congress report, October 1971; Juan Romero, "The Chicano Culture and Pastoral Theology: A Summary of PADRES San Antonio Symposium" (report), May–June 1971; Mario J. Paredes, "Thirty Years of Pastoral Service: The Northeast Hispanic Catholic Center" (unpublished paper); Burgués, *SEPI 1978–2008*. Primary sources for PADRES are in the Juan Romero papers at the University of Notre Dame Archives, South Bend, Indiana.

[14] Mexican American Cultural Center brochure, 1977, Archives of the Mexican American Catholic College, San Antonio, Texas.

[15] "Planning Committee" and "Statement of Purpose," in NCCB Secretariat for Hispanic Affairs (hereafter, SHA), "Proceedings of the Primer Encuentro," sections A and B.

[16] Ibid.

[17] Patricio Flores, "The Church: Diocesan and National," in NCCB/SHA, "Proceedings of the Primer Encuentro," sect. C4.

[18] NCCB/SHA, "Proceedings of the Primer Encuentro," sect. J1, no. 26. See also the version in *Origins*. Both sources contain the conclusions of the First Hispanic Pastoral Encuentro as well as the Report of the Ad Hoc Committee for the Spanish Speaking of the National Conference of Catholic Bishops on those conclusions.

[19] Ibid., 1; Juan Hurtado to Archbishop Jean Jadot, 12 April 1976, as cited in *PADRES* (Summer 1976): 15. *PADRES* was the organization's newsletter.

[20] "Encuentro Movement," in NCCB/SHA, "Proceedings of the Primer Encuentro," sect. J4; James V. Casey, "Church Concerned," *Denver Catholic Register*, 29 March 1973, as cited in Sandoval, "Organization of a Hispanic Church," 143; Paredes, "Thirty Years of Pastoral Service."

[21] NCCB/SHA, *Proceedings of the II Encuentro*, 64–66.

[22] Ibid., 66, 76; "Participants at the Primer Encuentro," in NCCB/SHA, "Proceedings of the Primer Encuentro," sect. J5.

[23] Editorials on the Second Encuentro in *Cara a Cara* (September–October 1977) and Ada María Isasi-Díaz in *El Visitante Dominical* (18 September 1977), in Stevens-Arroyo, *Prophets Denied Honor*, 325–26, 329–33; Gastón Witchger, "Recent History," 192; Sandoval, "Organization of a Hispanic Church," 144; Mario J. Paredes, "Historia de los Encuentros Nacionales" (unpublished manuscript), 1996, part 2, pp. 48–49. *Cara a Cara* was the bulletin of the Midwest Regional Office for Hispanic Ministry.

[24] NCCB/SHA, *Proceedings of the II Encuentro*, 56, 58, 68–69, 82; Editorial on the Second Encuentro in *Cara a Cara*, 325.

[25] NCCB/SHA, *Proceedings of the II Encuentro*, 66, 70; Second General Conference of Latin American Bishops, *Church in the Present-Day Transformation*, esp. document 15 on Joint Pastoral Planning, nos. 10–12.

[26] NCCB/SHA, *Proceedings of the II Encuentro*, 68.

[27] NCCB/SHA, *Prophetic Voices*, 3; "Somos Hispanos"; *Bishops Speak with the Virgin*.

[28] NCCB, *Hispanic Presence: Challenge*, nos. 12, 18, 19; Paredes, "Historia de los Encuentros Nacionales," part 3, pp. 4–8.

[29] NCCB/SHA, *Prophetic Voices*, 4–5; David Scott Blanchard, "An Evaluation of the III Encuentro Nacional Hispano de Pastoral" (typescript report in possession of author), 1986, esp. 13–31; Blanchard, "*III Encuentro*."

[30] NCCB/SHA, *Prophetic Voices*, 21; *Informes de Las Hermanas* (January 1986), 7. *Informes* was Hermanas's organizational newsletter.

[31] Connors, *Inculturated Pastoral Planning*, 62–63; NCCB, *National Pastoral Plan*, no. 17.

[32] NCCB/SHA, *Proceedings of the II Encuentro*, 68; NCCB, *National Pastoral Plan*, 28; NCCB/SHA, *Prophetic Voices*, 20. Passages that mention *pastoral de conjunto* in *Prophetic Voices* are on pp. 6, 7, 12, 13, 21.

[33] Blanchard, "Evaluation of the III Encuentro," tables 54–56.

[34] Sandoval, "Organization of a Hispanic Church," 145–46, 160.

[35] NCCB, *Hispanic Presence in the New Evangelization*, 39; USCCB, *Encuentro and Mission*, nos. 25, 27.

[36] John Paul II, *Apostolos Suos*, no. 22, art. 1.

[37] "Catholic Sex Abuse Hits Home."

[38] "Hispanics Form National Council"; Allan Figueroa Deck, Grant application of the National Catholic Council for Hispanic Ministry, 1993 (copy in possession of author); *Puentes.*

[39] William D. Dinges, "National and Regional Hispanic Catholic Ministry Organizational Initiatives: An Assessment"( typescript report), 12, 17. An abbreviated version of this report is available in Dinges, "National and Regional Initiatives"; Johnson-Mondragon, "Ministry in Parishes," 16.

[40] USCCB, *Encuentro and Mission*, no. 8; Ron Cruz, interview by author, 19 November 2009; USCCB, "FAQS about Many Faces in God's House"; NCCB, *Encuentro 2000*.

[41] Pablo Sedillo, interview by author, 30 September 2009; Edgard Beltrán, interview by author, 6 October 2009; USCCB, *Encuentro and Mission*, no. 11.

[42] Cepeda Escobedo, *Por una espiritualidad laical*, 13.

[43] Two subsequent Latin American episcopal conferences, one at Santo Domingo, Dominican Republic, in 1992 and the other at Aparecida, Brazil, in 2007, occurred after the Encuentros and the promulgation of the National Pastoral Plan and thus are not cited in any of their documents nor in the 2002 *Encuentro and Mission* document.

[44] NCCB/SHA, *Prophetic Voices*, 20; Vatican II, *Ad Gentes*, no. 10.

[45] USCCB, *Encuentro and Mission*, nos. 64–75; Virgilio Elizondo, Presentation at "Camino a Emaús: The Word of God and Latino Catholics" conference, University of Notre Dame, South Bend, Indiana, August 2009.

[46] Froehle and Gautier, *Ministry in a Church*, 14, 17; USCCB, *Study on Best Practices*, 1; USCCB, *Encuentro and Mission*, nos. 71, 72.

## Chapter 4. Parishes and Apostolic Movements

[1] *Miami Herald*, 7 August 1983; Poyo, *Cuban Catholics*, 95–97, 112, 118, 144, 281.

[2] Román, "*Other* Latin Mass."

[3] NCCB, *Hispanic Presence: Challenge*, no. 12; NCCB, *National Pastoral Plan*, esp. nos. 37–50.

[4] NCCB/BCHA, *Leaven for the Kingdom*, no. 4.2; NCCB/BCHA, *Communion and Mission*, vi.

[5] E. Rodríguez, "Hispanic Community," 237; Azevedo, *Basic Ecclesial Communities*.

[6] NCCB, *National Pastoral Plan*, nos. 37–38, p. 29.

[7] Ibid., nos. 23, 28–29, 33, 40–50, 68, 74, 76–77, 90, quote at 47.

[8] "Statistics on Hispanic/Latino(a) Catholics," Hispanic Affairs, USCCB, http://www.usccb.org/hispanicaffairs/demo.shtml; Center for Applied Research in the Apostolate at Georgetown University (hereafter, CARA), "Frequently Requested Statistics"; Lee with D'Antonio et al., *Catholic Experience*, 34–35.

[9] For an analysis of the challenging social context for Hispanic ministry in one Chicago parish, see Dahm, *Parish Ministry*, chap. 2, "Mexican Families in an American City."

[10] Greeley, "Defection among Hispanics"; Pew Hispanic Center and the Henry J. Kaiser Family Foundation, *2002 National Survey of Latinos*, 53; PHC/PFRPL, *Changing Faiths*, 42; Greeley, "Defection among Hispanics (Updated)." In this latter article Greeley calculated the annual defection rate as one-half of 1 percent of an estimated 12 million Hispanics in the 1988 U.S. population, which computes to sixty thousand, not six hundred thousand.

[11] Greeley, "Defection among Hispanics (Updated)," 12; Pew Forum on Religion and Public Life (hereafter, PFRPL), *U.S. Religious Landscape Survey*, esp. 25–26; Gray and Perl, *Sacraments Today*, 173; Putnam and Campbell, *American Grace*, 141, 301.

[12] Rosin, "Did Christianity Cause the Crash?"; NCCB/BCHA, *Hispanic Ministry*, On-Site Interview section, no. 4.

[13] Stevens-Arroyo, "National Survey," part 1, p. 1.

[14] Católico defiende tu fe Cristiana, http://www.defiendetufe.org; NCCB/BCHA, *Hispanic Ministry*, On-Site Interview section, no. 1.

[15] Espín, *Building Bridges*; J. González, *Mañana*.

[16] Rausch, "Ecumenism for Christians"; Gros, "Ecumenism in the U.S. Hispanic/Latino Community"; Stevens-Arroyo, "National Survey," part 1, pp. 11–17; R. Ramírez, "Crisis in Ecumenism," 666.

[17] PHC/PFRPL, *Changing Faiths*, 42, 44; Wuthnow, *After Heaven*.

[18] Stevens-Arroyo, "National Survey," part 3, p. 8; Matovina, *Guadalupe and Her Faithful*, 137; G. Espinosa, "Pentecostalization," 268.

[19] G. Espinosa, "Latinizing American Christianity," 30–31; Kosmin and Keysar, *Religion in a Free Market*, 247; Navarro-Rivera, Kosmin, and Keysar, *U.S. Latino Religious Identification*, 1. The Pew Latino religion survey showed an 8 percent "no religion" Latino response rate, while the 2010 Associated Press–Univision Poll found an 11 percent rate. PHC/PFRPL, *Changing Faiths*, 7; National Opinion Research Center (hereafter, NORC), *Associated Press–Univision Poll*, 37.

[20] Navarro-Rivera, Kosmin, and Keysar, *U.S. Latino Religious Identification*, 22; Bowen, *Evangelism and Apostasy*, 70–71.

[21] Stevens-Arroyo, "Correction, *Sí*; Defection, *No*," 17. The cited estimates are consistent with the most recent pertinent surveys: the 2006 Faith Matters survey, the 2008 ARIS study, and the 2010 Associated Press–Univision Poll. They are also consistent with the conclusions of CARA researchers' comparative analysis of eleven national surveys conducted between 1990 and 2003. Putnam and Campbell, *American Grace*, 268, 285; Navarro-Rivera, Kosmin, and Keysar, *U.S. Latino Religious Identification*; NORC, *Associated Press–Univision Poll*, 37; Perl, Greely, and Gray, "What Proportion Are Catholic?"

[22] Matovina, *Guadalupe and Her Faithful*, 37–40, 107–14, 142; Torres, "Our Lady of Guadalupe"; Pitti, "Sociedades Guadalupanas"; Poyo, *Cuban Catholics*, 93, 96.

[23] E. Rodríguez, "Hispanic Community," 215–19; Díaz-Stevens, *Oxcart Catholicism*, 109–10; Poyo, *Cuban Catholics*, 99–101; R. González and La Velle, *Hispanic Catholic*, 133–34; NCCB/BCHA, *Hispanic Ministry*, tables 5 and 6; Stevens-Arroyo, "National Survey," part 3, p. 14.

[24] Stern, "Evolution of Hispanic Ministry," 2:312.

[25] Hinojosa, "Mexican-American Faith Communities," 116–19; Deck, *Second Wave*, 67–68.

[26] Deck, *Second Wave*, 68–69.

[27] Christian Family Movement Online, http://www.cfm.org; E. Rodríguez, "Hispanic Community," 220–21; Movimiento Familiar Cristiano, http://www.mfc.org.mxg; RENEW International, https://www.renewintl.org; Deck, *Second Wave*, 73–75.

[28] Lee, with D'Antonio et al., *Catholic Experience*, esp. tables 1–2, 14–15, 27–31, 35, quotes at 81, 109.

[29] International Catholic Charismatic Renewal Services, http://www.iccrs.org/CCR%20worldwide.htm; Comité Nacional de Servicio Hispano, http://www.rcchispana.com.

[30] G. Espinosa, "Pentecostalization," 266; NCCB/BCHA, *Hispanic Ministry*, tables 5 and 6; Stevens-Arroyo, "National Survey," part 3, p. 14.

[31] PHC/PFRPL, *Changing Faiths*, 1, 28, 31–33.

[32] Ibid., 28.

[33] Aponte, "*Coritos* as Active Symbol"; Barton, *Hispanic Methodists, Presbyterians,* 94–98.

[34] NCCB/BCHA, *Hispanic Ministry,* On-Site Interview section, no. 3; Andrés Arango, interview by author, 8 July 2008.

[35] DePalma, "Hispanics Still Backing Leaders"; PHC/PFRPL, *Changing Faiths,* 37; NCCB/BCHA, *Hispanic Ministry,* On-Site Interview section, part 2.

[36] Arango, interview by author; Manetto, "Charismatic Spirit Spreads"; Deck, "Hispanic Ministry: New Realities," 410.

[37] G. Espinosa, "Marilynn Kramar," ; G. Espinosa, "Pentecostalization," 273; Charisma in Missions, http://carismaenmisiones.com; El Sembrador, http://www.elsembrador .org.

[38] As cited in Fierro, "Devil Must Be Laughing"; E. Rodríguez, "Hispanic Community," 219.

[39] Deck, "Where the Laity Flourish," 6; O'Connor, "Catholic Common Ground Initiative."

[40] USCCB, *Encuentro and Mission,* nos. 47–48; K. Davis, "Hispanic Catholics Deserve More," 26; Dahm, *Parish Ministry,* 79–83.

[41] Deck, "Hispanic Ministry Comes of Age."

[42] R. Rodriguez, *Brown,* 224, 230; R. Rodriguez, *Days of Obligation,* 45–47; Levy, "Weekly Mass for Gays Ends." See also Espín, *Grace and Humanness,* chap. 2, "*Humanitas,* Identity, and Another Theological Anthropology of (Catholic) Tradition."

[43] Stevens-Arroyo, "National Survey," part 1, pp. 8, 34–35.

[44] Davidson, *Catholicism in Motion,* 69; Dougherty, "How Monochromatic Is Church Membership?"; Emerson with Woo, *People of the Dream,* 35, 39; Stevens-Arroyo, "National Survey," part 1, pp. 3, 8, 34. See also Chaves, *Congregations in America,* 226.

[45] Johnson-Mondragón, "Ministry in Parishes," 9–10; Hoover, "Negotiating the Church."

[46] Wall, "Schism Hits Church"; NCCB/BCHA, *Hispanic Ministry,* On-Site Interview section, no. 8; Dahm, *Parish Ministry,* 294.

[47] NCCB, Committee on African American Catholics and Committee on Hispanic Affairs, *Reconciled through Christ,* 39, 45.

[48] Johnson-Mondragón, "Ministry in Parishes," 23; Wall, "Schism Hits Church"; Duck, "Bishop Meets with Parishioners."

[49] Emerson with Woo, *People of the Dream,* 147–55.

[50] Information and quotations in this and the following three paragraphs are taken from Hoover, "Negotiating the Church." See also Hoover, "'What Are We Doing Here?'"; Putnam and Campbell, *American Grace,* 220–30, 305–306.

[51] Rutenbeck, *Scenes from a Parish,* synopsis; Burr, "In One Parish."

[52] Warner, "Place of the Congregation," 2:54, 73; Wuthnow, *"I Come Away Stronger."*

[53] "Saint Camillus: A Catholic Multicultural Parish," http://www.stcamilluschurch .org.

[54] Wilkes, *Excellent Catholic Parishes*, 19–38.

[55] Catholic Charismatic Center, Archdiocese of Galveston-Houston, http://catholic charismaticcenter.org; Marina Carrion, interview by author, 28 March 2010; Msgr. Joseph Malagreca, interview by author, 19 November 2009.

[56] Teens Encounter Christ, http://www.tecconference.org/1.html. Other quotations taken from book prospectus (typescript) of Nabhan-Warren, "De Colores: American Catholic and Protestant Cursillos and the 'Fourth Day' Movement" (2010). I gratefully acknowledge Dr. Nabhan-Warren for allowing me to read and cite the research for her forthcoming book. See also Nabhan-Warren, "'Blooming Where We're Planted.'"

## Chapter 5. Leadership

[1] Nabhan-Warren, *Virgin of El Barrio*, 82–89, 101.

[2] Ibid., 3, 24.

[3] Ibid., chap. 4, "'On Fire for Mary and Jesus!': Becoming New Men and Women in Mary's Ministries," and chap. 6, "Corporate Evangelizers: A Family's 'Vision' for South Phoenix," 165.

[4] Ibid., 11.

[5] Fitzpatrick, "Hispanic Poor," 11.

[6] NCCB, *Hispanic Presence: Challenge*, no. 12; NCCB, *National Pastoral Plan*, no. 67; USCCB, *Encuentro and Mission*, no. 30.

[7] Spanish-speaking Apostolate Leaders, Letter to Cardinal Terence Cooke, 13 March 1972, as cited in Stern, "Evolution of Hispanic Ministry," 2:334–35; Trinidad Sánchez, Circular letter promoting the appointment of Hispanic bishops, 20 October 1978, PA-DRES Collection, University of Notre Dame Archives, Notre Dame, Indiana; "Hispanic/ Latino Bishops in the United States (1970–present)," http://www.usccb.org/hispanic affairs/bishops.shtml.

[8] USCCB, "Hispanic Ministry at a Glance"; Instituto Fe y Vida, "Fast Facts"; Gray and Gautier, "Latino/a Catholic Leaders," 81.

[9] Flores, "Vocations," 506, 510, 512.

[10] Gray and Gautier, "Latino/a Catholic Leaders," 67–69.

[11] National Conference of Diocesan Vocation Directors, http://www.ncdvd.org; National Religious Vocation Conference, http://www.nrvc.net; Archdiocese of Santa Fe Pilgrimages for Vocations, http://www.pilgrimagesforvocations.org.

[12] Lucille Flores, "Hispanic Seminarians' Conference" (unpublished paper in possession of author); Zimanske, "Conference Explores Ministry."

[13] St. Vincent de Paul Regional Seminary 2009–2010 Seminary Catalogue, http://www .svdp.edu/_files/pdf/WebCatalog093009.pdf, p. 12; Oblate School of Theology 2009 Catalogue, http://www.ost.edu/Full_catalog/OST%20Catalog%202009%20Revision.pdf, p. 4.

[14] Seminario Hispano de Santa María de Guadalupe de la Arquidiócesis de México, http://www.seminariohispano.org; Gautier, *Catholic Ministry Enrollments*, 6.

[15] Archdiocese of Miami website, http://www.newmiamiarch.org; Gautier, Bendyna, and Cidade, *Class of 2009*, 4, 9–10; Gautier, *Catholic Ministry Enrollments*, 10–12, 17.

[16] Gautier, Bendyna, and Cidade, *Class of 2009*, 10–11; Gautier, *Catholic Ministry Enrollments*, 13; José Gomez, comment during group discussion, "Present and Future of Catholic Hispanic Ministry in the United States" symposium, Boston College, June 2009.

[17] Stevens-Arroyo, "National Survey," part 2, p. 7.

[18] K. Davis, "Neutering or Nurturing?," 83–84; PHC/PFRPL, *Changing Faiths*, 49.

[19] USCCB, *National Directory*, esp. nos. 3–7, 31–38; CARA, "Frequently Requested Statistics."

[20] Asociación Nacional de Diáconos Hispanos, http://www.diaconoshispanos.com/index.html; Gautier, *Catholic Ministry Enrollments*, 20–23; "Eight in Ten U.S. Permanent Deacons."

[21] CARA, "Frequently Requested Statistics"; Bendyna and Gautier, *Recent Vocations*, 24–25, 33–34.

[22] USCCB, *Co-Workers in the Vineyard*, 7–13.

[23] Ibid., 13; Gautier, *Catholic Ministry Enrollments*, 10, 25; Allen, "Feminization of the Church."

[24] Hoge and Jewell, *Next Generation*, 7; Gautier, *Catholic Ministry Enrollments*, 25, 33.

[25] USCCB, *Encuentro and Mission*, no. 56; Catholic Association of Latino Leaders, http://www.hispanicleaders.net.

[26] USCCB, *Encuentro and Mission*, no. 11.

[27] Caterine, *Conservative Catholicism*; e-mail correspondence with Sister Ruth Bolarte, I.H.M., May 2010; program for 2009 Conferencia Nacional de Diáconos Hispanos, http://www.diaconoshispanos.com/_fileCabinet/July232009_Schedule.pdf.

[28] Gray and Perl, *Sacraments Today*, 126; Hoge and Okure, *International Priests*, 40; NCCB/BCHA, *Hispanic Ministry*, On-Site Interview section, no. 1.

[29] NCCB/BCHA, *Hispanic Ministry*, On-Site Interview section, no. 1; Midwest parish leader, comment during group discussion, "Soy Catequista: The Dignity, Vocation and Mission of the Catechist" symposium, University of Notre Dame, November 2006; Hoge and Okure, *International Priests*, 54.

[30] Hoge and Okure, *International Priests*, 85–86, 91–92.

[31] Asociación Nacional de Sacerdotes Hispanos, http://www.ansh.org.

[32] USCCB, *Welcoming the Stranger*, 34–35.

[33] USCCB, *Encuentro and Mission*, no. 46; Gurza, "*Ni Aquí* Nor There."

[34] NCCB/BCHA, *Hispanic Ministry*, On-Site Interview section, no. 1.

[35] USCCB, *Study on Best Practices*, 4.

[36] K. Davis, "Neutering or Nurturing?"; USCCB, *Encuentro and Mission*, no. 55.

[37] USCCB, *Program of Priestly Formation*, no. 228; Hoge, *First Five Years*, 14, 160–61. I gratefully acknowledge Sister Katarina Schuth, O.S.F., who provided me with her compiled information on Hispanic programs in U.S. seminaries from their respective catalogues.

[38] Stevens-Arroyo, "National Survey," part 2, p. 14; "Priests Learning a Language."

[39] K. Davis, "Neutering or Nurturing?," 82–83; Hoge and Okure, *International Priests*, 15, 20, 22, 108–20, 157–58.

[40] USCCB, *Encuentro and Mission*, nos. 55, 75; Gautier, *Catholic Ministry Enrollments*, 25, 30.

[41] Burgués, *SEPI 1978–2008*, 84–85.

[42] USCCB, *Encuentro and Mission*, no. 55, Presmanes and Marill, "Hispanic Ministry and Theology"; Ospino and Miranda, "Hispanic Ministry and Leadership Formation."

[43] Federación de Institutos Pastorales, http://www.fipusa.com/index.html; USCCB, *Study on Best Practices*, 5.

## Chapter 6. Worship and Devotion

[1] Alvaro Dávila, "Re-discovering My Spiritual History," 89–90.

[2] Ibid., 91.

[3] Ibid., 91–92.

[4] Elizondo, "Educación religiosa"; Deck, *Frontiers of Hispanic Theology*, xxi–xxiv; Espín, *Faith of the People*, 2; Elizondo, "Popular Religion," 37; Fernández, *La Cosecha*.

[5] De la Torre, *Santería*; León, "'Soy una Curandera.'"

[6] Davalos, "*La Quinceañera*"; Empereur and Fernández, *Vida Sacra*, 112–23; USCCB, *Bendición al Cumplir Quince Años*; Gómez, *Quinceañeras*.

[7] *Sacrosanctum Concilium*, nos. 13, 14, 37; Chupungco, "Liturgical Inculturation," 339; Chupungco, *Liturgies of the Future*.

[8] Congregation for Divine Worship and the Discipline of the Sacraments, *Directory on Popular Piety and the Liturgy*, no. 93; Phan, *Directory on Popular Piety and the Liturgy*.

[9] Elizondo, *God of Incredible Surprises*, 1. See also Espín and García, "Lilies of the Field."

[10] Elizondo, *Galilean Journey*, 41.

[11] Trexler, *Reliving Golgotha*, viii.

[12] "Perdona a Tu Pueblo," in *Cantos del Pueblo de Dios*, no. 36; Parker, "'Roman Soldier' Asks Forgiveness."

[13] Virgilio Elizondo, "San Fernando Cathedral's Way of the Cross through the Streets of San Antonio" (unpublished booklet of meditations), San Antonio, 1997; Kelly, "On Good Friday, Faithful Follow."

[14] Stingl, "Good Friday Procession."

[15] Montana, "Passion Play Unites Pilsen"; Davalos, "'Real Way of Praying,'" esp. 46–48.

[16] Gálvez, *Guadalupe in New York*, 60–71, 107, 129–39.

[17] Bell, *Ritual: Perspectives and Dimensions*, 38; Davalos, " 'Real Way of Praying,' " 68.

[18] Sadovi, "Cicero Rejects Parade"; Sadovi, "Deal Falters over Religious Procession"; Sadovi, "Cicero Procession Draws Crowd."

[19] Ashley, "Stations of the Cross," 362–63.

[20] Davalos, " 'Real Way of Praying,' " 60–61. Davalos followed the ethnographic practice of employing pseudonyms for her interviewees, such as Claudia and Patricia.

[21] Espín, *Faith of the People*, 49.

[22] Davalos, " 'Real Way of Praying,' " 50.

[23] Espín, *Faith of the People*, 73; Odem, "Our Lady of Guadalupe," 48; Odem, "Latino Immigrants," 122.

[24] *Mary Throughout Latin America*, 11, 23.

[25] M. E. Díaz, *Virgin, the King, and the Royal Slaves*, 116. Juan Moreno's account of the discovery of Our Lady of Charity's image is transcribed in appendix 4 of this work.

[26] Zúñiga, *La Virgen de la Caridad del Cobre*; Tweed, *Our Lady of the Exile*, 119, 126. A transcription of the veterans' petition and Benedict XV's response are in Vizcaíno, *Virgen de la Caridad*, 28–29.

[27] Citations are taken from a *Nican mopohua* translation popular among Guadalupan devotees in Elizondo, *Guadalupe: Mother of the New Creation*, 5–22. For a presentation of the original Nahuatl version with an accompanying English translation, see Sousa, Poole, and Lockhart, *Story of Guadalupe*, 60–93.

[28] Matovina, *Guadalupe and Her Faithful*, 128–30.

[29] "Buenos Días, Paloma Blanca," in *Cantos del Pueblo de Dios*, no. 201.

[30] M. Ramirez, "Mexican Icon Blossoms in U.S."; Matovina, *Guadalupe and Her Faithful*, 177; Durán, "Great Sign."

[31] Matovina, *Guadalupe and Her Faithful*, 157; Engh, "With Her People"; Gálvez, *Guadalupe in New York*, chap. 6, "La Antorcha Guadalupana/The Guadalupan Torch Run: Messengers for a People Divided by the Border," 149, 150, 155. Gálvez used pseudonyms for nearly all of her interviewees.

[32] Hall, *Mary, Mother and Warrior*, 284–88; Schuetz, "Religion and Art"; Coday, "Denver Catholics Fight."

[33] M. Navarro, "In Many Churches, Icons Compete"; Tabares, "Pastoral Care," 275, 279–80.

[34] NCCB/BCHA, *Hispanic Ministry*, On-Site Interview section, no. 6; Father John Koelsch, letter to the author, 22 September 2009; Matovina, "Capilla de Nuestro Señor de los Milagros," 198; Johnson, "Mary and the Female Face of God"; Johnson, *Truly Our Sister*, 71–92.

[35] García-Rivera, "Let's Capture the Hispanic Imagination."

[36] A. Pérez, "History of Hispanic Liturgy," 370–76.

[37] Ibid., 372–75; Sosa, *One Voice, Many Rhythms*, 68–72, 79–83; Instituto Nacional Hispano de Liturgia, http://liturgia.cua.edu.

[38] Sosa, *One Voice, Many Rhythms*, 19; Francis, *Shape a Circle*, 103–108; Francis, *Guidelines*; Reza, "Crosscultural Music Making"; Burke, "Facing the Bilingual Challenge."

[39] Sosa, *One Voice, Many Rhythms*, 68–71, 87–95; A. Pérez, "History of Hispanic Liturgy," 381–93; *Flor y Canto*; *Cantos del Pueblo de Dios*.

[40] "Ofertorio Nicaragüense" and "Un Pueblo que Camina," in *Cantos del Pueblo de Dios*, nos. 579 and 706.

[41] A. Pérez, "History of Hispanic Liturgy," 378–81.

[42] K. Davis, "Presiding in Spanish," 82; K. Davis and Presmanes, *Preaching and Culture*, 18.

[43] Deck, "Seized and Saturated," 12, 13, 17; Elizondo, "Converted by Beauty," 78.

[44] Arias, Francis, and Pérez-Rodríguez, *La Navidad Hispana*, 55–67; Elizondo, *Galilean Journey*, 34–38; Sosa, *One Voice, Many Rhythms*, 62.

[45] Isasi-Díaz, *En la Lucha*, 180; Goizueta, "Symbolic World," 121–22; Matovina, "Capilla de Nuestro Señor de los Milagros," 196.

[46] Goizueta, *Caminemos con Jesús*; Goizueta, *Christ Our Companion*.

[47] M. H. Díaz, "*Dime con quién andas*," 154, 156; Goizueta, "Resurrection at Tepeyac," 341, 343.

[48] Empereur and Fernández, *Vida Sacra*, 25, 300; R. Gómez, "Preaching the Ritual Masses," 109.

[49] Hoge, Dinges, Johnson, and Gonzalez, *Young Adult Catholics*, 43, 50, 126–27; Putnam and Campbell, *American Grace*, 156, 525.

[50] Matovina, *Guadalupe and Her Faithful*, 166–67; DeJesús Sáenz, "Church and Youth Ministry Participation," 100.

[51] Icaza, "Do We Have Inculturated Liturgies?," 22–23; A. Pérez, *Popular Catholicism*, 27; NCCB/BCHA, *Hispanic Ministry*, On-Site Interview section, no. 1.

[52] Committee on Divine Worship, USCCB, "Third Edition Roman Missal, Frequently Asked Questions," http://usccb.org/romanmissal/faqs2.shtml.

[53] Sosa, "Liturgical Piety?," 8; *Sacrosanctum Concilium*, no. 34; USCCB, *Encuentro and Mission*, nos. 34, 58.

[54] Pecklers, *Unread Vision*.

[55] Parker, "Lady of Guadalupe."

[56] Gálvez, *Guadalupe in New York*, 120–22; Matovina, "Latino Catholics," 68; Carter, *Culture of Disbelief*; Rourke, "Return to Ritual."

## Chapter 7. Public Catholicism

[1] Interfaith Funders, *1999 Annual Report*, 18–20.

[2] Matovina, *Tejano Religion and Ethnicity*, 70–74; J. Navarro, *Defending Mexican Valor*, 21.

[3] Wood, "Fe y Acción Social"; Warren and Wood, *Faith-Based Community Organizing*; Wood and Warren, "Different Face of Faith-Based Politics"; Wood, "Higher Power," 164; Swarts, *Organizing Urban America*, xxi.

[4] Wood, "Fe y Acción Social," 149–52; Swarts, *Organizing Urban America*, 23.

[5] Rogers, *Cold Anger*, 105–26; Warren, *Dry Bones Rattling*, esp. 47–57, 233–34; Wood, "Fe y Acción Social," 146; *Power, Action, Justice: 1974–1999* (COPS 25th anniversary program), 21.

[6] Warren, *Dry Bones Rattling*, 42; Wood, "Fe y Acción Social," 146; Rogers, *Cold Anger*, 124.

[7] Wood, *Faith in Action*, 162, 183–85; Wilson, *Politics of Latino Faith*, 8; Wood and Flaherty, *Renewing Congregations*, 27.

[8] Swarts, *Organizing Urban America*, xxiii, chap. 2, "Religion and Progressive Politics: Congregation-Based Community Organizing's Innovative Cultural Strategy"; Wood, *Faith in Action*, 185, 194.

[9] Catholic Campaign for Human Development, http://www.usccb.org/cchd/index.shtml; Warren and Wood, *Faith-Based Community Organizing*, table 2.

[10] Report on CCHD and ACORN; Reform CCHD Now coalition, http://www.reformcchdnow.com.

[11] Report of Bishop Roger Morin; Filteau, "10 Dioceses Quit Campaign."

[12] Dahm, *Parish Ministry*, 258–62; Wood, *Faith in Action*, 15.

[13] Richard L. Wood, "Raising the Bar: Organizing Capacity in 2009 and Beyond, A Report for the Neighborhood Funders Group" (typescript report in possession of author, available from rlwood@unm.edu), 3; Swarts, *Organizing Urban America*, 175–76, 207–15; Wood, "Higher Power," 180.

[14] Bishops' statements on immigration prior to 1988 are in NCCB, *Pastoral Letters*. See also USCCB, *Welcoming the Stranger*; USCCB/Catholic Bishops of Mexico and the United States, *Strangers No Longer*; Justice for Immigrants, http://www.justiceforimmigrants.org.

[15] G. Pitti, "To 'Hear about God,'" 301, esp. chap. 8, "'At the Cost of the Poorest of Our Own Citizens'? Catholic Migrant Ministry and the Bracero Program, 1942–1955," and chap. 9, "'A Ghastly International Racket': Catholic Opposition to the Bracero Program in California, 1954–1964"; USCCB/Catholic Bishops of Mexico and the United States, *Strangers No Longer*.

[16] M. T. García, *Católicos*, chap. 7, "¡Presente! Father Luis Olivares and the Sanctuary Movement in Los Angeles"; Agustín A. Román and Enríque San Pedro, Statement on Cuban exiles in federal penitentiaries, 21 December 1986 (typescript), Archdiocese of Miami Archives; Gabino Zavala, Address to the Los Angeles County School Board, 18 August 1994, Personal files of Gabino Zavala, Irwindale, California (copy in possession of author). Cardinal Roger Mahony's numerous public statements on immigration include "Immigration," and "Viewing Immigration."

[17] J. Gomez, "Immigration Reform."

[18] USCCB Migration and Refugee Services, http://www.usccb.org/mrs; Catholic Legal Immigration Network, Inc., http://www.cliniclegal.org; Yamane, *Catholic Church in*

*State Politics*, 9–13, 41, 62–69; Maryland Bishops, "Where All Find a Home"; Maryland Catholic Conference immigration page, http://www.mdcathcon.org/Immigration; Kicanas, "Arizona Immigration Law"; "USCCB Migration Chairman."

[19] Neuhaus, "Immigration and the Aliens," 64; Neuhaus, "When Bishops Speak," 63.

[20] Quoted in Wall, "Bishops Begin Campaign."

[21] Lord, "Parish Uses Dialogue Process"; Groody, *Border of Death*; Groody and Campese, *Promised Land*; Groody and Groody, *Dying to Live*; Kerwin and Gerschutz, *And You Welcomed Me*; Theology of Migration Project, http://woodstock.georgetown.edu/programs/Theology-of-Migration.html.

[22] PHC/PFRPL, *Changing Faiths*, 61–63; Lawton, "Immigration Fuels Church Activity."

[23] "UFW's AgJobs"; Schultze, *Strangers in a Foreign Land*; Hondagneu-Sotelo, *God's Heart Has No Borders*, chap. 4, "Take Your Good Friday to the Streets!," 93.

[24] Dahm, *Parish Ministry*, 61; Freedman, "Immigrants Find Solace."

[25] National Association of Latino Elected and Appointed Officials, *Profile of Latino Elected Officials*; Hero et al., "Latino Participation"; Gibson, "Is Sonia Sotomayor Catholic?"

[26] "Governor Bill Richardson Signs Repeal"; Wooden, "State's Decision to Abolish Death Penalty."

[27] M. Martinez with Breslin, *Sense of Belonging*, 24.

[28] Arlene Dávila, *Latino Spin*, 60–66; Pratt, "Parallel Presidential Campaign."

[29] D. Morris, "Hispanic Vote Elects Bush."

[30] Kettle, "Hispanic Vote."

[31] Leal, et al., "Latino Vote in the 2004 Election"; National Election Pool, 2004 exit poll; De la Garza, DeSipio, and Leal, *Beyond the Barrio*.

[32] 2004 presidential election results, http://www.cnn.com/ELECTION/2004/pages/results; 2008 presidential election results, http://www.cnn.com/ELECTION/2008/results/president.

[33] 2004 and 2008 presidential election results; Kromm, "Election 2008."

[34] Leal et al., "Latino Vote," 41; Mark Hugo Lopez, "How Hispanics Voted in the 2008 Election," 5 November 2008, http://pewresearch.org/pubs/1024/exit-poll-analysis-hispanics; De la Garza, "*El Cuento de los Números.*"

[35] William C. Velasquez Institute, "William C. Velásquez: 1944–1988," and "Latino Voter Statistics."

[36] Kosmin and Keysar, *Religion in a Free Market*, 230–31; J. Green, Smidt, Guth, and Kellstedt, "American Religious Landscape," 17; Leal et al., "Latino Vote," 46–47; PHC/PFRPL, *Changing Faiths*, 77–80; J. Green, *Faith Factor*, 9, 60; *National Survey of Latino Protestants*, 4; *Secular and Security-Minded*.

[37] G. Espinosa, "Latino Clergy and Churches," 282–88; Pantoja, Barreto, and Anderson, "Politics *y la Iglesia*"; Arturo Chávez, "Social and Political Involvement," 250–52.

[38] Suarez, *Holy Vote*, 217–18; NCCB, *Hispanic Presence in the New Evangelization*, 23, 39–41; Hispanic ministry leader, comment during group discussion, National Catholic Council for Hispanic Ministry Raíces y alas/Roots and Wings national Hispanic leadership congress, University of Notre Dame, May 2003.

[39] G. Espinosa, Elizondo, and Miranda, *Hispanic Churches*, 17.

[40] Pew Hispanic Center and the Henry J. Kaiser Family Foundation, *2002 National Survey of Latinos*, 55; PFRPL, "Portrait of American Catholics"; Alonso-Zaldivar and Tompson, "Poll: Young Hispanics"; Pew Hispanic Center, *Between Two Worlds*, 65–66.

[41] J. Green, *Faith Factor*, 13; J. Green et al., "American Religious Landscape," 11; William C. Velasquez Institute, 2008 WCVI Exit Poll Results.

[42] "Hispanic Bishops Visit Congressmen"; Zapor, "Bishops Talk Health Care."

[43] Benedict XVI, *Caritas in veritate*, no. 6.

[44] Henshaw and Kost, *Trends in the Characteristics of Women*, 11–13.

## Chapter 8. Passing on the Faith

[1] Wuthnow, *After the Baby Boomers*; Heft, *Passing on the Faith*; C. Carroll, *New Faithful*; C. Smith with Denton, *Soul Searching*, 194, 210–15; C. Smith with Snell, *Souls in Transition*, 104, 106; Hoge, Dinges, Johnson, and Gonzalez, *Young Adult Catholics*, 228.

[2] DeJesús Sáenz, "Church and Youth Ministry Participation," 86; Johnson-Mondragón, "Second Wave," 281; Hoge, Dinges, Johnson, and Gonzalez, *Young Adult Catholics*, 51; G. Espinosa, Elizondo, and Miranda, *Hispanic Churches*, 15; Perl, Greely, and Gray, "What Proportion Are Catholic?," 428; Navarro-Rivera, Kosmin, and Keysar, *U.S. Latino Religious Identification*, 16–17; Pew Hispanic Center, *Between Two Worlds*, 64; Alonso-Zaldivar and Tompson, "Poll: Young Hispanics"; Johnson-Mondragón, "Socioreligious Demographics," 21.

[3] National Catholic Network de Pastoral Juvenil Hispana–La Red (hereafter, La Red), *Conclusiones*, 92; Johnson-Mondragón, "Socioreligious Demographics," 16; G. Rodriguez, *Mongrels, Bastards, Orphans*, 254.

[4] Putnam and Campbell, *American Grace*, 300; Glauber, "Arizona Immigration Law"; Pew Hispanic Center, *Between Two Worlds*, 1.

[5] La Red, *Conclusiones*, 6, 11–12, 30, 89.

[6] USCCB, *Encuentro and Mission*, no.70; NCCB/BCHA, *Hispanic Ministry*, Bishops Survey section, question 4; USCCB, *Renewing Our Commitment*, 9.

[7] Foner, *Across Generations*, esp. 9–12; Suárez-Orozco and Todorova, "Social Worlds," 20–21; Hoge, Dinges, Johnson, and Gonzalez, *Young Adult Catholics*, 125.

[8] M. Sanchez, "Don't Tread on Amendment"; D. Gonzalez, "Family Divided."

[9] Marill, "Youth and Culture," 49–50; Foner, *Across Generations*, esp. 3–9; Carrillo, "Faith and Culture," 132.

[10] Pew Hispanic Center, *Between Two Worlds*, 82–91.

[11] Ibid., 4, 38, 49, 56; DeParle, "Struggling to Rise."

[12] Johnson-Mondragón, "Socioreligious Demographics," 33–39; Johnson-Mondragón, *Status of Hispanic Youth*, chap. 1 "The Pastoral Reality of Hispanic Youth and Young Adults."

[13] La Red, *Conclusiones*, 11.

[14] Ibid., 19, 23, 30, 113; Cervantes and Johnson-Mondragón, *Pastoral Juvenil Hispana*.

[15] USCCB, *Encuentro and Mission*, no. 70; Johnson-Mondragón, "Hispanic Youth," 9; La Red, *Conclusiones*, 64.

[16] NCCB, *Renewing the Vision*; NCCB, *Sons and Daughters of the Light*; Hayes, *Googling God*, 98–106.

[17] Baez-Chávez and Chávez, *RESPETO*; USCCB, *Encuentro and Mission*, no. 70.

[18] Pew Hispanic Center, *Between Two Worlds*, 89–92; National Youth Gang Survey Analysis, Demographics, http://www.nationalgangcenter.gov/Survey-Analysis/Demo graphics#anchorregm. I gratefully acknowledge Ken Johnson-Mondragón for calculating the cited percent estimates from the National Youth Gang Survey data.

[19] Fremon, *G-Dog and the Homeboys*; Boyle, *Tattoos on the Heart*.

[20] La Red, *Conclusiones*, 14, 33; USCCB, *Encuentro and Mission*, no. 70; Johnson-Mondragón, *Youth Ministry*, 9.

[21] Cervantes with Johnson-Mondragón, "Passing the Faith," 333–39, 345–52; Aguilera-Titus, "Youth Ministry"; Aguilera-Titus, "Ministry with Youth."

[22] La Red, *Conclusiones*, 96–106.

[23] Díez de Sollano, "Perceptions of Popular Religiosity," 31.

[24] La Red, *Conclusiones*, 20–21; Burgués, *SEPI 1978–2008*, 93–99; Prophets of Hope Editorial Team, *Hispanic Young People*, 190–98.

[25] La Red, *Conclusiones*, 21–22, 27–28.

[26] De Luna, *Faith Formation and Popular Religion*; Valenzuela, "Emergence of Hispanic Catechesis."

[27] Buckley, "Maria de la Cruz Aymes"; Aymes and Buckley, "Case-Study: Catechesis."

[28] Dahm, *Parish Ministry*, 215–16.

[29] "Hispanic Outreach and Faith Formation Considered."

[30] Notre Dame Task Force, *To Nurture the Soul*, 11, 20, 33, 51, 54.

[31] Information on all of these organizations and initiatives is taken from their respective websites, which can be easily found using Internet search engines.

[32] Notre Dame Task Force, *To Nurture the Soul*, 8–9, 19–20; Benedict XVI, Address to Catholic Educators.

[33] Notre Dame Task Force, *To Nurture the Soul*, 21–60.

[34] Hispanic Scholarship Fund, http://www.hsf.net; Association of Catholic Colleges and Universities, "Catholic Higher Education and Hispanic Students."

[35] Fry, *Latinos in Higher Education*, 5; CARA, *Impact of Campus Ministry*, 6–8; Gray and Bendyna, *Catholic Campus Ministry*, 12.

[36] Notre Dame Task Force, *To Nurture the Soul*, 8–9, 60; Froehle and Gautier, *Catholicism USA*, 68–73; T. Dolan, "Catholic Schools We Need," 14; George, "Latinos and Education," 746.

[37] "Hispanic Outreach and Faith Formation."

[38] Sáenz, "Church and Youth Ministry Participation," 102–7; La Red, *Conclusiones*, 34, 57.

[39] Johnson-Mondragón and Cervantes, *Dynamics of Culture*, 10; La Red, *Conclusiones*, 64–76.

[40] Johnson-Mondragón, *Youth Ministry*, 13, 16; Johnson-Mondragón, "Hispanic Youth," 7; Johnson-Mondragón, *Welcoming Hispanic Youth*, 3.

[41] Johnson-Mondragón, *Youth Ministry*, 8; Johnson-Mondragón, "Hispanic Youth," 10.

[42] C. Smith with Denton, *Soul Searching*, 162–63; Wuthnow, *After the Baby Boomers*, 54–56, 62.

[43] R. Ramírez, "My Vocation as a Catechist," 419. See also R. Ramírez, *Go and Teach*.

## Epilogue: Transformation in America's Largest Church

[1] Steinfels, "Further Adrift," 17.

[2] Badillo, *Latinos and the Church*; Fitzpatrick, "Hispanic Poor."

[3] NCCB, *Hispanic Presence: Challenge*, no. 3; USCCB, *Encuentro and Mission*, no. 6.

[4] Avery Dulles, "The Impact of the Catholic Church on American Culture," address at the John Paul II Cultural Center, Washington, D.C., 13 November 2001, as reported in *America* 185 (3 December 2001): 5; Dulles, "Impact of the Catholic Church," 24.

[5] NCCB/SHA, *Proceedings of the II Encuentro Nacional*, 61.

# BIBLIOGRAPHY

Abbott, Walter M., ed. *The Documents of Vatican II.* New York: America Press, 1966.

Acuña, Rodolfo. *Occupied America: A History of Chicanos.* 1972; 3rd ed., New York: Harper and Row, 1988.

Aguilera-Titus, Alejandro. "Ministry with Youth in a Culturally Diverse Church." In *Leadership for Catholic Youth Ministry: A Comprehensive Resource,* ed. Thomas East, 71–98. New London, CT: Twenty-Third Publications, 2009.

———. *Weaving Together a Culturally Diverse Church.* http://usccb.org/hispanicaffairs/ bestpractices/RegisteredNineSteps.ppt. November 2009.

———. "Youth Ministry in a Culturally Diverse Church." *Origins* 36 (12 October 2006): 277–83.

Alba, Richard, and Victor Nee. *Remaking the American Mainstream: Assimilation and Contemporary Immigration.* Cambridge, MA: Harvard University Press, 2003.

Allen, John L. "The Feminization of the Church." *National Catholic Reporter.* 17 August 2007.

Allsup, Carl. *The American G.I. Forum: Origins and Evolution.* Austin: Center for Mexican American Studies / University of Texas Press, 1982.

Alonso-Zaldivar, Ricardo, and Trevor Tompson. "Poll: Young Hispanics Less Likely to Be Catholic." Associated Press posting. 10 August 2010. http://www.usatoday.com/ news/religion/2010-08-11-hispanic10_ST_N.htm.

Aponte, Edwin David. "*Coritos* as Active Symbol in Latino Protestant Popular Religion." *Journal of Hispanic/Latino Theology* 2 (February 1995): 57–66.

Archambault, Marie Therese, Mark G. Thiel, and Christopher Vecsey, eds. *The Crossing of Two Roads: Being Catholic and Native in the United States.* Maryknoll, NY: Orbis, 2003.

Archdiocese of Newark. Office of Research and Planning. *Presencia Nueva: Knowledge for Service and Hope: A Study of Hispanics in the Archdiocese of Newark.* Newark, NJ: Archdiocese of Newark, 1988.

Arias, Miguel, Mark R. Francis, and Arturo J. Pérez-Rodríguez. *La Navidad Hispana at Home and at Church.* Chicago: Liturgy Training Publications, 2000.

Ashley, Wayne. "The Stations of the Cross: Christ, Politics, and Processions on New York City's Lower East Side." In *Gods of the City: Religion and the American Urban Landscape.* ed. Robert A. Orsi, 341–66. Bloomington: Indiana University Press, 1999.

Association of Catholic Colleges and Universities. "Catholic Higher Education and Hispanic Students." Web posting. 11 August 2008. http://www.accunet.org/files/public/NP_8-11-08.pdf.

Aymes, Sister Maria de la Cruz, and Francis J. Buckley. "Case-Study: Catechesis of Hispanics in the United States Today." In *Effective Inculturation and Ethnic Identity,* 1–28. Rome: Pontifical Gregorian University, 1987.

Azevedo, Marcelo de Carvalho. *Basic Ecclesial Communities in Brazil: The Challenge of a New Way of Being Church,* trans. John Drury. Washington, DC: Georgetown University Press, 1987.

Badillo, David A. *Latinos and the New Immigrant Church.* Baltimore: Johns Hopkins University Press, 2006.

Baez-Chávez, Mary, and Arturo Chávez. *RESPETO: Latino Youth Leadership Formation.* San Antonio: Mexican American Cultural Center, 2002.

Bardeck, Phillip. "Problems of Religious Practice among Puerto Ricans on the Mainland." In Ferrée, Illich, and Fitzpatrick, *Spiritual Care,* sec. 2, pp. 7–12.

Barton, Paul. *Hispanic Methodists, Presbyterians, and Baptists in Texas.* Austin: University of Texas Press, 2006.

Baxter, Michael J. "Writing History in a World without Ends: An Evangelical Catholic Critique of United States Catholic History." *Pro Ecclesia* 5 (Fall 1996): 440–69.

Baylies, Francis. *A Narrative of Major General Wool's Campaign in Mexico.* Albany, NY: Little, 1851.

Bell, Catherine. *Ritual: Perspectives and Dimensions.* New York: Oxford University Press, 1997.

Bendyna, Mary E., and Mary L. Gautier. *Recent Vocations to Religious Life: A Report for the National Religious Vocation Conference,* 2009. http://nrvc.net/english _version/?return_url=english_version.

Benedict XVI. Address to Catholic Educators. 17 April 2008. http://www.vatican. va/holy_father/benedict_xvi/speeches/2008/april/documents/hf_ben-xvi_ spe_20080417_cath-univ-washington_en.html.

——. *Caritas in veritate* (Charity in Truth). 2009. http://www.vatican.va/holy _father/benedict_xvi/encyclicals/documents/hf_ben-xvi_enc_20090629_caritas -in-veritate_en.html.

"The Bishops Speak with the Virgin." Reprinted as "Pastoral Message of U.S. Hispanic Bishops." *Origins* 12 (12 August 1982): 145–52.

Blanchard, David S. "The *III Encuentro:* A Theological Reflection on a Classic Church Event." In Galerón, Icaza, and Urrabazo, *Prophetic Vision,* 200–217.

Bowen, Kurt. *Evangelism and Apostasy: The Evolution and Impact of Evangelicals in Modern Mexico.* Montreal: McGill-Queen's University Press, 1996.

Boyle, Gregory. *Tattoos on the Heart: The Power of Boundless Compassion.* New York: Free Press, 2010.

Brekus, Catherine A., ed. *The Religious History of American Women: Reimagining the Past.* Chapel Hill: University of North Carolina Press, 2007.

Buckley, Francis J. "Maria de la Cruz Aymes." http://www2.talbot.edu/ce20/educators/view.cfm?n=maria_aymes.

Burgués, José P. *SEPI 1978–2008: 30 Años de Evangelización en el Sureste y en la Nación.* Miami: Centro de Artes Gráficas, 2008.

Burke, John Francis. "Facing the Bilingual Challenge: Spanish and English Choirs Share Practice Time." *Church* 23 (Summer 2007): 41–43.

Burns, Jeffrey M. "The Mexican Catholic Community in California." In J. Dolan and Hinojosa, *Mexican Americans and the Catholic Church,* 127–233.

Burr, Ty. "In One Parish, the State of the Church." *Boston Globe.* 8 April 2009. http://www.boston.com/ae/movies/articles/2009/04/08/in_one_parish_the_state_of_the_church.

Camarillo, Albert. *Chicanos in a Changing Society: From Mexican Pueblos to American Barrios in Santa Barbara and Southern California, 1848–1930.* Cambridge, MA: Harvard University Press, 1979.

*Cantos del Pueblo de Dios.* 2nd ed., Franklin Park, IL: World Library Publications, 2001.

Carrasco, Davíd. "Borderlands and the 'Biblical Hurricane': Images and Stories of Latin American Rhythms of Life." *Harvard Theological Review* 101, nos. 3–4 (2008): 353–76.

Carrillo, Carlos. "Faith and Culture in Hispanic Families." In Johnson-Mondragón, *Pathways of Hope and Faith,* 113–59.

Carroll, Colleen. *The New Faithful: Why Young Adults Are Embracing Christian Orthodoxy.* Chicago: Loyola Press, 2002.

Carroll, Michael P. *The Penitente Brotherhood: Patriarchy and Hispano-Catholicism in New Mexico.* Baltimore: Johns Hopkins University Press, 2002.

Carter, Stephen L. *The Culture of Disbelief: How American Law and Politics Trivialize Religious Devotion.* New York: Basic Books, 1993.

Caterine, Darryl V. *Conservative Catholicism and the Carmelites: Identity, Ethnicity, and Tradition in the Modern Church.* Bloomington: Indiana University Press, 2001.

Cather, Willa. *Death Comes for the Archbishop.* New York: Alfred A. Knopf, 1927.

"Catholic Sex Abuse Hits Home for Latinos." National Public Radio broadcast. 19 July 2007. http://www.npr.org/templates/story/story.php?storyId=12098261.

Center for Applied Research in the Apostolate at Georgetown University. "Frequently Requested Catholic Church Statistics." http://cara.georgetown.edu/bulletin.

———. "The Impact of Catholic Campus Ministry on the Beliefs and Worship Practices of U.S. Catholics." Washington, DC: Center for Applied Research in the Apostolate, 2005. http://www.usccb.org/education/highered/CARACMSpecialReport.pdf.

Cepeda Escobedo, José Arturo. *Por una espiritualidad laical en el contexto de la comunidad hispana de los Estados Unidos de América.* Roma: Pont. Universitatem S. Thomae, 2005.

Cervantes, Carmen M., with Ken Johnson-Mondragón. "Passing the Faith to Latino/a Catholic Teens in the U.S." In Johnson-Mondragón, *Pathways of Hope and Faith,* 321–59.

———. "*Pastoral Juvenil Hispana,* Youth Ministry, and Young Adult Ministry: An Updated Perspective on Three Different Pastoral Realities." Report of the National Research and Resource Center for Hispanic Youth and Young Adult Ministry. Instituto Fe y Vida, Stockton, CA, 2007.

César, Julio. "Recollections of My Youth at San Luís Rey Mission." In *Spanish Borderlands Sourcebook: Native American Perspectives on the Hispanic Colonization of Alta California,* ed. Edward D. Castillo, 13–15. New York: Garland, 1991.

Chaves, Mark. *Congregations in America.* Cambridge, MA: Harvard University Press, 2004.

Chávez, Angélico. *But Time and Chance: The Story of Padre Martínez of Taos, 1793–1867.* Santa Fe: Sunstone, 1981.

Chávez, Arturo. "The Social and Political Involvement of Latino/a Youth." In Johnson-Mondragón, *Pathways of Hope and Faith,* 239–65.

Chavez, Leo R. *The Latino Threat: Constructing Immigrants, Citizens, and the Nation.* Stanford, CA: Stanford University Press, 2008.

Chupungco, Anscar J. "Liturgical Inculturation." In *Handbook for Liturgical Studies II: Fundamental Liturgy,* ed. Anscar J. Chupungco, 337–74. Collegeville, MN: Liturgical Press, 1998.

———. *Liturgies of the Future: The Process and Methods of Inculturation.* Mahwah, NJ: Paulist Press, 1989.

Coday, Dennis. "Denver Catholics Fight to Restore Guadalupe Mural." *National Catholic Reporter.* 29 October 2010.

Colton, Walter. *Three Years in California.* Stanford, CA: Stanford University Press, 1949.

Congregation for Divine Worship and the Discipline of the Sacraments. *Directory on Popular Piety and the Liturgy: Principles and Guidelines* (2001). http://www.vatican.va/roman_curia/congregations/ccdds/documents/rc_con_ccdds_doc_20020513_vers-direttorio_en.html.

Connors, Michael. *Inculturated Pastoral Planning: The U.S. Hispanic Experience.* Rome: Editrice Pontificia Università Gregoriana, 2001.

Cooke, Vincent W. Archdiocese of Chicago [Report]. In Ferrée, Illich, and Fitzpatrick, *Spiritual Care*, sec. 3, pp. 3–5.

Costello, Damian. *Black Elk: Colonialism and Lakota Catholicism*. Maryknoll, NY: Orbis, 2005.

Cruz, Gilbert R. *Let There Be Towns: Spanish Municipal Origins in the American Southwest, 1610–1810*. College Station: Texas A&M University Press, 1988.

D'Agostino, Peter R. *Rome in America: Transnational Catholic Ideology from the Risorgimento to Fascism*. Chapel Hill: University of North Carolina Press, 2004.

Dahm, Charles W. *Parish Ministry in a Hispanic Community*. Mahwah, NJ: Paulist Press, 2004.

D'Antonio, William V., James D. Davidson, Dean R. Hoge, and Mary L. Gautier. *American Catholics Today: New Realities of Their Faith and Their Church*. Lanham, MD: Rowman and Littlefield, 2007.

Davalos, Karen Mary. "*La Quinceañera*: Making Gender and Ethnic Identities." *Frontiers: A Journal of Women Studies* 16, no. 2/3 (1996): 101–27.

———. "'The Real Way of Praying': The Via Crucis, *Mexicano* Sacred Space, and the Architecture of Domination." In Matovina and Riebe-Estrella, *Horizons of the Sacred*, 41–68.

Davidson, James D. *Catholicism in Motion: The Church in American Society*. Liguori, MO: Liguori/Triumph, 2005.

Dávila, Alvaro. "Re-discovering My Spiritual History: Exodus and Exile." In *Así Es: Stories of Hispanic Spirituality*, ed. Arturo Pérez, Consuelo Covarrubias, and Edward Foley, 87–92. Collegeville, MN: Liturgical Press, 1994.

Dávila, Arlene. *Latino Spin: Public Image and the Whitewashing of Race*. New York: New York University Press, 2008.

Davis, Cyprian. *Henriette Delille: Servant of Slaves, Witness to the Poor*. New Orleans: Archives of the Archdiocese of New Orleans, 2004.

———. *The History of Black Catholics in the United States*. New York: Crossroad, 1990.

Davis, Cyprian, and Jamie Phelps, eds. *"Stamped with the Image of God": African Americans as God's Image in Black*. Maryknoll, NY: Orbis, 2003.

Davis, Kenneth G. "Hispanic Catholics Deserve More from Their Church." *U.S. Catholic* 73 (February 2008): 24–26.

———, ed. *Misa, Mesa y Musa: Liturgy in the U.S. Hispanic Church*. Schiller Park, IL: World Library Publications, 1997.

———. "Neutering or Nurturing? Preparing Leaders for a Changing Church." *Seminary Journal* 14 (Fall 2008): 79–87.

———. "Presiding in Spanish as a Second Language." In K. Davis, *Misa, Mesa y Musa*, 79–84.

Davis, Kenneth G., and Jorge L. Presmanes, eds. *Preaching and Culture in Latino Congregations*. Chicago: Liturgy Training Publications, 2000.

Deck, Allan Figueroa. "At the Crossroads: North American and Hispanic." In *We Are a People! Initiatives in Hispanic American Theology,* ed. Roberto S. Goizueta, 1–20. Minneapolis: Fortress, 1992.

———, ed. *Frontiers of Hispanic Theology in the United States.* Maryknoll, NY: Orbis, 1992.

———. "Hispanic Ministry Comes of Age." *America* 154 (17 May 1986): 400–402.

———. "Hispanic Ministry: New Realities and Choices." *Origins* 38 (4 December 2008): 405–11.

———. *The Second Wave: Hispanic Ministry and the Evangelization of Cultures.* Mahwah, NJ: Paulist Press, 1989.

———. "Seized and Saturated by Gift: Living for Others." In Elizondo, Deck, and Matovina, *Treasure of Guadalupe,* 11–17.

———. "Where the Laity Flourish." *America* 195 (14–21 August 2006): 14–16.

DeJesús Sáenz, Lynette. "Church and Youth Ministry Participation: Creating a Welcoming Environment for Latino/a Teenagers." In Johnson-Mondragón, *Pathways of Hope and Faith,* 81–112.

De la Garza, Rodolfo O. "*El Cuento de los Números* and Other Latino Political Myths." In *Latino Politics in California,* ed. Aníbal Yáñez-Chávez, 11–32. San Diego: Center for U.S.–Mexican Studies, University of California, San Diego, 1996.

De la Garza, Rodolfo O., Louis DeSipio, and David L. Leal, eds. *Beyond the Barrio: Latinos in the 2004 Elections.* Notre Dame, IN: University of Notre Dame Press, 2010.

De la Guerra, Pablo. Speech to the California legislature, 26 April 1856. Reprinted in *El Grito: A Journal of Contemporary Mexican-American Thought* 5 (Fall 1971): 19–22.

De la Torre, Miguel A. *Santería: The Beliefs and Rituals of a Growing Religion in America.* Grand Rapids, MI: Eerdmans, 2004.

De la Torre, Miguel A., and Gastón Espinosa, eds. *Rethinking Latino(a) Religion and Identity.* Cleveland: Pilgrim, 2006.

De Luna, Anita. "*Evangelizadoras del barrio:* The Rise of the Missionary Catechists of Divine Providence." *U.S. Catholic Historian* 21 (Winter 2003): 53–71.

———. *Faith Formation and Popular Religion: Lessons from the Tejano Experience.* Lanham, MD: Rowman and Littlefield, 2002.

"Denies Catholics Oppose Separation: Archbishop McNicholas Says Protestant Group Erred in Recent Manifesto." *New York Times.* 26 January 1948.

DePalma, Anthony. "Hispanics Still Backing Catholic Leaders, for Now." *New York Times.* 1 May 2002.

DeParle, Jason. "Struggling to Rise in Suburbs Where Failing Means Fitting In." *New York Times.* 18 April 2009.

Díaz, María Elena. *The Virgin, the King, and the Royal Slaves of El Cobre: Negotiating Freedom in Colonial Cuba, 1670–1780.* Stanford, CA: Stanford University Press, 2000.

Díaz, Miguel H. *"Dime con quién andas y te diré quién eres:* We Walk with Our Lady of Charity." In *From the Heart of Our People: Latino/a Explorations in Catholic Systematic Theology,* ed. Orlando O. Espín and Miguel H. Díaz, 153–71. Maryknoll, NY: Orbis, 1999.

Díaz-Stevens, Ana María. *Oxcart Catholicism on Fifth Avenue: The Impact of the Puerto Rican Migration upon the Archdiocese of New York.* Notre Dame, IN: University of Notre Dame Press, 1993.

———. "The Saving Grace: The Matriarchal Core of Latino Catholicism." *Latino Studies Journal* 4 (September 1993): 60–78.

Díaz-Stevens, Ana María, and Anthony M. Stevens-Arroyo. *Recognizing the Latino Resurgence in U.S. Religion: The Emmaus Paradigm.* Boulder, CO: Westview, 1998.

Díez de Sollano, Dolores. "Perceptions of Popular Religiosity among Latino *Jóvenes.*" In *Latino Catholic Youth and Young Adults in the United States: Their Faith and Their Culture,* ed. Carmen María Cervantes, 28–33. Stockton, CA: Instituto Fe y Vida, 2001.

Dinges, William D. "National and Regional Hispanic Catholic Ministry Organizational Initiatives: An Assessment." *Origins* 39 (25 February 2010): 608–10.

Dolan, Jay P. *The American Catholic Experience: A History from Colonial Times to the Present.* 1985; reprint, Notre Dame, IN: University of Notre Dame Press, 1992.

Dolan, Jay P., and Allan Figueroa Deck, eds. *Hispanic Catholic Culture in the U.S.: Issues and Concerns.* Notre Dame, IN: University of Notre Dame Press, 1994.

Dolan, Jay P., and Gilberto M. Hinojosa, eds. *Mexican Americans and the Catholic Church, 1900–1965.* Notre Dame, IN: University of Notre Dame Press, 1994.

Dolan, Jay P., and Jaime R. Vidal, eds. *Puerto Rican and Cuban Catholics in the U. S., 1900–1965.* Notre Dame, IN: University of Notre Dame Press, 1994.

Dolan, Timothy M. "The Catholic Schools We Need." *America* 203 (13–20 September 2010): 11–14.

Domenech, Abbe [Emanuel]. *Missionary Adventures in Texas and Mexico.* London: Longman, Brown, Green, Longmans, and Roberts, 1858.

Dougherty, Kevin J. "How Monochromatic Is Church Membership? Racial-Ethnic Diversity in Religious Community." *Sociology of Religion* 64 (Spring 2003): 65–85.

Doyle, Ruth T., et al. *Hispanics in New York: Religious, Cultural and Social Experiences.* 2 vols. New York: Archdiocese of New York Office of Pastoral Research, 1982.

Duarte, Cynthia. "The Negotiation of 3rd+ Generation Mexican American Ethnicity in Los Angeles." PhD diss., Columbia University, New York, 2008.

Duck, Marilyn. "Bishop Meets with Parishioners Angry over Perceived Slight." *National Catholic Reporter.* 26 July 2006. http://www.nationalcatholicreporter.org/update/nt072606.htm.

Dulles, Avery. "The Impact of the Catholic Church on American Culture." In *Evangelizing America,* ed. Thomas P. Rausch, 11–27. Mahwah, NJ: Paulist Press, 2004.

Duncan, Brian, and Stephen J. Trejo. "Who Remains Mexican? Selective Ethnic Attrition and the Intergenerational Progress of Mexican Americans." In *Latinos and the Economy: Integration and Impact in Schools, Labor Markets, and Beyond,* ed. David L. Leal and Stephen J. Trejo. 285–320. New York: Springer, 2010.

Durán, Socorro. "A Great Sign Appeared in the Sky." In Elizondo, Deck, and Matovina, *Treasure of Guadalupe,* 97–100.

Düssel, Enrique, ed. *The Church in Latin America, 1492–1992.* Maryknoll, NY: Orbis, 1992.

Dysart, Jane. "Mexican Women in San Antonio, 1830–1860: The Assimilation Process." *Western Historical Quarterly* 7 (October 1976): 365–75.

"Eight in Ten U.S. Permanent Deacons in Active Ministry." *CARA Report* 15 (Summer 2009): 1.

Elizondo, Virgilio. "Converted by Beauty." In Elizondo, Deck, and Matovina, *Treasure of Guadalupe,* 73–78.

———. "Educación religiosa para el México-Norteamericano." *Catequesis Latinoamericana* 4 (January-March 1972): 83–86.

———. *The Future Is Mestizo: Life Where Cultures Meet.* 1988; rev. ed., Boulder: University Press of Colorado, 2000.

———. *Galilean Journey: The Mexican-American Promise.* 1983; rev. ed., Maryknoll, NY: Orbis, 2000.

———. *A God of Incredible Surprises: Jesus of Galilee.* Lanham, MD: Rowman and Littlefield, 2003.

———. *Guadalupe: Mother of the New Creation.* Maryknoll, NY: Orbis, 1997.

———. "Popular Religion as Support of Identity: A Pastoral-Psychological Case-Study Based on the Mexican American Experience in the USA." In *Popular Religion,* ed. Norbert Greinacher and Norbert Mette, 36–43. Edinburgh: T & T Clark, 1986.

———. *Virgilio Elizondo: Spiritual Writings,* ed. Timothy Matovina. Maryknoll, NY: Orbis, 2010.

Elizondo, Virgilio, Allan Figueroa Deck, and Timothy Matovina, eds. *The Treasure of Guadalupe.* Lanham, MD: Rowman and Littlefield, 2006.

Ellis, John Tracy. *American Catholicism.* 1956; 2nd ed., Chicago: University of Chicago Press, 1969.

Emerson, Michael O., with Rodney M. Woo. *People of the Dream: Multiracial Congregations in the United States.* Princeton, NJ: Princeton University Press, 2006.

Empereur, James, and Eduardo Fernández. *La Vida Sacra: Contemporary Hispanic Sacramental Theology.* Lanham, MD: Rowman and Littlefield, 2006.

Engh, Michael E. "From the City of Angels to the Parishes of San Antonio: Catholic Organization, Women Activists, and Racial Intersections, 1900–1950." In *Catholicism in the American West: A Rosary of Hidden Voices,* ed. Roberto R. Treviño and Richard V. Francaviglio, 42–71. College Station: Texas A&M University Press, 2008.

———. "From *Frontera* Faith to Roman Rubrics: Altering Hispanic Religious Customs in Los Angeles, 1855–1880." *U.S. Catholic Historian* 12 (Fall 1994): 85–105.

———. *Frontier Faiths: Church, Temple, and Synagogue in Los Angeles, 1846–1888.* Albuquerque: University of New Mexico Press, 1992.

———. "With Her People." *America* 188 (6 January 2003): 15–16.

Espín, Orlando O., ed. *Building Bridges, Doing Justice: Constructing a Latino/a Ecumenical Theology.* Maryknoll, NY: Orbis, 2009.

———. *The Faith of the People: Theological Reflections on Popular Catholicism.* Maryknoll, NY: Orbis, 1997.

———. *Grace and Humanness: Theological Reflections Because of Culture.* Maryknoll, NY: Orbis, 2007.

Espín, Orlando O., and Sixto J. García. "Lilies of the Field: A Hispanic Theology of Providence and Human Responsibility." *Catholic Theological Society of America Proceedings* 44 (1989): 70–90.

Espinosa, Gastón. "Latinizing American Christianity: Pluralism, Pentecostalism, and the Future of American Catholicism." *Conscience* 28 (Summer 2007): 28–31.

———. "Latino Clergy and Churches in Faith-Based Political and Social Action in the United States." In Espinosa, Elizondo, and Miranda, *Latino Religions and Civic Activism*, 279–306.

———. "Marilynn Kramar." In *The New International Dictionary of Pentecostal and Charismatic Movements,* ed. Stanley M. Burgess, 825–26. Grand Rapids, MI: Zondervan, 2002.

———. "The Pentecostalization of Latin American and U.S. Latino Christianity." *Pneuma: The Journal of the Society for Pentecostal Studies* 26, no. 2 (2004): 262–92.

Espinosa, Gastón, Virgilio Elizondo, and Jesse Miranda. *Hispanic Churches in American Public Life: Summary of Findings.* Interim Report, Institute for Latino Studies, University of Notre Dame, 2003.

———, eds. *Latino Religions and Civic Activism in the United States.* New York: Oxford University Press, 2005.

Espinosa, J. Manuel. "The Origins of the Penitentes of New Mexico: Separating Fact from Fiction." *Catholic Historical Review* 79 (July 1993): 454–77.

Fernández, Eduardo C. *La Cosecha: Harvesting Contemporary United States Hispanic Theology (1972–1998).* Collegeville, MN: Liturgical Press, 2000.

———. *Mexican-American Catholics.* Mahwah, NJ: Paulist Press, 2007.

Ferrée, William, Ivan Illich, and Joseph P. Fitzpatrick, eds. *Spiritual Care of Puerto Rican Migrants: Report on the First Conference, Held in San Juan, Puerto Rico, April 11th to 16th, 1955.* New York: Arno, 1980.

Fierro, Jonathan. "The Devil Must Be Laughing: The Archdiocese and Latino Charismatic Ministry." Los Angeles Lay Catholic Mission (February 2003). www.losangeles mission.com/ed/articles/2003/0203jf.htm.

Filteau, Jerry. "Bishops Downsize Their National Conference, Reduce Assessments." Catholic News Service posting. 15 November 2006. http://www.catholicnews.com/data/stories/cns/0606525.htm.

———. "10 Dioceses Quit Bishops' Antipoverty Campaign." *National Catholic Reporter*, 9 July 2010.

Fisher, James T. *Communion of Immigrants: A History of Catholics in America.* 2000; new ed., New York: Oxford University Press, 2008.

Fitzpatrick, Joseph P. "The Hispanic Poor in a Middle-Class Church." *America* 159 (2 July 1988): 11–13.

———. "No Place to Grieve: A Honduran Tragedy." *America* 163 (21 July 1990): 37–38.

———. *Puerto Rican Americans: The Meaning of Migration to the Mainland.* 1971; 2nd ed., Englewood Cliffs, NJ: Prentice-Hall, 1987.

———. "Sociological Aspects of Migration and Their Impact on Religious Practice." In Ferrée, Illich, and Fitzpatrick, *Spiritual Care*, sec. 2, pp. 41–45.

———. *The Stranger Is Our Own: Reflections on the Journey of Puerto Rican Migrants.* Kansas City, MO: Sheed and Ward, 1996.

*Flor y Canto.* 2nd ed. Portland, OR: OCP Publications, 2001.

Flores, Daniel. "Vocations in the Hispanic Communities of the United States." *Origins* 38 (22 January 2009): 505–12.

Foner, Nancy, ed. *Across Generations: Immigrant Families in America.* New York: New York University Press, 2009.

Fraga, Luis Ricardo, et al. *Latino Lives in America: Making It Home.* Philadelphia: Temple University Press, 2010.

Franchot, Jenny. *Roads to Rome: The Antebellum Protestant Encounter with Catholicism.* Berkeley: University of California Press, 1994.

Francis, Mark R. *Guidelines for Multicultural Celebrations.* Washington, DC: Federation of Diocesan Liturgical Commissions, 1998.

———. *Shape a Circle Ever Wider: Liturgical Inculturation in the United States.* Chicago: Liturgy Training Publications, 2000.

Freedman, Samuel G. "Immigrants Find Solace after Storm of Arrests." *New York Times.* 12 July 2008.

Fremon, Celeste. *G-Dog and the Homeboys: Father Greg Doyle and the Gangs of East Los Angeles.* 1995; updated ed., Albuquerque: University of New Mexico Press, 2004.

Froehle, Bryan T., and Mary L. Gautier. *Catholicism USA: A Portrait of the Catholic Church in the United States.* Maryknoll, NY: Orbis, 2000.

———. *Ministry in a Church of Increasing Diversity: A Profile of Diocesan Hispanic/Latino Ministry.* Washington, DC: Center for Applied Research in the Apostolate, 2002.

Fry, Richard. *Latinos in Higher Education: Many Enroll, Too Few Graduate.* Washington, DC: Pew Hispanic Center, 2002. http://pewhispanic.org/files/reports/11.pdf.

Galerón, Soledad, Rosa María Icaza, and Rosendo Urrabazo. *Prophetic Vision: Pastoral Reflections on the National Pastoral Plan for Hispanic Ministry*. Kansas City, MO: Sheed and Ward, 1992.

Gálvez, Alyshia. *Guadalupe in New York: Devotion and the Struggle for Citizenship Rights among Mexican Immigrants*. New York: New York University Press, 2010.

García, María Cristina. *Seeking Refuge: Central American Immigration to Mexico, the United States, and Canada*. Berkeley: University of California Press, 2006.

García, Mario T. *Católicos: Resistance and Affirmation in Chicano Catholic History*. Austin: University of Texas Press, 2008.

García-Rivera, Alejandro. "Let's Capture the Hispanic Imagination." *U.S. Catholic* 57 (July 1994): 34–35.

Gastón Witchger, María Teresa. "Recent History of Hispanic Ministry in the United States." In Galerón, Icaza, and Urrabazo, *Prophetic Vision*, 183–99.

Gautier, Mary L. *Catholic Ministry Formation Enrollments: Statistical Overview for 2008–2009*. Washington, DC: Center for Applied Research in the Apostolate, 2009.

Gautier, Mary L., Mary E. Bendyna, and Melissa A. Cidade. *The Class of 2009: Survey of Ordinands to the Priesthood*. Washington, DC: Center for Applied Research in the Apostolate, 2009. http://www.usccb.org/vocations/classof2009/class_of_2009 _report.pdf.

George, Francis. "Latinos and Education: Bonds of Solidarity." *Origins* 38 (7 May 2009): 744–49.

Gibson, David. "Is Sonia Sotomayor Catholic? UPDATE: Yes." Web posting. 26 May 2009. http://blog.beliefnet.com/pontifications/2009/05/is-sonia-sotomayor-catholic .html.

Glauber, Bill. "Arizona Immigration Law and Illegal Immigrants: State of Extremes." *Christian Science Monitor*. 17 May 2010. http://www.csmonitor.com/USA/Society/ 2010/0517/Arizona-immigration-law-and-illegal-immigrants-state-of-extremes.

Gleason, Philip. "American Identity and Americanization." In *Harvard Encyclopedia of American Ethnic Groups*, 31–58. Cambridge, MA: Harvard University Press, 1980.

Goizueta, Roberto S. *Caminemos con Jesús: Toward a Hispanic/Latino Theology of Accompaniment*. Maryknoll, NY: Orbis, 1995.

———. *Christ Our Companion: Toward a Theological Aesthetics of Liberation*. Maryknoll, NY: Orbis, 2009.

———. "Resurrection at Tepeyac: The Guadalupan Encounter." *Theology Today* 56 (October 1999): 336–45.

———. "The Symbolic World of Mexican American Religion." In Matovina and Riebe-Estrella, *Horizons of the Sacred*, 119–38.

Goldstein, Amy, and Roberto Suro. "A Journey in Stages: Assimilation's Pull Is Still Strong, But Its Pace Varies." *Washington Post*. 16 January 2000.

Gomez, José. "The Encounter with Christ and the Future of Hispanic Ministry." *Origins* 37 (10 January 2008): 477–81.

———. "Evangelization, Education and the Hispanic Catholic Future." *Origins* 39 (13 August 2009): 185–89.

———. "Immigration Reform after the Election." *Origins* 38 (13 November 2008): 363–66.

Gómez, Raúl. "Preaching the Ritual Masses among Latinos." In K. Davis and Presmanes, *Preaching and Culture in Latino Congregations,* 103–19.

———. *Quinceañeras: Order for the Blessing on the Fifteenth Birthday.* Liguori, MO: Liguori Publications, 2010.

Gonzalez, David. "A Family Divided by Two Words, Legal and Illegal." *New York Times.* 26 April 2009. http://www.nytimes.com/2009/04/26/nyregion/26immig.html.

González, Justo L. *Mañana: Christian Theology from a Hispanic Perspective.* Nashville: Abingdon, 1990.

Gonzales, Michael J. *The Mexican Revolution, 1910–1940.* Albuquerque: University of New Mexico Press, 2002.

González, Roberto O., and Michael La Velle. *The Hispanic Catholic in the United States: A Socio-Cultural and Religious Profile.* New York: Northeast Catholic Pastoral Center for Hispanics, 1985.

Gordon, Milton M. *Assimilation in American Life: The Role of Race, Religion, and National Origins.* New York: Oxford University Press, 1964.

"Governor Bill Richardson Signs Repeal of the Death Penalty." Official press release. 18 March 2009. http://www.deathpenaltyinfo.org/documents/richardsonstatement .pdf.

Granjon, Henry. *Along the Rio Grande: A Pastoral Visit to Southwest New Mexico in 1902,* ed. Michael Romero Taylor, trans. Mary W. de López. Albuquerque: University of New Mexico Press, 1986.

Gray, Mark M., and Mary E. Bendyna. *Catholic Campus Ministry: A Report of Findings from CARA's Catholic Campus Ministry Inventory.* Washington, DC: Center for Applied Research in the Apostolate, 2003.

Gray, Mark M., and Mary L. Gautier. "Latino/a Catholic Leaders in the United States." In *Emerging Voices, Urgent Choices: Essays on Latino/a Religious Leadership,* ed. Edwin I. Hernández, Milagros Peña, Kenneth G. Davis, and Elizabeth Station, 65–89. Boston: Brill, 2006.

Gray, Mark M., and Paul M. Perl. *Sacraments Today: Belief and Practice among U.S. Catholics,* Washington, DC: Center for Applied Research in the Apostolate, 2008. http://cara.georgetown.edu/sacramentsreport.pdf.

Grebler, Leo, Joan W. Moore, and Ralph Guzmán. *The Mexican American People: The Nation's Second Largest Minority.* New York: Free Press, 1970.

Greeley, Andrew M. "Defection among Hispanics." *America* 159 (30 July 1988): 61–62.

——. "Defection among Hispanics (Updated)." *America* 177 (27 September 1997): 12–13.

Green, John C. *The Faith Factor: How Religion Influences American Elections*. Westport, CT: Praeger, 2007.

Green, John C., Corwin E. Smidt, James L. Guth, and Lyman A Kellstedt. "The American Religious Landscape and the 2004 Presidential Vote: Increased Polarization." http://www.pewcenteronthestates.org/uploadedFiles/wwwpewtrustsorg/News/Press_Releases/Religion_in_public_life/pew_religion_religiousland_020305.pdf.

Green, Rena Maverick, ed. *Memoirs of Mary A. Maverick*. San Antonio: Alamo, 1921.

Greer, Allan. *Mohawk Saint: Catherine Tekakwitha and the Jesuits*. New York: Oxford University Press, 2005.

Griswold del Castillo, Richard. *The Los Angeles Barrio, 1850–1890: A Social History*. Berkeley: University of California Press, 1979.

Groody, Daniel G. *Border of Death, Valley of Life: An Immigrant Journey of Heart and Spirit*. Lanham, MD: Rowman and Littlefield, 2002.

Groody, Daniel G., and Bill Groody. *Dying to Live: A Migrant's Journey*. Videorecording. Groody River Films in collaboration with the University of Notre Dame Center for Latino Spirituality and Culture, 2005.

Groody, Daniel G., and Gioacchino Campese, eds. *A Promised Land, a Perilous Journey: Theological Perspectives on Migration*. Notre Dame, IN: University of Notre Dame Press, 2008.

Gros, Jeffrey. "Ecumenism in the U.S. Hispanic/Latino Community: Challenge and Promise." In *El Cuerpo de Cristo: The Hispanic Presence in the U.S. Catholic Church*, ed. Peter Casarella and Raúl Gómez, 197–212. New York: Crossroad, 1998.

Gurza, Agustin. "*Ni Aquí* Nor There." *U.S. Catholic* 73 (February 2008): 12–17.

Gutiérrez, David G. *Walls and Mirrors: Mexican Americans, Mexican Immigrants, and the Politics of Ethnicity*. Berkeley: University of California Press, 1995.

Gutiérrez, Ramón A. "Hispanic Identities in the Southwestern United States." In *Race and Classification: The Case of Mexican America*, ed. Ilona Katzew and Susan Deans-Smith, 174–93. Stanford, CA: Stanford University Press, 2009.

——. "El Santuario de Chimayó: A Syncretic Shrine in New Mexico." In *Feasts and Celebrations in North American Ethnic Communities*, ed. Ramón A. Gutiérrez and Geneviève Fabre, 71–86. Albuquerque: University of New Mexico Press, 1995.

Hall, Linda B. *Mary, Mother and Warrior: The Virgin in Spain and the Americas*. Austin: University of Texas Press, 2004.

Handlin, Oscar. *The Uprooted: The Epic Story of the Great Migration That Made the American People*. Boston: Little, Brown, 1951.

Hanson, Victor Davis. *Mexifornia: A State of Becoming*. San Francisco: Encounter Books, 2003.

Hayes, Mike. *Googling God: The Religious Landscape of People in Their 20s and 30s.* Mahwah, NJ: Paulist Press, 2007.

Hayes-Bautista, David E. *La Nueva California: Latinos in the Golden State.* Berkeley: University of California Press, 2004.

Heft, James L. *Passing on the Faith: Transforming Traditions for the Next Generation of Jews, Christians, and Muslims.* New York: Fordham University Press, 2006.

Hennesey, James. *American Catholics: A History of the Roman Catholic Community in the United States.* New York: Oxford University Press, 1981.

Henshaw, Stanley K., and Kathryn Kost. *Trends in the Characteristics of Women Obtaining Abortions, 1974–2004.* New York: Guttmacher Institute, 2008.

Hernández, Edwin, with Rebecca Burwell and Jeffrey Smith. "A Study of Hispanic Catholics: Why Are They Leaving the Church? Implications for the New Evangelization." In *The New Evangelization: Overcoming the Obstacles,* ed. Steven Boguslawski and Ralph Martin, 109–41. Mahwah, NJ: Paulist Press, 2008.

Hernández, José M. "The ACU: Transplanting a Cuban Lay Organization to the United States." *U.S. Catholic Historian* 21 (Winter 2003): 99–114.

Hero, Rodney, et al. "Latino Participation, Partisanship, and Office Holding." *PS: Political Science and Politics* 23 (September 2000): 529–34.

Hinojosa, Gilberto M. "The Enduring Hispanic Faith Communities: Spanish and Texas Church Historiography." *Journal of Texas Catholic History and Culture* 1 (March 1990): 20–41.

——. "Friars and Indians: Towards a Perspective of Cultural Interaction in the San Antonio Mission." *U.S. Catholic Historian* 9 (Winter/Spring 1990): 7–26.

——. "Mexican-American Faith Communities in Texas and the Southwest." In J. Dolan and Hinojosa, *Mexican Americans and the Catholic Church,* 9–125.

Hinojosa, Gilberto M., and Anne A. Fox. "Indians and Their Culture in San Fernando de Béxar." In *Tejano Origins in Eighteenth-Century San Antonio,* ed. Gerald E. Poyo and Gilberto M. Hinojosa, 105–20. Austin: University of Texas Press, 1991.

"Hispanic Bishops Visit Congressmen, Link Health Care and Immigration Reform." Catholic News Agency posting. 17 September 2009. http://www.catholicnews agency.com/news/hispanic_bishops_visit_congressmen_link_health_care_and _immigration_reform.

"Hispanic Outreach and Faith Formation Considered at National Meeting." Catholic News Agency posting. 9 December 2008. http://www.catholicnewsagency .com/news/hispanic_outreach_and_faith_formation_considered_at_national _meeting.

"Hispanics Form National Council." *National Catholic Reporter.* 8 February 1991.

Hoge, Dean R. *The First Five Years of the Priesthood: A Study of Newly Ordained Catholic Priests.* Collegeville, MN: Liturgical Press, 2002.

Hoge, Dean R., William D. Dinges, Mary Johnson, and Juan L. Gonzalez Jr. *Young Adult Catholics: Religion in the Culture of Choice*. Notre Dame, IN: University of Notre Dame Press, 2001.

Hoge, Dean R., and Marti R. Jewell. *The Next Generation of Pastoral Leaders: What the Church Needs to Know*. Chicago: Loyola Press, 2010.

Hoge, Dean R., and Aniedi Okure. *International Priests in America: Challenges and Opportunities*. Collegeville, MN: Liturgical Press, 2006.

Hondagneu-Sotelo, Pierrette. *God's Heart Has No Borders: How Religious Activists Are Working for Immigrant Rights*. Berkeley: University of California Press, 2008.

Hoover, Brett C. "Negotiating the Church: The Separate and Interconnected Worlds of Latino/a Immigrant Catholics and Euro-American Catholics in a Shared Parish in the Midwest, 1990–2008." Presentation to the American Academy of Religion annual meeting. November 2008.

———. "'What Are We Doing Here?' Local Theologies of Mission from a Shared Catholic Parish in the Midwest, 1990–2008." PhD diss., Graduate Theological Union, Berkeley, California, 2009.

Huntington, Samuel, *Who Are We? The Challenges to America's National Identity*. New York: Simon and Schuster, 2004.

Icaza, Rosa María. "Do We Have Inculturated Liturgies?" In K. Davis, *Misa, Mesa y Musa*, 17–24.

Ingalls, Robert P. *Urban Vigilantes in the New South: Tampa, 1882–1936*. Knoxville: University of Tennessee Press, 1988.

Instituto Fe y Vida. "Fast Facts about U.S. Hispanic Catholics." http://feyvida.org/research/fastfacts.html.

Interfaith Funders. *1999 Annual Report*. Jericho, NY: Interfaith Funders, 2000.

Isasi-Díaz, Ada María. *En la Lucha/In the Struggle: Elaborating a Mujerista Theology*. 1993; anniversary ed., Minneapolis: Fortress, 2004.

Jackson, Helen Hunt. *Ramona: A Story*. Boston: Roberts Brothers, 1884.

Jaramillo, Cleofas M. *Shadows of the Past (Sombras del Pasado)*. Santa Fe: Seton Village Press, 1941.

John Paul II. *Apostolos Suos* (On the Theological and Juridical Nature of Episcopal Conferences). 21 May 1998. http://www.vatican.va/holy_father/john_paul_ii/motu_proprio/documents/hf_jp-ii_motu-proprio_22071998_apostolos-suos_en.html.

———. "Do Not Leave to the Poor the Crumbs of Your Feast: Homily of Pope John Paul II at Yankee Stadium (October 2, 1979)." *The Pope Speaks* 24 (1979): 312–17.

———. *Ecclesia in America* (1999). In *Origins* 28 (4 February 1999): 565–92.

Johnson, Elizabeth A. "Mary and the Female Face of God." *Theological Studies* 50 (September 1989): 500–26.

————. *Truly Our Sister: A Theology of Mary in the Communion of Saints.* New York: Continuum, 2003.

Johnson-Mondragón, Ken. "Hispanic Youth and Young Adult Ministry in the United States: Bridging Hispanic and Mainstream Ministry to Forge the Church Anew in 21st Century America." Report of the National Research and Resource Center for Hispanic Youth and Young Adult Ministry. Instituto Fe y Vida, Stockton, CA, 2010.

————. "Ministry in Multicultural and National/Ethnic Parishes: Evaluating the Findings of the Emerging Models of Pastoral Leadership Project." Report and presentation to the National Ministry Summit: Emerging Models of Pastoral Leadership conference. April 2008. http://www.emergingmodels.org/doc/Multicultural%20Report%20(2).pdf.

————, ed. *Pathways of Hope and Faith among Hispanic Teens: Pastoral Reflections and Strategies Inspired by the National Study of Youth and Religion.* Stockton, CA: Instituto Fe y Vida, 2007.

————. "The Second Wave of the National Study of Youth and Religion." In Johnson-Mondragón, *Pathways of Hope and Faith,* 267–89.

————. "Socioreligious Demographics of Hispanic Teenagers." In Johnson-Mondragón, *Pathways of Hope and Faith,* 11–39.

————. *The Status of Hispanic Youth and Young Adult Ministry in the United States: A Preliminary Study.* Stockton, CA: Instituto Fe y Vida, 2002.

————. *Welcoming Hispanic Youth/Jóvenes in Catholic Parishes and Dioceses.* Report of the National Research and Resource Center for Hispanic Youth and Young Adult Ministry. Instituto Fe y Vida, Stockton, CA, 2003.

————. *Youth Ministry and the Socioreligious Lives of Hispanic and White Catholic Teens in the U.S.* Report of the National Research and Resource Center for Hispanic Youth and Young Adult Ministry. Instituto Fe y Vida, Stockton, CA, 2005.

Johnson-Mondragón, Ken, and Carmen M. Cervantes. *The Dynamics of Culture, Faith, and Family in the Lives of Hispanic Teens, and Their Implications for Youth Ministry.* Report of the National Research and Resource Center for Hispanic Youth and Young Adult Ministry. Instituto Fe y Vida, Stockton, CA, 2008.

Jones, Arthur. *Pierre Toussaint.* New York: Doubleday, 2003.

Juárez, José Roberto. "La iglesia Católica y el Chicano en sud Texas, 1836–1911." *Aztlán* 4 (Fall 1973): 217–55.

Kauffman, Christopher J., gen. ed. *American Catholic Identities: A Documentary History.* 9 vols., Maryknoll, NY: Orbis, 1999–2004.

Kelly, Maura. "On Good Friday, Faithful Follow in Christ's Footsteps." *Chicago Tribune.* 22 April 2000.

Kennedy, John F. Speech to the Greater Houston Ministerial Association. 12 September 1960. http://www.presidency.ucsb.edu/ws/index.php?pid=25773.

Kerwin, Donald, and Jill Marie Gerschutz, eds. *And You Welcomed Me: Migration and Catholic Social Teaching.* Lanham, MD: Lexington, 2009.

Kettle, Martin. "The Hispanic Vote Shaped the Contours of This Election." *Guardian.* 7 November 2008. http://www.guardian.co.uk/commentisfree/2008/nov/07/barack-obama-south-west-hispanic.

Kicanas, Gerald. "Arizona Immigration Law Is Flawed." *Origins* 40 (13 May 2010): 3–5.

Kosmin, Barry A., and Ariela Keysar. *American Religious Identification Survey 2008.* Summary Report. www.americanreligionsurvey-aris.org.

———. *Religion in a Free Market: Religious and Non-Religious Americans.* Ithaca, NY: Paramount, 2006.

Kromm, Chris. "Election 2008: Shifting Latino Vote Helped Obama Win in Florida." Web posting. 17 November 2008. http://www.southernstudies.org/2008/11/election-2008-shifting-fla-latino-vote.html.

Lawrence, A. B. Introduction to *Texas in 1840.* New York: William W. Allen, 1840.

Lawton, Kim. "Immigration Fuels Hispanic Church Activity." *Christianity Today.* 2 November 2006. http://www.christianitytoday.com/ct/2006/novemberweb-only/144-42.0.html.

Leal, David L., Matt A. Barreto, Jongho Lee, and Rodolfo O. de la Garza. "The Latino Vote in the 2004 Election." *PSOnline* (January 2005): 41–49. http://faculty.washington.edu/mbarreto/papers/2004vote.pdf.

Lee, Bernard J., and William V. D'Antonio et al. *The Catholic Experience of Small Christian Communities.* Mahwah, NJ: Paulist Press, 2000.

León, Luis D. *La Llorona's Children: Religion, Life, and Death in the U.S.-Mexican Borderlands.* Berkeley: University of California Press, 2004.

———. "'Soy una Curandera y Soy una Católica': The Poetics of a Mexican Healing Tradition." In Matovina and Riebe-Estrella, *Horizons of the Sacred*, 95–118.

Levy, Abe. "Weekly Mass for Gays Ends in San Antonio." *San Antonio Express-News.* 22 October 2010. http://www.chron.com/disp/story.mpl/metropolitan/7260317.html.

Lopez, Mark Hugo. "How Hispanics Voted in the 2008 Election." 5 November 2008. http://pewresearch.org/pubs/1024/exit-poll-analysis-hispanics.

Lord, Edna V. "Parish Uses Dialogue Process to Explore Immigration." *Initiative Report* 12 (August 2008): 1–2.

Lucey, Robert E. "'Christianizing' Mexican Catholics." *America* 77 (16 August 1947): 541–42.

Lummis, Charles F. *The Land of Poco Tiempo.* New York: C. Scribner's Sons, 1893.

Mahony, Roger. "Immigration, the American Economy and the Constitution." *Origins* 37 (31 May 2007): 33–37.

———. "Viewing Immigration through a Moral Lens." *Origins* 37 (25 October 2007): 320–23.

Manetto, Nick. "Charismatic Spirit Spreads with Latino Catholics." *Our Sunday Visitor.* 19 August 2007.

Marill, Alicia C. "Youth and Culture." In *Perspectivas: Hispanic Ministry,* ed. Allan Figueroa Deck, Yolanda Tarango, and Timothy Matovina, 46–52. Kansas City: Sheed and Ward, 1995.

Márquez, Benjamin. *LULAC: The Evolution of a Mexican American Political Organization.* Austin: University of Texas Press, 1993.

Martinez, Mel, with Ed Breslin. *A Sense of Belonging: From Castro's Cuba to the U.S. Senate, One Man's Pursuit of the American Dream.* New York: Crown Forum, 2008.

Martínez, Richard Edward. *PADRES: The National Chicano Priest Movement.* Austin: University of Texas Press, 2005.

Maryland Bishops. "Where All Find a Home." *Origins* 37 (6 December 2007): 418–19.

*Mary Throughout Latin America.* Liguori, MO: Liguori Publications, 2005.

Massey, Douglas. Review of *Who Are We?* by Samuel P. Huntington. *Population and Development Review* 30 (September 2004): 543–48.

Matovina, Timothy. "Beyond the Missions: The Diocesan Church in the Hispanic Southwest." *American Catholic Studies* 117 (Fall 2006): 1–15.

———. "La Capilla de Nuestro Señor de los Milagros: Encountering Christ at a Texas Shrine." In *Jesus in the Hispanic Community: Images of Christ from Theology to Popular Religion,* ed. Harold J. Recinos and Hugo Magallanes, 190–206. Louisville: Westminster John Knox, 2010.

———. *Guadalupe and Her Faithful: Latino Catholics in San Antonio, from Colonial Origins to the Present.* Baltimore: Johns Hopkins University Press, 2005.

———. "Latino Catholics and American Public Life." In *Can Charitable Choice Work? Covering Religion's Impact on Urban Affairs and Social Services,* ed. Andrew Walsh, 56–77. Hartford, CT: Leonard E. Greenberg Center for the Study of Religion in Public Life, 2001.

———. "Lay Initiatives in Worship on the Texas *Frontera,* 1830–1860." *U.S. Catholic Historian* 12 (Fall 1994): 107–20.

———. "Sacred Place and Collective Memory: San Fernando Cathedral, San Antonio, Texas." *U.S. Catholic Historian* 15 (Winter 1997): 33–50.

———. *Tejano Religion and Ethnicity: San Antonio, 1821–1860.* Austin: University of Texas Press, 1995.

Matovina, Timothy, and Gerald E. Poyo, eds. *¡Presente! U.S. Latino Catholics from Colonial Origins to the Present.* Maryknoll, NY: Orbis, 2000.

Matovina, Timothy, and Gary Riebe-Estrella, eds. *Horizons of the Sacred: Mexican Traditions in U.S. Catholicism.* Ithaca, NY: Cornell University Press, 2002.

McKevitt, Gerald. *Brokers of Culture: Italian Jesuits in the American West, 1848–1919.* Stanford, CA: Stanford University Press, 2007.

Medina, Lara. *Las Hermanas: Chicana/Latina Religious-Political Activism in the U.S. Catholic Church*. Philadelphia: Temple University Press, 2004.

Medina, Néstor. *Mestizaje: (Re)mapping Race, Culture, and Faith in Latina/o Catholicism*. Maryknoll, NY: Orbis, 2009.

Monroe, Laurence. *États-Unis, la métamorphose hispanique: Une bonne nouvelle pour l'Amérique et pour le monde*. Paris: Les Éditions du Cerf, 2008.

Montana, Constanza. "Passion Play Unites Pilsen: Way of the Cross Is a Community Tradition." *Chicago Tribune*. 26 March 1991.

Montejano, David. *Anglos and Mexicans in the Making of Texas, 1836–1986*. Austin: University of Texas Press, 1987.

Morris, Charles R. *American Catholic: The Saints and Sinners Who Built America's Most Powerful Church*. New York: Times Books, 1997.

Morris, Dick. "The Hispanic Vote Elects Bush." Web posting. 5 November 2004. www.newsmax.com/archives/articles/2004/11/4/203450.shtml.

Murillo, Luis E. "Tamales on the Fourth of July: The Transnational Parish of Coeneo, Michoacán." *Religion and American Culture: A Journal of Interpretation* 19 (Summer 2009): 137–68.

Nabhan-Warren, Kristy. "'Blooming Where We're Planted': Mexican-descent Catholics Living Out *Cursillo de Cristiandad*." *U.S. Catholic Historian* 28 (Fall 2010): 99–125.

———. *The Virgin of El Barrio: Marian Apparitions, Catholic Evangelizing, and Mexican American Activism*. New York: New York University Press, 2005.

National Association of Latino Elected and Appointed Officials. "A Profile of Latino Elected Officials in the United States and Their Progress since 1996." http://www.naleo.org/downloads/NALEOFactSheet07.pdf.

National Catholic Council for Hispanic Ministry. "Response to the USCCB Reorganization." *Origins* 37 (10 January 2008): 486–87.

National Catholic Network de Pastoral Juvenil Hispana–La Red. *Conclusiones: Primer Encuentro Nacional de Pastoral Juvenil Hispana, PENPJH*. Washington, DC: United States Conference of Catholic Bishops, 2008.

National Conference of Catholic Bishops (NCCB; now the United States Conference of Catholic Bishops [USCCB]). *Encuentro 2000, Many Faces in God's House: A Catholic Vision for the Third Millennium*. Washington, DC: United States Catholic Conference, 1999.

———. *The Hispanic Presence: Challenge and Commitment*. Washington, DC: United States Catholic Conference, 1984.

———. *The Hispanic Presence in the New Evangelization in the United States*. Washington, DC: United States Catholic Conference, 1996.

———. *National Pastoral Plan for Hispanic Ministry*. Washington, DC: United States Catholic Conference, 1988.

——. *Pastoral Letters of the United States Catholic Bishops, 1792–1988.* 5 vols., Washington, DC: United States Catholic Conference, 1983–1989).

——. *Renewing the Vision: A Framework for Catholic Youth Ministry.* Washington, DC: United States Catholic Conference, 1997.

——. *Sons and Daughters of the Light: A Pastoral Plan for Ministry with Young Adults.* Washington, DC: United States Catholic Conference, 1997.

NCCB Bishops' Committee on Hispanic Affairs (BCHA). *Communion and Mission: A Guide for Bishops and Pastoral Leaders on Small Church Communities.* Washington, DC: United States Catholic Conference, 1995.

——. *Hispanic Ministry at the Turn of the New Millennium.* Washington, DC: United States Conference of Catholic Bishops, 1999. http://www.nccbuscc.org/hispanic affairs/study.shtml.

——. *Leaven for the Kingdom of God.* Washington, DC: United States Catholic Conference, 1990.

NCCB Committee on African American Catholics and Committee on Hispanic Affairs. *Reconciled through Christ: On Reconciliation and Greater Collaboration between Hispanic American Catholics and African American Catholics.* Washington, DC: United States Catholic Conference, 1997.

NCCB Secretariat for Hispanic Affairs (SHA). "Proceedings of the Primer Encuentro Hispano de Pastoral." Typescript report. Washington, DC: Division for the Spanish Speaking, United States Catholic Conference, 1974. Encuentro conclusions published as "The Church and the Spanish-Speaking: A Dialogue" in *Origins* 3 (31 May 1973): 1–14.

——. *Proceedings of the II Encuentro Nacional Hispano de Pastoral.* Washington, DC: United States Catholic Conference, 1978.

——. *Prophetic Voices: The Document on the Process of the III Encuentro Nacional Hispano de Pastoral.* Washington, DC: United States Catholic Conference, 1986.

National Election Pool. 2004 exit poll. http://www.icpsr.umich.edu/icpsrweb/ICPSR/studies/04181.

National Opinion Research Center (NORC), University of Chicago. *The Associated Press-Univision Poll.* August 2010. http://surveys.ap.org/data%5CNORC%5CAP-Univision%20Topline_posting.pdf.

*National Survey of Latino Protestants: Immigration and the 2008 Election.* 16 October 2008. http://www.nhclc.org/about/pdf/poll_NHCLC08.pdf.

Navarro, José Antonio. *Defending Mexican Valor in Texas: José Antonio Navarro's Historical Writings, 1853–1857,* ed. David R. McDonald and Timothy Matovina. Austin: State House, 1995.

Navarro, Mireya. "In Many Churches, Icons Compete for Space." *New York Times.* 29 May 2002.

Navarro-Rivera, Juhem, Barry A. Kosmin, and Ariela Keysar. *U.S. Latino Religious Identification, 1990–2008: Growth, Diversity, and Transformation, A Report Based on the American Religious Identification Survey 2008.* http://www.americanreligionsurvey-aris.org/latinos2008.pdf.

Navia, Juan M. *An Apostle for the Immigrants: The Exile Years of Father Félix Varela y Morales, 1823–1853.* Salisbury, MD: Factor Press, 2002.

Neuhaus, Richard John. "Immigration and the Aliens among Us." *First Things* (August/September 1993): 63–65.

———. "When Bishops Speak." *First Things* (February 2001): 60–64.

Notre Dame Task Force on the Participation of Latino Children and Families in Catholic Schools. *To Nurture the Soul of a Nation: Latino Families, Catholic Schools, and Educational Opportunity.* Notre Dame, IN: Alliance for Catholic Education Press, 2009.

O'Connor, Liz. "The Catholic Common Ground Initiative Explores Lay Ecclesial Movements." *Initiative Report* 12 (August 2008): 3–6.

Odem, Mary E. "Latino Immigrants and the Politics of Space in Atlanta." In *Latino Immigrants and the Transformation of the U.S. South,* ed. Mary E. Odem and Elaine Lacy, 112-25. Athens: University of Georgia Press, 2009.

———. "Our Lady of Guadalupe in the New South: Latino Immigrants and the Politics of Integration in the Catholic Church." *Journal of American Ethnic History* 24 (Fall 2004): 26–57.

Odin, Jean Marie, to Jean-Baptiste Étienne, 7 February 1842. In *United States Catholic Magazine and Monthly Review* 3 (October 1844): 727–30.

Ospino, Hosffman, ed. *Hispanic Ministry in the 21st Century: Present and Future.* Miami: Convivium, 2010.

Ospino, Hosffman, and Elsie Miranda. "Hispanic Ministry and Leadership Formation." In Ospino, *Hispanic Ministry,* 173–200.

O'Toole, James M. *The Faithful: A History of Catholics in America.* Cambridge: Belknap Press of Harvard University Press, 2008.

Pantoja, Adrian, Matthew Barreto, and Richard Anderson. "Politics *y la Iglesia:* Attitudes toward the Role of Religion in Politics among Latino Catholics." In *Catholics and Politics: The Dynamic Tension between Faith and Power,* ed. Kristin E. Heyer, Mark J. Rozell, and Michael A. Genovese, 113–26. Washington, DC: Georgetown University Press, 2008.

Parker, J. Michael. "Lady of Guadalupe Crosses Cultural Lines." *San Antonio Express.* 11 December 2006.

———. "'Roman Soldier' Asks Forgiveness for Role as Jesus' Tormenter." *San Antonio Express.* 15 April 1995.

Pecklers, Keith F. *The Unread Vision: The Liturgical Movement in the United States of America, 1926–1955.* Collegeville, MN: Liturgical Press, 1998.

Perales, Alonso S. *Are We Good Neighbors?* San Antonio: Artes Graficas, 1948.

Pérez, Arturo J. "The History of Hispanic Liturgy since 1965." In J. Dolan and Deck, *Hispanic Catholic Culture in the U.S.*, 360–408.

———. *Popular Catholicism: A Hispanic Perspective.* Washington, DC: Pastoral Press, 1988.

Pérez, Lisandro. "Cuban Catholics in the United States." In J. Dolan and Vidal, *Puerto Rican and Cuban Catholics*, 145–208.

Perl, Paul M., Jennifer Z. Greely, and Mark M. Gray. "What Proportion of Adult Hispanics Are Catholic? A Review of Survey Data and Methodology." *Journal for the Scientific Study of Religion* 45 (September 2006): 419–36.

Peterson, Anna L., and Manuel A. Vásquez. *Latin American Religions: Histories and Documents in Context.* New York: New York University Press, 2008.

Pew Forum on Religion and Public Life. "A Portrait of American Catholics on the Eve of Pope Benedict's Visit." 27 March 2008. http://pewresearch.org/pubs/778/a-portrait-of-american-catholics-on-the-eve-of-pope-benedicts-visit.

———. *U.S. Religious Landscape Survey, Religious Beliefs and Practices: Diverse and Politically Relevant.* Washington, DC: Pew Forum on Religion and Public Life, 2008. http://religions.pewforum.org/pdf/report2-religious-landscape-study-full.pdf.

Pew Hispanic Center. *Between Two Worlds: How Young Latinos Come of Age in America.* Washington, DC: Pew Hispanic Center, 2009. http://pewhispanic.org/files/reports/117.pdf.

Pew Hispanic Center and Pew Forum on Religion and Public Life. *Changing Faiths: Latinos and the Transformation of American Religion.* Washington, DC: Pew Hispanic Center and Pew Forum on Religion and Public Life, 2007. http://pewhispanic.org/files/reports/75.pdf.

Pew Hispanic Center and the Henry J. Kaiser Family Foundation. *2002 National Survey of Latinos.* Washington, DC: Pew Hispanic Center and the Henry J. Kaiser Family Foundation, 2002. http://pewhispanic.org/files/reports/15.pdf.

Phan, Peter C., ed. *Directory on Popular Piety and the Liturgy: Principles and Guidelines, A Commentary.* Collegeville, MN: Liturgical Press, 2005.

Pitt, Leonard. *The Decline of the Californios: A Social History of the Spanish-Speaking Californians, 1846–1890.* Berkeley: University of California Press, 1966.

Pitti, Gina Marie. "The Sociedades Guadalupanas in the San Francisco Archdiocese, 1942–1962." *U.S. Catholic Historian* 21 (Winter 2003): 83–98.

———. "To 'Hear about God in Spanish': Ethnicity, Church, and Community Activism in the San Francisco Archdiocese's Mexican American Colonias, 1942–1965." PhD diss., Stanford University, Stanford, California, 2003.

Pitti, Steven J. *The Devil in Silicon Valley: Northern California, Race, and Mexican Americans.* Princeton, NJ: Princeton University Press, 2003.

Portier, William L. "Americanism and Inculturation, 1899–1999," *Communio* 27 (Spring 2000): 139–60.

Poyo, Gerald E. *Cuban Catholics in the United States, 1960–1980: Exile and Integration.* Notre Dame, IN: University of Notre Dame Press, 2007.

———. *"With All, and for the Good of All": The Emergence of Popular Nationalism in the Cuban Communities of the United States, 1848–1898.* Durham, NC: Duke University Press, 1989.

Pratt, Timothy. "The Parallel Presidential Campaign in Spanish." *Las Vegas Sun.* 31 October 2008. http://www.lasvegassun.com/news/2008/oct/31/parallel-presidential -campaign-spanish.

Prescott, William Hickling. *History of the Conquest of Mexico.* New York: Harper, 1843.

Presmanes, Jorge, and Alicia Marill. "Hispanic Ministry and Theology." In Ospino, *Hispanic Ministry*, 81–97.

"Priests Learning a Language and People: Hispanic Immersion Course Helps Priests Minister to Their Spanish-speaking Flocks." Sacerdos Institute web posting, 2008. http://www.sacerdos.org/english/articulos/articulo.phtml?id=14028.

Prophets of Hope Editorial Team. *Hispanic Young People and the Church's Pastoral Response.* Winona, MN: Saint Mary's Press, 1994.

*Puentes: NCCHM Official Newsletter.* Summer 2008. http://www.ncchm.org/files/ NCCHM09_FINAL/index.html#.

Pulido, Alberto López. *The Sacred World of the Penitentes.* Washington, DC: Smithsonian Institution Press, 2000.

Putnam, Robert D., and David E. Campbell. *American Grace: How Religion Divides and Unites Us.* New York: Simon and Schuster, 2010.

Quiñones Martínez, Sylvia. Presentation (untitled). In *Proceedings of the Forty-first Meeting of the National Conference of Catholic Charities,* 74–77. Washington, DC: National Conference of Catholic Charities, 1956.

Ramirez, Margaret. "Mexican Icon Blossoms in U.S." *Chicago Tribune.* 10 December 2006.

Ramírez, Ricardo. "The Crisis in Ecumenism among Hispanic Christians." *Origins* 24 (23 March 1995): 660–67.

———. *Go and Teach: A Pastoral Letter on Handing on the Faith* (18 October 2007). http://www.dioceseoflascruces.org/document_page.php?num=1.

———. "My Vocation as a Catechist." *Origins* 36 (7 December 2006): 414–19.

Rausch, Thomas. "Ecumenism for America's Hispanic Christians." *Origins* 36 (1 June 2006): 41–46.

Reimers, David M. *Still the Golden Door: The Third World Comes to America.* 1985; 2nd ed., New York: Columbia University Press, 1992.

Report of Bishop Roger Morin, Chairman, USCCB Subcommittee on the Catholic Campaign for Human Development. 17 November 2009. http://www.usccb.org/ cchd/morin_report_2009.shtml.

Report on CCHD and ACORN of Bishop Roger Morin, Chairman, Subcommittee On Catholic Campaign For Human Development. 11 November 2008. http://www .usccb.org/cchd/acorn-faq.shtml.

Reséndez, Andrés. *A Land So Strange: The Epic Journey of Cabeza de Vaca.* New York: Basic Books, 2007.

Reza, Mary Frances. "Crosscultural Music Making." In K. Davis, *Misa, Mesa y Musa,* 85–98.

Rieff, David. "Nuevo Catholics." *New York Times Magazine* (24 December 2006): 40–45, 85–87.

Rodríguez, Edmundo. "The Hispanic Community and Church Movements: Schools of Leadership." In J. Dolan and Deck, *Hispanic Catholic Culture in the U.S.,* 206–39.

Rodriguez, Gregory. *Mongrels, Bastards, Orphans, and Vagabonds: Mexican Immigration and the Future of Race in America.* New York: Pantheon, 2007.

Rodriguez, Richard. *Brown: The Last Discovery of America.* New York: Viking, 2002.

———. *Days of Obligation: An Argument with My Mexican Father.* New York: Viking, 1992.

Rogers, Mary Beth. *Cold Anger: A Story of Faith and Power Politics.* Denton: University of North Texas Press, 1990.

Román, Elisabeth. "The *Other* Latin Mass." *U.S. Catholic* 73 (February 2008): 30–33.

Romero, Juan. "Begetting the Mexican American: Padre Martínez and the 1847 Rebellion." In Steele, Rhetts, and Awalt, *Seeds of Struggle/Harvest of Faith,* 345–71.

Romero, Juan, with Moises Sandoval. *Reluctant Dawn: Historia del Padre A. J. Martínez, Cura de Taos.* San Antonio: Mexican American Cultural Center, 1976.

Ronstadt, Federico José María. *Borderman: Memoirs of Federico José María Ronstadt,* ed. Edward F. Ronstadt. Albuquerque: University of New Mexico Press, 1993.

Rosales, F. Arturo. *Chicano! The History of the Mexican American Civil Rights Movement.* Houston: University of Houston Press, 1996.

Rosin, Hanna. "Did Christianity Cause the Crash?" *Atlantic* (December 2009). http:// www.theatlantic.com/magazine/archive/2009/12/did-christianity-cause-the -crash/7764.

Rourke, Mary. "A Return to Ritual." *Los Angeles Times.* 28 March 1997.

Rutenbeck, James. *Scenes from a Parish* (film). 2009. Synopsis at http://scenesfroma parish.com/synopsis.html.

Sadovi, Carlos. "Cicero Procession Draws Big Crowd." *Chicago Sun-Times,* 3 April 1999.

———. "Cicero Rejects Good Friday Church Parade: Officials Fear Encouraging Clan." *Chicago Sun-Times,* 27 March 1999.

———. "Deal Falters over Religious Procession: Town Now Wants Participants Confined to Sidewalk." *Chicago Sun-Times,* 1 April 1999.

Sagarena, Roberto Lint. "Building California's Past: Mission Revival Architecture and Regional Identity." *Journal of Urban History* 28 (May 2002): 429–44.

Sanchez, Mary. "Don't Tread on the 14th Amendment." *Worthington Daily Globe*. 31 August 2010. http://www.dglobe.com/event/article/id/40274/group/Opinion.

Sánchez, Rosaura, Beatrice Pita, and Bárbara Reyes, eds. *Nineteenth-Century Californio Testimonials*. San Diego: University of California at San Diego Ethnic Studies/ Third World Studies, 1994.

Sánchez Korrol, Virginia E. *From Colonia to Community: The History of Puerto Ricans in New York City, 1917–1948*. Westport, CT: Greenwood, 1983.

Sandoval, Moises, ed. *Fronteras: A History of the Latin American Church in the USA since 1513*. San Antonio: Mexican American Cultural Center, 1983.

———. *On the Move: A History of the Hispanic Church in the United States*. 1990; 2nd ed., Maryknoll, NY: Orbis, 2006.

———. "The Organization of a Hispanic Church." In J. Dolan and Deck, *Hispanic Catholic Culture in the U.S.*, 131–65.

Schuetz, Janice. "Religion and Art: The Santa Fe Art Controversy about the Imprint of Our Lady of Guadalupe." In *Religion as Art: Guadalupe, Orishas, and Sufi*, ed. Steven Loza, 275–95. Albuquerque: University of New Mexico Press, 2009.

Schultze, George E. *Strangers in a Foreign Land: The Organization of Catholic Latinos in the United States*. Lanham, MD: Lexington, 2007.

Second General Conference of Latin American Bishops. *The Church in the Present-Day Transformation of Latin America in the Light of the Council*. Washington, DC: National Conference of Catholic Bishops, Secretariat, Committee for the Church in Latin American, 1979.

*Secular and Security-Minded: The Catholic Vote in Summer 2008, a National Opinion Survey of Likely Catholic Voters*. http://www.thefreelibrary.com/Secular+and+security -minded:+the+Catholic+vote+in+summer+2008:+a...-a0189832268.

Seguín, Juan N. *Personal Memoirs of John N. Seguín from the Year 1834 to the Retreat of General Woll from the City of San Antonio in 1842*. San Antonio: Ledger Book and Job Office, 1858. Reprinted in *A Revolution Remembered: The Memoirs and Selected Correspondence of Juan N. Seguín*, ed. Jesús F. de la Teja. Austin: State House, 1991.

Shannon, William V. *The American Irish*. New York: Macmillan, 1963.

Shaughnessy, Gerald. *Has the Immigrant Kept the Faith? A Study of Immigration and Catholic Growth in the United States, 1790–1920*. New York: Macmillan, 1925.

Silk, Mark, gen. ed. *Religion by Region*. 8 vols., Walnut Creek, CA: AltaMira Press, 2004– 2006.

Smith, Alfred E. "Catholic and Patriotic: Governor Smith Replies." *Atlantic Monthly* 39 (May 1927): 721–28.

Smith, Christian, with Melinda Lundquist Denton. *Soul Searching: The Religious and Spiritual Lives of American Teenagers*. New York: Oxford University Press, 2005.

Smith, Christian, with Patricia Snell. *Souls in Transition: The Religious and Spiritual Lives of Emerging Adults*. New York: Oxford University Press, 2009.

Smith, Robert Courtney. *Mexican New York: Transnational Lives of New Immigrants*. Berkeley: University of California Press, 2006.

Smith, Timothy L. "Religion and Ethnicity in America." *American Historical Review* 83 (December 1978): 1155–85.

"Somos Hispanos: Message of the U.S. Spanish-Speaking Bishops." *Origins* 7 (1 September 1977): 171–72.

Sorensen, Theodore C. *Kennedy*. New York: Harper and Row, 1965.

Sosa, Juan J. "Liturgical Piety or Popular Piety?" *Liturgy* 24 (November–December 1979): 7–9.

———. *One Voice, Many Rhythms*. Portland, OR: Pastoral Press, 2008.

Sousa, Lisa, Stafford Poole, and James Lockhart, eds. and trans. *The Story of Guadalupe: Luis Laso de la Vega's Huei tlamahuiçoltica of 1649*. Stanford, CA: Stanford University Press, 1998.

Steele, Thomas J., ed. and trans. *New Mexican Spanish Religious Oratory, 1800–1900*. Albuquerque: University of New Mexico Press, 1997.

Steele, Thomas J., Paul Rhetts, and Barbe Awalt. *Seeds of Struggle/Harvest of Faith: The Papers of the Archdiocese of Santa Fe Catholic Cuarto Centennial Conference on the History of the Catholic Church in New Mexico*. Albuquerque: LPD Press, 1998.

Steinfels, Peter. "Further Adrift: The American Church's Crisis of Attrition." *Commonweal* 137 (22 October 2010): 16–20.

Stern, Robert L. "Evolution of Hispanic Ministry in the New York Archdiocese." In Doyle et al., *Hispanics in New York*, 2:283–357.

Stevens-Arroyo, Anthony M. "Correction, *Si;* Defection, *No:* Hispanics and U.S. Catholicism." *America* 189 (7–14 July 2003): 16–18.

———. *The National Survey of Leadership in Latino Parishes and Congregations*. Brooklyn, NY: Religion in Society and Culture, 2002.

———. *Prophets Denied Honor: An Anthology on the Hispano Church in the United States*. Maryknoll, NY: Orbis, 1980.

Stingl, Jim. "Good Friday Procession Ties Traditions to Today's Sorrows." *Milwaukee Journal Sentinel*. 11 April 1998.

Stoller, Marianne L., and Thomas J. Steele, eds. *Diary of the Jesuit Residence of Our Lady of Guadalupe Parish, Conejos, Colorado: December 1871-December 1875*. Colorado Springs: Colorado College Press, 1982.

Strauss, Lilo T., et al. *Abortion Surveillance—United States, 2001*. Atlanta: Centers for Disease Control and Prevention, 2004. http://www.cdc.gov/mmwr/preview/mmwrhtml/ss5309a1.htm.

Suarez, Ray. *The Holy Vote: The Politics of Faith in America*. New York: HarperCollins, 2006.

Suárez-Orozco, Carola, and Irina Todorova. "The Social Worlds of Immigrant Youth." In *Understanding the Social Worlds of Immigrant Youth, Issue 100--New Directions for Youth Development: Theory, Practice, and Research*, ed. Carola Suárez-Orozco and Irina Todorova, 15–24. San Francisco: Jossey-Bass, 2003.

Swarts, Heidi J. *Organizing Urban America: Secular and Faith-based Progressive Movements*. Minneapolis: University of Minnesota Press, 2008.

Tabares, Fanny. "Pastoral Care of Catholic South Americans Living in the United States." *Chicago Studies* 36 (December 1997): 269–81.

Taylor, Alan. *American Colonies*. New York: Viking, 2001.

Taylor, Mary D. "Cura de la Frontera, Ramón Ortiz." *U.S. Catholic Historian* 9 (Winter/ Spring 1990): 67–85.

Telles, Edward E. "Mexican Americans and the American Nation: A Response to Professor Huntington." *Aztlán: A Journal of Chicano Studies* 31 (Fall 2006): 7–23.

Telles, Edward E., and Vilma Ortiz. *Generations of Exclusion: Mexican Americans, Assimilation, and Race*. New York: Russell Sage Foundation, 2008.

Texas State Historical Association. "The First Thanksgiving?" *Texas Almanac*. http://www.texasalmanac.com/history/highlights/thanksgiving.

Thompson, Joseph A. *El Gran Capitán, José de la Guerra: A Historical Biographical Study*. Los Angeles: Cabrera and Sons, 1961.

Tomasi, Silvano M. *Piety and Power: The Role of Italian Parishes in the New York Metropolitan Area, 1880–1930*. Staten Island, NY: Center for Migration Studies, 1975.

Torres, Theresa. "Our Lady of Guadalupe in the Society of the Guadalupanas in Kansas City, Missouri: An Empirical and Theological Analysis." PhD diss., Catholic University of America, Washington, DC, 2002.

Torres-Saillant, Silvio, and Ramona Hernández. *The Dominican Americans*. Westport, CT: Greenwood, 1998.

Travieso, Antonio Hernández. *El Padre Varela: Biografía del Forjador de la Conciencia Cubana*. 2nd ed., Miami: Ediciones Universal, 1984.

Treviño, Roberto R. *The Church in the Barrio: Mexican American Ethno-Catholicism in Houston*. Chapel Hill: University of North Carolina Press, 2006.

Trexler, Richard C. *Reliving Golgotha: The Passion Play of Iztapalapa*. Cambridge, MA: Harvard University Press, 2003.

Tweed, Thomas A. *Our Lady of the Exile: Diasporic Religion at a Cuban Catholic Shrine in Miami*. New York: Oxford University Press, 1997.

———, ed. *Retelling U.S. Religious History*. Berkeley: University of California Press, 1997.

"UFW's AgJobs Measure Part of Comprehensive Immigration Reform Bill Introduced by Rep. Gutierrez." Press release. 14 December 2009. http://www.ufw.org /_board.php?mode=view&b_code=news_press&b_no=5822&page=1&field=&ke y=&n=624.

United States Conference of Catholic Bishops (USCCB; formerly National Conference of Catholic Bishops [NCCB]). *Bendición al Cumplir Quince Años. Order for the*

*Blessing on the Fifteenth Birthday.* Washington, DC: United States Conference of Catholic Bishops, 2008.

——. *Co-Workers in the Vineyard of the Lord: A Resource for Guiding the Development of Lay Ecclesial Ministry.* Washington, DC: United States Conference of Catholic Bishops, 2005.

——. *Encuentro and Mission: A Renewed Pastoral Framework for Hispanic Ministry.* Washington, DC: United States Conference of Catholic Bishops, 2002.

——. "FAQS about Many Faces in God's House: *Encuentro 2000.*" 20 January 2000. http://www.nccbuscc.org/encuentro2000/questions.htm.

——. "Hispanic Ministry at a Glance." USCCB website. Hispanic Affairs page. http://www.usccb.org/hispanicaffairs/rememberingpast.shtml.

——. *National Directory for the Formation, Ministry, and Life of Permanent Deacons in the United States.* Washington, DC: United States Conference of Catholic Bishops, 2005.

——. *Program of Priestly Formation.* 5th ed., Washington, DC: United States Conference of Catholic Bishops, 2006.

——. *Renewing Our Commitment to Catholic Elementary and Secondary Schools in the Third Millennium.* Washington, DC: United States Conference of Catholic Bishops, 2005.

——. *Study on Best Practices for Diocesan Ministry among Hispanics/Latinos.* November 2006. http://www.usccb.org/hispanicaffairs/BestPractices2.pdf.

——. *Welcoming the Stranger among Us: Unity in Diversity.* Washington, DC: United States Conference of Catholic Bishops, 2000.

USCCB Catholic Bishops of Mexico and the United States. *Strangers No Longer: Together on the Journey of Hope.* Washington, DC: United States Conference of Catholic Bishops, 2003.

*U.S. Catholic Historian* 28 (Fall 2010). Issue titled "Remembering the Past, Engaging the Present: Essays in Honor of Moises Sandoval."

"USCCB Migration Chairman Joins Arizona Bishops in Decrying Anti-Immigrant Measure, Calls for Comprehensive Reform." USCCB news release. 27 April 2010. http://www.usccb.org/comm/archives/2010/10-080.shtml.

Valenzuela, Victor M. "The Emergence of Hispanic Catechesis: A Review of Literature from 1940–1980." MA thesis, University of San Francisco, 2008.

Varacalli, Joseph A. *The Catholic Experience in America.* Westport, CT: Greenwood, 2006.

Varela, Félix. *Letters to Elpidio,* ed. Felipe J. Estévez. Mahwah, NJ: Paulist Press, 1989.

Vatican II. *Ad Gentes (Decree on the Missionary Activity of the Church).* In Abbott, *Documents of Vatican II.* 584–630.

——. *Sacrosanctum Concilium (Constitution on the Sacred Liturgy).* In Abbott, *Documents of Vatican II.* 137–78.

Vecoli, Rudolph J. "Prelates and Peasants: Italian Immigrants and the Catholic Church." *Journal of Social History* 2 (1969): 217–67.

Vecsey, Christopher. *American Indian Catholics.* 3 vols. Notre Dame, IN: University of Notre Dame Press, 1996–1999.

Vidal, Jaime R. "Citizens Yet Strangers: The Puerto Rican Experience." In J. Dolan and Vidal, *Puerto Rican and Cuban Catholics,* 9–143.

Vizcaíno, Mario, ed. *Virgen de la Caridad: Patrona de Cuba.* Miami: Instituto Pastoral del Sureste, 1981.

Wall, Stephen. "Bishops Begin Campaign." *San Bernardino County Sun.* 10 January 2010.

———. "Schism Hits Church: Some Feel Left Out by Latino Culture Shift." *San Bernardino County Sun.* 13 March 2010. http://oneoldvet.com/?p=17799.

Warner, R. Stephen. "The Place of the Congregation in the Contemporary American Religious Configuration." In *American Congregations,* ed. James P. Wind and James W. Lewis. 2:54–99. Chicago: University of Chicago Press, 1994.

Warren, Mark R. *Dry Bones Rattling: Community Building to Revitalize American Democracy.* Princeton, NJ: Princeton University Press, 2001.

Warren, Mark R., and Richard L. Wood. *Faith-Based Community Organizing: The State of the Field.* Jericho, NY: Interfaith Funders, 2001.

Weber, David J. *On the Edge of Empire: The Taos Hacienda of los Martínez.* Santa Fe: Museum of New Mexico Press, 1996.

———. *The Spanish Frontier in North America.* New Haven, CT: Yale University Press, 1992.

———, ed. *What Caused the Pueblo Revolt of 1680?* Boston: Bedford/St. Martin's, 1999.

Wilkes, Paul. *Excellent Catholic Parishes: The Guide to Best Places and Practices.* Mahwah, NJ: Paulist Press, 2001.

"Willa Cather." *Catholic Library World* (15 January 1932): 30, 32.

William C. Velasquez Institute. "Latino Voter Statistics." http://www.wcvi.org/latino_voter_research/latino_voter_statistics.html.

———. "William C. Velásquez: 1944–1988." http://www.wcvi.org/wcvbio.htm.

———. 2008 WCVI Exit Poll Results. http://www.wcvi.org/latino_voter_research/polls/national/2008/2008exitpoll.html.

Williams, Michael. "Willa Cather's Masterpiece." *Commonweal* (28 September 1927): 490–92.

Wilson, Catherine E. *The Politics of Latino Faith: Religion, Identity, and Urban Community.* New York: New York University Press, 2008.

Wood, Richard L. *Faith in Action: Religion, Race, and Democratic Organizing in America.* Chicago: University of Chicago Press, 2002.

———. "*Fe y Acción Social:* Hispanic Churches in Faith-Based Community Organizing." In Espinosa, Elizondo, and Miranda, *Latino Religions and Civic Activism,* 145–58.

———. "Higher Power: Strategic Capacity for State and National Organizing." In *Transforming the City: Community Organizing and the Challenge of Political Change,* ed. Marion Orr, 162–92. Lawrence: University Press of Kansas, 2007.

Wood, Richard L., and Mary Ann Flaherty. *Renewing Congregations: The Contribution of Faith-Based Community Organizing.* New York: Interfaith Funders and the Ford Foundation, 2003.

Wood, Richard L., and Mark R. Warren. "A Different Face of Faith-Based Politics: Social Capital and Community Organizing in the Public Arena." *International Journal of Sociology and Social Policy* 22 (Fall 2002): 6–54.

Wooden, Cindy. "State's Decision to Abolish Death Penalty Marked at Rome's Colosseum." Catholic News Service posting. 15 April 2009. http://www.catholicnews .com/data/stories/cns/0901704.htm.

Wright, Robert E. "Father Refugio de la Garza: Controverted Religious Leader." In *Tejano Leadership in Mexican and Revolutionary Texas.* ed. Jesús F. de la Teja, 76–101. College Station: Texas A&M University Press, 2010.

———. "How Many Are 'A Few'? Catholic Clergy in Central and Northern New Mexico, 1780–1851." In Steele, Rhetts, and Awalt, *Seeds of Struggle/Harvest of Faith,* 219–61.

———. "Local Church Emergence and Mission Decline: The Historiography of the Catholic Church in the Southwest during the Spanish and Mexican Periods." *U.S. Catholic Historian* 9 (Winter/Spring 1990): 27–48.

Wuthnow, Robert. *After the Baby Boomers: How Twenty- and Thirty-Somethings Are Shaping the Future of American Religion.* Princeton, NJ: Princeton University Press, 2007.

———. *After Heaven: Spirituality in America since the 1950s.* Berkeley: University of California Press, 1998.

———. ed. *"I Come Away Stronger": How Small Groups Are Shaping American Religion.* Grand Rapids, MI: Eerdmans, 1994.

Yamane, David. *The Catholic Church in State Politics: Negotiating Prophetic Demands and Political Realities.* Lanham, MD: Sheed and Ward, 2005.

Zangwill, Israel. *The Melting-Pot: Drama in Four Acts.* New York: Macmillan, 1909.

Zapor, Patricia. "Bishops Talk Health Care, Immigration with Members of Congress." Catholic News Service posting. 18 September 2009. http://www.catholicnews.com/ data/stories/cns/0904169.htm.

Zimanske, Jessica. "Conference Explores Multicultural Ministry." *Aquin* (University of St. Thomas student newspaper). 2 November 2007. http://jessicazimanske.efoliomn .com/Uploads/Conference%20explores%20multicultural%20ministry.pdf.

Zúñiga, Olga Portuondo. *La Virgen de la Caridad del Cobre: Símbolo de cubanía.* Madrid: Agualarga, 2001.

# INDEX